KINC … ASTLES

SONS IN THE SADDLE

MARY DURACK

BANTAM BOOKS
SYDNEY • AUCKLAND • TORONTO • NEW YORK • LONDON

KINGS IN GRASS CASTLES
SONS IN THE SADDLE
A BANTAM BOOK

This omnibus edition first published in Australia and New Zealand in 2000
by Bantam

Kings in Grass Castles first published in Great Britain by Constable & Co. Ltd in 1959
Corgi Edition published 1967
Bantam Edition published 1997

Sons in the Saddle first published in Great Britain by Constable & Co. Ltd in 1983
Corgi Edition published 1985
Bantam Edition published 1998

National Library of Australia
Cataloguing-in-Publication Entry

Durack, Mary, 1913–1994.
Kings in grass castles ; Sons in the saddle.

Includes index.
ISBN 1 86325 297 5.

1. Durack family. 2. Pioneers –Australia – Biography. 3. Ranchers – Australia – Biography. 4. Ranches – Australia. I. Title.

994.0099

Transworld Publishers,
a division of Random House Australia Pty Ltd
20 Alfred Street, Milsons Point, NSW 2061

Random House New Zealand Limited
18 Poland Road, Glenfield, Auckland

Transworld Publishers,
a division of The Random House Group Ltd
61-63 Uxbridge Road, London W5 5SA

Random House Inc
1540 Broadway, New York, New York 10036

Cover photograph by Grenville Turner courtesy of Wildlight Photo Agency
Historical photographs courtesy of the Durack family
Typeset by Midland Typesetters
Printed and bound by Griffin Press, Netley, South Australia

10 9 8 7 6 5 4 3 2 1

KINGS IN GRASS CASTLES

'Cattle Kings' ye call us, then we are Kings in grass castles that may be blown away upon a puff of wind . . .

PATRICK DURACK 1878

TO THE MEMORY OF MY GRANDFATHER

PATRICK DURACK

AND TO THE SUCCESS OF MY BROTHER

KIMBERLEY MICHAEL DURACK

IN HIS WORK FOR THE DEVELOPMENT OF

THE KIMBERLEY DISTRICT OF WESTERN AUSTRALIA

I DEDICATE THIS BOOK

Contents

Maps and Tables

ACKNOWLEDGEMENTS

For helping me in the preparation of this book I have particularly to thank Mr Jas Jervis of History House, Sydney, and his colleagues of the Mitchell Library for their patient search in unearthing information from the Immigration files of the late 1840s and early fifties. To Mr Garth Mansfield of Sydney I am in debt for discovering the location and procuring photostat copies of early maps of holdings in the Goulburn district and for putting me on the track of many sources of information relating to the contemporary life of the area.

Miss Miriam Chisholm of Kippilaw, NSW, a descendant of the original owner of the estate, was most co-operative in sending me details of the terms and conditions under which members of the family were contracted for farm work on arrival in the colony.

To the Oxley Memorial Library, the Land Administration Board of Brisbane, and to the Lands Department, Public Library and Battye Archives of Perth, I owe yet another debt for unfailing patience and for much precise information and data.

I must also mention in particular Geoffrey Bolton, MA, (later Professor Bolton, AO) who, in preparing his thesis on the Kimberley Pastoral Industry, sifted from masses of family business records many facts relevant to this document.

To relatives throughout the continent, particularly to my Tully cousins in the Quilpie district of western Queensland, to Kathleen MacArthur of Caloundra, Queensland, granddaughter of my father's uncle 'Stumpy' Michael, to Mrs Peppin, daughter of 'Big Pat' Scanlan of Springfield, I owe more than I can say for hospitality, information, letters, documents and photographs. Nor should I forget the advice and help of my sister Elizabeth, the valuable contribution of my brother Kim in preparing the maps found in this book, the information supplied by my cousins Gerald Durack of Harvey, whose careful filing system of old letters and newspaper cuttings proved invaluable, Eric Durack of Darwin and Walter Durack of Arrino. I owe much also to my late Aunt Mary's sons, Kenneth and Douglas Davidson (then the owner of the Dunham Station outside Wyndham), who burned the midnight oil with me in resurrecting the past from our grandfather's records and making sense for me out of a bewildering tangle of legal documents.

For information regarding family origins I am indebted to my late Uncle Dermot (Professor J. J. Durack), who died in Dublin in 1956 and to those scholars and historians, notably Father John Clancy of County Clare, who helped him in his search.

For measuring the areas of various family holdings I owe sincere thanks to Mr Maurice Mulcahy of Perth, and for their valuable assistance with photographic illustration West Australian Newspapers Ltd, *Walkabout Magazine* and Mr Phillip Mathews.

Of the many people I have called on for odd pieces of information I would like to mention especially Mr Tom Owen of the State Steamship Co, WA, for information on early ships and costs of charter, Mr Sydney Emanuel of London, representative for Emanuel Estates in Kimberley, WA, and a grandson of the late Mr Solomon Emanuel of Goulburn who figures in this book, and Mr W. MacDonald, present owner of Fossil Downs Station, nephew of pioneer Willie MacDonald of the 3,500-mile overland trail from Goulburn to West Kimberley.

The Reverend Mother and nuns of Loreto Convent, Nedlands, WA, I sincerely thank for access to the historical section of their library and for the help and inspiration they have been at all times.

My particular thanks are due also to my friends Florence James and Dr Phyllis Kaberry who read my manuscript in the rough and gave so much helpful advice, at least *some* of which I hope I have been able to carry out.

Lastly I must thank that most efficient, indefatigable and always encouraging midwife of so many shaggy manuscripts of West Australian writers—our friend and typist Marjorie Rees.

And also my beloved husband and six children who have suffered this seemingly unending project.

M.D.

Introduction

For many years now I have lived in three generations, following vague and winding tracks in search of missing clues and facts long buried in the drifts of time. My father often remarked upon the shortness and fallibility of human memory but even he, I think, would have been surprised to find how many aspects of his father's life had either completely eluded his generation or become distorted with the passing years. He had always wanted me some day to write of the family's pioneering efforts but it was not until after his death that I discovered the collection of Grandfather Patsy's old account books, stock records, cheque-butts, random jottings, and letters to his family, and I set about putting them together, like the pieces of a jigsaw puzzle, against the background of his times. While so doing, this man who died so long before my birth, drew towards me out of the fog of years until I seemed to know him more intimately than I had my own father. Only then could I understand the drive and purpose that had goaded him into the wilderness, and the yearning and sadness of his eyes in that last portrait.

I believed the story should be recorded if only for archival purposes, and I attacked the process of research and compilation with something of the dogged spirit of those overlanding drovers who, having undertaken the job, were committed come what might to see it through. As it happened it took me considerably longer than that cattle trek from Queensland to the Kimberley, with delays caused not by drought and flood but by the inevitable crises of family life, including the birth of children along the track.

My publisher considered the resulting volume worth producing, even if unlikely to sell beyond a limited edition, and it was to our mutual surprise that the book, first published in 1959, met with such an appreciative public. I had not intended continuing the family story beyond my grandfather's lifetime but in the early 1970s I felt impelled to take up the task again, and completed a sequel—*Sons in the Saddle*—which was published in 1983. This book begins at the time of my grandfather's death in 1898, when my father took over as head of his branch of the family. With a background of world and local events and the ever-changing economic and political situation, it follows the fluctuating fortunes of surviving family members and their associates, including a steadily increasing younger generation.

My father, as general manager of Connor, Doherty & Durack's widespread northern properties, company director, politician and indefatigable traveller, lived a full and active life until his death in 1950, at the age of eighty-five.

An unexpected outcome of these publications has been the drawing together of far-flung branches of the family, not only throughout Australia but also in the United States, Canada, South Africa and New Zealand. Ensuing correspondence has revealed family characteristics that have survived time, distance and diverse circumstances and has also stimulated mutual interest in the causes influencing our different national characters and constitutions. It is an interesting subject, and a few observations on the development of these factors in Australia might place the context of this book in better general perspective.

Impossible though it be to parallel the turbulent complex of United States history with Australia's comparatively short and simple story, it can at least be said that both cultures have been largely inclined by the productivity of the land and that the frontier conditions of each country left a lasting impression on its national character and government.

After the penetration of the Great Dividing Range in the early 1820s Australia's westward drive was as rapid and vigorous as the American, and in both countries early land laws were desperately contrived to accommodate individuals who were impatient—even contemptuous—of official restraint. Hopes of Australia's westward flowing streams emptying into a vast inland sea were, however, soon dispelled, the harsh truth being that the total annual run-off of her rivers was a mere 200 million acre feet, compared with 1,300 million in the United States. Therefore while America's frontier moved into a fertile west before consolidating ranks of small farming families, in Australia thin spearheads of settlement strung on into the mirage of an increasingly arid interior. Britain's demand for wool and the land's suitability for sheep-raising strongly influenced early Australian enterprise, especially since agriculture, possible only in the higher rainfall areas, was difficult and not very profitable.

The large areas required to run stock on an open range of natural pastures were readily available, but the Crown, mindful of its duty to posterity in dealing with land of untried potential, hesitated to confer extensive freehold rights. As the squatters increased in confidence and power, their demands secured them the tenure of restricted but vital areas, and by purchasing for a few pounds all permanent waterholes and river frontages they managed to tie up hundreds, sometimes thousands, of acres of grazing land.

The gold rushes of the 1850s brought a big influx of land-hungry men, a number from the diggings in California with stories of umhampered free selection on the American prairies, and these newcomers eventually broke the domination of the squatting minority. The Free Selection Act of the early sixties, designed to uphold the rights of the small settler, somewhat paralleled the United States Homestead Act of the same period but, though both were subject to similar abuse, the American Act was considerably more successful.

In Australia the development of small farms proved so costly and difficult that unscrupulous big men could readily find 'dummy' selectors to occupy resumed parts of their estates. The Act, however, had the overall effect of breaking up the higher rainfall areas and of pushing the frontier forward into arid 'marginal' regions where anything other than open-range grazing was impractical.

No one in this country was ever satisfied with the land laws. Every attempt to mollify the big holders in their demands for the greater security of tenure that would encourage them to improve their properties and develop the pastoral industry brought from the landless or small holders louder protests against 'favouritism' towards the grasping sheep or cattle 'kings'.

That Australia's land laws, rightly described as 'a jungle penetrable only to the initiate', *did* tend to favour the big holders was actually a reluctant concession to harsh reality. As many a determined trier or 'battler' learned to his sorrow, it was only men with enough capital to improve and maintain large pastoral leases who could make out in those drought-menaced, light-carrying areas.

In time, when the discovery of the artesian flow made smaller holdings practical, many of the larger properties were broken up, but the Australian frontier remained the province of the relatively big pastoral holder.

The country, however, was never really at ease with the situation or happily resigned to the fact that so few should control so much. The voice of Australian democracy was always the voice of the struggling majority against the more fortunate few.

Herein lies an essential difference between the two countries, for ours was not the American democracy of abundance but that of a land which, though roughly the size of the United States, was possessed of considerably poorer resources. In theory, free from the old-world restrictions of class and tradition, every man had an equal chance of getting on, but success was a lottery in which the prizes were few and far between.

People in these conditions developed, to be sure, a great deal of initiative, resourcefulness and self-reliance, but these were generally expended in the sheer struggle for survival that fostered collective security rather than the competitive individualism of the United States. The Australian tradition of 'mateship' had its roots in the mutual dependence of small, scattered communities in a tough and often hostile environment.

Sometimes individuals like Patsy Durack starting from scratch could, with a rare combination of luck, good timing, drive, and sagacity, win through to be prosperous landholders, but the average man had no such prospect, and the further out he got, the less were his chances of being anything other than a wage-earner.

The frontier, however, did attract a certain, perhaps uniquely Australian type: the itinerant stockman or drover, who, ambitious within the limitations of the bush, took pride in his horsemanship, his knowledge of handling stock and his 'bushmanship', which covered a variety of skills, such as setting a course in trackless country, living off the land, coping with the Aborigines and generally surviving in the toughest circumstances. Almost all these men, knowing their only chance of a break-through to lie in a stroke of phenomenal luck, combined their stockwork with a constant search for gold. With this added incentive there was no corner of the continent they were not prepared to probe, mapping with extraordinary perception the areas of possible settlement, blazing new trails in the big stock drives of the seventies and eighties. In their nomadic calling, few of them ever gathered moss or settled into normal domesticity. Some of them found gold, or indications of gold, and even started rushes to various remote parts of the country, but others usually got the credit and the reward for their discoveries. Others occupied the country they opened up while they rode on to ever-receding horizons and lonely graves.

That bush workers and employers alike were so matter of fact about their lives may have been due, in part, to a lack of Australian frontier literature, for they generally acknowledged the romance and excitement of America's 'Wild West'. For many it was the last retreat from the law, from society, from political intrigue. Some were survivors of the overland trails, among the best and toughest stock riders in the world, whose adventures would have outclassed the wildest fiction. Yet, while their American counterparts galloped the prairies with swinging lariats, creating legends to delight the world, these men were content to ride on in obscurity, performing feats of bushmanship and triumphs of endurance that left little country to be officially 'opened up' by the end of the last century.

The boundaries of Australian agricultural and pastoral settlement as defined by that time have not substantially changed. Over one million square miles, or approximately one-third of the continent, lacking the discovery of hitherto unknown scientific aids, can carry only a very sparse population, and Australia is therefore proportionately more highly urbanised than any other country in the world. Despite this, however, and despite the influence of subsequent European migration, her salient national characteristics are strikingly relevant to those of that early frontier. All in all, Australians remain less assertive, less competitive, less excitable than the people of the United States, and Australia even in her most congested urban areas is still comparatively a relaxed and silent land.

'The Lucky Country?' 'The Land of Opportunity?' That would depend entirely on the point of view, but it would be wrong to suppose that her future is bound to the limitations of her past. She is still a land of expanding frontiers, although the outriders of modern development are not the tough and often illiterate bushmen of yesterday. They are the scientists and engineers, the pioneers of modern invention and industrial methods, the scholars and artists, tackling old problems with new skills, their horizons wide from the summit of every new discovery.

MARY DURACK
Perth, Western Australia
February 1985

KINGS IN GRASS CASTLES

JOHN DURACK
of County Galway, Ireland
m 1806 Amy Forde 'Mammie Amy'

- **MICHAEL** b 1808, m Bridget Dillon, to Australia 1853, d 1853 Goulburn
  - **MARY** b 1833, m Denis Skeahan, d 1920 ↓
  - **PATRICK** 'Patsy' b 1834, m 1862 Mary Costello, d 1898
    - **MARY** b 1863, d 1865
    - **MICHAEL** 'M.P.' 'Miguel' b 1865, m Bessie Johnstone, d 1950 ↓
    - **JOHN** 'J.W.' b 1867, d 1936
    - **JEREMIAH** b 1869, d 1869
    - **PATRICK** 'P.B.' b 1870, m Eva Hughes, d 1933 ↓
    - **MARY** b 1872, m James Davidson, d 1948 ↓
    - **BRIDGET** 'Birdie' b 1874, d 1949
    - **JEREMIAH** 'Dermot' b 1877, m Diana Wentworth, d 1956 ↓
  - **MARGARET** b 1837, m 1860 John Bennet, d 1864 ↓
  - **BRIDGET** b 1839, m Patrick Scanlan, d 1873
  - **SARAH** b 1841, m Patrick Tully, d 1914 ↓
  - **ANNE** b 1845, m John Redgrave, d 1874 ↓
  - **MICHAEL** 'Stumpy' b 1846, m 1873 Catherine McInnes, d 1895
    - **AMBROSE** b 1875, m Nancy Tiddy, d 1954 ↓
    - **MARGARET** b 1877, m Marchant, d 1953 ↓
    - **BARBARA** b 1879, d 1901
  - **JEREMIAH** 'Galway Jerry' b 1853, m 1879 Frances Neal, d 1901 →
- **DARBY** b 1819, m Margaret Kilfoyle, to Australia 1849, d 1873
  - **BRIDGET** b 1848 at sea, m Michael Cahill, d 1934 ↓
  - **JOHN** 'Big Johnnie' b 1849, d 1886. Speared by native
  - **PATRICK** 'Mantinea' or 'Black Pat' b 1851, m Susan Downes, d 1933 ↓
  - **MICHAEL** 'Long Michael' b 1854, m Bertha Levinson, d 1937
  - **CATHERINE** b ?, m John Nesbit, d ?
  - **THOMAS** b 1857, d 1922

The entries in this abbreviated Durack family tree are limited to those members who are contemporary with this story.

JEREMIAH	MARGARET	MARYANNE	JAMES	LAWRENCE	SARAH	WILL
'Jerry Brice' b 1858 m Agnes O'Hara d 1952	b ? m Gus McEvilly d 1938	b 1862 d 1939	b 1863 d 1907	b 1865 d 1933	b 1867 m J. Stokes d 1925	b 1869 d 1911

CATHERINE	JESSIE	CHRISTINA	SARAH	CLARE	FERGUS	FLORA
'Kathleen', 'Kit' b 1881 m Dan Evans d 1951	b 1883 m Helion d 1916	b 1884 d 1978	b 1885 d 1947	b 1887 d 1940	b 1889 d 1915	b 1892 d 1968(?)

JANE	BRIDGET	PATSY	ANNIE	JACK	NEAL	MOLLIE	VERA	FRANK
b 1880 d 1883	b 1881 d 1884	b 1882 m Lillas Mulligan d 1933	b 1884 d 1898	'J.P.' b 1888 m Rowe d 1978	b 1892 m Imelda Sellenger d 1920	b 1894 m Leslie Brockman d 1962	b 1896 d 1898	b 1901 m Wertheimer d 1972

1

Roots

Family origins and conditions of life in Western Ireland.
The Great Famine of '45 and the departure of Darby Durack and his wife for New South Wales in 1849.

From the bridge across the River Bow which once divided the counties of Galway and Clare you may see on one side the green valley of Magerareagh and on the other the little town of Cappabaun in the ancient parish of Moynoe where the graves of my forebears lie tumbled and overgrown. Generations of Duracks were born around Magerareagh, which belonged to Galway until 1899, when it was moved within the boundary of Clare, and the farm on which they paid rent to some 'upstart landlord' lay close by on the slopes of Slieve Aughty Mountain. The land was poor and subject to the whims of shifting bog, serving as a constant reminder to my people of the chip they had carried on their shoulders since the year 1542 when their ancient heritage of Ogoneloe had been granted, in fee simple, to their traditional enemies.

The past was always real and close to them, and their pride of race throve on the retelling of ancient wrongs and of glories still more remote. It seemed none so long ago to them that the Duracks, as a Dalcassian family, had fought beside Brian Boru, High King of all Ireland, against the invading Danes. 'O'Dubraic', the nearest translation of the name from the original Gaelic characters, was variously translated 'dark prosperity' or 'dark outlook'. Their outlook, like that of all followers of the great Boru after his death at Clontarf, would have been dark enough, but if the inference was personal they must assuredly have changed, for whatever else they may show themselves in this story they were not pessimists.

In the Book of Ballymote, one of the world's oldest documents, the name is given as 'O'Dubraic of Dun Braine', and it is quoted in the history of County Clare as among Irish names existing before the fourteenth century: 'O'Dubraic, dynast UiConghail, now Durack, a name still locally known and applied to a district co-extensive with the parish of Ogoneloe, verging on Lough Deirgheirc, i.e. L. Derg.'

It was here, on the slopes of Mount Bernagh, overlooking Scariff Bay that they held sway in ancient times:

Family O'Durack of Dun Brain
[sang the bard O'Heerin in about 1400]
Are chieftains of Ogoneloe,
Their forts about the good Boru
Locks of hair like gold on their heads.

In 1300 O'Duracks and O'Kennedys, backed by the Anglo-Norman de Grey, had fought against the powerful MacNamaras, backed by another Anglo-Norman, de Burge, a skirmish in keeping with the Norman policy of setting the Celtic clans at each other's throats. Turlogh O'Brian, the ruling monarch of Thomond who disapproved of de Grey, banished O'Duracks and O'Kennedys for having had truck with him, but their exile was short-lived and they were soon back in possession of their land.

When Henry VIII set about the conquest of the Irish nobility by granting confiscated monastic property to his supporters the ruling O'Briens, who accepted Henry as sovereign and head of the Church, were created earls and granted further estates. At the same time Sheeda, head of the MacNamaras, was granted a knighthood with the land of Ogoneloe thrown in, so that the O'Duracks, for their stubborn refusal to bend the knee to a Protestant overlord, not only became the tenant farmers of their ancient enemies but were stripped of all privileges, at last even the O' prefix to their name. It is not to be supposed, however, that they settled down meekly under these humiliations. There were times when the MacNamaras must have wondered whether they had the best of the bargain, after all, for somewhere in the course of the long vendetta a certain 'Red Mac', in a fit of exasperation at their persistent sabotage, was said to have uttered a curse of such potency that any of the name to die in his bed past the prime of life was considered fortunate. When the family first came to Australia they could reel off 'Red Mac's' victims for generations back, but such legends were given short shrift in this matter-of-fact land. The young people paid so little attention to the reminiscences of their elders that some became convinced, when none remained to deny it, of a link between the Gaelic name Durack and the French Du Roc, while an obliging armorial firm actually produced, for a fee, testimony of their relationship to Napoleon's famous marshal! Fortunately for this record Irish documents and long-forgotten letters leave no shadow of doubt that if a French family named Du Roc sought refuge in Ireland after the revocation of the Edict of Nantes in 1685 they assuredly had no connection with the clan O'Dubraic that for over one thousand years had tilled their fields and pastured their stock on the green banks of the Shannon at Ogoneloe. The French heresy was not without a shadow of reason though, for some of the first Australian generation vaguely recalled their old people's references to stirring events in French history and to forebears who had perished on French battlefields. Had the long-cherished background of their people been less of a blank to these Australian born they might have connected such fragments with the story of the 'wild geese' who, after the signing of the Treaty of Limerick in 1691, went off to fight the cause of Irish liberty under Catholic flags in France, Italy and Spain. A certain Captain Will Durack of Limerick is listed as having died at Dettingen as a member of the famous 'Irish Brigade' that, under the motto *'Semper et Ubique Fideles'* fought with the French armies for one hundred years.

My great-great-grandfather, in accordance with the homely advice to 'choose your wife and cow from your own county', married a Connemara lass named Amy Forde in 1806 and they reared a large and sturdy family. 'Himself' found compensation for the bitter restrictions of his tenancy in the production of a fine, fiery brew of 'potheen', the proceeds of which he gambled on the turf or put to the breeding of hunters that he rode to hounds and sometimes sold to English squires.

The head shaking that had accompanied the recital of the exploits of 'Daddy Jack', as the old people called him, was mingled with pride of his wit and daring and the popularity clearly shown by the memorable success of his wake. He was killed (the vindictive 'Red Mac' again!) in the hunting field shortly before the birth of his tenth child in 1829, and his funeral rites ended only with his supply of 'the crathur' that was cannily cellared in the mountain turf. His widow, 'Mammie Amy Forde' as they called her, was of sterner stuff, though she had a weakness for fortune tellers and a strong belief in omens and signs. She had lain each of her babies, naked, in the furrows of the newly tilled soil in a ritual as ancient as the pagan Celts, while she prayed to the Mother of God that they might draw strength from the good earth to withstand evil and adversity. After their father's death no more 'potheen' was brewed that side of Slieve Aughty Mountain and her children minded their business when the huntsman's horn echoed across the countryside. They grew up with their hands on the plough but steeped in the traditions of their Gaelic ancestry, attending, whenever possible, the forbidden 'hedge schools' where fugitive Irish scholars passed on at least a love of the learning for which their land had once been famed.

When the eldest son, Michael, married Bridget Dillon of Cappabaun in 1831 he took up a farm near the village of Scariff, on the Clare side of Loch Derg, which, like the Slieve Aughty land, had been part of the original family holding of Ogoneloe. My grandfather, Patsy, the second of their eight children and the central figure of this story, handed down to us a few glimpses of their life in Ireland, of how their small black cattle and thin, black-faced sheep had grazed on the slopes of Mount Bernagh, finding pickings among the heather and bog cotton and after harvest among the stubble of the thin crops in the fields below; of how the soil, worked out in the tilling and reaping of centuries, still yielded generously an unending crop of bald, grey rocks to be levered out and added to the long crisscross pattern of stone walls. Between the tasks of shepherding, milking, sowing, harvesting and cutting the wet turf slabs from the hillside to be stacked and dried for fuel, young Patsy and his sisters went to school. Their letters, although not lacking in a natural fluency, indicate that they received no more than the rudiments of learning but they had from their parents a sound practical training in the use of tools, the art of thatching and of devising all manner of things from limited resources.

There had been the joy of trout fishing in the Shannon or at the salmon leap beyond Lough Derg where the river tumbled in foaming cataracts; visits to the ruined shrines of Ireland's monastic past, where like his people of ancient times Grandfather had looked down from the mound of Dun Brian to where his river narrowed from the Lough on its last stretch to Limerick and the sea. He would tell of the excitement of market days in Gort, the men with their ashwood sticks, their peak caps and gay home-knit mufflers, driving their cattle through the mud, bumping and lurching in their donkey carts, calling the time of day, bargaining, brawling and exchanging ribald jests. He would live again the heated political discussions, issues of awful moment that had little meaning for his children—Daniel O'Connell and Young Ireland, moderation or 'blood and iron'. He would talk of the tests of skill and strength, wielding the cudgels, the sport of hurling, of dancing 'The Walls of Limerick' in the market square; and, dearest of all, the Galway Blazers, the great Irish hunters with yapping hounds at hoof that flashed through soft grey mornings across misty fields taking walls and hedges in their splendid stride.

During his childhood there had been a steady exodus of friends and relatives to America, for there were too many people in Ireland when, having previously subdivided the country into small lots to multiply their rents, the landlords found that tillage no longer paid and they must again restore the land to pasture. The small tenants must be cleared, they said, and the land 'consolidated' or Ireland would be ruined, but no one took into account the ruin of the poor Irish through this saving policy. Evicted tenants, their cottages razed to the ground, came crowding in around what little soil remained to them until there was no option but to thin themselves out by emigration, hoping that some further change of the wind would restore the land to the idle ploughs. But it was an ill wind after all that next turned the course of history, for the bitter blight of '45 that struck at the potato crops struck deeper still at the roots of Irish life. There had been famines in the past when the death bells had pealed incessantly and funerals were black upon the roads, but never before were the people so dependent upon potatoes as their staple diet. Now there was starvation in the midst of plenty, since cattle and other produce must be sold to meet the crippling rents and 'famine rates' that were 'squeezed out of the very blood and vitals and clothes and dwellings of the tenants'. Three successive years of hunger, bitterness and pestilence, when dead and dying lay huddled in doorways and ditches on the frozen highways to be buried in common graves, divested the people of the laughing spirit that had stood to them through all the troubles of the past. Emigration was on everyone's lips. 'You cannot live in Ireland. To get up you must first get out.' This exodus was no 'flight of the wild geese', that flocking of Ireland's finest sons to the battlefields of France, for now the women, children and old people were going too until the English press rejoiced that 'So complete is the rush of departing marauders . . . a silence reigns over the vast solitude of Ireland'. The steady stream that had been flowing away for half a century swelled to a flood of desperate people who must needs get out or starve.

Mammie Amy lost four of her ten children in the famine years, and the rest, except for a married daughter and a son, set sail for other lands. Her boy, Cornelius, attracted by the romance of the diamond fields, hied himself to South Africa about the same time as three first cousins, the brothers Michael, William and Walter Durack, left for America. My grandfather's Uncle Darby, Mammie Amy's tenth and youngest child, was the first of the family to leave for Australia, which up to this time had been eschewed by most emigrating Irish with any choice in the matter as a destination of felons and paupers. During the late forties it had become known that the colony of New South Wales had succeeded in capturing England's wool market and that a wealth of new pasture land had been opened to the settler. Assisted emigration schemes that had flourished after the suspension of convict transportation in 1840 almost ceased during the depression of the following years, to burgeon again as the clouds lifted and the story spread of expanding possibilities in the new south land.

In 1848 Darby Durack married a handsome colleen named Margaret Kilfoyle whose family had recently migrated to New South Wales. Darby, having scraped together, therefore, the princely sum of £5 10s and agreed to pay the remaining £35 from wages earned under a system of indentured labour, the couple set sail from Plymouth on the *Duke of Roxborough* in May 1849. Most of their two hundred and twenty fellow passengers, carefully listed in the emigration files, were English people, including forty-eight agricultural labourers, seven shepherds, three blacksmiths, three gardeners, two carpenters, two shoemakers, two bookbinders, one wheelwright, one shipwright, one coachman, one clerk and one miner.

Out of this fairly typical mixed bag it is to be hoped that the single, unknown optimist at the end kept faith with fortune to rise in two years' time on the colony's golden wave. More likely he joined the ranks of earlier settlers, who, as the *Duke of Roxborough* arrived in Sydney, were leaving for the gold rush to California, shouting disparagement of the colony from the ship's rails.

Darby and Margaret Durack, nursing their infant Bridget, born upon the voyage, looked on in bewilderment. They had been told that the colonial depression had lifted and that opportunity awaited any with a will to work in this great country. Why, then, should these earlier comers appear so eager to try their luck elsewhere? It would be understood only when background came into focus and the topsy-turvy world of strange stars and seasons in reverse turned slowly right-side-up.

2
Colonial Background

The year 1849. Darby Durack, his wife and infant arrive in New South Wales. A brief background of progress in the colony, limits of penetration, the manner of early settlement. The work of John Dunmore Lang and Caroline Chisholm for immigration. Suspension of convict transportation. Depression of the forties. Revival of immigration and rise of the smaller settlers. Departure of the new arrivals for Goulburn.

Darby and Margaret had promised with simple confidence to write home the truth about the colony. 'Sure, and we'll be letting you know just the way it is.' But what were they to say when contradictions faced them at every turn and they could form no picture whatever of this vast continent, roughly the size of the United States and into which the British Isles, complete with Ireland, would have fitted comfortably twenty-five times over? The colony of New South Wales, still unshorn of Victoria, Queensland and the Northern Territory, sprawled between the tropical Arafura and Coral seas and the cold waters of Bass Strait for over one and a half million square miles and yet contained, in the year 1849, no more than 400,000 people.

The shape and area of settlement was still largely undefined, the boundaries of occupation blurred with the straying feet of sheep and cattle in a fenceless land. The story of Australian settlement was yet to be written, and the inland penetration of the squatters and their herds could be traced only with uncertain fingers on the unformed maps. No one knew how far a man was going when he set out from the nearest depot with his loaded bullock waggons and his stock, nor did he know himself. He was off in search of good grazing and good waters for his herds, like as not beyond the last man out before, who would indicate to him the arbitrary boundaries of his 'run'—a blazed tree, a ploughed furrow, a range or a river.

When the Duracks arrived in 1849 the process had been going on for thirty-six years, since 1813, when men had at last crossed the Great Dividing Range that had held settlement in check for twenty-five years after the arrival of the first fleet. Later Australian bushmen, reflecting on the tremendous obstacles they themselves had overcome, would wonder that the pioneers had remained daunted for so long, but the mountains had been a psychological as well as a physical barrier to settlement. Beyond had lain the great unknown believed by many to be an arid, wind-swept waste inhabited by wild cannibal tribes, and it was even thought among the convicts that if a man crossed the range and kept walking he might reach China or Tibet. When a pass was found at last and the explorers gazed enraptured on the vast sweep of the rich Australian prairies there appeared the first symptoms of a land fever that was to burn in men's blood, driving them into the remotest and most forbidding wilderness.

The government had done its best to satisfy this urge in an organised way by issuing land grants to approved settlers within surveyed areas, but by the early twenties when the surveyors could no longer keep pace with the demand for land the flood of settlement had broken through. The land takers, with their herds and assigned servants, were over the hills and far away, past the reach of the law. Breathlesslv the authorities set about the establishment of nineteen counties where, it was declared, settlement must be contained. With the vision of tidy farms and patchwork fields, of county squires and a sturdy, respectful yeomanry they named their counties nostalgically—Gloucester, Cumberland, Glamorgan, Buckingham, Argyle, Durham, Northumberland—but only in name were they to resemble those of the old land. Fast as they worked, the pioneers on their indomitable westward march were even faster, pushing out the boundaries of settlement in a policy of their own. Undaunted by the government challenge that no police protection would be provided outside the authorised limits, they made their own rules, fighting out the battles of their boundaries with rifles, stockwhips and stirrup irons.

The Home Office was outraged, demanding that the colonial government recall these 'self styled pastoralists', these 'lawless gypsies' to within surveyed limits. Little they knew the conditions of the country or the fibre of the 'gypsies' they would have brought to heel. 'Not all the armies in England,' replied Governor Bourke, 'not a hundred thousand soldiers scattered through the bush could drive back those herds within the limits of the Nineteen Counties.' And so the tide of settlement, pressing on the tracks of the explorers, followed the rivers and tributary creeks, spreading fanwise across the countryside.

Provision depots became stores and shanty hotels that in turn burgeoned into dusty little towns. The settlers cut the tracks between them with their waggon wheels, and in time, as the centres grew, the convict gangs came out and built the roads. Within a decade the squatters, rising on the success of John Macarthur's experiments in pure merino fleece, and the toil of their assigned labourers, had become virtually the ruling voice in the colony and were clamouring for title to the land they had commandeered. The term 'squatter', in its first Australian application, had referred to an illicit occupier of Crown land who plundered stock from legal holders. A squatter was then a common thief, 'a bushranger with a base', but the term became confused when robust and otherwise law-abiding pioneers broke bounds and 'squatted' where they pleased, wresting their little kingdoms from the virgin bush. In time, as their status became recognised and their demands for security of tenure were granted, the term lost all its earlier implication and tooth on the respectability that they had won for themselves.

They were the big men now, and governments were swayed by their insistence that what Australia needed was not more free settlers but more labourers, the cheaper the better, and convicts for preference. For the first fifty years free emigration had been discouraged in the colony, but during the thirties public conscience began to stir about 'the system' whereby men were reduced to the status of beasts and it was realised by the more far-seeing that, however the wool industry might prosper, Australia could never progress to nationhood without a healthy population of free settlers.

Among the most zealous advocates of family emigration were Dr John Dunmore Lang, a radical Presbyterian minister, and Mrs Caroline Chisholm, the English-born wife of an officer of the East India Company who had come to Sydney with her husband in 1839, ten years before the arrival of Darby and Margaret Durack. Mrs Chisholm, appalled at the miserable condition of many destitute women and young girls shipped out in a crude attempt to balance the colony's largely male population, at once established a home for them, set up a labour exchange and soon a colonisation bureau. Realising the desperate need for family life in the outback, she personally escorted groups of young girls to the scattered inland settlements. A pretty little woman on a big, white horse, she had ridden before her cavalcade of bullock drays on one of the most remarkable match-making campaigns in history, teaching her timid charges how to live and like it in the Australian bush, prompting the squatter with his duty to his employees.

Only Dr Lang's violently sectarian bias separated his aims from those of this Catholic woman whom he described as 'an artful female Jesuit' whose sole object was 'to Romanise this great colony by means of a land flood of Irish popery'. Like others before him, Lang had striven hard to preserve Australia as a strictly Protestant dominion and was outraged to observe how the Catholics were quietly consolidating themselves in the colony with a growing network of churches and schools, and—worst of all—an Archbishop named John Polding who was as zealous and hard-riding as himself. His antipathy to Caroline Chisholm was, if not unfounded, at least unjust, for her message was quite unpartisan and carried no less to the poor crofters of Scotland and the struggling industrial workers of England and Wales than to the destitute of Ireland. Nonetheless, the combined voices of these two forceful personalities contributed largely to the suspension of convict transportation in 1840 and to the furtherance of a policy that in fifteen months brought over 26,000 assisted emigrants to New South Wales.

This triumph of reason and humanity over the viciousness of an inhuman policy was not, however, without its reverse side. 'The bounty system' and other schemes, too hastily devised, had brought out the undernourished and backward overflow of workhouses, orphanages and depressed industrial towns. People long since sapped of the qualities needed in a pioneering land had clung to the outskirts of Sydney town, living squalidly in bark huts, eking out a meagre living from their little plots. Timid and suspicious, confident only that 'the lordly men', 'the squatters' as they called them here, would somehow contrive to have all the good things for themselves, they believed nothing that had been told them of opportunities outback. Even the venturesome spirits, disillusioned by conditions not yet reassessed in terms of free labour, came flocking back, some to enter trades and build up little businesses, most to swell the ranks of the unemployed about the port.

The sale of Crown lands for the financing of immigration had encouraged land sharks to buy up tracts of country for the fleecing of small settlers, and the government, its funds 'completely deranged', was forced to suspend further assisted immigration. Drought struck the colony. Agriculture made no progress. The price of wool dropped and sheep were hardly worth the price of getting them to market. The pastoral industry, suddenly bereft of convict labour, hard hit in other ways, teetered for half a decade on the edge of ruin. Many pioneers walked off their properties. Others clung on, pinning their faith to a turn of the tide. Someone hit upon the plan of rendering down the sheep for their fat and reeking 'boiling-down works' sprang up in the outback towns.

When the price of tallow, mutton hams and hides rose from next to nothing to 16s a head, and good rains revived the land, salvation was in sight. The depression was already lifting by '43, but it left behind it empty pockets and heavy hearts. It was none so easy to start again, and the call to gold and easy money in California fell upon eager ears. Now that the shackled mutes were no longer there to cushion the impact of men against the land Australia was seen for the hard precarious virgin country that she was.

Without labour, progress was impossible. Convicts were no more and free emigration seemed patently to have failed. Yet through all the chaos and seeming contradictions Dr Lang and Caroline Chisholm had plugged on. By 1846, having failed to enlist the support of a disillusioned government in her own improved colonisation scheme, Mrs Chisholm had personally settled 2,000 men and women in the colony and had returned to England to establish her own Family Colonisation Loan Society and charter her own ships, properly equipped and supervised. The first of these, the *Slains Castle*, was not to leave England until 1850, by which time many like the Durack couple and their Kilfoyle relatives, influenced by her propaganda for emigration to New South Wales, had already come out.

How much of this great continent, they asked, was still unexplored? A simple question, but no one could answer it precisely. The landseekers, moving swiftly out along the big westward-flowing streams, had left untouched wastes between, and all the while explorers had been slowly solving the mystery of what lay in the unmapped emptiness beyond. In 1840 a valiant Yorkshireman named John Eyre had forced his way towards the centre of the continent in search of a fabulous inland sea, but finding nothing more promising than the great, shimmering salt lake that bears his name, struck west along the blighted southern coast towards Swan River Settlement. Although he did not succeed in reaching his objective over land, the desert miles he covered threw another shaft of light into the unknown.

In '44 Charles Sturt had penetrated to within 150 miles of the centre of the continent, and in '48 the German scientist Ludwig Leichhardt, who had previously made his way from Moreton Bay over three thousand miles of hitherto unknown country to the central northern coast at Port Essington, disappeared for ever with his entire party when attempting to cross the continent from his previous starting-point to Perth on the far west coast.

By '49, the year of the Duracks' arrival, the more fertile river tracts as far south as Port Phillip were occupied and pioneers had pushed up the Darling in the far west of New South Wales almost to Menindee, but still the 'great grey lands' to the north and west lay largely unexplored. From Moreton Bay Settlement, six hundred miles up the coast from Sydney, pastoral occupation was spreading more slowly west to the Condamine River and north to the Burnett, but the remainder of that vast land, to be declared the independent colony of Queensland ten years later, lay empty and challenging. Scattered groups of 'shepherd kings' were expanding in the colony of South Australia with as yet little evidence of permanent occupation, while on the western side of the continent settlement clung sparsely to the southernmost corner between Swan River and the little port of Albany. For the rest, nomad Aboriginal tribespeople were still the undisputed occupants, those furthest from the line of settlement only half-believing the rumours of a new race, part human and part animal, like the tribal heroes of olden time, who strode upon four legs with long tails blowing in the wind.

The newcomers could not yet write home to Ireland of a land of opportunity for the little man, but it could not be said that the big men had it all their own way here. They had been defeated only a few weeks before in an issue that was still being much talked about. The pastoralists had kept appealing for the revival of transportation, but public opinion had been so loud in its disfavour that their requests had been reconsidered only when the gaols at home became full to overflowing. The humanitarians had their point, but there was another side of it. Not only would transportation put the colonial wool industry again on its feet but would give hundreds of lost men, rotting in overcrowded cells, a chance to reprieve themselves as had so many 'emancipists' or 'ticket of leave men' now successfully established in New South Wales. When news came that a shipload of convicts had been despatched to Sydney such a hue and cry broke out as had not been heard before in the colony. By this time the protests of disinterested idealists were joined by a chorus of thoroughly interested small people—shopkeepers dependent on the custom of free men, immigrants who could not compete against slave labour. Each side couched its arguments in high-sounding phrases. The big men talked of the 'ideals of national development' and of 'giving the unfortunate convict a chance to redeem himself', so the little men had talked back in the same coin. The transportation system was a 'menace to the slowly emerging ideals of a young nation' and a song of freedom had rung out in the streets:

> Sons of the soil arise! Let this your anthem be,
> Shout 'til it rend the skies—'Australia shall be free!'

It was a crude strain but with a ring of triumph so different from the yearning songs of the Irish, conditioned to the unrequited wrong, protesting always, but with little hope of redress. It seemed that in this country the small men stood as much chance of gaining their point as the proud and powerful. They had laughed to scorn the suggestion of establishing a hereditary Australian aristocracy and, shaking their fists as the convict hulk *Hashemy* sailed into Sydney Harbour in June '49, they had again won the day. The passengers were let ashore, quietly, as work was found for them, granted immediate 'tickets of leave' and let go their way as free men. It was the end of an epoch, for transportation was never to be revived in New South Wales.

By 1849 reception depots for immigrants were an established feature and bewildered newcomers were now met and organised. Immigration lists were published in the *Sydney Morning Herald* for the benefit of intending employers, and on August 14, 1849, the arrival of the *Duke of Roxborough* was duly noted with the information that:

> Tomorrow the hiring of immigrants will be proceeded with . . . Besides the above there are about ten unmarried females by this vessel who will be lodged in the depot at Hyde Park where they can be hired between two and four o'clock tomorrow and on succeeding days.

Darby Durack, who had signed up for farm work, was forced to await the departure of immigrant coaches for inland, an irksome two weeks' delay, since the raw and rowdy port of Sydney was hardly to the taste of these Irish country folk. The overcrowding of the town served only to stress the emptiness of the vast colony. The ill-sewered, dray-made thoroughfares were noisy with swaggering sailors, red-coated soldiers brawling with the native-born 'currency lads', hucksters, jugglers, street dancers and gaudy prostitutes. Chinese coolies—another unsuccessful experiment in servile labour—shuffled past with poles of fish, black men in tattered clothing sold wooden props, rush-made brooms and wild honey. Bullock-drawn waggons swayed through slushy wheel ruts with their top-heavy loads of wool and hides from far inland. And on everything the light, even in winter, fell hard and harsh.

On August 28 it was further announced in the press that thirty-seven immigrants per ship *Duke of Roxborough* were that day sent from the immigration barracks at Parramatta to the town of Goulburn, and Darby with his wife and infant faced their first inland journey with mingled sensations of relief and apprehension.

3

THE GOLDEN YEARS

The years 1849 to 1853. Journey to Goulburn, where Darby Durack finds employment with James Chisholm of Kippilaw. Impressions and conditions of labour. The discovery of gold in '51 and its effects upon the colony. Michael Durack and his family leave Ireland for New South Wales.

The carriages, overloaded with passengers and luggage, jolted and bogged on their way, over Razor Back Mountain, a two-day stage from the smokes and clamour of the town to where the old road swung south so that the ranges lay upon the west and rolling hills subsided to the coast.

Prepared for a land of perpetual sunshine, the immigrants found themselves exposed to wild rains and winds blowing bleakly from mountain snows, as cold or colder than any they had known. They found it no land for loving at first sight. Only time would make friends of the unbending gums whose branches with their thin perennial leaves spread stiffly above the reach of man. Familiarity would give shape and meaning to the twisting, tattered paperbarks and confusion of the lesser forest as it would bring joy of its bright, hard flowers and bright, harsh birds. A journey of 130 miles inland had seemed a great distance to the newcomers, not yet adjusted to the vast perspectives of this empty continent.

Incidents, soon to become the commonplace of everyday life, seemed perilous adventures—floating coaches on empty hogsheads across swollen streams or easing down steep inclines with logs hitched on behind; unharnessing the horses in drenching rain, the women and children sleeping, if sleep they could, inside the carriages, the men underneath on beds of canvas laid over heaps of bark.

The arrival of the immigrant coaches, rattling through the unmade streets, caused some stir in the little bush town on the edge of the great plain. To Darby Durack and his wife, Goulburn had seemed at first flat, crude and ugly with its slab-built, bark-roofed humpies and shanty hotels, its roads that were no more than winding waggon ruts, noisy and congested with creaking drays and bullock teams and herds of sheep and cattle being driven to the boiling-down works, whose pungent smell pervaded the atmosphere.

They could hardly have believed with what affection they would watch the little frontier town grow to a centre of importance and dignity—Goulburn, city of the big plains. Already it had become a lively focus for the roads of the south and south-western districts and for the surrounding bush community. Since its foundation in 1820 it had seen the growth of a great pastoral industry as well as some of the worst evils of the convict system, since the chain gang had been stationed for thirteen years at the Towang stockade, only six miles south. Public executions had been frequent during the twenties and thirties when corpses had been left to blacken on the gibbet on Gallows Hill. The triangle could still be seen in the town where Billy O'Rourke, 'The Towang Flogger', and the vicious negro 'Black Francis' had flaked the flesh from men's backs so that if they lived to be free men they were branded as 'shellbacks' who had worn the yellow garb of misery and shame. Desperate men, goaded beyond endurance, had escaped into the bush and formed themselves into lawless bands that infested the southern roads, sticking up the mail coaches, robbing isolated settlements and molesting travellers. The hanging of Whitton, leader of the local outlaws, in Goulburn in 1840 had marked the end of that first era of bushranging, and it seemed then that the menace had been finally dealt with and the roads made safe for travellers. Its recurrence from another strata of society was not then foreseen.

So keen was the competition for labour at this time that a crowd had gathered at the immigrant reception depot for the arrival of the coaches. Squatters, for the most part big, bearded men in broad-brimmed cabbage-tree hats and moleskin trousers, smoking heavy pipes, flicking at the flies with the crops of their stockwhips, appraised the newcomers descending stiffly from the muddy carriages. The man who at once drew Darby and his wife aside was hardly typical of the early 'squattocracy', being tall, spare and clean-shaven except for side-whiskers, and of a quiet, considerate manner that contrasted with the bluff heartiness of the majority. In Darby he would have seen a strongly built young fellow, also clean-shaven at that time, with dark curly hair and clear-cut features, while his wife was a fresh-faced, capable-looking girl with a quirk of unfailing good humour about her mouth. A few formal questions and the couple found themselves engaged in the service of James Chisholm, clipping along beside him in his smart four-in-hand on the road to his Kippilaw estate.

They learned that their employer was not, as far as he knew, related to Caroline Chisholm, the Emigrants' Friend, but he knew her well and proudly claimed her as a kinswoman. Unlike most big landholders of the time, he admired and approved her work, even her encouragement of small settlers, and did all he could to assist her, acting as treasurer of her fund for the Emigrant Friends' Society in the Goulburn district. As time went on they would know much of the kindness and generosity of this man with whom they had been lucky enough to find a home. His father had come to the colony as a member of the New South Wales Corps but had avoided the disrepute of many members of that body during the years when rum, in the control of the army, was colonial currency. In the same way his son James had never earned the opprobrium attached to so many employers of convict labour. He had publicly denounced the flogging of minor offenders and the laying of trumped-up charges against more useful assigned convicts in order to prolong their servitude. Fortunate indeed had been the bond men and women assigned to Kippilaw, for Mr Chisholm and his good wife had helped many a lost soul to a new start in life. No bushranger ever molested his property or those belonging to it. Sometimes they had been held up on the road but when recognised had been allowed to keep their money and valuables and go on their way.

The estate of Kippilaw, spread about the fertile valley of the Wollondilly River at the head of the Hawkesbury, had begun as a cattle station in 1832, but was soon growing also wool, wheat and maize. The homestead enclosure, its lawns and gardens stretching to the river banks, was like a little village with a two-storey 'Government House' of white stone, its four wings surrounding a courtyard, convict-built with shingled roof, gables, long shuttered windows and creeper-shaded verandahs. Other buildings included a small stone church, stables, a store, a butchery and a blacksmith's 'shop' and a long barracks that had housed assigned servants of earlier years and now accommodated free labourers. Married couples and their families occupied smaller stone buildings, each with kitchen-living-room below and loft above, equipped with straw palliasses for sleeping. It was one of these that became for some years the home of Darby and his Margaret and the birthplace of their first three Australian sons. James Chisholm had chosen wisely, for Darby was not one to break his contract and return to the huddle of the port town. He knew the value of these years at Kippilaw, learning how to work stock under Australian conditions, becoming accustomed to the climate and seasons of the southern hemisphere, saving from his princely wage of £40 a year, against the day when he would follow the advice of the solid old hands and 'put everything into four legs' and a good piece of land. Out of this wage he also managed to send home a regular remittance, at the same time urging his family to emigrate, but an underlying note of sadness in the letters did not escape his people. He felt obliged to explain that the young colony was in many ways a strange, harsh land where men and manners were very different from those of the old country. It was an uphill struggle to become one's own master, and for this reason the would-be settler, fighting for a place in the sun, was aptly dubbed 'a battler'. Agriculture was backward in the colony, for although most properties had their cultivated plots of barley, maize and vegetables, large-scale cultivation was difficult. Labour was not only short but expensive because every acre must first be cleared of heavy scrub and trees. Therefore men became graziers, using the unfenced virgin country for their stock in a free and easy style that was difficult to understand. Many of the big squatters and merchants, early on the scene, had become rich, but newcomers, without capital, could succeed only through great patience, hard work and the long-range plan.

Darby had been almost two years at Kippilaw when the colonial picture changed with dramatic suddenness. In May '51 gold was discovered at the Turon and the tough, prosaic outpost of empire became a continent of fabulous romance.

In convict times Australian gold had been a whisper and a fear. The wealth of the colony was the golden fleece of her sheep and woe betide it if their shackled tenders should break to dig for treasure among the tumbled hills. A man who was warned to put away the nugget he had found lest the free men of the colony had their throats cut had prudently complied. When transportation ceased, Australian settlers, in their slough of despond, were too intent upon scanning the skies for rain and the press for news of better times to seek a glint of gold about their feet. Colourful stories of gold rushes in America had seemed a far cry from this humdrum south land until a man who had walked off his bankrupt property in '48 and sailed to California one day looked up from washing dirt in the bed of Sacramento River and was reminded of the Bathurst scene he had left behind. If this was gold country—why not that? A simple-hearted fellow, he told everyone he met, all the way back to New South Wales and out on horseback across the mountains. Nobody paid much attention to his naïve talk, but his hunch had not played him false. He found his gold in the first dishful he washed and the next and the next. And so a merry chain of campfires swung out from Sydney across the mountains to the plains beyond, the mushroom roaring canvas towns sprang up and the gold fever mounted to delirium. There was buried treasure in the river beds and among the sunbaked hills and valleys of this old-new land and quick as news could travel the word went round the world.

Darby Durack, coming in from Kippilaw for stores, saw men near mad in Goulburn the day the news came through. The big Scot McKensie, blowing on his pibroch like some outsize pied piper, had led off the first lot of diggers to a wild accompaniment of singing and shouting and waving of hats, leaving Goulburn like a plague spot, shops closed, houses deserted, the bootmaker's bench unoccupied with a lady's shoe upon the last, bread in the baker's oven left to ruin. What a crazy march that had been—men and women, even children, goods and equipment piled into any sort of vehicle from a four-in-hand to a gin case on wheels!

It was not easy, in that moment of infectious excitement, when all over Australia men were exchanging their tools of trade for miner's shovels and picks, and in Sydney entire crews were deserting their ships, to resist the temptation to join the rush to the Turon, but Darby, prudently weighing the risks against the value of a steady job and a good home for his family, carried on at Kippilaw. More than half Chisholm's other labourers made off, and every shepherd on the place rolled his swag, whistled up his dogs and went on his way. All over the countryside the squatters met in frantic consultation. How to carry on? Optimists declared it a flash in the pan and predicted that before long the importunate fellows would be back again, caps in hand, begging for their old jobs. Others felt that a great tide of change had turned in the colony and that landholders must think up other ways and means of holding their flocks and working their runs.

In Goulburn excitement ebbed and flowed. Many after only a few weeks returned from the diggings, disillusioned, but there was scarcely a day without fresh rumours of gold in some new place that kept a section of the populace rushing from place to place like shuttle-cocks. Darby observed that, of them all, but a few made good: the majority would have done better to stay at home and attend to their ordinary work. He saw the gold rush as a madness that would pass and, sensitive of the Irish reputation for rashness and instability, took pride in keeping a cool head until things returned to normal. Some said, 'He's a steady fellow, that Irishman at Kippilaw. Chisholm's lucky to have a chap like that,' but many squatters were suspicious of a saving, steady labourer. 'Give me the improvident fellow—the man who gambles or hands his cheque over the bar counter,' they would say. 'As long as he's broke he'll stick to the job, but once he has a few pounds put by he begins to fancy himself as a landholder.'

Pastoralists had talked big about Australia's need for more people and more capital to swell the labour pool and raise the price of meat, but with the gold rush their wish came true with a vengeance. It was some twelve months after the discovery of gold before the first mining immigrants could reach Australian shores. By this time the southern portion of the colony, comprising about 87,900 square miles, had been declared the separate State of Victoria and more sensational gold finds around Ballarat had sent the gold seekers rushing in that direction. Rising 95,000 people flocked to Victoria from other parts of Australia in '51 and 20,000 from overseas surged into Melbourne in September '52. Thereafter immigrants swelled from a previous average of 500 to many thousands a month. The money and the population had materialised. Meat soared to the dizzy height of 5d a pound and all the produce of the land was in keen demand. So far so good, but where was the labour to replace the stockmen and the poor, rum-besotted shepherds who had rushed off at the first clarion call of gold? Soon it became apparent that what the landholder had gained on the roundabouts he had lost on the swings. The money he made he must now put into fences, since it soon became obvious that shepherds would be from henceforth an extinct race in the land, while an ever-hungrier pack of small men clamoured about the borders of his run.

Conflicting though the situation was, it emerged clearly enough that the day of the little man had dawned in the colony. Unable to realise the vastness of Australia and the potential of her still unopened wilderness, it seemed to the newcomer that all unclaimed land must soon run out in this latest scramble, and Darby Durack wrote entreating his family to delay no longer. Mr Chisholm had promised them all employment, but he was not one to stand in a man's way when he wished to branch out for himself. In two years they might, between them, have saved enough to secure a small block and sufficient stock to make a modest start.

Up to this time Darby's elder brother, Michael, shocked by stories of entire families dying on 'coffin ships' on the long voyage to the colonies, had been reluctant to leave his native land. Although his family, then numbering five girls and two boys, had survived the rigours of famine, some of them had been left far from strong. The fifth child, Sarah, seven years old when her uncle migrated to Australia, could not, they believed, have survived even a reasonable voyage and although 'Mammie Amy Forde' urged them to go, leaving the sickly child in her care, they clung on in the desperate hope of better times. The hope proved vain, for although the famine had lifted by '48, its main causes—the wholesale evictions and land clearances—went on. Ireland sank deeper in the mire of pessimism and bitterness, the hatred of England and the landlords stronger than ever before. 'To get up you must first get out,' and everywhere deserted fields and the ruins of little homes betokened a broken-hearted land.

By the end of '52 Michael Durack also faced the fact that he and his family must emigrate or starve, but they had virtually nothing with which to make even a small down payment on their fare. My grandfather Patsy, already introduced as the eldest son, who longed to join his uncle Darby in the golden colony of New South Wales, often told his children how chance had come to their assistance. The great Lord Dunraven of Adare, probably the father of the man who, some forty years later, was to join forces with other fighters in the cause of Irish liberty, was travelling to Limerick when his coach became embedded in the mire. Patsy, seventeen years old and deceptively strong for his light build, had put his shoulder under the hub of the vehicle and quickly had it free. The great man had called him back as he turned away and asked whether he was so rich that he had no need of a reward. Blushing with confusion, Patsy had declared himself the eldest son of a large family hoping soon to emigrate to Australia and dig for gold.

'Then here's a piece to go on with,' said his Lordship, pressing a sovereign into the boy's hand.

To one who had counted a few pence handsome payment for a day's toil this was riches indeed, and it was not long before he had translated it into two hens, a sow and the present of a holy picture for each member of his family. He told his children in later years how that sovereign had proved a magic coin, for the hens laid well and the sow brought forth a fine litter, so that in twelve months there was enough money to bring them all to Australia. Besides this, little Sarah seemed stronger by the autumn of '52 and the die was cast.

A prospect of exciting change and adventure for the young people, for their parents the leave-taking was fraught with grief and anxiety. Mammie Amy at the last refused to leave the now impoverished farm at Scariff. She would not desert the graves of her dead but would pray out her life for their souls and for those who had been spared to start life anew in distant lands. She had good friends left who would visit and care for her, and someday perhaps there would be a letter to say that one very dear had found that pot of gold she had dreamt of at the rainbow's end.

So they were gathered at last, with a host of other migrating families guarding their bundles, the spinning wheels and wooden cradles and rocking chairs tied up together with their patched and homespun clothes, waiting in the cold for the sailing packet that would carry them to Plymouth on the first stage of their 13,000-mile journey to the strange south land.

4
Digging In

The years 1853 to 1855. Michael Durack and his family arrive in New South Wales. Arrival and death of Michael at Kippilaw. His son Patsy makes £1,000 at the Ovens goldfields.

The good ship *Harriet*'s three and a half months' voyage was shadowed by the death of eleven children in an epidemic of measles, an ordeal the Durack family managed to survive intact. The vessel, which arrived at the end of May '53, was held in quarantine until the middle of June when the passengers gathered at the immigration barracks at Parramatta where an officer recorded a few brief details of family history.

Michael Durack, born at Magerareagh, County Galway, aged forty-four, eldest son of John (deceased) and Amy Durack (living), of the same county, had been nominated as a farm labourer by Mr James Chisholm of Kippilaw, Goulburn. He had paid £8 passage money in all for himself and eight dependants and undertook to refund the remaining £115 within two years.

No doubt the recording officer took this guarantee with a grain of salt, as the colonial balance sheet was clear proof of the frailty of migrant promises. In no time at all newcomers found out that Jack was as good as his master here and they need not be pushed around by anyone. Forced labour in the colony had gone by the board with the transportation system and the high-sounding '52 Bill of Indenture with its dire threats of legal action for failure to fulfil contracts and refund passage money stood precious little chance of catching up with elusive defaulters in so vast a land. Even the humble Chinese coolies soon went their own way here: those who braved the outback made a beeline for the goldfields, while the rest lived huddled together in a little China at the far end of the town, with joss-sticks, opium dens and all the trimmings of Oriental life.

It was officially stated that the seven Durack children, all described as 'farm servants', could read and write and were in good health, although, probably undernourished and still suffering from the after-effects of measles, they would have been a wan-looking little group. Strangers often expressed surprise at the mixed appearance of this brood, black Irish and red Irish from the same tree, though others declared that apart from obvious differences of colouring and character they were stamped with an unmistakable brand of family. The dark strain had come down from Mammie Amy's side, a throwback, some said, to the survivors of Spain's wrecked Armada whom many a west Ireland family had taken into their hearts and homes; though Mammie Amy herself said her forebears had been 'Claddagh folk', survivors of the oldest race in Ireland who had built the great dun of Aran—a dark, wild people, but good builders and extremely proud of their great antiquity.

Mary, aged twenty, had the gaunt, anxious features and the too-large, grey eyes of one grown to womanhood in hungry years. Because she had always borne the brunt of eldest girl in a large, struggling family they called her 'Poor Mary' even then, and as though it set the seal on her hard and ill-starred life, she was never known as anything else but that. Her brother Patsy, my grandfather, then eighteen years old, was blue-eyed with a mass of dark, curly hair, a thin boy, nimble on his feet, who loved to dance and could play by ear any instrument from a tin whistle to the fiddle he had inherited from his rollicking grandfather 'Daddy Jack' and that he guarded like his honour. Fifteen-year-old Margaret was pretty as a wax doll, but her long, fair plaits seemed too heavy a frame for her wistful face. Bridget, at thirteen, was an undersized waif with reddish hair, while the eleven-year-old Sarah, small too, was gypsy dark with lively, bright eyes that shone from a face of transparent whiteness. Then came little Anne, nine years old, blue-eyed, auburn-haired and even then inseparable from the seven-year-old Michael. This last boy, like his sister Sarah one of 'the black Duracks', was later to be known as 'Stumpy Michael' to distinguish him from other, Australian-born 'cornstalks' of the same name, and as such, to avoid confusion, I must refer to him from the beginning.

Young Patsy, his precious fiddle tucked under his arm, viewed the pageant of life in the raw young colony with eager eyes. He was a little awed by the immigration formalities and the sight of his father in his Sunday clothes, the bowler hat, the long dark coat, the striped, stove-pipe trousers, coloured waistcoat and cravat, his long hair sleekly brushed and curling decorously about his ears, his lean, clean-shaven features portentously solemn as he answered the sharp barrage of personal questions. The boy sensed that life in a new land would not be easy for the proud, conservative Galwayman who had seemed at times over-stern with his family, over-insistent on mannerly deportment, over-meticulous about details that seemed of little importance, and who stiffened now as he replied that his good wife, aged forty, could neither read nor write. What did they know of this woman who had been 'The Rose of Cappabaun'? What was it to them that she was an exponent of Irish lore and of her native Gael, learned of a scholarly priest who had said Mass in the barn of her parents' farm, or that she was a sweet singer and had dancing feet and was known throughout two counties as a woman with 'the healing hands'? Bridget Dillon had been well schooled in many things, but the eldest daughter of a poor farming family stood little chance of formal learning in the erratic 'hedge schools' of her youth.

Difficult though it might prove for his parents to adjust themselves to colonial life, young Patsy had felt himself at once a part of it, thrilling to every unaccustomed sight and sound, to the fine horses that even working men rode here as a matter of course, to the varied and colourful people, European, Oriental, Kanaka, that had figured only in the legends and stories of his childhood.

Also at the barracks this day was a shipload of bearded, Gaelic-speaking highlanders and Skye-men who, the newcomers learned, had been brought out under the auspices of John Dunmore Lang as an antidote to the weakling Irish, many of whom had been encouraged to migrate by the incorrigible Caroline Chisholm. Disappointment awaited him in this, for many of the Irish 'marauders and malcontents' he so reviled and distrusted were to prove among the finest and hardiest pioneers of the land, while most of his own bluff peasant Scots who were to have provided the backbone of the nation went flocking back to the mists and rigours of Highland winters before they had learned to love the sun or had discovered that unremitting poverty and toil was not necessarily the lot of man born of woman. Ironically the Irish, whose low standards of living had been so deplored and who had nothing to return to but destitution, remained to blend in the making of a people some day to enjoy one of the highest living standards in the world.

Darby Durack had come to Sydney from Kippilaw with a waggon-load of wool to meet his family, but since the ship had been quarantined he had perforce returned without seeing them. The good Mr Chisholm, however, had arranged for him to come a second time and the family found accommodation meanwhile at a modest inn on the outskirts of the town. Years later Grandfather Patsy would point out the spot and wonder at the changes he had seen in his own time, telling how before these buildings and pavements it had been a swampy place where teamsters and drovers pastured their animals while they regaled themselves at the Woolpack, the Square and Compass or the Dog and Duck.

Two years of gold had already made a mark on the sprawling settlement of Sydney town among the hilly coves. The business premises and homes of the newly rich were dwarfing humble shops and cottages and there were breathtaking signs of easy money and wanton extravagance. Although excessive drinking was no new sight to the Irish, it shocked them to see fiery Bengal spirit swilled neat from wine glasses in the foetid grog-houses that throve in every street. Successful merchants in smart phaetons and gentlemen squatters in carriages went clattering past with their families, shut off by their prosperity from the harsher aspects of colonial living. Their homes, glimpsed through stately wrought-iron gateways past curved carriage drives, were little islands of orderly Victorian life, where ladies plied their gentle accomplishments and men in velvet smoking-jackets sipped old brandy from fine-cut goblets and discussed such weighty colonial topics as the iniquities of free labour, the bad effects of easy money on the masses, the shiftlessness and audacity of the 'currency' and the benefits of educating their own sons abroad.

'How soon you have become a colonial!' Michael told his brother when they met at last amid all the tears and embracings of Irish reunion. The fresh-faced young man of three years before was weather-beaten and wore a beard, moleskin trousers, stockman's boots and broad-brimmed hat. He was besides, he proudly told them, now the father of three children, the girl Bridget and two sons whom they had called John and Patrick, both born at Kippilaw.

Plans were made to divide the family for a time, since an invasion of nine newcomers was felt to be too great a strain even on the well-known kindness of the Chisholms. Bridget Durack with the younger children was to remain with friends in Goulburn until after the birth of her eighth child. Poor Mary and Margaret were to take positions as farm servants on a nearby property while young Patsy and his father returned with Darby to Kippilaw. Even temporary separations were always painful to my grandfather and the idea of working steadily with the hope of acquiring land and a home of their own in the remote future chafed his impatient spirit. With the glorious optimism that was to stand by him through the bitterest reverses he believed that he had only to take a pick and shovel to the goldfields and he would have them all set up in no time at all. His father and uncle, however, dismissed his ambition as romantic nonsense and said he must get a good grounding in the working of sheep and cattle under Australian conditions. He liked the life well enough at Kippilaw, delighting in the splendid horses and other stock, feasting his eyes on the rolling natural pastures of the Wollondilly, on the blue Australian hills and the tall gums, but always with a restlessness in his heart, dreaming of gold that would buy him land of his own. As it happened he was not destined to spend more than a few weeks of his life working for a master, for in one swift stroke of fate his status in life was changed from that of a dutiful son to head of his family.

He and his father had been set to work felling timber for a fence near Rose Lagoon, a picturesque part of the property abounding in wild game. The older man had been holding open a gate while the boy drove through with a dray-load of wood, when a kangaroo, bounding from a patch of scrub, had startled the blinkered horse. As the animal jibbed a piece of timber slipped to one side hitting Michael a stunning blow. He fell across the track, the dray lurched backwards and jolted over him with its crushing load. There was no cry, only a sickening bump and silence and the boy on his knees in the sand, his arms around the broken, lifeless body.

The *Goulburn Herald* of August 27, 1853, made a note of the inquest:

> ... held at Gatton Park, near Mummel, on the body of Michael Durick [*sic*] who met his death on the previous day, by a cart and horse running over him at Rose Lagoon. The deceased had been only two months in the country and has left a widow and eight children to deplore his loss ...

So it is that great-grandfather Michael remains only a shadowy figure in family memory, a proud, prudent, hardworking Galwayman who made the few, strong, simple pieces of household furniture that were to travel many thousands of miles to the lonely outposts he did not live to see. The only photo we have of him is a faded tin type in a plush-lined case, taken before he left his native land, but in which we can discern the Irish features and fine-boned hands with the crooked small fingers that have come down through the generations. A poor farmer, he clasps in his right hand a gold-tinted quill like a symbol of the learning he revered.

To the simple Irish widow the cry of the Australian curlew was always the banshee wail of her native bogs. She had heard it on the eve of her husband's death and had known then, she said, that the wrath of 'Red Mac' had followed them to the end of the earth. It was a tragic start for their life in the new land, but had his father lived Grandfather might never have become the man he was or have done the things he did. He would no doubt have remained to work out his apprenticeship at Kippilaw and perhaps after some years, his ambitions clipped to modest proportions, gone into land under the prudent guidance of the elder man, to become a quiet, steady fellow of the same mind. As it happened he plunged headlong at eighteen into the swift current of his times so that in surveying his life one is constantly amazed at the speed at which he travelled and the zest with which he lived.

'I had no boyhood,' Grandfather told his children. 'I was a child one day and a man the next, with the cares of the world on my shoulders.' But although given to these occasional flashes of self-pity, that was the way he must have wanted it or he would not so consistently have gathered troubles to himself.

He quickly organised his family, the older girls in jobs not far from Goulburn, his bereaved mother with the younger children, including the new-born Jeremiah, boarding in that town; and with the warmth of Mr Chisholm's blessing and the chill of his Uncle Darby's disapproval he set out for the goldfields. He had acquired a horse, covered cart and merchandise on commission basis from Mr Samuel Emanuel of Goulburn, little knowing this to be but the beginning of a long and far-reaching association.

The Emanuels belonged to a prosperous Jewish community that, with uncanny business instinct, had gathered around Goulburn in the depressed forties. The *Sydney Morning Herald* summed the situation up by saying that 'the ten tribes had not been lost, only mislaid into Goulburn' and a successful man of the time was often said to be as 'solid as a Goulburn Jew'.

This family, long established in the legal profession in Southampton, had immigrated during the thirties and had sold out of what was bluntly described as 'a slop clothing business' in Sydney to take on a variety of new interests in the centre of the rich pastoral tablelands, and were prominent in the far-seeing group that financed and organised the Sydney Gold Escort more than a year before the great discovery. Some said it was intuition, others that they had 'been in the know'.

They had seen Goulburn grow from a little frontier village of slab-built, bark-roofed humpies and shanty hotels to a sizeable and prosperous town. The roads were still no more than the winding waggon ruts, always noisy and congested with creaking drays and bullock teams, and herds of sheep and cattle being driven to boiling-down works or saleyard, but business premises and hostelries were now numerous and flourishing. The Emanuels had a finger in many pies. They were gold buyers, bankers, shareholders in the Gold Escort, proprietors of the Steam Flour Mills, the Beehive Store and the Beehive Hotel, whose swinging sign sported an appropriate ditty:

In this house we're all alive,
Good liquor makes us funny.
If you are dry, come in and try
The virtue of our honey.

It was from the Beehive Store that Grandfather stocked his vehicle for the fields, having been assured that, although past the first flush of excitement when fabulous fortunes had been made, the Ovens diggings, some 220 miles south of Goulburn, and about 25 miles below the border of New South Wales and Victoria, were still flourishing enough and that, while covering himself with the sale of his goods, he could equip and work a claim of his own. Emanuel advised him that with the credit he could raise on, say, £1,000 capital, he might set himself and his family up with land and stock, though if he stayed on in the hopes of making more he might well find himself back where he started.

Already thinking in figures and distances that would have staggered him on arrival in the colony only fourteen weeks before, young Patsy went on his way south through the straggling, dusty country towns of Tarago, Collector, Gunning, Yass and across the Murrumbidgee at Gundagai.

Life at Albury, the border town, and Beechworth, the miners' centre on Ovens River, seemed wildly exciting and extravagant to the newcomer, though the old hands remembered even livelier times.

'You should have been here last year, when we played skittles with bottles of champagne and a crowd of Yanks spread butter between pound notes and fed them to their dog!'

Since the first rush to the district in '52 mining had sown a wide, sporadic growth of calico tents, windlasses, ventilators, shafts and mounds of earth about the once lonely countryside. The roar of the diggings—Mopoke Hill, Chinaman's Lead, Wooragee, Napoleon's Flat, Snake Valley—ominous as the noise of a tidal wave, could be heard for miles on a still day. Later Patsy would come to know each separate sound, to distinguish the busy rattle of the 'Long Toms'—the cradles that sifted dross from gold, the ringing of anvil and pick, the thud of shovel, the bang and jangle of tin dish and bucket. He would know the groan and creak of the waggons and the bellowing of the teams under the sharp crack of whips, the raised, urgent voices, the trundling of barrows and the clatter of horses' hoofs.

Never had he seen such a motley crowd, faces and beards heavily begrimed, an impression of red shirts and blue dungaree trousers under a spattering of caked mud and dust. Nets, and here and there a dancing circle of corks, dangled from the brims of cabbage-tree hats to disperse the persistent flies. Most of the women, in poke bonnets and faded dresses, were as grimy and weather-beaten as the men, but they became animated at sight of the goods in the dray and eager fingers tested the quality of tarlatan, of ribbon and lace, while the men clamoured for picks and shovels, tin dishes, billycans and camp ovens.

Patsy's trade was brisk, and payment came in gold dust and raw nuggets, one in the shape of a horseshoe which he had set as a brooch for his mother. For the first time he fingered and knew the fascination of raw gold and realised something of how men could grow to love even the pursuit of it.

In a short time he was a miner along with the rest, at home with the vernacular, the nicknames, the passwords, the grievances. He shared resentment of the 'miner's fee', now increased out of all proportion to £3 a month, burned with indignation at the sight of diggers who had failed to produce their licences on demand chained to logs like felons. He learned the password signalling the coming of the police, remembered how the single warning syllable would echo round the diggings from claim to claim and down into the shafts—'Joe! Joe! Joe!'

Many things he saw in those days—violent death, men killed in greed, in anger or in drink, men crushed or trapped and smothered in the shafts. He saw men prepared to give up the chance of a lifetime for mateship, quixotic deeds of unselfishness and courage. He worked beside ex-convicts and immigrants from many lands—English, Scottish, German, French, Afghan and Chinese—rubbed shoulders with Anglican, Lutheran, Jew, with followers of Buddha, Confucius, Muhammad or simply the god of gold. He learned a wide tolerance and a respect for the beliefs of all men of good faith.

On Saturdays he joined the diggers who flocked into Beechworth to quench their thirsts at nineteen shanty pubs. What went into the miners' liquor was nobody's business. Wood spirit in casks was coloured with tobacco and livened up with a dash of vitriol. They drank Bengal and Jamaica rum and 'barley bree', and sometimes, to celebrate some great occasion—champagne.

Irishmen gathered in hundreds at the Harp of Erin, the Shamrock, the Albion to swap yarns, sing and dance to the wheeze of accordion, fiddle, gum-leaf or tin whistle, but there were no great national distinctions drawn. Irishmen were as likely to barrack 'The Tasmanian Bruiser' or a Scotsman in a fight, as Tom Coughlin, 'The Freckled Irishman', famed for his 'hit wid the left'.

All his life Grandfather would speak of the personalities of these impressionable days—Wallace, 'The Golden King', who made his pile at Beechworth store, 'Sandy' Cameron his clerk, Will Quinlan who died at Eureka Stockade in '54, Charles McAlister and his brother George, whose rough-hewn ballads of current happenings were among the first folk songs of the land. Then there was Don Cameron, boss sluicer of Woolshed Creek, candidate for the Ovens electorate, whose supporters contributed a matchbox full of gold apiece to his campaign, and whose victory march, beginning with the ceremonial fitting of his horse with golden shoes, was a highlight of Ovens history. Tip-drays hitched to heavy miners' horses, fours-in-hand, dog-carts and waggonettes were filled with cheering, singing diggers who followed their hero across the red carpet spread in the main street.

Cameron's mate 'Woolshed Johnson', two years before a shepherd earning 7s a week, now sluicing £600 a month, shouted champagne for the town, and at the banquet that followed the successful candidate was presented with 2,000 sovereigns in expectation of his political services. The confidence was misplaced, for the popular member had mistaken his obvious vocation as a showman for that of politician and it was not long before the miners were complaining of his 'poor effort on behalf of the Ovens electorate'. Faithful supporters joined his detractors in a brawl that Superintendent Robert O'Hara Burke at the head of twenty mounted police was called upon to quell. Soon afterwards Cameron resigned, leaving as the only glorious memory of his political career the time he rode through the diggings on a horse shod with gold—and even that was disputed, for some declared the shoes as bogus as his promises, that they had been appropriated from a circus then on tour of the diggings and were made of brass!

Robert Burke, late of the Irish Constabulary of County Galway, was one of the few policemen who managed to remain reasonably popular with the miners. Grandfather was proud, in after years, to have known the man whose tracks he was to follow into the unknown of a new State. They hailed from much the same part of Ireland and shared a passion for horses, but when they discussed the Irish hunters Burke spoke as a man who had ridden them and Grandfather as a wistful spectator. For all that, Burke was a modest fellow, as Grandfather remembered him, neither officious nor class-conscious—rather an odd man out in the Force with his informality of dress and manner, his love of literature and his romantic talk. Hardened bushmen had smiled in their beards when the fresh-faced Irish youth, who could 'lose himself in a paddock', they said, spoke of his longing to lay bare the mysteries of the interior.

There, too, Grandfather met two young Irishmen, Dinny Skeahan and Pat Tully, who were to become his brothers-in-law. Dinny was a young miner who had sought his fortune 'with more optimism than encouragement' on every goldfield in the country. Patsy enjoyed his rollicking stories and his scurrilous topical songs, but was apparently none so pleased when the unstable fellow turned up at a later date to capture Poor Mary's sentimental heart.

Pat Tully, although also an incorrigible miner, was a very different kettle of fish. A thoughtful, gently mannered Galway youth, he and his brother had come to the Ovens after battling their way through all the fields from

Adelong to Bendigo and Ballarat. Their people too had been farmers on the banks of the Shannon and had fought the cause of Ireland in every battle back to Clontarf and beyond. From Sydney the brothers had carried their swags over the mountain roads to join their uncle on a little property near Goulburn, but a few weeks later the gold fever broke out in the colony and all three had taken the road to the diggings. Somehow nothing had gone to plan. Their horses were stolen and in eight months they scratched no more than a meagre living while some men, working alongside, had grown rich. But therein lay the fascination of the golden years that were to leave an indelible mark on the Australian character. Long after the big rushes the restlessness would remain, the yearning for change, excitement, independence and wider opportunity, a love of wager and hazard—the fall of a coin, the form of a horse.

Grandfather made £1,000 in eighteen months on the goldfields. It can hardly be imagined that he was 'satisfied' (for what digger ever was?) or that he was not sorely tempted to go on, but it was the sum he had fixed as his goal and he stuck to it. No doubt, too, he saw that the day of the individual miner was drawing to a close, for already the shallow shaft and the tub-and-cradle of the little man were giving place to the horse-drawn harrows of parties with capital. Soon these, too, would go under before the crushing machines and steam batteries of the big companies, and the independent prospector must either give the game away or hump his bluey and move on—to Queensland, Kimberley, Nullagine, Kalgoorlie, on the fugitive trail of 'the alluvial'.

Grandfather never quite lost his nostalgia for the mining life. These eighteen months in which he had grown from a smooth-faced boy to a bearded man had been formative ones for him and he would always look back to them as happy and exciting times. Nor would he ever lose hope, in later years, of retrieving his fortunes as he had founded them.

5

LAND OF THEIR OWN

The years 1855 to 1857. Patsy and Darby Durack obtain land on Dixon's Creek in the county of Argyle and settle into farming life.

During the fifties in New South Wales getting information about unoccupied land amounted to something of a fine art. There were still no fences to mark the boundaries of the runs, nothing to distinguish private from Crown land and sheep as well as horses and cattle now roamed where they would. When shepherds faded from the picture the landholders, desperate at first, soon discovered that sheep did very well in this country left to their own devices, so with his stock roaming at large it was not hard for a settler to give the impression of owning all the country in his vicinity. Grandfather knew that a landseeker naïve enough to announce his intention was likely to be sent on a wild-goose chase from run to run, so, like many another would-be selector of his time, he rode the countryside ostensibly on business of another kind, keeping his eyes and ears open. He had been warned by shrewd oldtimers that he would learn less in a week at a comfortable homestead than in an evening spent in the men's hut, joining in a game of 'all fours' played for plugs of tobacco and listening to the brisk exchange of local yarns and gossip.

More than ever now the squatter had reason to fear and resent the up-and-coming little man. From the beginning it had been a country of 'every man for himself' but before the golden year of '51 the squatters, representing one-tenth of the community, wielded more power than all the rest—labourers, small farmers, merchants, shopkeepers and professional men—put together. In a series of heated battles they had won the purchase rights to the plums of their districts and by buying up all permanent waterholes and river frontages for a few pounds, could tie up hundreds of acres of grazing land. If, however, a big man, either through negligence, good nature or over-confidence should leave a waterhole unclaimed the small settlers would be on to it like a flock of thirsty cockatoos and sometimes, having got a toe in, one of these so-called 'cockies' would succeed in worming himself into the original owner's shoes. To protect himself, therefore, the wary squatter made haste to purchase every likely watering place until he had spotted the map like a peacock's tail.

With righteous indignation these 'peacockers' now found the whiphand slipping from their grasp. No longer a tenth but a mere fortieth of the swiftly rising population, the rights the pioneers had won in the days of their ascendancy were being filched from them by a new influx of ever more confident little men. Was it fair, the squatters demanded, that this marauding horde, without capital or experience and not willing to serve an honest apprenticeship to gain either, should be allowed to sabotage the industry that had been the backbone of the colony? How could men who had pushed out the frontiers of settlement, subdued the forests, dealt with the savage blacks and marked out the roads with their waggon wheels, be tolerant of the shiftless scroungers on the borders of their runs, killing their sheep, laying claim to their unbranded calves and tampering with the earmarks of their other stock? 'Faking' had become an art in the colony. Earmarks were easily disguised, if necessary by docking the whole ear, and if there was a stamp devised that could not be changed by the overlaying of crosses, bars, half circles or figures of eight, the branded hide could be flayed off in the flash of a jack-knife. Most butchers and 'cattle-jobbers' were connivers too, receiving cross-branded stock at cut prices, and newspapers were full of bitter indictments against such as the Goulburn pound-keeper of '52 who acquired a run and suddenly jumped up the owner of 1,000 head of prime stock.

But the small man had his case too, and was voicing it to good effect, for some of the best radical blood of the English Chartist Movement and the European revolutions of '48 had been swept to the colony on the golden wave. The squatters had spoiled things for themselves and everyone else by greedily 'peacocking' the countryside, 'locking the land' far beyond the requirements of their herds, merely to keep others out. The government, alarmed both by the inordinate claims of the squatters and the threatening voices of the little men, compromised by reserving large tracts of land 'in the general interest', its policy being to let them out by degrees to smaller settlers. Meanwhile, however, the squatters' herds still wandered at large as before on the reserves, eating out the pastures around the waterholes.

So on all sides rose a perpetual chorus of 'Unfair! Unfair!' Nobody was satisfied. Big holder, small holder and landseeker each pushed and jostled the other, loudly stating his grievances while the lawmakers clapped their hands to their ears thinking up the next move and vainly seeking precedents. Try as they would, through much familiar claptrap of 'ideals and principles of true democracy', 'rights of the individual', 'progressive thinking', and 'nation planning', the Australian land settlement policy was being built upon jungle law.

In December '55, some months after his return from the goldfields, Grandfather discovered that blocks of Crown land were open to purchase in the vicinity of Dixon's Creek that ran between the parishes of Mummel and Baw Baw in the county of Argyle, about twelve miles north-east of Goulburn. This information he shared with his Uncle Darby and his aunt's relatives the Kilfoyles who were then also looking out for land and who in turn shared the good news with other friends and relatives so that a flock of Irish cockies, all connected in some way, came noisily flapping down around Dixon's Creek Meadow and proceeded, to the consternation of neighbouring big holders, to make themselves at home.

Grandfather purchased 273 acres at about £1 each in blocks of 30 to 50 acres in this vicinity and about the same time registered in his mother's name another 240 acres for the same price on Lake Bathurst near Tarago, some twenty miles south of Goulburn and about thirty-two miles from his other holding.

Having obtained the land the next step was to procure stock and equipment, building materials, a buggy, dray and stores and to hire a teamster and a couple of stockmen. Grandfather's £1,000 would not have gone far without further finance from Samuel Emanuel. At first the sound of the word 'mortgage' had frightened him, but he quickly learned that few had been able to make a start in New South Wales without some such help.

The Dixon's Creek property, to be the family headquarters, Grandfather planned as a mixed farm where they would run a small herd of good dairy cows, rear pigs, poultry and a few stud horses. The Lake Bathurst country, still surrounded with a few thousand acres of Crown land, he saw as the nucleus of a cattle run.

That he had always concentrated on cattle his family thought a matter of temperament, but Grandfather would no doubt have gone in for raising performing seals if this had seemed the most practical way to success. A man who let himself be ruled by preferences or sat back expecting the slow evolutionary processes of older lands would find himself run over the top of in no time at all. Success in Australia depended largely on one's talent for quick adaptability and rapid summing up of the implications of changing times. Where cattle had long been subservient to wool-growing, the sudden influx of population during the gold rush had greatly increased the demand for beef. Cattle needed less handling than sheep, therefore less labour. They required more country but once a man had built up some capital in a restricted area he could look further afield to newly opened country in the far west or north that, while not then considered suitable for sheep, had been recommended for cattle. Here a new generation of pioneers, no less tough and determined than the last, would have scope for their ambitions, and avoid for many years to come the problems and expenses of closer settlement.

Apart from all this, one could at that time build up at least the basis of a herd for very little outlay. Stock could be bought for a song from the Goulburn pound, and though it might look fit only for boiling down, a shrewd observer could see that much of it was well-bred and needed only a spell on good grass to treble its purchase price.

Grandfather also took advantage of a policy by which landowners, in an effort to clear their holdings of cattle and horses that had been let run wild during the depression years and were now menacing their herds, issued 'musterers' licences'. This they hoped would not only clear up the menace of outlaw stock but might remove from some of the smaller men the excuse of being unable to obtain a herd by honest means. Whatever they mustered they could keep for themselves and there were some good young breeders among the wild cattle, as well as horses of good strain gone brumby in the ranges. Grandfather often spoke to his family of the days when he had 'mustered the wilds' around the Lachlan and the Murrumbidgee Rivers.

'I learned in a hard school,' he told his sons, 'and with some of the best stockriders in Australia. None of the young fellows these days could hold a candle to them.'

When he became known as a breeder of fine horses he would tell how some of their progenitors had been the sturdy Arab strain brumbies he had mustered in his youth. For these expeditions he had joined forces with groups of experienced stockmen whose exploits have been recounted in song and story.

We picture them as they rode, bewhiskered and bearded, all in their cabbage-tree hats, blue Crimean shirts and tight-fitting moleskin trousers, pouches for tobacco, pistols and knives in heavy belts, and elastic-sided boots with high 'larrikin heels'. Among them were 'old lags' and sons of squires, remittance men, ex-army officers from Indian regiments, Highland Scots and madcap Irishmen, some in the game of hard necessity and some for the sheer thrill of breakneck rides after the 'Rooshian' cattle of scrub and range, wild as hawks, with sweeping horns and shaggy hides. Their passion for horses amounted almost to a cult. Their conversation was mostly of horses and of how they came into possession of the brave mounts they rode—one from a brumby mob mustered along the Murrumbidgee, another a thoroughbred that had belonged to a bushranger, another bought, near perishing, from a pound.

With horses trained to 'turn on a plate', to wheel and dodge, they mustered cattle in hundreds from gully to scrub. Many animals, reverted to their hump-backed, long-haired progenitors, were of use only as working bullocks. The older, fiercer bulls were shot down and the better animals tailed to hastily erected trap yards and drafting crushes. There, with horns lassoed by greenhide ropes, the bellowing animals went down in the dust to rise enraged, branded, earmarked, emasculated. It was here, among the plains and ranges of the south, that those methods and mannerisms were developed that could be traced a century later on an overland trail from the Lachlan to the Ord.

Great-grandmother Bridget had remained in Goulburn with her three youngest until the Dixon's Creek house was built. The younger boy, Stumpy Michael, who was to be a tower of strength in years to come, was still hardly more than ten years old and then attending a bush school, for Patsy insisted he should not be 'unlearned'. It didn't matter so much about the girls. They could already read and write. They told their children how they had worked with Patsy like men to build the houses and the yards both at Dixon's Creek and at Lake Bathurst where an overseer remained in charge when Grandfather was not there.

Each homestead was of slab timber and stringybark, with thatched roof and shutters swung on greenhide hinges. One room served as sleeping and dressing quarters for the women and little ones, the other as living room where the men slept at night in their swags on the floor. The kitchen was an open lean-to. Floors were of hard beaten mud and strewn with hides. Furniture was rough-hewn and the barest minimum—table, chairs, one or two bedsteads with timber framework interlaced with greenhide and covered with sheep and possum skins. Bed coverings were the pelts of furred animals, often pieced together from the skins of koala bears, so plentiful in those days. It was a makeshift dwelling of a makeshift age—a generation in a hurry. Someday they would build a fine house—a mansion indeed—and there would be time for the proper husbanding and cultivation of the land. For the present, as was the custom in this country of prodigal, fenceless acres and labour shortage, they would turn their stock loose to pasture on the virgin land and would 'tail' their cattle until they became accustomed to their legitimate boundaries. After that any 'boxing up' of stock could be adjusted at regular boundary musters, which, so long as one kept in with one's neighbours, were fine fun.

Grandfather's Uncle Darby was of a different mind and considered his nephew reckless and improvident in having raised a mortgage and purchased more land and stock than a man could reasonably keep under his eye. For himself Darby was satisfied with the modest eighty acres and the little herd of dairy cows he had purchased, cash down, from the hard-earned savings of seven years at Kippilaw. He planned to fence his property and clear twenty to forty acres for the cultivation that was so wantonly neglected in the colonial haste to get rich quick. He would have his sons good practical farmers, not afraid to put their hands to the axe, the spade and the plough, not like so many of the younger generation, for ever galloping about the countryside after wild stock or hell-bound droving into some waterless wilderness. Alas for the irony of fate that was to mould the sons of this careful farmer into some of the most daring and dedicated stockmen ever to trail cattle over trackless country.

Grandfather, however, was far from scornful of his uncle's respect for the plough, his delight of tilled fields, his thought for the rotation of crops and the proper use of God's good soil. A knowledge of land husbandry had been part of his Irish heritage but in dealing with hard, virgin country, it must, he felt, be laid aside for another, more leisurely day. In a sense he never lost it, for he always loved his kitchen gardens and cherished his little crops of lucerne, barley and maize, but any thought he may have entertained of agriculture in a broader way was overridden in the haste and urgency of his growing hunger for land. Already the outlook of the cowherd was becoming that of the pastoralist, the dream of acres swelling to a vision of square miles.

A landmark in their new lives had been the day that Grandfather and his Uncle Darby registered their brands. Darby used his wife's initials cunningly placed $\frac{M}{D}$ to make them more difficult to fake. Grandfather chose his lucky number 7 followed by his initials PD and at the same time had a goldsmith cast the brand from a nugget as a brooch for his mother.

After this transaction, as his buggy jogged home across the great Goulburn plain Grandfather saw seven crows in a tree which he took to be the sign of a wish.

'I make a wish to see stock with the 7PD brand grazing over plains like this—as far as the eye can see,' he told his mother.

'And you will, Patsy boy,' she said. 'God help you, so you will.'

When the dairy was finished the women began making and selling butter and cheese and Great-grandmother Bridget was able to teach her daughters many of the frugal household skills of her homeland. The family had not been long established at Dixon's Creek before this Irish widow's fame as a midwife and a doctor of sick animals had spread about the district. Although some of her remedies savour quaintly of witchcraft they were mixed with a deal of sound sense and practical skill, even, so they say, to turning a misplaced calf in the mother. People came from miles around seeking her advice about fowls that would not lay, cows that would not give milk and ills that beset their pigs, their horses, their dogs and cats. As sprightly as a girl at forty-three she received so many proposals of marriage from lonely bachelors that her daughters complained they stood little chance of gaining attention from the men while their mother was about. That was family banter, for like most unmarried girls in a predominantly masculine population they were courted from a very early age, and might have married even earlier but that most Irishmen who presented themselves were not, in Patsy's eyes, fine enough for his sisters, while the more eligible English and Scottish young bloods of the district were not of their faith.

Of these crowded and eventful years, however, most of the actual incidents handed down were trivialities.

'Oh yes indeed,' the great-aunts would say, when pestered for their memories, 'there were some exciting times in those very early days. We had to wash our clothes in the creek and spread them over the bushes and were always having to keep watch for fear the men would see our underwear!'

'Were you never bothered by wild blacks?' they were asked.

'Oh dearie no,' they replied, 'there was no fight in the poor things by that time—not in those parts,' and they would tell how the wandering bands would appear from time to time, offering to lend a hand in exchange for food, clothing and tobacco. A few were clad in cast-off rags, others in flapping possum-skin cloaks, sewn up with fibre of the stringybark tree. Remnants of the proud old tribes of the Tablelands—Mulwarrie, Tarlo and Burra-burra—they watched the 'dreaming' of their forefathers lose shape and meaning under the axe and ploughshare of the new people. Gone were the days when they had thought to discourage the newcomers by attacking their shepherds and spearing their stock. They knew themselves beaten now, and the dreamy, changeless philosophy of the old tribes was superseded by a vigorous new way of life of which change was the keynote. A few men who had been responsible for a mass destruction of the tribespeople had been hanged for their deeds in accordance with a capricious whiteman sense of justice, but this did not bring back life to the dead nor spirit to the living. Even the cumbersome half-moon brass plates given as marks of special favour from the 'big fella gubberment' were soon found to possess no magic nor special virtue but were worn with a smile to please the givers.

The new settlers found their dark-skinned visitors good-humoured and amusing, even helpful in a desultory fashion, until a whim seized them and they were on their way.

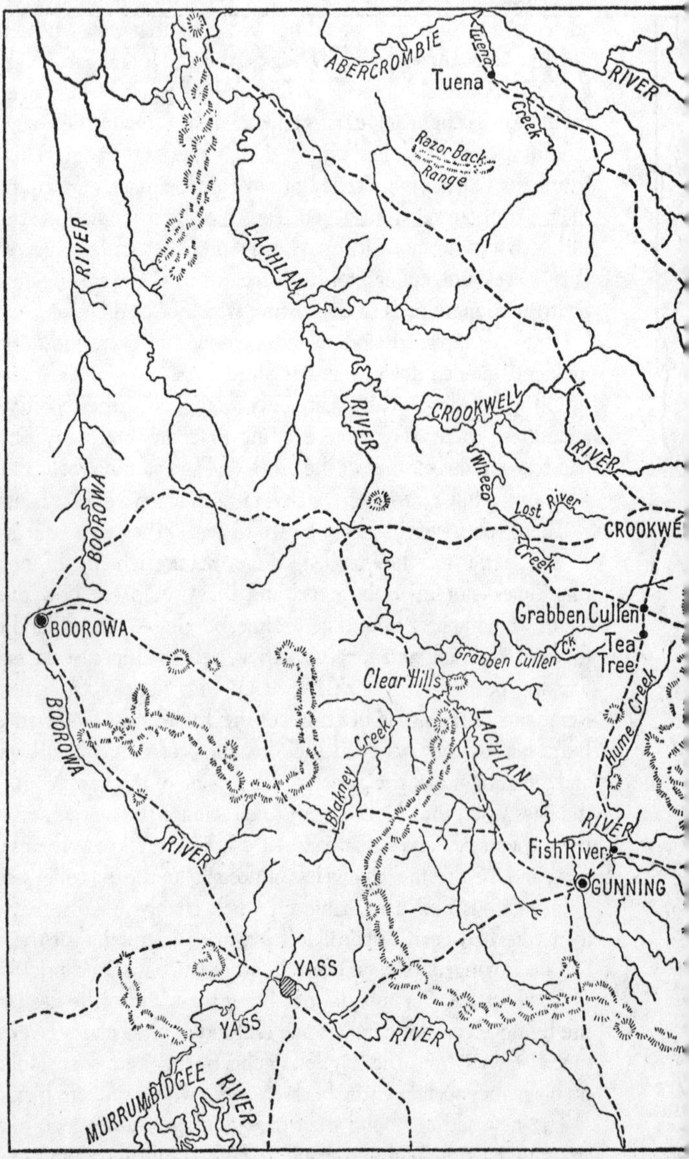
ABERCROMBIE
RIVER
Tuena
Tuena
Creek
Razor Back
Range
LACHLAN
RIVER
CROOKWELL
RIVER
Wheeo
Lost River
Creek
CROOKWE
RIVER
BOOROWA
BOOROWA
Grabben Cullen
Tea
Tree
Grabben Cullen
Ck
Clear Hills
BOOROWA
LACHLAN
Hume Creek
Blakney Creek
RIVER
Fish River
RIVER
GUNNING
YASS
YASS
RIVER
MURRUMBIDGEE
RIVER

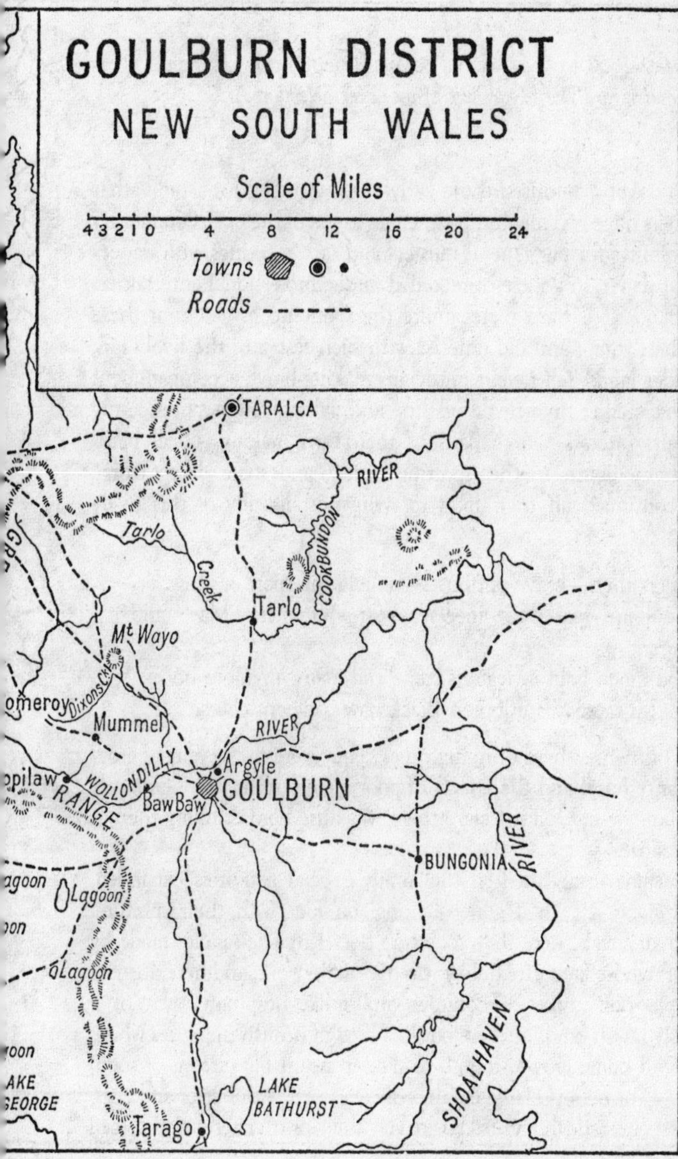
GOULBURN DISTRICT
NEW SOUTH WALES
Scale of Miles
4 3 2 1 0 4 8 12 16 20 24
Towns
Roads
TARALCA
RIVER
Tarlo
Creek
COOKBUNDON
Tarlo
Mt Wayo
Dixons Ck
omeroy
Mummel
RIVER
WOLLONDILLY
Argyle
GOULBURN
opilaw
RANGE
Baw Baw
BUNGONIA
RIVER
agoon
Lagoon
Lagoon
LAKE BATHURST
SHOALHAVEN
AKE
EORGE
Tarago

6
Goulburn Days

The years 1857 to 1862. Social occasions, family courtships and marriages. The beginnings of the 'Free Selection Act'.

Time no doubt glamorised those early Goulburn days for Grandfather but others have had much the same tale to tell of the brisk community life, the gatherings for big general musters and race meetings with dances that ended at dawn. In an age of recorded music, professional entertainers and dance bands it is hard to recapture the spontaneous gaiety of these occasions when young and old entered with such zest into the lively folk dances of older lands, self-taught musicians making brave accompaniment on concertina, fiddle, tin whistle or flute and willing songsters rendering traditional airs often set to ballads of their own making. Local bards flourished in Goulburn in the 'sporting fifties', and some, like George McAlister, continued all their lives to write nostalgically of this lively decade:

> Our fathers then—brave optimists—upheld the sport of kings,
> And Goulburn had three meets a year—Summer's, May's and
> Spring's,
> When bushmen bold in legions came and many a famous horse
> O'ertook his fated Waterloo on Blackshaw's ancient course . . .

Some speak of them as hard drinking times. They were the heyday of grog-house or shanty hotel and the effects of poor quality spirits were certainly deplorable, but the old folks declare there was little hard drinking then at dances and parties.

As life became established so the family's social activities expanded. Where in Ireland they had gone 'keating' on foot with their spinning wheels on their heads, here they rode fine horses in side-saddles made by their brother, whose favourite hobby was his saddle-work; and here, instead of the simple home fare of potatoes and milk, hospitality was of a comparatively lavish kind. In these outdoor days of healthy appetites where produce was all home grown, friends to dinner meant big tureens of soup, whole roast pig or poultry, large batches of cakes rich with butter and eggs. There were scones and home-baked loaves, their own cheeses and spiced meats, and guests went on their way with baskets of preserves, pickles and samples of this and that. Often, when some special dish or cake was produced by Aunt Sarah's daughters in later years, they would tell how it was one of their mother's recipes from her early Goulburn days.

Besides heavier work in the dairy, the stockyards or on the run with their brother, they managed to produce elaborate trousseaux of fine embroidery, lace and crochet work, some of which survives today. The third sister, Margaret, was an especially clever needlewoman and was in great demand as a dressmaker with friends and relatives. She made elaborate wedding gowns for the brides and in due course exquisite layettes for the little ones.

Even Poor Mary was gay in these expansive years between the bitter memories of her childhood and the hard knockabout life that lay before her.

It had been a great solace to my widowed great-grandmother Bridget in her grief to see how quickly the Australian life had brought strength and vigour to her sickly brood. Her baby, Jerry, Goulburn-born so soon after her husband's death, was a merry, sturdy child who was in the saddle before he had learned to walk. The girls too, although small built, were all splendid horsewomen. Sarah who had been thought not long for this world soon became her brother's right-hand 'man', riding everywhere with him and working stock with the cunning of an old hand. Everyone who knew Sarah, either then or later as the matriarch of Cooper's Creek, spoke of her riding prowess, of her pluck and spirit and sometimes also of her sharp, Irish tongue. Perhaps because she had been so delicate as a child she was always her brother Patsy's favourite while her devotion to him was fierce and absolute. In Sarah's eyes Patsy was as infallible as the Pope.

The more memories I unearth of my little great-aunts and their mother the more I wonder at the fullness of their lives, at their gaiety and their industry. Simple folk though they were I feel it would be a cliché to say that they led simple lives—unsophisticated certainly, but how simple would it have been to establish and maintain the standards they set themselves in their rough and ready bush community?

Despite all that is said of increasing prejudice against the Irish, our own family at least had almost as many friends in the Scottish, English and Jewish sections of the community as among their own. Only the occasional visits of a church dignitary such as the pioneer Archbishop Polding called for more or less exclusive Irish gatherings. Their religion meant a great deal to these Irish immigrants and there was much rivalry among the Catholic outback community for the honour of acting host to a member of the clergy. Parish priests were few and far between and the Archbishop, an Englishman of the Benedictine Order, to keep the faith alive over his enormous diocese was constantly travelling on horseback or by buggy, celebrating Mass in dusty bush townships, under trees and on riverbanks, in lonely settlers' cabins or among the earth dumps of the mining centres. Sometimes he led the worship of his Catholic flock within earshot of his rival in zeal, the Reverend John Dunmore Lang who preached the near approach of the Day of Judgement and denounced the work of all such 'agents of the Beast of Apocalypse'. A contemporary wrote of John Polding that 'no monk ever looked more of a monk than he with his benign, loveable countenance, the trailing, grey hair tumbling down his neck like snow, the deep-set blue eyes, the mouth showing power and patience and an almost terrible rectitude . . .'

He found warm support in the Irish community for his ambitious projects of enlarging the little bush church in Goulburn to a splendid cathedral and later of establishing a fine college in the town for the sons of a people long starved for learning.

For one memorable fortnight this venerable figure and his little retinue had made their headquarters with the Costello family of Tea-tree Station near Grabben Gullen, and Catholic families for many miles around gathered to meet him and share in the religious rites and general festivities. Mass was celebrated daily on the homestead verandah; there was much delayed baptising and confirming of bush-born offspring, and finally the presentation to the Costellos of a water-colour portrait of His Grace which hung ever afterwards in a place of honour in their home.

The Costellos and Duracks had met before, but this is the first remembered occasion of Grandfather's family having visited their station home. It left a lasting impression and had far-reaching results.

The Costellos had come to Australia from Tipperary in 1837 on one of the overcrowded, disease-ridden emigrant hulks of the day, and their four Irish-born children had died on the voyage. They had settled in Yass, a small town about fifty miles south-east of Goulburn, opened a small store and within the next few years had been blessed with some prosperity and two further children, John and Mary. This they believed to be 'a heavenly miracle and an answer to prayer' since they were no longer young. Mr Michael Costello was a hard-working, good-natured man rather under the domination of his strong-willed, pious and ambitious wife. During the gold rush the sleepy town of Yass had sprung to life as a stopping stage on the diggers' route from New South Wales to the big mining centres of Victoria. Their business had flourished and when their son was thirteen years old they sold out for a good price and took up 1,000 acres of first-class pastoral country around Grabben Gullen and Clear Hills about ten miles from the Duracks' property on Dixon's Creek. The herds of both families grazed over a good deal of reserve land between, and the return of the straying Costello stock later gave Grandfather his most plausible excuse for visiting their homestead.

Grandfather claimed to have fallen in love with Mary Costello at first sight, when she was only fourteen years old, but for some years he saw a great deal more of her brother John, a keen, lean youngster whose restless disposition was already causing his parents some concern. He was not, from all accounts, a wild youth, or an undutiful son, but simply adventurous, and by the time he was sixteen had already ranged the country with droving parties, was a seasoned stockman and had made a local name for himself as a rider and breaker of wild horses. Although four years his senior and bent on courting his sister, Grandfather enjoyed the company of young John Costello for they had a strong common interest in horses and spent hours together tracing on a map the latest tracks of the explorers.

During this time many family members were courting and marrying. Poor Mary had been swept off her feet by the devil-may-care Dinny Skeahan, friend of Patsy's mining days. There was some head-shaking over the match, for Dinny was declared 'a wild one entirely' and rather too fond of the convivial company of the mining towns and the turf to make a steady husband. Mary, however, captivated by a pair of bold blue eyes and a voice to melt the heart, had ridden blithely off in a buggy to the goldfields where Dinny was confident of 'being on a good thing at last'.

Margaret had fallen in love with a young man named John Bennet who, although eligible enough, was, to her mother's distress, a Protestant. There was division of feeling in the family about this romance but Margaret had the support of her brother Patsy who while firm in his faith disliked all social, religious and geographical barriers on principle. This meant that Sarah approved also, so Margaret, whom they called 'the flower of the flock' with her fragile prettiness and her ropes of golden hair, sewed herself an exquisite bridal dress and, married with the priest's blessing, went off to Sydney with her husband.

Bridget, the third girl, soon afterwards married a big Irish farmer named Pat Scanlan who had come from County Clare with his two brothers some years before and taken up land in the Argyle district. Pat was a big, red-bearded young fellow locally renowned for the freak strength he demonstrated in the most original ways. His broad shoulders could carry a twenty-eight-gallon barrel of spirits with ease, and sometimes on bush roads he would take over from the buggy horse between the shafts!

Grandfather's other mining friend, Pat Tully, was a first cousin of Mrs Costello and when visiting his many relatives in the district called at Dixon's Creek, at first to see Patsy, and later because he had been captivated by the sprightly Sarah. He had stuck doggedly to the mining life though no great luck had ever come his way. Sarah lectured him for his foolishness and refused to consider his proposal unless he gave up mining for the land, for unlike her trusting sister Mary she believed in reforming her man before going to the altar.

John Costello was courting Pat Scanlan's sister Mary, a spirited girl who had recently followed her brothers from Ireland. She was said to have been pretty, quick-witted and well versed in current affairs, but the attachment seems to have found little favour in Mrs Costello's eyes as the girl was suspected of encouraging John's ambition to strike out for himself on new country past the frontiers of settlement.

The anxious mother regarded Patsy Durack's growing interest in her gentle daughter with less favour still. She had never wanted Mary to be like other bush-bred girls—horse-riding young women like Mary Scanlan and the Durack sisters. Weather-beaten herself, Mrs Costello was determined that Mary should keep the peaches and cream complexion of an Irish colleen. At the slightest touch of sunburn her skin was treated with oatmeal packs and she was sent to bed in gloves over hands smeared with mutton fat, for Mrs Costello cherished ambitions for her of a good match with a city man. Unfortunately, however, the various hired governesses with whom her education had been entrusted proved less interested in equipping their pupil for a successful marriage than in finding husbands for themselves. Mary had had little interest in lessons and later admitted that she had aided and abetted many a romance by disappearing at convenient times into the kitchen where she picked up from the capable Scottish cook, Annie McTavish, most of those practical and frugal skills that served her in good stead in years to come. She was already seventeen when, in '59, a pioneer band of Irish Mercy nuns opened their first little weather-board establishment in Goulburn, and Mrs Costello, seizing the opportunity of removing her daughter from the attention of unsuitable admirers and improving her education, enrolled her as their first pupil. Mary remained very happily with the good nuns for two years, and for a short time even considered joining them in their self-effacing lives. This project, however, Mrs Costello nipped in the bud.

'Glory be to God,' she said, 'after taking four of our little ones already He'll not be asking for another!'

But she was delighted with her daughter's progress, for Mary had become an exquisite needlewoman, and although quite unmusical could struggle through a few little 'pieces' on the piano, which seemed to her mother the height of maidenly accomplishment. No one considered it to her discredit that Mary still had the greatest difficulty in writing a letter and had probably read nothing beyond her Bible and the abridged lives of selected saints. Enough that she spoke and conducted herself with dignity and had a simple and endearing charm. Before there could be any further interference with her plan, Mrs Costello whisked her darling off to Sydney to introduce her to the social life of the metropolis. Her plan, however, was of no avail, for Grandfather found urgent business in Sydney and there, between inevitable visits to the races and the stock sales, continued his courtship. Grandmother Costello, a formidable figure in her city finery, always complete with button-up boots and goose-head umbrella, was outraged and from the storehouse of her remarkable Irish memory and often unscrupulous imagination produced stories to the discredit of the Durack name throughout the centuries. She flung a heritage of drunkards, gamblers, wastrels, informers and turncoats at Grandfather's head and he, never the mildest-tempered or most forbearing of men, had little good to say of the 'MacCostellos', the invading Norman de Angulas of remote history.

'It's no use Patsy,' the gentle Mary said at last, 'for think of the criminals we might rear with such ancestors on both sides!'

This delighted Grandfather who often quoted it with relish long after parental opposition had crumbled under the dogged persistence of true love.

Meanwhile, a discordant background to these social and romantic activities, raged the battle of the landless against the landed. Far, far away the Crimean War, the Indian Mutiny, the Second Chinese War were fought and finished but scarcely an echo penetrated the consciousness of these remote colonials absorbed in their own struggles towards nationhood. From a medley of people drawn to these shores by crime or poverty, to find living space, adventure, freedom, land or gold or who had come simply for the hell of it, out of many creeds and many races, preponderantly English, Irish and Scottish, was emerging the Australian people. The land was moulding them already to a certain uniformity, shading the raven hair to brown, the flaxen to honey gold, blending dark eyes and blue to a tawny hazel, a smoky grey. Even their voices were losing the distinguishing traits of country, county and class, Australia imposing an intonation and emphasis of her own, abhorrent to the outside ear, inescapable within her frontiers.

The uprooted progeny of a revolutionary age, they were a people struggling lustily but without focus within the crucible of their new environment to find a way of life that was reasonably fair and compatible to all, a people who, in their unique isolation, from the fire of their idealism, the power of their lust, the very strength of their individualism were already clearing the way for a mighty mediocrity.

Men had brought catch cries snatched hot from the cauldrons of English industrial strife and European social upheaval, while the 'forty-niners' who had flocked to California returned to tell how the prairies of America had been opened by free selectors unhampered, as in New South Wales and Victoria, by the widespread pre-emptions of the squatters and the locked acres of Crown reserve. The tentative land reforms following the gold rush years were not enough to satisfy the needs of the ever-growing horde demanding not vast leasehold kingdoms but small freehold 'selections' to clear and cultivate. Unexpectedly, a powerful champion of the little men arose from the ranks of the squatters themselves, a big, bluff, handsome fellow with a cleft palate and a quick, blunt wit. He was John Robertson, London-born and among those early settlers who broke 'beyond the bounds' in New South Wales. An idealist with a burning faith in humanity and a zeal for the cause of the under-dog, he succeeded in '61 in pushing through both Houses of Parliament bills designed to give every family that so desired a stake in the agricultural revolution that was to provide land and a living for thousands where only hundreds could exist before.

His Acts appeared on the surface to be just, democratic and far-seeing, providing, by throwing open all Crown lands, limiting the squatter's pre-emptive rights and curtailing his term of pastoral leases to five years, agricultural 'selections' of from 40 to 320 acres for all applicants. For this the only conditions required were an advance payment of £10 and the signing of a declaration that one would reside on the land as a genuine settler.

Throughout the colony hitherto landless little men joined a merry chorus of 'The Ballad of Free Selection':

Come all of you Cornstalks, the victory's won,
John Robertson's triumphed and the lean days are gone.
No more through the bush we'll go humping the drum,
For the Land Bill has passed and the good times have come.

We will sow our own gardens and till our own field
And eat of the fruit that our labour doth yield
And be independent in right long denied
By those who have ruled us and robbed us beside . . .

So, amid the groans and forebodings of the squatters and the excited clamour of the free selectors, the Acts were put into effect. Faster, however, than the wheel of the Great Agricultural Revolution wheels began turning in the minds of all sections of the community to discover how the trusting conditions of the new land laws might be circumvented to their own advantage.

It could hardly be expected that the squatters were to be so easily deprived of the lands they now regarded as their hard-won heritage, or that the little men would not soon discover easier ways of making a living on their 'selections' than by clearing and cultivating the land. Honest John Robertson, in perceiving the weakness and injustice of the existing land laws, had not taken into equal account the frailty of human nature.

7

WEDDING BELLS

The year 1862. Patsy Durack marries Mary Costello. The Free Selection Act turned to travesty. Bushranging reappears.

Grandfather and Grandmother were married in the spring of 1862 at Tea-tree, the Costellos' station home to which settlers and townsfolk from far and wide rolled up in their buggies and fours-in-hand, since, whether or not she approved the match, Mrs Costello was determined that her daughter should have the biggest bush wedding of the year.

What a flurry there was, smoothing down crinolines and adjusting millinery—prim leghorn hats for the younger girls, confections of flowers and feathers for the matrons whose tightly corseted bosoms bore a proud display of brooches and heavy cameos, festoons of gold chains over tucks and frills and bows. The men were scarcely less gorgeously arrayed in coloured waistcoats, flowing ties and a fashionable profusion of whisker and moustache. Even the small boys were splendid for the occasion in checked pantaloons, tight-fitting trousers, peaked caps or ribboned boaters. Fortunately for family records a maker of daguerreotypes—an enterprising American—had made his way to the district about this time. He must have done a roaring business, for the wonder of photography was novel and irresistible. Everyone was taken—babies decked like little high priests in long lace surplices, spread out upon skin rugs or precariously propped against pieces of baroque furniture, grandparents seated with hands upon knees or on heavily bound family Bibles. Maidens clasped posies of flowers or leant rounded chins upon drooping hands with elbows resting on betasselled plush table covers. Young men in party finery or riding attire stood stiffly ill at ease before painted forests of English trees, or amid a clutter of pot plants and ornate Victorian bric-à-brac.

It was clear from Mrs Costello's picture that her stiffly boned, flounced and fringed taffeta would, as her family claimed, have 'stood alone'.

Officiating at the ceremony was Father Michael McAlroy, one of those splendid apostles of the saddle who did so much to bring civilisation and community life to the scattered back-block settlements. He had known the Costellos since earlier days in Yass when they had been storekeepers and, although Mrs Costello would prefer to have forgotten these humble beginnings, her husband, mellowed with wine and sentiment, recalled the days when the big, practical priest had shown him how to keep his ledger and get in some of the money owing to him. The Costellos were not the only members of his flock for whom he had combined the roles of father confessor and business adviser, while everyone knew of the incident at Lambing Flat. A judge sent down to quell a miners' riot had found himself trembling in the midst of 10,000 angry men shouting to have him strung up, when into the medley strode Father McAlroy. The hubbub quickly ceased and the crowd dispersed, for the influence of 'the fighting Father of Kildare' went far beyond the limits of his own flock, and men of many creeds contributed to the schools and churches he called to life in every country town within his sprawling parish.

The occasion of the wedding was marked with all the laughter, song and dancing of typically Irish gatherings, for the linking of the clans Costello and Durack had connected half the Irish population of the district. Mrs Costello's four sisters, my grandmother's aunts, were all married and living with ever-increasing offspring around the county of Argyle. These included the families Hammond, Abbey, Kelly and Moore with another big clan named Hackett related somewhere on the side. Add to this the families Skeahan, Scanlan and Kilfoyle with all their spreading branches and one will not wonder that in these days it is hardly possible to name a town or district in Australia in which we cannot unearth some family connection. Grandfather embraced them all, to the last link in the long chain, and as this expansive trait was hardly less marked in his wife's family the stage was now set for the mass migration of the clans that was to follow. Grandmother's chief bridesmaid was her cousin Frances Hammond who was later to spend so much time with her relatives in western Queensland. Best man and groomsman were the brothers Michael and Stephen Brogan, cousins of Grandfather whom he had recently persuaded to join him from County Clare, and who were later to figure among the young bloods of Cooper's Creek and the early droving tracks.

But there were many besides Irish among the wedding guests, some also to remain associated with the family in various ways. These included the Emanuels from Goulburn and the MacDonalds from the Isle of Skye who had a property near Grabben Gullen and were, like the Duracks, to be part of the big westward cattle drive of '83. The McInnes family who had come from Tarlo River were also destined to be relatives by marriage but the sixteen-year-old Stumpy Michael was then too gauche and shy to reveal any interest in their daughter Kate, a close friend of his youngest sister Anne. Anne, however, had already made up her mind about the match and was to play a leading role in bringing it off. At eighteen, petite and bright as a bird, she was now the only unmarried girl in the family. Unlike her elder sisters, who regarded such pursuits as waste of precious time, she was an avid reader and although she shared the others' passion for horses had taken a position as teacher in a little Goulburn school. Naturally her qualifications for this job were modest but she was a fine needlewoman and wrote a good, clear hand.

The three married sisters, Poor Mary Skeahan, Bridget Scanlan and Sarah Tully, were there each with a first-born son, Poor Mary looking wan and tired from an unsettled anxious life with Dinny, the rolling stone, Bridget developing the forthright character of a bush matron. Sarah, married in Goulburn a year before to Mrs Costello's cousin Pat Tully, had been more successful than her sister in persuading her husband of the folly of a miner's life, and they had taken up mixed farming on a free selector's block at Hume Creek, twenty-five miles from Goulburn.

Darby and Margaret Durack arrived from Dixon's Creek with their brood of five sons and four daughters, having been 'blessed' in almost every year of their married life. Everyone remarked the sturdy good looks of their offspring, the usual Durack mixture of fair and dark. The eldest, already known at twelve years old as 'Big Johnnie' to distinguish him from a number of other smaller Johnnies coming on behind, already earned money when harassed station owners needed an extra hand. His father swelled with pride to hear the boy praised for his horsemanship and the younger brother 'Black Pat' lauded as a game young buck jump rider. Even the third boy, the 'Long Michael' of after years, was already at home in the saddle, but it had not then occurred to Darby that his 'brood of young eagles' as people called them would not long content themselves within the confines of his nest on Dixon's Creek. His determination never to resort to anything that savoured of borrowing had been maintained only by almost superhuman toil. Since he had also to keep his dairy business going it had taken him some years to clear even a few acres of trees and wattle scrub and sometimes, to make ends meet, he had taken well-paid carrying jobs to the goldfields.

When Grandfather brought his bride to Dixon's Creek his mother planned to spend most of her time with her married daughters but it never worked out that way. The two women lived always in complete harmony and grieved for each other in the years they were apart. The same can hardly be said for Grandfather and his mother-in-law who never made much pretence of getting on. Their frank antagonism, however, seems to have provided a good deal of popular interest and amusement. When she considered an argument had gone far enough, Grandmother, a placid woman herself but accustomed from childhood to the uninhibited venom and eloquence of Irish tongues, would clang the horse bell that served as a dinner gong.

'Come now,' she would say, 'what diference will it make atall in a few years' time?'

How right she was, for although her children always remembered their mother's quiet rebuke and her ringing of the bell, the momentous issues that threatened to raise the homestead roof were forgotten long ago.

We do know, however, one point on which they argued frequently and that was Grandfather's wish to 'poke along up north', as he called it, into the new colony of Queensland which had been separated from New South Wales in 1859. The unfolding of Robertson's Free Selection Act was proving particularly unsatisfactory to men in Grandfather's position who were neither big established squatters nor free selectors, but who were ambitious to expand without circumventing the law.

Two successive bad seasons had done nothing to help the successful working of the 'agricultural revolution' and many who had come in good faith to clear and cultivate the land, unable to grow wheat without rain, either set themselves up as small pastoralists or turned to 'dummying' for the squatters. It was soon obvious how the radical new Act, conceived by an upright man, was being turned to a travesty by the manipulation of rogues, although it is hardly to be wondered that Robertson's simple conditions, carrying no penalty for default, put temptation in everyone's way. The squatters, in order to even up the score against them, found little difficulty in bribing discouraged selectors to bid and sign on their behalf at the land sales, so that the old evil of 'pre-emption', outlawed in theory, was in fact continuing under another name. Many of these 'dummies' were only too happy to take up residence on 'their' selections thereby complying with the conditions of the Act while turning their houses into grog shanties and acting as go-betweens for horse thieves and cattle duffers. Other selectors meanwhile had hit upon the profitable ideas of making such nuisances of themselves, thieving stock, firing hay-stacks, poisoning water and similar merry pranks that their neighbours were forced to buy them out, often at a great price.

There was a song about it now outback that put the situation in a nutshell:

> If we find a mob of horses when the paddock rails are down,
> Though before they were never known to stray,
> When the moon is up we drive them to a distant inland town

And we sell them into slav'ry far away:
To Jack Robertson we'll say:
'We're on a better lay
And we'll never go a-farming any more,
For it's easier duffing cattle on the little piece of land
Free selected by the Eumerella Shore.'

In these conditions the old bushranging bogy, long since decapitated, had grown a secondary head and the settlers were menaced as never before. The new outlaws were of a different type, however, from the refugees of chain gangs, and their lawlessness sprang from a combination of other causes. Many were colonial-born sons of poor settlers, some feckless, some genuinely frustrated by the conditions of their times. Often spirited and resourceful, they were frankly sceptical that crime would not pay in a country of ever-expanding frontiers, where many small settlers were willing collaborators in stock-lifting exploits directed against the domination of the squatter class and where it required no great feat of strategy to hold up a gold escort or a mail coach on a lonely bush road. Names such as 'Darkie' Gardiner, Ben Hall and O'Meally became household words in the outback. Robin Hoods of the Australian forest, Dick Turpins of the southern highways, feared and hunted, they were as often sheltered and admired.

About the time of Grandfather's marriage, Darby Durack, his brother-in-law Tom Kilfoyle and their neighbour Con MacNamara had been held up by bushrangers while returning with their teams from the Forbes gold rush. The outlaws proved none other than the notorious 'Darkie' Gardiner and his gang, who, on hearing that they were working for Charlie McAlister had let them pass unmolested.

'A decent chap, McAlister,' Gardiner told them, 'once sold me a good horse, dirt cheap, when I was near down and out. That was before I made my way up in the world. You can tell him Frank Gardiner don't forget a good turn.'

This well-worn family anecdote is also related by Charles McAlister himself in his autobiography *Old Pioneering Days in the Sunny South* where he reminds his readers how the same gang soon after got off with £7,000 of gold dust from the Eugowra gold escort.

It is not to be wondered that Grandfather, irked and restricted by his turmoil of conflicting interests, yearned to strike out into a new area that promised just such limitless grazing land as had lured the first squatters into the unknown of New South Wales. Although Australia throughout the fifties was still too absorbed in gold to give much attention to official exploration, the tracks of men and stock had been pushing slowly out, following the rivers and tributary creeks, skirting the gibber plains in search of permanent water and grazing country. Unsung pioneers were mapping many a new river and mountain range, filling in the details of maps outlined, remaining to make their terms with the land and its original inhabitants.

Since the disappearance of Leichhardt's party in '48 a lot of country had been opened up in vain attempts to throw some light on their fate, and also by Thomas Mitchell moving around the interior of Queensland intent upon solving the mystery of the inland streams. In '46 Mitchell had described a land of pasture and water to satisfy all the needs of man and his herds, but Gregory, returning in '58 from another fruitless search for Leichhardt's party, had reported Mitchell's paradise in the grip of drought, his mighty Cooper river system a chain of lost and dwindling waterholes. Still, up to '61 the continent had not been crossed except around the southern coast and men were still haunted with the phantom of an inland sea. In that year two men had come forward to contest the prize for the first to accomplish this tremendous task. One had been the Scot, John McDouall Stuart, the other Galway-born Robert O'Hara Burke, lately police officer, with whom Grandfather had become acquainted at the Ovens diggings.

The fifty-year-old Scot, less heavily supported than the dashing young Irishman, was the more experienced bushman—and a scientist. A small man, with sun-calloused skin and eyes red-rimmed with 'sandy blight', he had taken up the challenge of the interior before and having been several times defeated, knew what he was up against. He had known when to turn back and when to start again, while his rival was bravely pushing himself and his party on to nemesis. Stuart, a walking skeleton, scarcely human and half-blind, returned 2,000 miles from Van Dieman's Gulf to Adelaide on the same day that the remains of Burke were brought to the same city by the men who had solved the mystery of his fate. Stuart had lived to receive the prize money, but not long enough to claim the grant of land that went with it.

So at last the secret of the inland had been made known. Let them come now, knowing that her fabled inland sea was lost in the drifting sands of geological time, its bed the pebbled gibber plains that had ground down the hard hoofs of the explorers' horses to bleeding quicks. Let them come knowing the state in which she had cast back the men who claimed to have 'conquered' her, and how others had fared following the mock waters of her mirage.

But that was not the whole picture. Stuart had found fertile valleys in a central range, and farther north a well-watered tropical wilderness of unknown potential, while search parties combing the hinterland for Burke and his men, converging on Cooper's Creek from three States, reported upon thousands of square miles of good grazing land.

But Queensland had a bad name, especially with the womenfolk who associated it still with the ill-famed 'Moreton Bay Settlement', selected in '23 as the dumping place of the tougher convict types—those 'thrice convicted felons', who, under the merciless regime of Captain Logan, had been reduced to murdering their mates so that they might end their hopeless misery on the gallows. Some who had escaped into the bush were befriended by the blacks, others tortured and killed while the blacks themselves had been shot at, fed strychnine in bread and flour, skinned and set up as scarecrows in the paddocks. It was not long since men were publicly flogged in the streets of Brisbane and up to a year before, coin of the realm being still unknown in the settlement, people had dealt in flimsy paper currency—IOUs payable in Sydney and sometimes scribbled cannily on tissue paper, or baked so that they would crumble in the pocket.

But into the muddle and viciousness of its beginnings, when the district stagnated in 'the dead sleep of inane criminality', had ridden the free men, the landseekers. In defiance of the ban on free settlement they had followed on the tracks of that Aberdonian 'Prince of Bushmen', Pat Leslie, who in 1840 pushed out with his bullock teams and his flocks to wrest a holding from the Darling Downs. Knowing from past experience the futility of calling back these tough first-footers in a tough land, cut off from control in Sydney by 500 miles, the government had officially thrown open the interior of this region in '42, but already the sheep and cattle were spreading up along the coast, inland to the Thompson River, over the Plains of Promise and soon into the hinterland of Carpentaria where cotton and sugar plantations had sprung up on the alluvial lands along the coastal rivers and creeks. Since it seemed that men of enterprise should be encouraged into this vast and empty land, no effort had been made, as in the days of 'The Nineteen Counties' of New South Wales, to keep the pastoralists within definite bounds and during the forties and fifties the frontiers had expanded rapidly. Nor was it long before these sturdy pioneers of the north had begun to express themselves as a group whose special problems of isolation, climate, lack of labour and other hardships separated them from their fellows of the south. They held indignation meetings, clamouring for the re-establishment of transportation, pointing out how the southern counties, smug in their prosperity, had been built on the convict labour they now self-righteously denied the pioneers of the north. There was fierce opposition to their demands, but in '59 the mother colony decided that this noisy minority had best be allowed to work out its own salvation.

At the time of her separation from New South Wales, Queensland, covering an area of 670,500 square miles, could boast no more than 25,000 of Australia's population that had topped the million mark a year before and labour was still her most crying need. She began with the ludicrous sum of sevenpence-halfpenny in her treasury, but with an infectious optimism and faith in her future that brought in vast sums of borrowed capital to start her public works and encourage immigration.

John Dunmore Lang, still zealous in the cause of free settlement, had tried to solve the labour problem by a much advertised system of 'land orders' that in the next few years brought a motley collection of unfortunates flocking to Queensland as previously to New South Wales and Victoria. From the manufacturing towns of northern England came families driven from the cotton famine caused by the American Civil War, came more Irish drafted from the poorhouses, came assigned labourers, German farmers, Italian peasants, Kanakas 'blackbirded' from islands and sold to the sugar planters. The population more than doubled itself by '61 but, as in New South Wales, too few were disposed to push out past the coastal areas to solve the labour problems of the squatters. Still, the lure of new country, coupled with an encouraging land policy that had profited by many mistakes of the mother colony, was strong enough to outweigh the inconveniences. The Queensland system of 'supervised selection' favoured the small man while an ideal of 'expansion without speculation' gave encouragement to bigger settlers by issuing fourteen-year leases only to those who, by stocking their land during a year's probation, had proved themselves not mere speculators but genuine pioneers.

In a dogged regime of 'do it yourself', the root no doubt of the often ingenious but crude and inelegant Australian 'makeshift', the lonely advance guard pushed west to Cambridge Downs on the Flinders, out to Julia Creek, on the Cloncurry district of the State's north-west. Further south stock had pressed out to Enniskillen on the upper Barcoo River by '62 and Tambo and Terrick Stations quickly followed on its eastern tributary, but south and west of these outposts was still a no-man's-land crying out, or so it seemed to Grandfather and John Costello, to be taken up.

'Out there,' Grandfather declared, 'between the Warrego and the Paroo, are kingdoms waiting to be claimed.'

'Out there,' said Grandmother Costello, 'ye will be having your bones picked white by the dingoes and the crows like those poor fellows Burke and Wills if ye haven't the sense to know when you're well off.'

Mrs Costello contended moreover that Patsy Durack was an unsettling influence on her son John but the boot may well have been on the other foot, for John Costello had the wanderlust and the land hunger in his veins long before Grandfather spoke with him of those empty kingdoms a thousand miles north.

8

Prophet of the New Colony

The years 1862 to 1863. A meeting in Sydney with William Landsborough and discussion of the possibilities for Queensland settlement. With cattle and horses into Queensland. Retreat.

From the time of his marriage Grandfather's personality clearly emerged as the expansive, impatient, gregarious, organising fellow, who was to take himself and a lot of other people a long way fast. His mother, distressed at his restless energy, once complained that he worked as though he had 'the devil on his tail'. 'And so I have,' he said, 'but he'll not be catching up with me this side of tomorrow.' That was a favourite phrase of his and if he said he wanted a job finished 'this side of tomorrow' a wise man would get it done that day.

Although he must often have appeared an autocrat, time was to prove him sincere in saying that he wanted nothing more than to see his dependants standing firmly on their own feet. He was quick to recognise where talent and ability in others excelled his own and gladly gave to his younger brothers and cousins credit for superior bushcraft and horsemanship. He would defer to them on such matters but he knew he was on his own ground when it came to planning, to seeing ahead and examining a problem from all sides. Friends and family respected his discernment, his capacity for clear thinking and decisive action, and were so submissive to his guiding influence that they would often travel for miles over rough bush roads to consult him about such things as the purchase or sale of land and stud and the juggling of finance. He had a fair head for figures and enjoyed adding up sums on scraps of paper to show people how well off they could be in a few years if they did as he suggested and kept their fingers crossed. In this it must be admitted that his natural optimism often outpaced his better judgement for although he made certain deductions against 'Acts of God' he gave credit for a restraint the Almighty did not always show.

From the time of free selection he was unable to pass a likely looking unclaimed block without wanting to take it up for somebody and would frequently do so if time was limited, without as much as consulting the people concerned. From this time too he began writing home to friends and relatives in Galway and Clare about 'a bit of a selection' he had his eye on if they were 'minded' to come out. Mostly they came—Doyles, Murphys and Brogans—to swell the Irish communities between Bathurst, Goulburn and Yass. A letter, many years later given to his sons by a family that has prospered through his thoughtfulness, is typical of his approach. I quote it as written:

Dixon's Creek Meadow,
Mummel, near Goulburn, N.S.W.
2nd Feb. 1863.

> Dear John, I sed I would let you know when it was a good time to come out, well no time is to good if ye look at it from the shady side but this will be as good as eny time and I have a smawl block taken up forty acres about thirty mile from Goulburn good country somewhat high and a creek through the top end, will need hard work and clearing but yere boys will be getting big chaps now and ye have the girls for to milk the cows. I have a bit of a house on it and a man who is not minded to stop as frikened to blister his hands no good for this country so the selection is yers John if ye like to come and also the bit of stock for a start orf five milking cows two good drafts for the dray and some hens if ye want them from this place. Enclosed find £10 for part passage mony or expences and if ye decide not to come keep it for the help ye have all been to poor old Grandma dear old Mammie Amy in her last days God rest her soul. Come strate to Goulburn if ye come and let me know and I will be there to meet ye awl for sure. I have a wife now Mary Costello a fine girl and ye know her mother's people the Tullys who are at Drimnaugh, Costello was from Tipperary.

Yours faithfully,
Patrick Durack.

His protégés were not all such a credit to him though. Some, to Grandfather's anger and disgust, disheartened by the long uphill struggle to clear the land, took the easier way of 'dummying' for some big holder. Once he heard that a man he had helped was not only acting as go-between for a gang of horse thieves but was using the name of Patrick Durack to get credit at a local store. Grandfather bore down on the big Irishman in a towering rage, laid about him with a stockwhip and ordered him out of the district.

There was a deceptive power in his light-boned frame, and his eyes, habitually mild or merry, could flash with dangerous fire. Men who had dealings with him soon learned to avoid the hard spots in his good nature. If a man blasphemed that was between himself and his Maker but if he used in vain the name of Saint Patrick or the Duracks, Grandfather made it his own business. Saint Patrick was his special patron and he always celebrated his own birthday on March 17, the Saint's feast, while he defended his inordinate pride of family by reasoning that a man who had respect for his own name could be trusted to respect the law.

A loyal son of Ireland, he felt keenly for the rising prejudice against his people that their behaviour often warranted and had little patience with the excuses they made for themselves. The following fragment from a letter written home during one of his journeys, while quoting the views of a certain Mr Billings, gives a good indication of his own:

> I met today at Bathurst a Mr Billings a very amiable nice gentleman, he is with the Government in the Lands Office and had his education received at the Univarsity at Oxford. His Mother was Irish he tells me her people turned Protestant in the thrubles and he has been in Ireland though not in the west. He has had some throuble with the Irish in this country but is not narrow knowing what is behind us and the want of will that is found in many and we have had the example of our parents and other good people or would be the same way. Mr Billings ses it is not the caracter of the Irish they are idle and not to be thrusted with the thruth or to keep in the law but we have the chance in this country to shew the caracter of the Irish and not up against the government for no reson but the love of fite and argument and we will do better to work for the way we would have it here than what it was not in the past and there are some I can think of will do well to mind what he ses. He did me the honor to have a drink with me and we talked up to six . . .

It can be understood with what respect he listened to this no doubt rather pompous discourse for he was deeply impressed by people of education and good breeding whatever their failings may have been. In later years in Queensland he employed a rum-soaking book-keeper who was supposed to be the son of a lord and sacked him reluctantly only after he had been discovered forging the name of Patrick Durack on a cheque for the second time.

In '62 Grandfather had purchased by auction at Goulburn some 300 acres in the name of his younger brother Stumpy Michael, then rising seventeen. His policy at this time was to raise as much capital as possible by improving and part-stocking selections for sale to other settlers, but this block he declared young Stumpy must develop on his own initiative.

'It's yere own selection now. Ye must be working out all the problems for yourself.'

His brother had examined the land and pegged out a site for a shack but that was as far as his initiative was allowed to go.

'Now what sort of a kippenhead will be wanting to perch on the roof-top wheniver the creek's in flood?' Grandfather expostulated. 'There's only one place to build and it's yonder on the flat.'

He was right, of course, but it is hardly to be wondered that Stumpy Michael, although anything but a weak character, just never had much to say.

'The boy must be got out of his shell a bit,' Grandfather decided. 'He should be off to Sydney and seeing a bit of life, maybe buying some stud for that run of his.'

Others agreed that it might give the shy boy confidence to feel his feet in the city away from the family, but Grandfather had meant nothing of the kind.

'And what,' he asked, 'would a boy of that age be doing with himself in the city on his own?'

So it was a family party as usual.

To Grandfather's delight other branches of the Durack family had now come out from Ireland, some to settle in the Bathurst district, others to go into hotel business in Sydney so that when he arrived in the city with his wife, brother-in-law John Costello and brother Stumpy there was no question as to where they should stay. (It might be of interest here to mention that little Fanny, a daughter of his hotel-keeping distant cousin Tom, was one day to win fame as the world's champion woman swimmer.)

Sydney had seen many changes in that golden decade. Old landmarks had been either dwarfed or demolished. Black wattle swamp, where the teams had grazed on the edge of the town, lay reclaimed under a busy thoroughfare to the Quay. The first railway had been laid and everywhere was an air of prosperity, solidity and assurance that had been lacking ten years before. There now seemed as many steamships as sailing vessels on the harbour and the whaling ships of other days had disappeared. In a population more varied even than before were people of obvious opulence, dandies in embroidered waistcoats and extravagant ties, lifting bell toppers to ladies in crinolines stepping fastidiously from monogrammed carriages.

It was as well Grandmother had city friends to visit, since her menfolk spent most of their time at the stock sales where their attention was one day drawn to a lean, bearded bushman, outstanding even in this gathering of weather-beaten inlanders for the unusual penetration and brightness of his wide-set eyes.

'That's Will Landsborough!' they were told.

Next thing they were pumping him by the hand like long lost brothers, and meeting his companion Nat Buchanan, to be better remembered as 'old Bluey' of the overland trails.

Patsy and his companions had followed Landsborough's movements closely over the past few years. They knew him for one of the Fathers of the new colony of Queensland who a year or so before had discovered the Camooweal district, followed the Gregory to its source, named the rich Barkly Tableland and returned via the big rivers—Thompson, Barcoo and Warrego. Buchanan had been with him on the trip and was now his partner on the Thompson River. They had come down to Sydney to purchase stud sheep for their property to which Buchanan was returning soon with his bride, Kitty Gordon, a fine bush girl and daughter of the manager of Banban Station.

Their mutual interest established, they had dined together and talked on into the small hours. Landsborough, now an agent for the land he had opened up, was a stirring but sincere propagandist for Queensland settlement and his words fell on fertile soil with Patsy and his brother-in-law.

I picture Landsborough with his bright, wide prophet's gaze summing up the situation, knowing that the best 'pioneering spirit' was just this combination of ambitious drive and dissatisfaction with existing circumstances.

'So it is a failure after all, this Free Selection, but the law is made now. The people have come and the pattern has changed. The little men with their stringybark huts and their chock and log fences, firing the forests and cutting the scrub, have come to stay. Men who hanker for the open range, breathing space and boundaries marked by ridge or river have either to resign themselves to a changed order or move out.'

The explorers maintained that although transport difficulties on a 600-mile trek from the nearest depot, and a superstition that the climate, so far inland, would turn wool to the coarse hair of the common goat, had called a halt to settlement in south-western Queensland, the area could not much longer remain unoccupied. Already cattle and sheep were moving northwards from Victoria and New South Wales and the land boom was in full swing. Any person might apply for a year's occupation licence for a run of 100 square miles and within nine months, if he had by then stocked his run to one-fourth of its assumed carrying capacity of one hundred sheep or twenty head of cattle to the square mile, for a fourteen-year lease at an annual rental of 10s per square mile.

For himself Landsborough believed sheep would do well enough out there and put little credence in the theory of their fleece turning to hair. Sheep would survive drought seasons where cattle perished, but owing to the scab disease so prevalent in New South Wales the Queensland Government had recently put an embargo on all sheep crossing the border of that colony. For the cattle man, however, there were other advantages. He would need less labour and no fences for many years.

Conversation turned to the Queensland blacks who from the beginning had seemed more virile and spirited than those of the south. There had already been isolated instances of serious trouble—nineteen men, women and children massacred at Cullin-la-ringo in '61 and another disaster near Taroom where a pioneer family of thirteen had been wiped out. Landsborough pointed out, however, that experienced settlers might well expect more help than hindrance from the Aborigines if they started off on the right foot. Exploring parties had had little trouble from the blacks and much to thank them for. In the Barcoo district the natives seemed mild-mannered, timid of white intruders though not hostile. But for Burke's foolishness in flourishing his firearm, causing the tribe to disappear, they might well have saved the whole party from their miserable fate of slow starvation. As it was, the blacks did not show up again until only one man named King remained, but him they had taken at the point of death and cared for to the best of their ability. King had spoken highly of their kindness and of how they had searched over many miles to find food for him in a drought-stricken area from which be was too weak to travel.

Drought? But where in Australia, demanded the optimist, was this not a hazard to be faced? It was a misfortune as likely to fall upon the Murrumbidgee as upon the Barcoo and the first-footers out there could take so great an extent of country that in poor seasons they could shift their stock from badly affected areas. It was obviously a land of extraordinary recuperative qualities, capable of turning, almost overnight, from desolation into a waving pasture of fragrant clover and fine natural grasses.

As for distance from civilisation, with the tide of settlement so swiftly flowing out towns must soon follow.

When the party broke up at last they had covered so much ground they seemed already life-long friends. Their paths were to cross many times again until Landsborough, an old and honoured pioneer, was fatally thrown from his horse in '86 and 'Bluey' Buchanan had become that 'old man far-away', moving on into the Territory and first with cattle on the Ord—his wife, and Grandfather's, in the years to come, the first white women in the Kimberley hinterland.

This encounter supplied the spark to fire immediate action. In no time Grandfather had it totted up on paper how the natural increase from an original five or six hundred head of cattle, grazing on the lush pastures of the Cooper, would have them all wealthy squatters in about five years' time. Costello decided they should breed horses too and in a few minutes they were wealthier still. Finance was no great stumbling block for they could raise a mortgage on their existing properties and pay it off from the sale of the estates when they returned from staking and stocking their Queensland claims. Even though they ran themselves deep in debt it was agreed that any sparing of expense on essential equipment was false economy. The saddles and packs must be new and strong, the waggon solid and well stocked and their mounts the best procurable. Stockmen's wages were from £1 to 30s a week in those days but for droving trips of this distance and hazard they paid £2—and got their money's worth! Rations were worked out on the old bush scale of seven, two and a quarter'—seven pounds of flour, two of sugar and a quarter of tea per man per week. They would kill and salt beef on the track, and anything beyond these items was considered a luxury. They carried, however, a case of currants, some rice, mustard, curry powder and a few tins of jam.

It is not hard, from photographs and family descriptions, to picture the party that moved off with stock from Goulburn early in June '63. There was Grandfather, twenty-seven years old, slim, dark-bearded, upright in the saddle, his tender Irish skin permanently sunburned and peeling, his slim, strong hands scabbed with small sun sores. His brother Stumpy Michael, although darker than Grandfather, was also tender-skinned all his life. A quiet boy, still beardless with sensitive, chiselled features, too retiring to join the boastful displays of the other stockmen, young Stumpy had not yet proved the bushmanship that was to make his name. Growing in the shadow of his elder brother, listening and learning, he now faced for the first time the long, northward track that he was to travel so many times in the years to come. There was John Costello, twenty-three, lithe as lignum with a quick springing stockman's step and already a beard like a young bushranger. His almost dreamy eyes were as keen and trained as an Aboriginal's and his colonial drawl carried over from his parents an unmistakable Irish twist of tongue. Big, blond, bearded Jim Scanlan, whose sister Mary was soon to marry John Costello and whose brother Pat was married to Grandfather's sister Bridget, was already reckoned a good stockman, although no more than five years out from County Clare. Young Tom Kilfoyle, Darby Durack's brother-in-law, a veteran of the droving tracks at twenty-one, was a dashing-looking fellow on his fine stockhorse.

Besides the cook, who was a stolid German known as 'Vild Villy', only one member of the party was not related in some way. This was Jack Horrigan, Australian-born of Irish parents, whose name as a horseman is still a byword in parts of the outback. 'Poor old Horrigan was no oil painting even as a young fellow, when we first joined up,' Grandfather remarked many years later. 'But I never saw a man handle a horse as prettily.' Born to the saddle, he was bandy-legged, jockey-sized, keen-eyed, thin-featured with a scraggy red fringe of beard. Trousers low on his lean hips and tucked into his high-heeled elastic-sided boots, broad-brimmed hat fastened under his chin with a leather strap, he was the Australian stockman par excellence

With 100 horses valued at about £2,500 and 400 breeding cattle reckoned at £5 a head, they planned to push on past Bourke, 400 miles from Goulburn as the crow flew, nearer 600 following the rivers, and on into country recommended by Landsborough over the Queensland border. They agreed that Kilfoyle, Horrigan, Stumpy Michael and the cook would remain here at a selected depot while Grandfather, Costello and Jim Scanlan made south to sell up and return with the women, children, further stock and all the impedimenta of permanent settlement.

Costello, famed for his unerring sense of direction, was appointed leader of this expedition. Where Grandfather used his compass all the time, Costello seldom needed his, never when he had once covered a track and this was no mean feat over these vast, almost featureless inland plains. He could make back so precisely over his former tracks that his horse once put its foot on a compass he had previously dropped. He would display the dinted case with pride. 'How's that for a deadline now?' 'If ye'd the sense to dodge about a bit as I do,' Grandfather teased him, 'ye might have had your compass back intact.'

Both Costello and Kilfoyle were already familiar with the early stages of the route that wound for about 150 miles north-west along the Lachlan and up the Bogan River to its junction with the Darling some 200 miles due north. They made eight to ten miles a day over good country, the cook with his dray moving on ahead to strike camp, the horses following and the cattle bringing up the rear. Sometimes they camped for a day or two while the route ahead was examined for water and grass and men from scattered sheep and cattle runs dropped in on the camp for a yarn and to make sure, in passing, that they did not linger too long on the station waters. It was a dry year around the Lachlan and as the settlements fell behind and the track swung in a half turn down the Darling the outlook did not improve.

They were two and a half months to Bourke, last outpost of New South Wales settlement, where the explorer Thomas Mitchell, seeking the destination of the big river in 1835, had built his little fort against the blacks. Only lately gazetted as a frontier township, Bourke already promised to become a thriving centre. Its two enterprising storekeepers and three publicans predicted that it would soon be the Mecca of settlers, drovers and teamsters for hundreds of miles around. Almost every week another party went through, some to occupy land in the far north-western corner of New South Wales, others into Queensland, mostly via the Darling to the Culgoa, but when the Costello–Durack party cut out north-west they made fresh tracks

Feeling their way up the inconsistent stream of the Warrego and across the Cuttaburra, they moved on to the sandy, treeless plains of the Paroo into an area of seemingly permanent springs which they judged to be fair horse country but of little use for cattle. Here just south of the border they established a depot and left most of the horses in charge of three men whose instructions were to follow their tracks if they had not returned within a certain time. John Costello, Grandfather, his brother and Jack Horrigan then pushed on with the cattle, hoping to find better country a little farther to the north-west. Instead the outlook grew steadily more arid and desolate as, now about 150 miles past Bourke, they trailed the cattle through dusty mulga, gidgee and brigalow scrub, over parched plains broken into a crazy pavement of widening cracks.

Sixty years later my father and I travelled through this country in just such a drought, when hot winds stirred up a gritty film of dust, whirlwinds reared spinning, red columns against a cloudless sky and at evening the sun seemed to float like a huge, pale balloon above a desolate horizon.

'This is how poor Father first saw this country,' my father said. 'What a heart he must have had ever to come back to it!' and he recalled the story as he had heard it many years before.

With two dry stages behind, they had come at last to the drover's 'point of no return'. Scouts rode on ahead, located a little water in the Bulloo River and returned to bring on the thirsty stock, though by this time some of the horses had fallen in their tracks, and had to be shot where they lay.

The frenzied cattle smelt water on the wind from a mile away and broke into a stampede. Four men on weakened horses stood no chance of wheeling them as they plunged forward to the river, trampling fallen beasts to pulp under their frantic hoofs. Half were drowned in the milling turmoil, while the rest drank until they nuzzled the mud and then bogged, exhausted, too weak to pull themselves out. The drovers, forced to shoot what perishing stock remained, moved on up river and found a little water for themselves and their horses.

Only those who know the undying optimism that drives the seeker of gold or land will understand how practical men could find themselves in such a plight, how, gripped now with the doggedness of desperation, they plodded on another thirty or forty miles in the awful face of the drought. Their stock had perished, but if they found good country on ahead they could return for more when the season broke.

A patch of parakeelia, with succulent leaves and stems, provided a little moisture for men and horses as they plodded on, their hopes reduced at last to the discovery of a little water to sustain life.

Salvation lay in a party of blacks, striding like lean giants through the waters of mirage, dwindling as they drew near to the meagre proportions of the desert people. The men, naked but for belts of woven hair, emu feather head-dresses or dangling circlets of dingo tails to brush away the flies, carried bundles of long, thin spears and throwing sticks. The women wore armlets of possum skin, necklets of clustered kangaroo teeth or small human bones—relics of drought-born babes, killed and eaten to be born again, they reasoned, in better times. One or two carried little ones, surprisingly fat and gazing mutely from bark coolamons swung about their mothers' backs.

As though sensing the helpless and sorry plight of the travellers, the warriors laid down their arms and stood quietly as the white men came on. Astonishingly one spoke a few words of garbled English and was later found to have been in contact with King, the sole survivor of Burke's party of two years before. Words, however, were scarcely necessary. The lives of the white men and their horses, with tongues swollen and turning black from thirst, lay in the hands of these people whose lot they might at other times have pitied or despised. They led the white men to a low, rocky outcrop and there, removing a cover of brushwood and stones, disclosed a well of stagnant water.

Later they brought food—*pinkunnas*, fat yellow grubs dug from the roots of the mulga, black goannas to be roasted in hot ashes with little hard cakes made from the pounded flour of the nardoo—a feast for starving men. They revived rapidly and began to question the blacks about country farther on. The leader shook his head, scowled and jutted his chin to the south.

'Go! Go!'

But whether or not the advice to return was given in concern for their safety, the white men, encouraged by a flight of parrots to the north-west, decided to push on. They ate crows and kangaroo rats, sucked moisture from parakeelia, but they found no water and soon there were only two horses left. They called and signalled for the blacks whose smoke fires had followed them, but nobody came. They found a pack saddle, half covered in sand on the bald plain, and inferred it to be one abandoned by Burke on his hurried death march over these same hungry plains. When the last horse was near death they shot it and drank from its jugular vein—the last desperate measure of perishing men. It was only then they turned back and suddenly the blacks were there again.

'Go?'

Heads nodded and white teeth flashed in dark faces. There was another well in a limestone outcrop not far away. More lizards and nardoo cakes, and a sign conference in which the blacks agreed to accompany the travellers, showing them the hidden waters until they rejoined their people.

One of the party, about to move on, dipped his leather water bag into the well. Instantly there were lowered brows and upraised spears, for the blacks were masters still in this timeless country where life was sustained by a stern discipline of mind and body uncomprehended by the white. These little reservoirs in an arid land had succoured the traveller from time beyond memory and were a sacred tribal trust, not to be camped on for unnecessary time, their contents never to be carried away. The water was tipped back and following the example of the blacks, the white men placed pebbles under their tongues.

From well to well they plodded south on blistered and swollen feet, until one morning the blacks had vanished, their tracks pointing north-west to the horizon, while from far down the course of a dry creek came the faint, hollow knocking of a horse bell. They sent up a smoke signal, fired a shot and presently riders and packs appeared out of the dust.

The time agreed upon for the return of news had elapsed and stockmen who had remained at the depot had set out in search. They carried flour, tea and hard 'jerked' beef in their tucker bags, but the water in their canteens was low and when these were filled and the horses watered for the return journey, the little native well was drained dry.

And already men were saying of a people whose lives had been pared and restrained to a system of survival remarkable among all races on earth—'The blacks have no thought for tomorrow.'

9

Of Plans Deferred

The years 1864 to 1867. Family events and tragedies. Political and sectarian strife in New South Wales. The flood of '64. Marriage of John Costello and Mary Scanlan and their departure for the north. Depression in Queensland. Patsy Durack makes preparations for the northward trek.

Incredible as it may sound after the experience they had just survived, both Grandfather and John Costello were resolved before they got back to Goulburn not only to return as soon as possible but to bring their families. Their heavy losses of stock and equipment were a bitter blow to family resources but they were somehow confident that when the current drought had broken they could soon retrieve their losses. Grandfather, for his part, was convinced that had they been able to continue in the direction of the flying birds they would have come upon good permanent water. Most of the surviving horses they had been forced to leave, running wild, below the border. Here, provided the blacks left them alone, it was thought they should do well enough until their return when they could have a grand horse muster and dispose of the increase for a small fortune.

Still, they had not reckoned on the barrage of family opposition that met their plan. Mrs Costello avowed that she and her husband would advance not a penny more on their son's wildcat schemes. Tea-tree was a good property and there he must settle down. The three Scanlan brothers were behind her at this stage and refused to sanction young John's marriage to their cherished only sister while he entertained the idea of returning with her to the desolate and lonely north. Grandfather's position was complicated too, for the little daughter, Mary, born shortly before his return did not seem robust enough to survive an expedition of this kind. Family troubles crowded in on all sides. One of the little Skeahan boys had been fatally injured by a horse and another died of 'a fever' within a few weeks. Poor Mary had come home with her grief and her remaining two sons while Dinny, weary of battling on the drought-stricken selection he had been persuaded to take up near Lambing Flat, talked of defying the family and trying his luck in a deep shaft on the Adelong River.

About the same time news came from Sydney that the second sister,

Margaret Bennet, had taken ill of 'a chest complaint' that had haunted the family since the famine years and Grandfather, in a frenzy of worry, went post-haste to fetch her home with her baby Mary Anne. As her husband's work had kept him so much away, Margaret had lived with his relatives in the formal atmosphere of an English household where both her religion and her friendly, outspoken Irish ways were little understood. She had pined badly for the boisterous hugger-mugger of family life, for the riding, romping and banter, the bluster of Irish argument, and the intoxication of her brother Patsy's quick enthusiasm for new schemes. It was thought that the dry inland air would soon restore her strength but she continued to decline as the weeks went by and the dress she had started to make for the Christmas races became her shroud when they crossed her hands on her rosary and braided her long fair hair for the last time.

There could be no prolonged wake in an Australian summer, but Irish families, determined to wring every ounce of emotion from 'the tragedy', came flocking from miles around with offerings of food and drink and blessed candles to burn beside the bier. The keening and the praying went on for a day and a night while the distracted husband pleaded with the family to turn 'the barbarians' away.

'But it is as she would have expected it,' Grandfather told him, 'for if these are barbarians then so was she.'

Anxious to remove his child from this environment, John Bennet announced that he would take her to his own family, but Great-grandmother Bridget would have none of it.

'And have her reared a Protestant!' she exclaimed. 'Over me own dead body!'

The Irishwoman, entrenched in her stronghold, won the first round of this classic and long-to-be-disputed issue, in which neither party could in conscience give way to the other. A host of well-meaning busybodies took up the cause on either side and Grandfather found himself embroiled in the only type of argument that was really anathema to him.

Already religion was at the bottom of most personal and political issues in the colony, the cause of frequent riots and fights. With every shipload of immigrants came a further influx of southern Irish, with a mingling of derelict and weak-willed falling easy prey to the temptations of the Free Selection Act. The prevalence of blackmail and perjury, the number of poor and disillusioned Irish now 'dummying' for big holders and turning farm-houses into grog shanties were used by political zealots in sweeping generalisations on the degeneracy of the Irish race and the iniquities of 'papism'. The fine radical spirit of Ireland found itself in the ironical position of supporting the more moderately conservative leaders since the left-wing elements led by Henry Parkes and Dr John Dunmore Lang embodied a bitter hatred of their faith.

Parkes had emigrated from Birmingham a few years before the discovery of gold in New South Wales and through his support of the anti-transportation movement had won a reputation for vigorous leadership. Unfortunately for the Irish, however, he had grown up in an overcrowded industrial area where labour problems had been aggravated by an influx of hungry and dispossessed from across the channel. British workers in the inevitable fight for self-preservation stirred an ancient anti-papism into a living fire which many, like Parkes himself, carried with them to vent upon the Irish in the new land.

In the late fifties open conflict had broken out on the education issue, with Parkes espousing the State school system divorced from sectarian influence and the Irish keenly supporting a policy of education combined with religious instruction. For a few years all sects came in behind the vigorous campaign of Catholic and Anglican Churches, but in the face of bitter opposition Parkes, then Premier of New South Wales, established his first secular public schools in 1866.

Still the fight raged on, complicated by inter-sectarian prejudice and strife, disrupting the harmony of every community. It was now no mere land hunger that pulled Grandfather and Costello to the empty north but a wish to start afresh where they could find wholesome expression of true Irish life and personality.

The drought years broke in the winter of '64 and the Mulwarrie came down in a mighty flood, drowning stock, sweeping through the settlements right into the streets of Goulburn. Life over the entire district was disorganised while families more fortunately situated took in the straggling bands of refugees. The house at Dixon's Creek was filled to overflowing with friends and relations whose homes were temporarily under water.

Grandfather's sister Bridget Scanlan had been giving birth to her third child while the water level rose steadily up the walls of their shack and big Pat stood by urging his wife to get up and swim for it.

'I tell ye it's drowned we'll be, woman, if we stop here another mortal minute.'

Poor Bridget, helpless in her extremity, expostulated: 'It's not so much that I won't get up as that I can't, but if it's scared you are there's nothing to keep yourself.'

No sooner was the child born than Pat wrapped it in a blanket with its mother and swam them all to safety.

After the confusion and excitement of the flood came the marriage early in 1865 of Pat Scanlan's sister Mary to John Costello, with Father MacAlroy, who had presided at so many of the family weddings, again officiating.

Mary Scanlan, the serene-looking girl from County Clare who had pioneered a selection with her brothers, was a fine rider, an efficient hand with stock and a crack shot with a rifle. She had besides the reputation of being 'an authority' on world affairs and local politics and contended that it was more important to know what was going on outside than to keep one's eyes constantly bent on household tasks. Before the marriage Great-grandmother Costello thought such views unwomanly, and the bright, wide-spaced gaze and confidence with which Mary Scanlan would discuss the affairs of the day a sign of unseemly boldness. Later on, when Mary became her daughter-in-law and the mother of her grandchildren it was a different story and Mary's virtues and intelligence were lauded to the skies.

No sooner were the couple married than the subject of the north country again raised its ugly head and the bride, far from shrinking from the prospect of such a pioneering adventure, urged it wholeheartedly. They were eager to make a start at their previous depot below the border and later expand into the new colony which was said still to be flourishing, albeit on borrowed money. It seemed a good sign that private investors were now following the example of the government which, with finance from London, continued its programme of public works and its wooing of immigration with glowing promises and advertisements in striking capitals:

WANTED: YOUNG MEN FOR QUEENSLAND!

For a time old Mr Michael Costello had done no more than vaguely shake his head over the 'beautiful, lovely horses' abandoned to their fate up north, but at last, no doubt under pressure from the young people, he quietly took action at the Lands Office. For a down-payment of £25 he obtained title to the lease of 32,000 acres between the Warrego and Paroo Rivers at that time occupied by a tribe of wild natives and a mob of near-brumby horses. He then wrote out a cheque for £3,000 to see his son on the road north with two hundred head of cattle, fifteen horses, two waggons, a dray, a bride, brother-in-law Jim Scanlan, two extra stockmen and a cook. Grandmother Costello was beside herself, berating in turns her husband, her son and any other relatives within earshot:

'It's soft in the head ye are, ye silly old man, and young John here with a heart of stone to be taking a young girl where there's niver a white woman in a thousand miles and lucky to have a black gin attend her in her time of trouble. Well, ye can be off the lot of ye and good riddance and I'll carry on at Tea-tree with a manager.'

Still when the time came for departure there was the senior Mrs Costello beside her husband in the family buggy, grim-faced under poke bonnet, the goose's-head umbrella from which she was inseparable at hand to ward off the sun over the long, hot miles. Meanwhile Tea-tree had been put under lease, for the old people loved their home and could not bring themselves to dispose of it.

'The day may come when you'll be glad of our "little cocky run", as ye call it,' Mrs Costello said. 'It will always be a roof over yere heads if ye've nowhere else to turn.'

John Costello and his wife would remember her words when, forty years later, an ageing couple with a big family, they would return to set up the neglected homestead and clear the land again of the encroaching scrub.

Eager as Grandfather was to follow them, family problems and financial difficulties tied him to the Goulburn district for a further two years. In July 1865 my father, Michael Patrick, was born but the joy of a son and heir was overshadowed by the sickness of the two-year-old girl. Grandfather, carrying her everywhere in his arms, crooning to her, willing her to life, scorned the women's forebodings.

'Wamen! It's a flock of ravens they are. The same they were saying of Sarah—"Ah, the little angel not long for this world" and all. God Almighty, look at her now, with her brood of giants!'

Sarah Tully felt no less cramped than himself under the conditions of close settlement. At twenty-five, a small, lean, brown-skinned woman, she had a forceful, almost terrible vitality and sometimes out of frustration or Irish indignation at some local incident, she would saddle up and ride like the devil across country to fling herself off, breathless and excited, at the gate of Dixon's Creek some fifteen miles away. Great-grandmother Bridget would come panting, full of joy and anxiety:

'Sarah child, ye'll have the bairn born dead if ye ride like that!' (There was mostly a babe in arms and another on the way.)

'Nonsense, Mother! Haven't I ridden with them all, and aren't they the finest children in the colony?'

The fierce devotion that Sarah lavished on all her family was almost fanatic with her offspring whom, following the example of her Grandmother Mammie Amy Forde in Ireland, she placed, soon after birth, on the fresh tilled soil to receive the goodness and strength of their mother earth. For all this two of her little ones already lay near her father and Poor Mary's two sons in the Goulburn cemetery.

'Please God we can all be going north soon,' she would say. 'Even Dinny Skeahan should be doing all right up there away from the gold and the pubs.'

By '66, however, Grandfather could no longer close his eyes to the fact that Queensland's rosy promise had grown somewhat pale. That the colony's debentures had become a drag on the London market by the middle of '65 had been considered of little account. 'Only to be expected,' men said, 'a temporary fluctuation', and in this frame of mind the government had plunged on with its ambitious schemes of development. But British investors had become wary of what they now knew from bitter experience in the defeated American Confederacy, in South American republics, in Spain and the Middle East, to be dangerous over-borrowing. The failure, in the middle of '66, of London banks that had made big advances to the new colony reflected at once on its affairs. There was chaos within a day of the news reaching Queensland. Unemployed and disillusioned rioted in the streets of Brisbane and bankruptcy spread like a bushfire through the Land of Promise.

Meanwhile, in the north of New South Wales, always at least three months out of touch with current affairs, the Costellos were fighting for foothold in an inhospitable land. Their station, which they had named Warroo Springs, gave little sense of security for the country was patchy from a pastoral point of view, and the blacks who had soon discovered the superiority of horseflesh to their native lizards and kangaroos were a constant menace to stock. John Costello had decided on a policy of killing beasts for them at regular intervals and of trying to explain the white man's views on personal property, but one of their young stockmen made a game of firing over the natives' heads for the fun of seeing their terrified retreat. One day he had been found speared in his swag some miles from the homestead, since when no natives had shown up for their beef ration but had increased their killing and chasing of stock on the run. Nonetheless, a few natives had attached themselves to the white settlers and were proving faithful helpers.

Not long after the family's arrival at Warroo Springs a son, John, had been delivered to the young couple by the capable hands of Great-grandmother Costello, and the infant's sturdy build seemed a good advertisement for the district. In letters to his relatives John Costello was careful always to temper news of their hardships and misfortunes with a note of optimism for the future and reports of 'the better country farther out' to which they would move as soon as other members of the family had joined them.

Early in '67, soon after the birth of a second son to my grandparents, their little girl's frail life ended. Consumed with grief—for how could there ever be such another angel child?—Grandfather determined to delay his departure no longer than it might take him to 'raise the wind'. The sale of their three Argyle district properties, about 900 acres in all for which they had paid £1 an acre, would not realise much more than twice the purchase price, even allowing for improvements, since their stock had been depleted since the '63 debacle and the best they had left was to go on the road with them. Grandfather estimated that he must have at least £4,000 behind him for this project, about £2,000 to see them on the road and as much again to tide over the first two or three years when little would be coming in and a good deal going out.

Bankers, hitherto fairly co-operative in advancing money to settlers, hesitated to finance a venture to a still unknown destination in an already depressed colony where the settlers had, moreover, only a flimsy lease title to the land. The problem was overcome at last by a deal of Irish juggling and the advice and assistance of the bankers Samuel Emanuel and his son Solomon who had recently joined his father in Goulburn. So, after fourteen years in Australia, Grandfather started on his thousand-mile trek north with a load of debt that would have bowed the shoulders of any but an incurable optimist.

Although this time he could afford only a small herd of breeding cattle and comparatively few horses, he had refused to stint on equipment. They had come into the district as penniless immigrants but at least they should move out in the grand manner, and Grandfather proudly displayed to curious droves of friends and relations the wonders of his four covered waggons, built to his own design, two with bunks that could be folded when not in use and complete with everything required for comfort on the road, the others stacked with goods, equipment and livestock. Everything they possessed was to go with them, even their fine Irish linen and lace, bulky feather mattresses, silver and brass, china and glassware, for this time there could be no turning back.

A rough estimate of their requirements and expenses for the expedition ran as follows:

	£	s	d
150 head of breeding cattle reckoned at £3 a head but fifty from our own place not counted in...........	300	0	0
Two four horse waggons at £55 each.....................	110	0	0
Two two horse waggons at £40 each	80	0	0

12 heavy team horses @ £35 per head	420	0	0
15 good stock horses @ £15 per head, but six from Dixon's Creek not counted in	135	0	0
Saddles, harness, packs and gear of which we have not already	100	0	0
Carpenter's equipment such as we have not already	35	0	0
One large kitchen range, for 20 loaves	10	0	0
Utensils required new	15	0	0
12 prs. boots, 12 trousers, 12 shirts........................	22	10	0
Provisions such as cannot be got on road...............	50	0	0
Wages for three stockmen for three months at 35/– per week	63	0	0
Wages for two men for teams @ £2	64	0	0
Wages for cook at 25/–..	15	0	0
Blacksmith's stuff (tools, horseshoes, horse nails etc.)	8	10	0
Blankets and canvas	6	15	0
Total	£1434	15	0

Buggy and buggy horses, furniture, crockery, cutlery, household linen, kitchen sundries, a number of tools, saddling and gear, 6 pigs, 6 milking goats, 14 laying hens, 3 roosters, 12 Muscovy ducks and 3 sows and boar and other sundries, not counted in exes. as already to hand.

Farewells went on amid final preparations for departure, Grandfather extending wholesale invitations to friends and relatives to join them later in Queensland. Already he was picturing a Beulah land of happy community life, roads and townships springing up in the empty wilderness. A simple-hearted man with a passion for 'fixing', Grandfather believed that life not only should but could be adjusted so that people were not constantly harassed and frustrated, where families could put down roots and spread thriving branches.

Any dismay Grandmother might have felt for this exodus was tempered by pleasure at the prospect of joining her parents and her brother John. It was true, as her mother maintained, that she was not like her brother's wife, Mary Costello, by nature or inclination a pioneer. She would have settled down very happily to an ordinary suburban life and if circumstances drew from her qualities of resource and endurance that made her seem born to the role, she at least had no such illusions. Once, when praised by a city friend for her courageous pioneering spirit, she replied simply:

'I had nothing of the sort, my dear, but when Patsy said we must go pioneering what else was I to do?'

While their relatives were packing up for Queensland, Darby Durack and his family were also moving out from Dixon's Creek to what they considered superior land near Boorowa, about sixty miles west of Goulburn. Now the parents of seven sons and five daughters, Darby and his wife, anxious that the younger children should have a better education than had been possible for the rest, did not aspire so far afield as their relatives. The two eldest boys, 'Big Johnnie' and 'Black Pat', as they were usually known for obvious reasons of identification, were now seventeen and fifteen years old and had already been on droving trips with their Uncle Tom Kilfoyle. Already men in size and practical experience, they were now determined to strike out for themselves on the Castlereagh where they had taken up two sheep selections which they called Gidyeagunbine and Muchenba.

'The old man will get nowhere with his scrub-bashing,' they declared. 'The only way to get anywhere in this country is leave the land as it is and run your stock on the natural pasture.'

The Irish farmer who had worked and cherished his land almost as a sacred trust had been unable to influence the outlook of his Australian-born sons.

'Ye must learn to know the land,' he had said. 'Ye must feel for it as a living thing or it will die.'

But his boys had shrugged:

'Better that than it should kill us first.'

Since Great-grandmother Bridget had promised her son-in-law John Bennet that she would not trail his little girl to Queensland, she now made her home with Darby's family at Boorowa. Her youngest boy—'Galway Jerry' as he was later called—was to remain with her and go to school for another year or two before joining his elder brothers, and the youngest daughter, Anne, to continue teaching in Goulburn where she was being ardently courted by a young Irishman named John Redgrave who gave his occupation as 'miner, horsebreaker and tutor'.

Sarah Tully had been all for joining the north-bound expedition but here her quiet-spoken husband exerted his authority. Without capital behind them another couple and five children would be nothing but a burden to poor Patsy. They must wait and see how things turned out before giving up their interests in the south. Pat had recently taken up a second free selection block near Adelong, about 150 miles south-west of Goulburn, a haunt of his early mining days where, since there had been fresh rumours of gold in deeper shafts, he dreamed of dropping on a lucky strike while tilling the land. Sarah, always suspicious of mining, said they would move from their place at Hume Creek only to go north, but Dinny Skeahan had happily agreed to fulfil the conditions of occupation by putting up a shanty on the Adelong block and working a shaft

Poor Mary, still vulnerable to the bright plans her husband so eloquently expounded, agreed to carry on the selection at Lambing Flat with her little sons while Dinny dug up enough gold to put them all on the road to Queensland. To these complicated plans Sarah vented her scepticism in the words of a popular song of the time:

So he built him an iligant pigstye
That made all the Munster boys stare,
And he builded likewise many castles
But alas! they were all in the air.

10
EXODUS

The year 1867 to 1868. Patsy Durack and his family leave Goulburn for the north of New South Wales. Reunion with the Costellos at Warroo Springs. Establishment of a station on Mobel Creek, Queensland. Breaking of the drought. Costello takes horses to South Australia and returns via Goulburn.

In June '67 the family cavalcade moved out of Goulburn to catch up with the stock already wending its way north along the Lachlan in charge of three hired hands. The cattle were all Herefords whose west England working ancestry had established a suitably robust and docile strain, with sturdy development of chest and hindquarter and good hoofs for hard travelling. Grandfather had become a keen stock breeder, always 'culling' the coarser animals that ran to sway backs, long heads and narrow eye spaces, selecting for straight, clean lines and good heads. He could judge the weight of a beast almost to the pound, a skill he handed on to my father, who, when describing either beast or human, never failed to add what the subject would probably 'go' on the scales.

Grandmother, with the two-year-old Michael and the baby Johnny in arms, travelled in the buggy with either Grandfather or young Stumpy Michael who took turn about with one of the larger horse-drawn waggons. Two hired teamsters and the cook, who travelled with the cattle, were in charge of the other three vehicles and after the parties joined up the buggy went lead each day to strike camp for the following cattle and teams. Fires were lit, billies, cooking pots and camp ovens in which bread had been rising on the way along, came rattling off the cook's waggon. Grandfather would set up a shade for his family while Grandmother fussed over her infants, bathing the hot, tired little bodies in sometimes no more than a pannikin of water. Every man took turn at night to watch around the cattle while the rest gathered at a communal fire where tea and coffee were kept brewing at all hours and where Grandfather and his brother enlivened the quiet evenings with fiddle and flute. Soothed by the sound of music and voices the cattle grazed peacefully, some edging close to the camp and throwing themselves down contentedly within a few yards of the fire.

The first stages were comparatively easy travelling, over wheel-made tracks and past farms and stations where they would sometimes linger for a day or so on the invitation of hospitable bush people touched to see the little family forging on into the never-never, recalling the Costello party of over two years before and eagerly inquiring how the brave young wife had fared with her expected little one. Most spoke pessimistically of conditions over the border. It was surely a bad time to be taking up country in the new colony when so many were getting out, they said. Had they not heard that the Bank of Queensland had failed, that in Brisbane police were called upon almost every day to quell riots among the unemployed? Did they realise that the price of livestock scarcely covered the cost of droving to market, that they were boiling down sheep and cattle for tallow as in the bad times in New South Wales, and that people said nothing short of a miracle could now save Queensland from complete disaster? Yes, Grandfather said, they had heard all this but depressions were passing phases of history. Besides, they believed in miracles.

Lifelong friendships were made on this journey, for through all their years in Queensland one or another of the family was frequently on the road back to Goulburn. Twelve years later when my father and his brother came south for the first time on their way to school they would be surprised at how many remembered this first meeting and how one woman, with more sentiment than tact, had clasped their mother, crying: 'What has it done to you, that terrible, cruel country? What has become of your lovely skin and the roses in your cheeks?' So we picture her, still young and slim and fair in her blue poke bonnet, high-necked blouse and neat gloved hands, a gentle, fastidious little woman facing a new life in that harsh and lonely land, and Grandfather, brisk-moving, dark-bearded, keen-eyed, telling with his Irish lilt of their hopes and plans. And there is young Stumpy Michael, whom people on this track would know best of all the family, a quietly spoken, courteous boy, twenty-one years old, five foot ten inches, strongly built, already encouraging a beard to protect his sensitive skin, but a tough man on the track, a skilled hand with the teams.

They stocked up at bush townships that grew sparser with the weeks and the miles. A month, by easy stages to the Bogan Gates, had brought them 200 travelling miles from Dixon's Creek, then as the low featureless scrub below the Darling spread about them all signs of settlement petered out, and they made a compass course through more or less trackless bush.

There were breathless days of aching heat and others when the hot winds bowed the pale grass, stirring up the dust and veiling the sun while the stock plodded doggedly with bowed heads, intent only upon reaching the next water. On black soil country over mile upon mile of raised

Mitchell grass tussocks the going was an agony in poorly sprung vehicles. Sometimes, in extreme heat, they travelled at night, steering a northern course by compass and by stars.

They reached Bourke, their last outpost, after about three months on the track, to find that the optimism of the township pioneers had been justified and it now boasted a number of stores and hotels, two banks, a Court of Petty Sessions and a hospital. Every road in the far west swung into this centre and residents spoke of its progress with pride.

'Bourke is not a town,' they said, 'but a city whose borders are hundreds of miles apart.'

After replenishing their stores for the last time, the party moved north on a roundabout trail of the Warrego and Cuttaburra and north-west towards the Paroo and the Costellos' station between the rivers.

Here was a flat world of little shape or colour, sparsely timbered, faded under torrid skies to dusty yellow and grey, unrelieved by mountain peak or range, and where even the water in the broken river holes was the colour of clay. Sometimes, knowing they might find no firewood before the day's end, they carried timber from camp to camp.

The letter telling of their coming had been still awaiting some erratic mailman when they got to Bourke so the dust of the buggy and the following waggons brought the Costellos running in excited surmise. Of what intriguing speculation and ecstatic surprise the party lines and pedal radios have deprived the bush in our enlightened times! There was no through track past Warroo Springs so these could be no mere travellers on some lonely trail north. Could it be that they had come at last?

'I believe that was one of the happiest moments of my life,' Grandmother told her children, 'to find my parents, my dear brother and his family safe and well in that lonely place.'

After the embracings and the tears, the babble of questions, and exchange of news, there were rapid plans to make, for the 'permanent' springs on Warroo had almost given out and only the hope of their relatives' coming had prevented their moving on already to a good waterhole John Costello had discovered some 200 miles north-west across the border.

'Of course we would have to strike another drought to start us off,' Costello said, 'but it can't go on much longer and when it breaks we shall all be on clover.'

Since there was no hope of 'selling out' in such times it was simply a matter of getting out—abandoning to the wilderness the work of two and a half years, of mustering and packing and moving on with their goods and chattels and stock. There was a great outcry among the few native families that had attached themselves to the station and quickly become used to the white man's ways and his good food. One young fellow whom Costello had named Soldier because of his fine physique and upright bearing had amazed the newcomers by a natural gift for handling horses. It was he who had gone with Costello to the good water on Mobel Creek, a camping place of his wife's people, so when the time came for moving on Soldier, his wife and two or three other relatives accompanied them.

The three hired teamsters, three of the stockmen and the cook returned from Warroo Springs, leaving a party of nine white men, three white women and three children to start off across the border. There was John Costello, his wife and child, his benign old father, his staunch but irascible mother, his brother-in-law Jim Scanlan and one stockman named Jack Farrar who had stuck to them on Warroo Springs. In Grandfather's party there was, besides himself, his wife and brother Stumpy, two hired stockmen and the two little boys, my father and baby Uncle John. This time native riders helped with cattle and horses, leaving the white men free to manage the waggon teams. Great-grandmother Costello 'manned' one buggy and her capable daughter-in-law the other, while Grandmother took charge of the little ones.

How many besides the blacks had been before them in this trackless land since the explorer Gregory, in '58, had discovered Mitchell's splendid Barcoo River to peter out into the shallow channels of Cooper's Creek? The Burke and Wills party had passed through the locality in '61. Landsborough had crossed it in search of them and they had themselves come part of the way in '63. A few thin lines of penetration in a vast, empty land. Here and there they passed the bleached and scattered bones of their own perished stock. There was more feed and water now than on their previous journey but as they pushed north from the border it was seen that drought was again closing in on Landsborough's pastoral paradise. Grass grew sparse and bad water thick with green slime lay in dwindling holes. Before the stock drank they drew off buckets for their own use, boiled and cleared it a little with a mixture of gidgee ash and Epsom salts; but fever and dysentery were already upon them and in heat rising to the limits of human endurance sick women nursed their fretful children while sick men fended for the precious stock.

The leaders must have wondered now, as did my own father in after years, how they had dared bring women and children into such a situation. Even explorers would have had more chance than they of rescue in a final extremity, for settlers put no time limit on their reappearance. Any who knew of their intention to move on from Warroo Springs would have had little idea of their possible destination. They were responsible to themselves alone, at the mercy of unpredictable tribespeople and an even less predictable land. Obsessed with an ambition to be first in an area that so far settlement had shunned, they had ventured into this pitiless country for the second time, confident that such a drought as they had struck before could not occur again so soon. Now once more before them stretched the parched, colourless plains, dotted with sparse and ragged timber, scarred with the sun-baked courses of shallow creeks where the only signs of life besides that they brought with them were the gathering flocks of hungry crows and eaglehawks, the erratic whirlwind spirals that darted with furnace breath across their trail or over their midday camps, scattering the fires, leaving a heavy scud of dust, dry grass and brittle leaves.

If this were fiction it might be said that I had at this stage overstepped the bounds of credulity and descended into bathos in having a child die in such a scene. But this is stark truth and it was here that the Costellos' sturdy two-year-old, wasted almost to a skeleton over the fevered miles, died pleading for water in the unquenchable thirst of delirium. They told how at the last he had roused himself in his mother's arms and smiled as the waggon jolted through mirage on the blistering plain: 'Water, mummy. Water!'

They dug a grave on the banks of the Bulloo River and placed above it a rough wooden cross, soon to be dispersed like the bones of their dying stock by the ravages of flood and wind.

The 'good hole' on Mobel Creek lay between drooping, flood-tattered paperbarks and raggy coolibahs where flocks of parrots ard white cockatoos clustered and cried. The water was opaque and uninviting but it was good water for a drought year and there was enough pasture to indicate promising possibilities. It would be 'sweet country' after rain, they said, and if, because of limited permanent water, it might not sustain a large herd, it was suitable at least for a temporary place. They ran up slab huts and a post and rail yard, 'tailed' the stock and watched out for the return of the blacks who had fled the water on their approach.

Knowing that if the natives turned against them everything could well be lost, they had sent Soldier and members of his family to make contact and explain that the white men would kill cattle for them provided they left the stock alone. Soon groups of natives came straggling in, received their beef, laughed, made unintelligible but seemingly friendly comments and set up camps on the far side of the waterhole. One good-humoured, grizzled-haired fellow with a bone through his nose and a body ornate with tribal scars at once attached himself to Grandfather and was given, along with the name of Cobby, a shirt and trousers, a hat and a pair of stockman's boots. He picked up the rudiments of English with surprising speed and although not young soon learned to ride a horse and tail cattle. Being 'Mr Durack's boy', as he called himself, he brought his section of the tribe to the station side of the creek with the crowd from Warroo Springs.

'I don't know how you can stand the sight of that terrible old Cobby,' Grandmother told her husband one day. 'Several times I've caught him lifting the mosquito net to peer at the baby and I don't like the look in his eye.'

'But Cobby was sent by my Guardian Angel,' Grandfather said, 'in the very minute I was praying for protection for the lot of us.'

Grandmother remained doubtful for although probably more deeply religious than her husband she was sceptical of the intimate terms on which he conversed with the hierarchy of heaven, and wondered how, while the family prayed to God and all His saints for rain, Grandfather could bring himself to promise the blacks an extra ration of tea, sugar and tobacco if they succeeded in influencing their tribal spirits to the same end. Grandfather felt no evangelical mission to the Aborigines. He displayed a keen and respectful interest in their beliefs and religious practices and related in exchange simple legends of his own faith so that his own particular 'boys' would call upon St Patrick in times of stress and St Anthony to help them track lost horses.

The family was not many weeks on Mobel Creek when the Costellos' second child was born—the first white baby of the Bulloo district. They christened her Mary, but the blacks called her Burtnagala—little girl of Burtna, their own name for the Mobel waterhole.

Rain fell like a benison with the coming of the child. The Bulloo ran overflowing its tributaries and soon the grass sprang sweet and succulent on the parched plains. The settlers watched the flanks of cattle and horses swell to curves of wellbeing and contentment, realising how truly Landsborough had described this as a country of swift, almost miraculous change.

The horses that, for all the ravages of the blacks, had increased considerably on Warroo Springs were soon again in wonderful condition and fearing they would quickly run wild and become a nuisance Costello decided to take a draft of 200 down to Adelaide where horses were said to be bringing a good price.

There were few details available of what lay between Mobel Creek and the settled parts of South Australia, but from his study of the explorer Gregory's track in '58 Costello knew that a creek—the Strzelecki—ran, when it did run, almost due south into Lake Blanche—part of Eyre's shimmering horseshoe of salt lakes. From there, he reasoned, a drover should find water enough in scattered creeks and soaks to see him to more reliable country south of Lake Frome. Undismayed by the prospect of some 860 trackless miles to market, he set out with his brother-in-law Jim Scanlan, his boy Soldier, and another Warroo native called Scrammy Jimmy.

They cut across from the Bulloo one hundred miles west to the Wilson River to find that selections there had been taken up at about the same time as the family came to Mobel Creek. Canbar East, Canbar West, Lubrina, Nockatunga, were tiny outposts in the wilderness where pioneer settlers S. D. Gordon, Alex Munroe and Pat Drynan were battling like themselves. Cheered on their way they struggled down the fitful stream of the Strzelecki and into the desolate sandhill country, the land of lost men. The thirsty horses, mostly unbroken and more imaginative than cattle, stampeded at mirage, quivered with fear of strange waters, started at shadows, thundering off night after night in moonlight frenzy. Young Soldier, with his uncanny understanding of the ways of the horse, galloped with his master, breakneck, to turn the lead of the frightened mob.

Three weeks to Lake Blanche, a month from there to Lake Frome and Wilpena Creek, they nursed the animals along, until they fell gradually into the hard rhythm of the track, taking up their self-selected places—the big black stallion always in the lead, paces ahead of the rest, others on the wings or in the body of the mob, the weaker bringing up the rear. Gradually they moved through more closely settled districts to Kapunda, north of Adelaide, where, not a beast short, they clattered through the dusty streets to the saleyards in the first week of 1868.

Costello interviewed the young auctioneer, Jenkin Coles—knight of later years—telling how he had travelled down on an unsurveyed route of over 800 miles.

In his auctioneer's stand Coles told the story of those horses and their drovers. The animals were all of thoroughbred Arab stock from around the Murrumbidgee, Lachlan and Wollondilly Rivers—a region already renowned for producing horses of great hardiness and spirit. They or their forebears had travelled north, nearly 1,000 miles to the Bulloo, had survived the drought to thrive on the grass and clover of a good season. Their hoofs were inured to rough travelling. Heat held no terrors for them. They had the speed of thoroughbreds, the intelligence and hardihood of brumby strain—in short the makings of superb Australian stockhorses.

The crowd was so stirred by Coles' eloquence that the horses averaged

£15 a head and Costello and his companions found themselves overwhelmed with hospitality.

Hailed everywhere as 'The Queenslanders' and congratulated on the news which they heard only on arrival at Kapunda, of a gold strike at Gympie in the new colony in September '67, Costello decided that the tide of family fortune had turned at last. With a cheque for £3,000 he changed his mind about making back over the dreary desert route. It would be more expensive but quicker in the long run, he reasoned, to ship men, stockhorses, gear and all from Port Augusta to Sydney, covering the 1,072 sea miles in comfort in about ten days, making inland for Goulburn to see the folks and returning to Queensland by the New South Wales track. So the two stockboys, Soldier and Scrammy Jimmy, who three years before had never seen a white man or worn anything more than a hair belt, a bunch of feathers and a nose bone, found themselves plunged into a bewildering world of busy thoroughfares, big buildings, noise and confusion all about something they would never understand. Costello, watching their reactions with interest, was surprised to find with what seeming *sang froid* they accepted the white man's world. The sight of the ocean surprised and excited them more than any of the wonders of man and where they had walked, not greatly impressed, through the streets of Adelaide, they stood on the sea-front gazing in awe at this immense water, vaster than any inland river in a big flood year. Running forward, they threw themselves down to drink and jumped up spluttering in disgust:

'Him chalt!'

From that moment the sea held no charms for them. It was useless—no good to drink, and horrible to travel on. They huddled in their blankets, sick and cold, moaning that they were about to die, so that Costello and Jim Scanlan had constantly to encourage and cheer them for fear they would.

'It was a lesson to me,' Costello admitted. 'I'd take a blackfellow anywhere short of hell on land, but never again on sea.'

In Sydney they rallied at once and in smart stockmen's outfits strode the streets with their white masters, again less curious of the sights and crowds than was the white population of them, for Aborigines of this type were now no common sight in Australian cities.

A curious crowd watched them pack up and ride out of Sydney on the Goulburn road, a mere step and a jump of 136 miles to these seasoned travellers, with the mountains and forest country awakening the lively interest and wonderment of the native boys.

Word had gone ahead of their coming and family and friends had flocked to meet them in Goulburn, hungry for news from the far north. There was Great-grandmother Bridget with the wide-eyed Mary Anne Bennet, and her youngest, Jerry, yearning to be off with these heroes to the new land of adventure. The Scanlans, Pat and Mick, were there to greet their brother Jim and this man Costello who had taken their sister into the wild, lost land. Sarah and Pat Tully had come with their family laden with parcels to be taken to the dear ones in the north and Poor Mary Skeahan to tell of how Dinny had every confidence in his latest deep shaft on the Adelong, and little Anne, the school teacher, to be teased about her diary and the young man John Redgrave who remained so attentive.

Costello registered the Mobel holding of about 40,000 acres, paid his cheque into the Goulburn bank, handed around some £5 notes and answered all protests with a breezy wave of the hand.

'The drought's broken and they've found gold at Gympie. They said it would take a miracle to set Queensland on her feet and here it is!'

11

A Land Loved by Birds

The year 1868. Patsy Durack and his brother find Thylungra on Kyabra Creek and return there with their own and the Costello family.

Grandfather loved to tell the story of his coming to Thylungra and his hunch about the birds. Although there were parrots, cockatoos, some duck and an odd pelican to be seen on Mobel Creek, great flocks passed over from time to time making for the north-west.

'They'd all be down here,' Grandfather reasoned, 'unless they knew of something better farther on.'

Patiently he had questioned old Cobby and the other blacks:

'Good country out that way?'

'You-eye, country all right, only here more better.'

This Grandfather took with a grain of salt, knowing that no native will admit any country being better than his tribal heritage.

'Plenty water over there?'

'Can't finish'm.'

'What about blackfellows?'

'No good. Proper wild fullas that way.'

'How far this good water?'

Thin arms swung to wide horizons. 'Oooo long way—two-three mile—might be fifty.'

'About fifty miles?'

'You-eyes. Might be t'ousand.'

'How many days' ride? How many sun go down?'

'Oooo mob. Not too many horseback.'

'You reckon you can show me this good water?' Grandfather asked Cobby. 'You been there before?'

This put the old man on his mettle. He knew all about this country—everything. As ambassador of the Murragon tribe he had often visited those carpet snake Boontamurra people who camped on the big Kyabra waterholes where there was fish and game all the year round. He could take him all right. He had a mother-in-law and a few other 'little bit' relatives over there but they were wild people. You had to look out for them, keep your hand on your gun. From the beginning of their short association Cobby had been so thrilled and fascinated by firearms that Grandfather had had to keep them locked away for fear the curious fellow would someday try one out for himself.

'No gun,' Grandfather said, for he had strong views on riding armed into the black man's country. 'Only maybe that shotgun in case we need some tucker.'

So, while Costello was on his way south with the horses, Grandfather, young Stumpy Michael and the native Cobby had set off for the camping place of the wild Boontamurra and the great flocks of wild birds. Flopping untidily in the saddle, reins flapping, old Cobby led off with confidence, sixty-five miles north up the sprawling course of the Bulloo to somewhere about the site of the present town of Quilpie, then away a hundred miles to the north and west until the low eroded slopes of the Grey Range, drab-coloured as their name, dropped away behind and in front stretched the mighty Cooper plains. The black man's arms embraced the vast horizons as he turned smiling in his saddle. Here were the pastures of a grazier's dream—Flinders, Mitchell, button, kangaroo and blue grasses, while gidgee, boree and coolibah trees made scattered shade and lignum sprouted succulent shoots along the courses of winding creeks and gullies. The foliage of these trees seemed stunted and thin to the unaccustomed eye. Not yet could the stranger find beauty in their supple hardiness, elegance in the dainty fan-like spread of boree branches limned against the sky, grace in the lithe growing lignum, swaying under the weight of perching birds. Here and there, dazzling red against a hard blue sky, were sandhills composed of fine quartz grains—monuments to a long-lost Cretaceous sea. The travellers made camp at the foot of one of these, under a gidgee that would remain, in years to come, a landmark beside the well-travelled track—'the Durack tree'.

While the white man surveyed the landscape the native tracked lizards and marsupials to their haunts, emerging from a wild scramble with a small blue rat and a spiny lizard which he introduced as 'Nai-ari'—a little *Moloch horridus*, gentle ant-eating miniature of a monster that might well have walked the earth when fish swam in Queensland's forgotten sea. From the trailing Nulloochia, a species of wild cotton, he pulled dry brittle fruit and chewed them with relish. 'Good tucker,' he said, for nothing, apart from poisonous plants, was ever despised by the wandering children of the hungry plains.

The black man pointed westward to a meandering smudge of timber, where, he said, lay the 'good water properly', camping place of the

Boontamurra. It had been different in the old days when Cobby had approached them as tribal messenger, bearing the carved letter sticks—the 'milli-milli'—and other peace symbols of the Murragon. Today he came in the white man's clothing and mounted on a white man's horse, his message not of some forthcoming ceremony, of birth, death or betrothal, but of the coming of a strange people to share their camping grounds. For himself Cobby had never questioned the new regime, but he could not answer for the reaction of these nighbouring tribespeople.

'You got that shotgun, boss?'

The timber grew less scattered as they drew towards the watercourse, and through the ragged arches of bordering coolibah and wild oranges the water shone polished bright in the setting sun.

The coming of the travellers had aroused a deafening clamour of birds, parrots and water fowl of all kinds, wild geese, plumed duck, spoonbill, avocets. Flocks of teal wheeled noisily with egrets, ibises, herons and pigmy geese, while pelicans, heavily rising, flapped off in the wake of low-flying brolgas. A land loved by birds must be good land, the travellers reasoned, marking the length of the waterhole bending away between ravaged timber with the grass and driftwood of flood-time in its topmost branches.

Cobby pointed to a bank of sand breaking the waterhole where fires, hurriedly covered, still smoked and smouldered.

'Big mob Boontamurra close up, Boss.'

The thirsty horses, sniffing the danger scent of the wild people, sipped the water nervously with lips and ears backturned. Grandfather and his brother walked to one of the deserted fires and raised hands in the peace signal they had learned from the Burtna blacks. Presently there was a stirring in the timber and timidly the people of Boontamurra emerged, men women and children, over 200 strong, streaked with ochre, decked with feathers, down of emu and wild duck in fantastic patterning stuck on with blood.

Soon Cobby was chattering away with them, telling the story of the white man's coming, the dawn of a new age of plenty and novelty. Already the name bestowed on the white man by natives in the south had spread to the far tribes, but 'Cooeebooroo', the man who cooees, was much of a mystery still. By some it was said that he was man and beast in one and went upon four legs, but now it was seen that he walked upright like themselves.

Cobby explained that his master was a great man, a brother —'Boonari'— and the reverential title was repeated in good faith.

'Boonari! Boonari! Taralee!' Everything was 'very good'.

Asked whether their waterhole was permanent, the blacks made a babble of assent.

'You-eye! Thillung-gurra.'

Cobby interpreted.

'Yes. Yes. Good water. Not go dry.'

Grandfather's Irish tongue fumbled with 'Thillung-gurra'.

'Thyloungra . . . Thylungra.'

There was good-humoured laughter at his efforts. An agile youth, decorated to indicate an early stage of tribal initiation, beckoned the white man to the water's edge where he displayed a device of stones and nets ingeniously arranged for trapping fish. From this he removed a fine specimen of golden perch or 'yellow belly', flapping alive on the end of his spear. Cobby translated his tumbling sentences. One knew the holding capacity of a waterhole by the size of the fish. The creeks that quickly dried allowed their creatures little time to grow. Smiling, the youth introduced himself, thumping his chest.

'Burrakin!'

He was five foot nine or ten inches, broad-shouldered, lean-hipped, his rippling dark skin slashed with protruding tribal scars that were accentuated with ochre and feathers. His face, with wide-set eyes, sloping forehead, broad nose pierced with a bone, and wide laughing mouth, was eager and intelligent.

'Him yabber you brother belong him,' Cobby said. 'Long time him brother die. Now him jump up white man.'

Grandfather smiled acknowledgement of the relationship, but 'Pumpkin' was the best he could do with Burrakin. Later he was often to remark that he had named this native better than he knew for in the vegetable kingdom the humble, hardy pumpkin was the bushman's best friend, his standby through good season and bad.

The lad's brothers were brought forward and christened Melon Head and Kangaroo. Now all were clamouring to be renamed—Jimmy, Willie, Jackie, for the lilting music of the tribal names, a few to be perpetuated in creeks and hills and billabongs—Murryaweatherloo, Wathagurra, Tongalerry, Gungaditchee, Warraboleyna, Waddi Mundoai. The last was a merry little man, his name meaning 'wooden foot'. When a child his leg had become crushed to pulp by a heavy piece of timber when swimming a flooded river but the gallant little fellow had devised himself a wooden stump on which he hopped about as lively as a cricket. He was witch doctor, sorcerer, comedian, renowned for his keen senses of sight, hearing and smell. In later years, when anything was lost on Thylungra, it was little Waddi

Mundoai who found it, covering the ground like a sparrow, his head cocked from side to side.

When night came down over the Thillung-gurra waterhole the travellers camped, without fear, within sight and sound of the Boontamurra and their gunyahs of mud and bark. Already familiar to them were the scents they breathed, the pungent reek of river mud, of smoke from aromatic woods, of roasting duck and kangaroo, of wild bodies rank with blood and fat.

The black people, for their part, unsuspecting the change that had dawned for them, had already returned to their past, with Cobby who had given warning of their savagery happily ensconced in their midst. Darkness vibrated with the savage rhythm of sand mounds beaten between the knees of the old men, with the hollow pulsing of didgeridoo, the clopping of cupped hands on naked thighs, the sharp calculated click of boomerangs and 'talking sticks'. Wild voices took up the throbbing measure in a song of earth and element, of time without beginning and without end, while the ground shook under the heavy stamping of the dancers' feet.

Firelight flickered on animated spectres, fantastically patterned with ochre and feathers, topped with crazy headgear designed to awe or to amuse.

'It is the blessing of Almighty God they are kindly and child-like savages,' Grandfather said and would never alter his estimate even when the simple people had turned fiends at last in blind thrusts of bewildered rage.

Morning brought a sense of driving urgency. The secret of success in this country was to get in first and who knew but that someone else was already riding out to claim the pick of the Cooper plains? There was no time to lose, they said, to the bewilderment of the blacks who spoke of wild goose cooking slowly in stone ovens. To them time was a magic and a mystic thing to be spoken of in awe—a time past and a time to come for which all things must be kept unchanged, whereas the white man spoke of it as something tangible that might be 'lost' or 'found' or even 'killed'.

So they returned to Mobel Creek with tidings of good pasture, permanent waters and friendly tribespeople. The blacks had drawn them a mud map indicating that the watercourse which they called Kyabra swung south and north again in a half ellipse finally junctioning into a big river of many channels, probably Cooper's Creek. There were good permanent waters all along and one they spoke of as 'Momminna', apparently not far distant, bigger than the hole they called 'Thillung-gurra'.

The return of Costello, Scanlan and the two native boys, a mere six weeks on the road from Goulburn, was hailed with delight and arrangements for moving on began at once.

It was sufficient within the law of the time that the newcomers ran their stock on the country they wished to occupy, provided they took steps to lodge official claim as soon as possible. That was interpreted as meaning anything from a few weeks to two years.

Stockmen rode out to comb the plains, the gullies, ridges, breakaways of the Mobel holding, gathering in the cattle from their self-selected camping places, the horses from their wider range. Meanwhile the women packed up the waggons and the drays, stacked in the rough-hewn furniture, the kitchen utensils, babies' cradles piled with clothing, tin trunks full of valued possessions from their old homes in New South Wales.

The natives, Cobby, Soldier and Jimmy with their wives and families, entered into the urgency of departure, electing cheerfully to make their homes on strange waters and among strange tribespeople.

So, by April 1868, the cavalcade of stock and waggons was once again on the move, following the watercourses on to the sweeping prairies between the western rivers. The mob, now dwarfed by the breadth of the great plains, was in fact pathetically small. Of the 150 head with which Grandfather had left Goulburn he had lost more than half in the drought trek from Warroo Springs, and although there had been a small increase on Mobel Creek the time-worn Thylungra stock book starts with the significant entry:

> Cattle
> Came from Goulburne in 1868
> 100 head.

Costello was starting with about twice this number, as he had mustered over 300 from Warroo Springs. Grandfather had about thirty head of horses and Costello, since he had taken the surplus to South Australia, about the same. Their stock, all told, was little enough on which to stake a future on untried country but their hopes rode high through the pastures of this first good season.

'Look at it!' Costello enthused. 'Didn't I say we'd be on clover in no time at all?'

The Boontamurra people, scaling the sandhills, gazed on the fantastic spectacle of moving cattle, horses and mounted men, open waggons drawn by yoked bullocks, covered waggons horse-drawn, a flock of goats, a dray-load of squealing pigs. A medley of new noises broke on the ancient silence of the plains, a bellowing and a neighing of stock, a thunder of hoofs, a cracking of whips, a clanging of bells and a rumble of wheels. The 'Cooee-booroo' had returned but there could be no eager welcome for such a fear-inspiring horde. There could only be hiding and watching ... watching the thirsty stock move in to drink, churning the clear waters into mud, urgent, clumsy hoofs trampling the fishing nets into the sand, scattering the stone fish traps, while birds in their thousands wheeled and screamed. Later, when all was peace again, and the strangers and their herds moved on, there would be a tale to tell, a new corroboree.

They did not know yet that the 'dreaming' was over for the Boontamurra and soon enough for all the wandering ancient tribes of the white man's big new colony.

12

LAND OF WAITING

The years 1868 to 1869. Drought and hard times haunt the settlers.

Into focus through the blur of years ride these hard, lean, bearded men, quick-moving in their days of slow travel, pitting human will and energy against a strange land's hostility, dotting its great grey empty plains with their stock, their homesteads, their fences and yards; and beside them their women, wind-burned, sun-browned, wrinkled before their time, coping, normalising, dedicating to the will of God griefs and anxieties that pedal radio and flying doctor would spare the bush people in years to come.

Grandfather and his family settled on the Thillung-gurra waterhole while the Costello party moved south on a pot-hook trail twenty-five miles downstream to where Kyabra Creek swelled into a lake, seven miles long by half a mile wide. This was 'Big Momminna', another favoured camping place of the natives, abounding in water fowl, pelicans, duck, herons and cormorants. They called their place 'Kyabra'.

During the months of settling in Grandfather and Costello must have driven themselves and others almost to breaking point. Stockmen were sent out to tail the cattle until they grew accustomed to their new camps, also as elsewhere to make friendly contact with the blacks and kill an occasional beast for them. A few they had met on first coming to Kyabra Creek, among them old Waddi Mundoai, Pumpkin and his brothers, Melon Head and Kangaroo, had turned up again soon after their arrival and remained as a matter of course. The three younger boys took readily to stockwork while Pumpkin also showed remarkable aptitude in the use of tools.

Drafting yards went up, barricades of split timber made to withstand the sieges of time, for Grandfather had become impatient of the colonial attitude of 'good enough'. He built defiantly, as though with every blow of his adze he would reassert his resolution and the permanence of his occupation, and others about him must do the same. He always held that shoddy workmanship was an attitude of mind and betokened lack of faith in the future. He worked fourteen or fifteen hours a day and expected others to do likewise, checking on their labours with eagle eye, testing the staying power of rails, the depth of post holes, the hanging of gates, pacing, measuring, contriving.

Even the 'temporary' mud residence on the river bank was made so well that it was still in use until demolished for a modern homestead seventy years later. It was built of mud mixed with dry leaves and grass, horse-churned to a sticky clay, shovelled between upright board frames and rammed firm. When the mixture dried the boards were removed and the walls stood rough, red and durable. The house was bungalow style with hard, mud floors and sloping coupled roof extending to wide verandahs and thatched with a waterproof interlacing of straw and paperbark—a typical Irish farmhouse in the Australian bush.

Bullock and goat hides were carefully pegged and salted and later softened by patient rubbing with rough stones to make floor mats and bed coverings. This was work at which the black women excelled, sitting for hours in the shade pounding away in the ancient manner of crushing the hard nardoo.

The furniture was solid and rough-hewn, the bunks of unplaned timber and rawhide, the big dining table built in the main room so that it could never be removed in one piece.

But the crudeness of bush living was softened for the men whose wives went with them into this voluntary exile. A generation later people would remember the homely charm and comfort of the first Thylungra, its shuttered windows gay with chintz, the dining table meticulously laid with spotless damask and shining silver cutlery, the heavy oil lamps with their elaborate silver bases and globes embossed with deers' heads.

There was no time yet for the relaxation and enjoyment of living that would come with the years, but through all the long months of toil Grandfather, his brother and John Costello learned to know the land they had claimed. Riding around, shifting and tailing stock, they had ranged as far out as the channel country—a vast flat area watered in good seasons by the westward-flowing system of the Cooper, Diamantina and Georgina Rivers. Only in time to come would the immensity and potential of these pastures be fully realised and man obtain a bird's eye view of that sixty thousand square mile plain, eroded to an intricate pattern of shallow, braided channels, swamps, gutters, billabongs—a natural irrigation system for the rich fodders and clovers that followed swiftly on the rains. However, even these earliest pioneers, jogging over a weary panorama of broken country too complex to map, sensed something of its unique quality.

In the higher stony ridges they had been puzzled to find a number of small pits, two or three feet deep, holding an even level of water and so regular in formation that they had thought them man-made, like the desert wells of other parts. The blacks insisted that this was 'dreaming water', and the wells made by sky heroes of the time long past. One of these 'spirit men', they said, had banished a great river underground where it flowed deep down in the dark, a seepage rising here and there in holes like these to succour thirsty travellers. Years later science would tap the resources of this legendary stream—the 'water underneath'—and bring it throbbing hot to the surface from deep artesian bores, but by that time these first pioneers had packed up and moved on.

Although they had put little credence in this story, the settlers were eager to learn all they could from the blacks of their country and its wild creatures, for like most bushmen they were ardent naturalists. They learned to distinguish the interlacing tracks of reptiles, insects and marsupials, to read significance in the habits and antics of birds.

At the end of August, Stumpy Michael and a native boy named Willie set off with two waggons to bring supplies from Bourke and put in their claim for the Kyabra Creek country. They had reckoned the journey of about five hundred miles there and five hundred back, as the track wound, would take them about three months but four months went by and there was still no sign of them.

When the wet weather clouds began banking up the family knew that if the travellers did not beat the rain, swollen rivers and boggy plains might hold them prisoners for months. Every day anxious eyes scanned the horizon for the homing waggons. Hopes were raised by spirals of whirlwind and dust, possibilities were endlessly discussed and hazards assessed. That they might be lost was hardly considered, for Willie was a native of exceptional intelligence and Stumpy himself a natural bushman. Sickness was a possibility, fever, snake bite, dysentery. Accident to one of the drays was a likelihood, for it was a simple thing to break an axle coming down a steep incline, over a gully or breakaway. Still, Stumpy was clever enough with his hands to have mended or improvised in a very short time. Attack by natives was a haunting fear and trusted scouts from the local tribe were sent out to discover whether any such rumour had circulated among their people. They returned always with the same story. The teams had passed unmolested on their way south but had not returned.

Sometimes settlers were beaten by nothing so much as the nervous strain of such interminable conjecture, of waiting for rain, for mail, for someone to turn up, by hope long deferred, or bitterly frustrated by clouds that passed away, the mail that was left behind, the man who did not come.

Beef and goat mutton was the settlers' staple diet for as the waterhole dwindled the fish disappeared and the water fowl took off to other haunts.

Sugar was down to the last few pounds, carefully rationed. There was no tea, no jam, no tobacco, little salt, and weevils riddled the few remaining bags of flour.

Scratches and insect bites festered and spread into big, oozing, scabby sores—'Barcoo rot' they called it, though other districts claimed and named the sickness as their own. It was not hard to diagnose the cause, but the yams, nardoo and parakeelia of the parched bush had little curative effect on the pampered constitution of the white. Grandfather quickly ploughed and fenced off a garden area and planted pumpkins, potatoes and runner beans and these, with patient hand watering, showed promise.

Through hard years of make-do Grandfather developed a number of pet economies and devised all manner of improbable substitutes, often convincing himself, if not others, that he had improved on the original product. When the tobacco gave out he made a dry hash of gum leaves and pituri, recommended by the blacks, not good, but better to some tastes than nothing at all. Tea was eked out with the dried leaves of wild marjoram and other herbs—a brew commonly known as 'posts and rails' because of the little sticks that always came floating to the top. There were endless experiments in preparing 'bush tucker' to give variety to the salt meat menu. Grandmother did her best with kangaroo, emu and even, under strong persuasion, with lizard, but she put her foot down when it came to snakes, frogs and witchetty grubs, which Grandfather insisted were delicacies if cooked on hot coals as the blacks advised.

In the station store there were always criss-cross stacks of home-made soap, concocted of a mixture of fat, caustic and resin stirred over a slow fire, candles made in moulds shaped to a point at one end with string wicks pulled through and held in place as the liquid tallow was poured around to set. Everything was grist to the settlers' mill. Even their ammunition was home-made—the leaden lining of the tea chests melted in a crucible and poured into bullet moulds, later to be filled with gunpowder. Grandfather also made 'gammon' bullets loaded with coarse salt or flour to fire at the marauding crows and eaglehawks.

The new year of 1869 came in under the shadow of two haunting fears, one for the safety of Stumpy Michael and black Willie, the other for rain. The hired stockmen, unable to tolerate the isolation, and the shortages, had soon gone on their way and neither Grandfather nor Costello could leave their places. They could only wait, watching the sky for clouds, the plain for the dust of the waggons. They could expect no news from passers-by for none came that way in those early days. Their nearest neighbours were over 200 miles north on the Thompson River, 150 miles south on the Wilson, 200 miles north-east at Tambo while out west lay only the mighty loneliness sweeping over 350 miles to meet the drifting sands and gibber plains of the Simpson Desert. Once during these heavy weeks of waiting and anxiety there had been a shrill outcry from the blacks as two horsemen emerged from the horizon dust.

At first they were thought to be Stumpy Michael and Willie riding home after for some reason abandoning the teams, but it was a stranger who dismounted and came to greet the family. His name was Welford, a polished young Englishman whose father was a judge in Birmingham and who had come to Australia in search of fortune and adventure. From a few thousand pounds capital he had purchased a mob of 500 breeding cattle and some horses from Roma, hired three white stockmen, two native boys and a cook and pushed out to take up the first good unoccupied country he could find west of the Condamine. From the Bulloo his party had picked up the tracks of waggons and stock and he and his boy had left the party some miles back to follow them into Thylungra.

My grandparents took this brave-hearted English boy at once to their hearts. He was their first contact with the outside world for many months and they were anxious to see him established as their first neighbour. Grandfather rode with him to the head of Kyabra Creek, about 120 miles north of Thylungra homestead, to a good piece of country he had thought of taking up for himself. Welford was pleased with its possibilities and having sold Grandfather twenty-five female calves to boost the small Thylungra herd, moved on to settle in.

Now the blacks predicted there would be no rain that season, for the chattering hordes of budgerigars that so delighted the eye with acrobatic displays, now darkening the sun like a storm cloud, now turning in a conjuror's vanishing trick on the knife edges of a million wings, were congregating too thickly about the remaining waterholes. The nankeen plovers, rising in the furnace blast of rainless summer with long-drawn cries of ecstasy to circle and dive through the racing whirlwinds, were no good omen either, for these birds revelled in drought. Aboriginal heads shook dolefully at sight of nests abandoned, half built, and others with broken eggs, at emus and brolgas rearing singleton chicks in the same law of the wild that prompted the tribespeople to kill the newborn babes of drought.

Every morning clouds piled up to the north to melt in midday heat and evening skies were agate-bright fading to amethyst. Cracks widened on the parched plains and hot winds filled them with the brittle remnants of precious grass. The kitchen garden languished and died.

Stock fed but did not fatten on mulga, spinifex, salt-bush, blue bush and cotton bush—hardy stand-bys of drought years. Wells were sunk into the creek beds and water fed by means of whip and bucket to lines of rough-hewn troughing.

In mid-January rain fell at last in an earth-shaking storm that raised a film of green on the bare plains. For two weeks thunder rumbled among threatening clouds, then came two days of searing wind, sweeping up the red dust and darkening the sun. Fat lamps burned all day in the stifling house while stockmen with handkerchiefs tied under their eyes rode out to urge the bewildered cattle on to water in the face of the stinging, howling gale.

Grandfather's horse stumbled in a breakaway and rolled on its rider as the maddened mob thundered past. He lay in agony until the tearing wind had spent itself and the sun blazed out on the red land turned white under a shroud of desert sand, when he was found by the blacks, half-conscious and almost buried alive. He was riding again before his ribs had mended or his cuts and bruises healed. He had no faith in the efficacy of lying up while one could still stand, but Grandmother contended that the 'sciatica' which was to plague him for the rest of his days dated from that time.

It was nearly six months before the long awaited waggons came swaying into sight with Stumpy Michael and Willie cracking the whips on the last stretch, smiling stiffly through the dust on their beards.

And oh, there were sacks of flour, casks of black sugar, cases of medicine—those panaceas of all ills, Holloway's ointment and Epsom salts—a cask of rum, kegs of salt, kegs of nails, bolts, cases of currants and raisins, garden seeds, spices, bolts of calico and turkey twill, needles and thread, men's slop clothing, barrels of gunpowder, clay pipes, rank plug tobacco, boots and tins of jam. There was prepared leather for saddles, and heavy saddle cloth, and for the children a tin of boiled sweets.

Stumpy related how, on reaching Bourke, he had found the single general store almost depleted by the rush of prospectors to the Gympie diggings.

Apparently few had learned caution from the Canouna stampede of '58 when 20,000 prospectors met with bitter disappointment, for no sooner had a fossicker named Nash reported rich specimens in the bed of the Mary River than settlers were again leaving their runs and labourers their assured jobs to join the rush.

Stumpy Michael had put his bullocks out to grass and settled down to await the further supplies expected any day. Three weeks passed and no one had shown up except a few impatient and frustrated settlers like himself. Tortured by thought of the family's need and anxiety he decided at last to push on down the Darling, 150 miles to Wilcannia, but here too provisions were short and many necessary items unprocurable.

It was three weeks before the supply boat came up the river, and then he and the faithful Willie had faced the long, hard home journey, zigzagging to find water in the drought-stricken land, toiling along the sandy courses of dried up rivers and creeks.

On steep inclines they had had to stage the load, bringing it on part at a time and toiling back for the rest, coping with panicking cattle when the ropes twisted or the load slipped. On abrupt declines they had felled trees and hitched them behind the drays. One of the leaders slipped and broke its leg and had to be shot and several others died from eating poison bush. Michael had purchased replacements from a station but these were unbroken to team work and the going was slower and tougher than before. It needed no more than one trip on the road with the drays to learn why bullockies were notoriously hard-mouthed men, but Michael was to face this journey until he became a familiar figure at every station and township on the road.

For twelve years his life was to be spent mostly on the track with the supply teams or droving stock. The Thylungra cash books are full of brief, revealing entries: 'Michael, for cash to Goulburn . . .' 'On the road Wilcannia . . .' 'Cash going Adelaide with cattle . . .' 'Exes on roads bringing cattle up.' 'Exes to Cootamundra with horses . . .' 'Cash to Sydney with cattle (flood-bound four weeks)'. Flood-bound—waiting for some river to subside, sandflies and mosquitoes torturing his permanently sun-burned skin, centipedes and scorpions crawling from the closing cracks in the ground, sometimes causing agonising bites, snakes wriggling in to share his refuge from the driving rain. 'Give it to Stumpy Michael,' people said. 'He always gets through,' and there was never a trip that his memory and his pockets were not taxed with special messages, letters and commissions.

A great load of anxiety had lifted with his return, but still the rains held off. Light showers, two months after the big dust storm, had brought another film of grass to wither on the plains in 112 degrees and after that the cold weather set in with a sudden drop of temperature to freezing point. In the mornings there was ice on the horse troughs and water frozen in the pails and they knew then that there could be no more rain before the next monsoon.

In July Great-grandmother Costello, who lived mostly with her son at Kyabra, came to Thylungra to her daughter Mary who gave birth in August '69 to her fourth child. Grandmother considered herself lucky to have had a white woman with her at a time when many bush women had no help at all. Sometimes a gin was summoned hurriedly from the camp, or a woman gave birth alone while a frantic husband rode to the nearest neighbour fifty to a hundred miles away, perhaps returning to find mother and baby dead. But these were times to be spoken of in whispers, in female company only, and a woman tried not to cry out in labour lest her intimate distress be heard by menfolk and children.

The baby Jeremiah had been lusty enough at birth, but he became fretful with prickly heat rash until too exhausted to suck or even to cry and died at six weeks old. Great-grandmother Costello, standing grim-faced beside the first grave in the little Thylungra cemetery, looking across at her son-in-law had voiced her reproach with terrible restraint:

'The poor bairn never had a chance!'

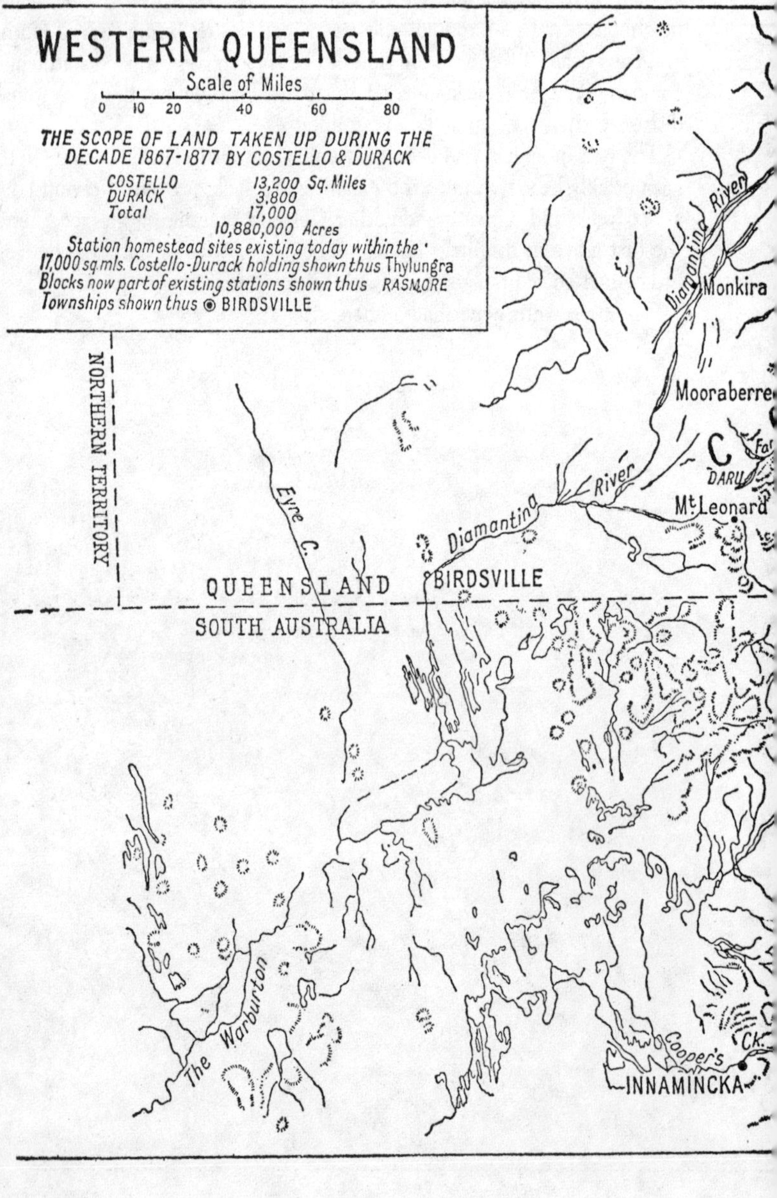
WESTERN QUEENSLAND
Scale of Miles
0 10 20 40 60 80
THE SCOPE OF LAND TAKEN UP DURING THE DECADE 1867-1877 BY COSTELLO & DURACK
COSTELLO 13,200 Sq. Miles
DURACK 3,800
Total 17,000
10,880,000 Acres
Station homestead sites existing today within the 17,000 sq.mls. Costello-Durack holding shown thus Thylungra
Blocks now part of existing stations shown thus RASMORE
Townships shown thus BIRDSVILLE
NORTHERN TERRITORY
QUEENSLAND
SOUTH AUSTRALIA
Diamantina River
Monkira
Mooraberre
DARU
Mt. Leonard
Diamantina River
Eyre C.
BIRDSVILLE
The Warburton
Cooper's Ck.
INNAMINCKA

Dunham Towers
Connemara
enport Downs
FARRARS RUN
GUNGABULLA
Gungabulla Ck.
Currawilla
The J.C.
orney
lains
Thomson R.
JUNDAH
Barcoo R.
Mt Marlow
Galway Downs
Welford
WINDORAH
Hammond
Downs
Thunda
STONELEIGH
SULTAN
WICHELOO
DALTON
Tenham
SPRINGFIELD
WHEEO
Bulgroo
RASMORE
ADAVALE
Keeroongooloo
Thylungra
Ray
(Wathagurra)
Kyabra Ck.
Mt Orthevan
Kyabra
Nickavilla
McIVER
Bulloo R.
Pinkilla
Lake
Yamma
Yamma
Cooper's Ck.
EROMANGA
QUILPIE
Comogin
KALAKE
CALLPIE
Mobel Creek
GRABENGULLEN
THE GREY RANGE
Conbar
pamerry
Nockatunga
Wilson River
THARGOMINDAH
COSTELLO
DURACK

13

The Battling Years

The years 1869 to 1873. The Pastoral Leases Act brings improved conditions for settlers. Patsy Durack and John Costello peg wide claims and wait for rain. A murder on Kyabra. The family at Thylungra threatened by blacks. Shortages and hard times. Family letters. Death of P. Durack's sister Bridget and Uncle Darby. The breaking of the drought.

Somehow they kept their faith in the land and the good times coming, although scraps of news from the outside world were far from encouraging. One thousand Queensland settlers had walked off their properties since '66, and were drifting to the goldfields, into the city and the outback towns. Some managed to find better land elsewhere, but most joined the ranks of the proletariat and the government began to fear that with so much bitterness and disillusionment abroad it would be none so easy to entice men back to the land. The discovery of gold had narrowly averted catastrophe to the young State but prosperity was still a long way off. Prices remained low, for stock had increased far beyond the needs of the population and although the outside world was clamouring for food the day of tinned and frozen meat had not yet dawned.

Many settlers, in order to realise something on stock that would otherwise have perished before the season broke, drove their cattle hundreds of miles to the nearest boiling down works, a desperate measure that had a far-reaching side issue, for the sight of these fellows from the furthermost frontiers poking their wasted stock along through the drought-stricken countryside touched many hearts.

Could nothing be done, it was asked, to keep them on the land where men of their calibre were so sorely needed? The advantages they had been promised amounted to practically nothing. They had no security, no guarantee that land opened up at such great risk and cost would not be resumed on twelve months' notice with nothing to show for their efforts. Moreover, there were too many impossible conditions attached to their fourteen-year leases, and rentals were absurdly high for untried country.

No doubt these struggling 'outsiders' were surprised and gratified to find their case so strongly espoused and eloquently pleaded. They could hardly have expected anything of the sort since squatters in New South Wales had aroused little sympathy from anyone and were in fact generally regarded as a national menace, an impenetrable barrier against the smaller man.

The fact was that these western Queensland settlers were too isolated and remote to have, as yet, antagonised anyone and their chances of making out at all seemed so slim as to awaken the sporting instincts of the Australian people. If the pioneers were surprised by the sympathy they aroused among so many strangers, the outcome of the appeal must have been even more astonishing, for it brought about a rapid reassessment of the land policy, and the heartening Pastoral Leases Act of '69. The bill increased the terms of leasehold from fourteen to twenty-one years and allowed renewal of leases for fourteen years instead of a meagre five. Settlers were permitted to purchase an area of 2,500 acres containing specified improvements. Rentals were reduced, rights of pre-emption, that had proved so disastrous in New South Wales, considerably extended and generous compensation offered for improvements on land at any time resumed.

On this right of resumption the State, mindful of its duty to posterity, had of course to stand firm, for although leases might be indefinitely extended even to ninety-nine years the title deeds remained with the Crown, together with the right to use the land for other purposes should the need arise.

Grandfather and John Costello knew that much of the area they had originally claimed could still be resumed by the government at twelve months' notice, but under the amended Act they should, by surrendering their leases within six months, receive back half their runs for ten years and were free to pasture their stock on the rest until it was sold. This suited them well enough and, anxious for closer settlement, believing that with the return of good seasons people would come flocking out eager to participate in the advantages of the new Act, they rode about throwing open thousands of square miles of country between Kyabra Creek and the Diamantina. Sometimes this 'throwing open' meant no more than riding through, making contact with the local tribespeople, observing the waters and general topography for future reference, but often it entailed the careful selection and pegging of properties for relatives, friends or possible purchasers. Something of the extent of their activities may be traced on the early maps by the names they gave the various blocks, Clare, Scariff, Galway, Lough Derg, Lough Isle, Lough Neagh, Shannon View, Limerick, Yass, Wheeo, Grabben Gullen, Goulburn. A few of these names are still in use today, but many of the smaller blocks have since been incorporated into larger properties and are not to be found on present-day maps.

Although the area was still almost a blank on official maps, they charted the land they rode with extraordinary accuracy and detail, marking the twists and turns of creeks and river channels that so seldom ran, plotting the good country, shading in the mulga scrub, marking the rocky belts of eroded range in elaborate 'herring bone', smudging in the sandhills.

Their methods of pegging boundaries were rough and ready, though the surveyors of later years were often surprised at the clarity with which they defined the dividing fences of the future. One of their devices was to light a fire on a dark night at either end of the intended boundary when two men, carrying lanterns, would walk towards each other, pegging as they went. In the morning they would run their line, straight as a die, into the ashes of the fires. Years later, when a surveyor found difficulty in laying a boundary on Pinkilla, one of the pioneers suggested this simple old-time method, which met with immediate success.

In the early years when the nearest post office was at the little town of Tambo, over 200 miles north-east of Kyabra Creek, it was often eighteen months or more before selected land was officially registered. Although the stock book shows that Thylungra was occupied by the middle of '68 the official registration was not made until June '71, and that of Kyabra in '72, but few serious disputes about the tenure of country arose between these early pioneers. A man had only to run a few head of stock on to a piece of unoccupied country to lay claim to it. His 'tracks' were on it and that was that, and before long the tracks of Thylungra and Kyabra stock fairly peppered the countryside.

While the drought prevailed Grandfather could not saddle himself with too much rental but he spread his 'tracks' liberally over an area of some two and a half million acres of mostly adjoining country divided, on his own maps, into holdings averaging 100,000 acres. On Thylungra's eastern boundary he selected land for his sister Sarah Tully and her family and pictured them with a nice little homestead on Wathagurra Creek. Immediately north-east of this he had pegged a block of country which he named Rasmore for his elder sister Poor Mary Skeahan, her husband and boys. He had blocks in mind also for his youngest sister Anne and his brother Jerry, while Jim Scanlan expected soon to be joined on a neighbouring property, Springfield, by his brother Pat and his wife Bridget, Grandfather's third sister.

John Costello meanwhile was laying wide territorial claims in all directions. Out along the Cooper, 120 miles west to the Diamantina and 150 miles upstream, he established a mighty pastoral empire of over eight and a half million acres on which no other white man but himself and his faithful head stockman Jack Farrar, after whom he had named the big Diamantina tributary Farrar's Creek, had as yet set foot. He and Grandfather were seldom at home in these days, never at rest.

They rode with their lives in their hands, in peril of death from thirst or native spears, but their feats of endurance and bushmanship were known only to their immediate associates. Like most happenings in this remote corner, Costello's remarkable trip with horses down the Strzelecki to Kapunda in '67 received no publicity and the credit for opening this desert stock route has been generally given to Harry Redford who got through the same way with 1,000 head of stolen cattle from Bowen Downs near Tambo in 1870. John Costello, riding out among the Cooper channels, picked up the tracks of this large mob of cattle that had passed through towards the south-west and soon afterwards asked patrol officer Gilmour whether he knew anything of these enterprising drovers. Gilmour was puzzled for he had heard of no new settlers moving in that direction or of any squatter who would be likely to send stock that way in a drought season. His enquiries caused western graziers to investigate their runs and Grandfather, riding some country he had recently taken up on the Bulloo River was intrigued to discover, hidden in the mulga, an ingenious contraption for watering stock. A timbered well had been put down and above it constructed a stub tank with outlet pipe that operated on an old time patent whereby a horse worked the whim, bringing one bucket up as another went down. The water was fed into a line of rough timber troughing and everything had been put together completely without nails. At the same time the manager of Bowen Downs about 200 miles north-east of Thylungra discovered that 1,000 head of cattle and a 500-guinea white bull were missing from the big station herd. Redford had worked on the reasonable assumption that a mere thousand would hardly be missed from such a property and that the Bowen Downs brand was unlikely to be recognised 700 miles away in another state. Most Australians are now familiar with the story of Redford's extraordinary manoeuvre, his sale of the cattle for 5,000 guineas, his subsequent arrest and return to Roma for trial with the incriminating white bull, and his acquittal by a sympathetic local jury in the face of overwhelming evidence. Much of the tale is incorporated in Rolf Boldrewood's classic *Robbery Under Arms*, but the part played by the Kyabra Creek settlers in putting the police on the alert is not generally known. That men could have got away with such a large mob of cattle and were detected only by accident serves to illustrate the vast emptiness of this part of western Queensland when Grandfather and Costello were staking their Cooper claims.

'And what are you wanting with all that country atall?' Great-grandmother Costello protested. 'Whatever can you be doing with it?'

'Don't you see, Mother,' her son would point out, 'we're in here first and when the drought breaks everyone will be rushing out taking up the land. We have to secure it for all the people we promised to bring up.'

'And what if they've sense enough in their heads to say "no" to yere kindness?'

'Then we can sell the rights to someone else. There'll be plenty after them when the drought breaks.'

And Great-grandmother Costello with a hopeless upward glance:

'When the drought breaks indeed! And who's to say we'll not all be broken first?'

In fact many men would break before that four-year drought and the children at Thylungra and Kyabra would ask what this rain was like that everyone spoke about and prayed and waited for.

Sometimes in the stillness of night and early morning anxious ears would catch a distant rumble, a pulsating roar or a sound like rising wind. The sleeping homestead would start awake to find it was nothing but the patient throbbing of a didgeridoo, the persistent beating of a sand drum or some Aboriginal rainmaker whirling his bull roarer to rouse the sleeping spirits of water and life. Day and night dark voices from the dry river beds, and gullies threatened and cajoled the drought spirit and her children who rode the desolate land in whirling spirals of dust.

By this time big encampments of natives had gathered within a few miles of Thylungra and Kyabra homesteads to receive regular rations from the station people. This pleased the blacks who had thrown in their lot with the settlers but were still bound by strong ties of loyalty and relationship to the outside natives and at night bush and station blacks joined in communal singing and dancing. On important ceremonial occasions as many as 600 might forgather on the far side of the big Thylungra waterhole but how easily they might have wiped out this first little handful of settlers seems not then to have occurred to either blacks or whites.

Sometimes the lean black women, naked and shyly smiling, would bring their new-born babies to the white women to be named and admired in their neat bark coolamons. After a fight they would be called upon to patch up cuts, broken limbs and split heads and to treat terrible burns caused by the native habit of sleeping too close to the fire and rolling into the embers. They had effective and homely panaceas for all these things and in tending them grew to love the strange, wild people whose ways they would never understand.

Disturbed by evidence of cruel rites and occasional cannibalism, the family had resolved by degrees to instruct the more civilised station natives in the virtues of monogamy and the evils of their savage practices. Realising they could get nowhere with the tribal elders, they started with the young men who had come into the stations before the final stages of initiation and who, if the black man's laws went against the grain with them, were willing enough to take the white man's word for it that they were evil or of little account.

About this time a youth had appealed to Costello for permision to marry a girl forbidden him by tribal law. The white man called an enquiry, found that the girl had been 'promised' to one of the old men who already had two or three wives anyway. In vain the elders expounded, in their limited pidgin phrases, on the intricate and complicated marriage system that governed not only the Boontamurra but every tribe in the continent. It was not, they argued, simply the selfish will of the older men to claim all the young girls for themselves, as Costello declared. This girl, according to the marriage class system, was 'mother' to this boy, and how could it be moral in any law for a man to marry his mother?

'Nonsense,' said Costello, 'how can a girl be mother to a boy older than herself? Be off with you now with your nonsense and leave the young people alone.'

He performed the marriage himself, blessing them and tying their wrists together with a piece of string, confident he had struck a blow against foolish superstition and heathen nonsense.

Ignoring the whisperings and warnings of the station blacks, he gave permission for the couple to camp in the saddle shed near the homestead until the affair had blown over. Some nights later, startled by terrible cries, he went out with his lantern and hurrying to the saddle shed stumbled over the headless body of the faithful native boy Soldier who had helped him take the horses to Kapunda in '67. Soldier had been sleeping across the doorway to protect the young people from attack and had kept the killers at bay while the bride and groom escaped.

In the morning Costello, grief-stricken and angry, rode off with Scrammy Jimmy to make enquiries at the outside camp.

The site, where 200 natives had been camped the day before, was deserted but Costello, determined to have the matter out, insisted on following the tracks until they petered out over stony ground. Some natives appeared on a ridge and while riding forward to question them Costello was hit on the side of the head by a well-aimed stone. As he fell, half stunned, from his saddle two blacks closed on him, but the agile Jimmy sprang from his saddle and split one man's head clean through with a tomahawk. The other vanished into the scrub while the station boy lifted his master in front of his saddle and rode home.

No one seems to have doubted that the stone was intended to kill Costello or wondered why the blacks had not ambushed the two riders in the ridges and made a proper job of them with spears.

Grandfather came galloping from Thylungra to find his brother-in-law laid up with a wound that was to leave an impression on his skull for life. Kyabra was pandemonium, the blacks wailing and elaborating shrilly on rumours of a plot to attack the homestead at night, to spear the inhabitants and burn the place to the ground. Costello and Grandfather, familiar though they were with the blacks' love of drama, knew that they must take steps to protect their families. Holes were made in the homestead walls to fit the muzzles of guns and the women were instructed in the use of firearms in case of trouble while the men were away. John Costello's wife had always been a good shot, but Grandmother was more terrified of firearms than of wild blacks and proved a poor pupil.

The Kyabra excitement fizzled out, but as the drought persisted there was a feeling of tension and growing resentment among the bush blacks. They believed that defiance of the old law must inevitably bring its punishment and that everyone must suffer for the stupidity and wrongdoing of the few. At the same time they were becoming disillusioned about the settlers' generosity and goodwill. Time was when they had distributed tobacco, tea, sugar and flour but they grew more and more niggardly with these good things and the blacks began to doubt the white man's word that his store was empty until the teams came back.

Old Cobby warned his master repeatedly of this distrustful attitude but as the bad seasons persisted it became imperative for all hands to be out on the run shifting cattle from waterless areas.

Every night, while his master was away, the old man and his gin slept with their swags across the doorway of the house. Nothing stirred that they did not hear and the track of every strange native within a mile of the homestead was noted and reported.

Even during the day Cobby was never far from his mistress and her children so that Grandmother, although now devoted to the old fellow she had at first distrusted, sometimes became impatient of his being forever under her busy feet. She had now three boys, for a little son, Patrick Bernard, had been born in September 1870.

It was Cobby who one day gave warning of a menacing shadow at the kitchen door. Grandmother turned, flushed and surprised from the stove, to see clustering dark figures streaked with white ochre, bedecked with emu feathers.

'Tea, chugar, tobacco! Gibbet!'

The teams were late back from Bourke again and supplies perilously low. Grandmother, on an inspiration, offered a pumpkin, and a few precious sweet potatoes, but the natives tossed them contemptuously aside and pointed to the containers along the kitchen shelves.

'Tobacco!'

Helplessly the white woman opened empty tins.

The blacks came swarming in, overturning packing cases, jeering as Cobby let forth a blood-curdling yell and disappeared. With mounting impatience they scattered things about the floor, so engrossed that they did not see the old man return until he had thrust a rifle into his mistress's hands.

'Kill'm missus! Shoot'm dead fulla!'

As Grandmother raised the rifle uncertainly the blacks retreated to the door, and her six-year-old Michael who had taken in his father's instructions shouted shrill advice.

'Cock it, Mother, like Father showed you!'

He snatched the rifle, adjusted expertly, and handed it back. There was a deafening explosion, a bedlam of terrified shrieks and cries and a kitchen full of smoke.

'It went off in my hands,' Grandmother said helplessly. 'Dear God, what have I done?'

'Nothing,' her eldest said in disappointed tones. 'They all got away.'

Cobby leapt about gesticulating wildly after the retreating blacks.

'Shoot'm again, Missus! Shoot'm again!'

'Never again,' Grandmother said. 'Not as long as I live.'

It was the first and last time she ever used a rifle, though every night until Grandfather returned, Cobby insisted on firing at intervals through a hole in the wall.

Grandfather and Costello now increased precautions when leaving home. However stifling the night no one was allowed to sleep on the homestead verandahs. The doors of the house were always barricaded after dark, weapons kept ready to hand and dogs trained to keep watch for prowlers. Anxious for the sense of security they felt could only come with closer settlement they wrote urging friends and relatives to stake their faith in the good times soon coming to the sweeping plains of 'the Cooper fall'.

The news that selections had been taken up in potentially rich 'outside' country was surprisingly quick to spread abroad and drought or no, by early

'71 although so many 'inside' settlers were still walking off their properties southern landseekers began to arrive in Queensland's far west. Among the first of these were Jim Hammond and his family, Mrs Hammond being one of the Tully clan and a younger sister of Great-grandmother Costello. These people took up one of the tentatively selected blocks on a north-western section of Kyabra Creek which they named Tenham after the Hammond home in England. Then came Syd Prout, one of the two well-known pioneer brothers, to be escorted by Costello to a promising strip of country which he at once took up and called 'Kangi'. Not many months later some half dozen landseeking parties from Victoria came to take up various blocks west of Kyabra Creek. These included the Tozers, Cottons, Bostocks and Frenches, not previously known to the family. These were soon followed by further Costello relatives named Roche, Sandy Abbey and Mike Tully with, close on their heels, two Irish clans named Doyle and Hackett who claimed some vague relationship and who had brought a herd of horses to selections Costello had taken up for them named Dalton and Castle Hackett.

Each party brought its stock, its waggons and equipment and it seemed that the lonely, silent land must quickly awaken to lively community life, but only meagre showers came to replenish the waterholes in '71. No rivers had come down since early '68. Horses, ranging far for feed and water, ran brumby among the Cooper channels and weak cattle perished in the mud of stagnant waterholes. Some of the settlers who had come with such brave hearts and high hopes decided to cut their losses and move out. The sight of their retreating waggons was a heart-breaking sight to the Durack and Costello families, now hand-watering their remaining stock from troughs fed by whip and bucket from the bed of the creek. There was little increase in these years for the cows were too weak to rear their drought-born calves and the Thylungra stock book from '69 to the end of '72 tells its own story:

April '68	branded calves on the Mobell	63
Oct. '68	" " at Thylungra	20
Jan. '69	female calves from Welford	25
Mar. "	branded	21
July "	"	25
Oct. "	store cattle	140
Dec. "	branded	36
May '70	"	76
Aug. "	"	35

Dec. "	"	68
May '71	"	71
Oct. "	"	89
Nov. "	store cattle	143
April '72	branded	99
Oct. "	"	135
	Total cattle on Thylungra at end of '72	
	– losses 200 approx =	946

From this it will be seen that there were too few adult cattle to market during these years. In '69 Grandfather had gone to Roma, 350 miles east, then the nearest town of any consequence, to purchase store cattle to build up the Thylungra herd, and in '70 and '71 Stumpy Michael, John Costello and Jim Scanlan had gone south to Goulburn, returning with further stock.

Journeys such as this had kept family members in New South Wales in touch with those in Queensland during these years of separation. They also gave the two unmarried boys a chance to court their sweethearts. Stumpy Michael's romance with Kate McInnes was being firmly aided and abetted by his sister Anne who, fearful that they might lose touch and become otherwise attached, kept up a vigorous correspondence constantly informing brother and friend of the other's activities and splendid character. Kate kept all Anne's letters with loving care and handed them down to her family so that we are able to follow Stumpy Michael's activities over this period in some detail. In May '72 Anne wrote from Gullen, near Goulburn:

> My dear Kate,
>
> Michael told me the day before he went away to write to you. He did not start on Tuesday as Mr Costello was not ready, but they started early on Wednesday morning. He said that he was going to write to you from 'the Darling'. Will you be so good as to write to me when you get this letter and tell me how they are getting on, for he said that he would not have time to write but the one letter and that should be to you . . .
>
> Mother sends love and hopes to have the pleasure of embracing you as a *Daughter* 'ere long. I hope dear when you have your photo taken you will send me one and I will send you mine . . .
>
> Your sincere friend
> Annie A. Durack.

In June the same year Anne wrote flutteringly of her own romance:

> I am sure you have heard of my flight to Sydney long before this. So now you see I am out of Michael's road and the sooner he goes off the hooks the better: He has not heard the news yet.
>
> My dear Kate I did not think when I last wrote to you that I would be married so soon. Mr Redgrave came to Goulburn to see me and he would not go back without a companion so it was all done in a hurry—the best way. So here I am, one of the happiest little wives in the world. It is no use me trying to praise him dear Kate for I could not do him justice. I will send you his portrait and my own as soon as we have them taken.
>
> Dear Kate you must write and tell me how you are all getting on and if you have heard from that old man of yours lately. You know you must not forget him while he is away for I am certain that he will make a kind good husband since he is a good fond brother. My dear Kate I could not tell you how happy I am. The more I see of my husband the more I love him for I am now beginning to know him better and can see that he is a fine and a noble hearted fellow . . . He has been prospecting this long time for Merchants in Sydney and if he finds anything he has as much interest in it as they and they find him the money to work it. We are beginning with but very little, so you see dear, it was not for riches that I married . . .

By December a forlorn note was creeping into Anne's letters to her friend:

> . . . Well dear I am almost tired of Sydney and begin to long for a ride. It is now six months since I was on a horse so you will understand how I feel. I would like the city better if Mr Redgrave's business did not take him so much away, but think it will be soon all done, for I see by the paper today that he has found something very rich. Have you heard from my darling brother lately? I have had but the one letter from him since I came to Sydney but I had last night a letter dated Nov. 5th from Miss Hammond of Tenham, then staying at Thylungra. They were all well out there and some signs of rain when she wrote. My brother Jerry was starting for Goulburn next morning so she said, so I think he must be home by this time. She also said that Michael was away at the time at Charleville on business . . .

Young 'Galway Jerry', now aged nineteen, had gone north to Thylungra a year before, leaving his mother and little niece, Mary Anne Bennet, with

Darby's family at Boorowa, and not long afterwards the child's father had forthrightly settled the much-vexed question of her upbringing. Two of Darby's younger children, the only witnesses of the episode, told of an important looking gentleman in a frock-coat and top hat who had alighted from a carriage, swooped upon the little girl and vanished with her in a cloud of dust. Great-grandmother Bridget, having no legal claims to the child, was without redress and inconsolable when further tragedies were heaped upon her. Poor Mary Skeahan, still struggling at Lambing Flat while Dinny sank shaft after shaft on the Adelong, lost yet another little boy, leaving her, in '72, with only three out of six sons. Soon after this came the sudden death of Bridget Scanlan, Great-grandmother's fourth child, from what was described as 'a chest complaint' such as had taken her sister Margaret Bennet some years before. Great-grandmother had gone at once to the Scanlan selection outside Goulburn to help big Pat with his four motherless children.

Soon after this Darby Durack, while hacking away at the relentless scrub on his Boorowa selection, was smitten with sunstroke and died at the age of fifty-three. After all his years of struggle he had little or nothing to leave his widow and family of thirteen sons and daughters. The all-pervading drought had closed in around the Castlereagh and for over two years the elder boys had been keeping their few remaining sheep alive on agistment, trailing them around the countryside in search of water and grass. After their father's death they gave up their fruitless battle, sold their stock and took on droving and carrying contracts to support the family.

Sarah and Pat Tully, now both eager enough to join their relatives in the north, could not face the expense of such a move and Grandfather, while the drought persisted, was in no position to finance them. In fact the family at that time, with a mounting overdraft, was almost as poor as it had ever been. At Thylungra living expenses were cut to bedrock. Scarcely any clothing was bought. Grandmother made shirts from calico and patched the stockmen's moleskins with canvas from old tent flies. Boots were home-made from kangaroo skin and goat hides, with elastic let into the sides.

Though their men might rove abroad the women remained locked in their forgotten world, bearing and rearing their children, maintaining the home base for their men. Fashions passed them by, but twice a year with the station stores they received mail and bundles of papers from the outside world. Grandmother read no more than the births, deaths and marriages of the Goulburn district and snippets of church news, but Mary Costello at Kyabra read everything systematically, one paper a day from first to last, discussing the pros, cons and possible outcome of world issues long before resolved.

'I knew it,' she said on a visit to Thylungra in the middle of '71, 'it's come to war between Prussia and France just as I predicted.'

'I told you about that when I got back from Roma three months ago,' her husband said. 'It's probably blown over by now.'

'Never mind,' his wife replied, 'as far as I'm concerned it started last week, when I got up to it in the papers.'

'Rain come soon now,' the blacks said when in November '72 the cockatoos, swifts and martins were seen to be flying low again and the big grass spiders in the lower branches of the mulga began fortifying their webs.

Then came a rumble of thunder in the afternoon. Clouds from the north, indigo dark, scudded before a driving wind; great drops flattened the curling edges of the cracked, parched soil and washed the salt pans clean of the sickening phantoms of mirage. A wild triumphant chanting rose from the native camps with shrieks of excited terror when blazing forks of lightning shattered the sky and splintered a tree on the storm-lashed plain.

Before the homestead area was fairly wet storms in the upper reaches of the Thompson and Barcoo sent a wall of water racing south-west down the shallow rivercourse, swirling in a thousand tributaries. A breathless rider came in from stock shifting around the junction of the big river and Kyabra Creek.

'The Cooper's coming!'

With the flood roar already in their ears men rushed to saddle horses and move stock to higher ground, up into the ridges and sandhills. Kyabra Creek came down like thunder with rain swirling to meet it through gullies, cracks and breakaways. Frogs roused from their long torpor in the hard-baked river mud and rifts in the drought-cracked plains gave voice in deafening chorus with the shrill, returning birds.

Soon the creek was lost in an inland sea where the earth buildings seemed to float like little Noah's Arks. A few outhouses, newly built, came down like stacks of cards, but the homestead stood firm as the water rose, frighteningly, to the window ledges and subsided slowly to the confines of the creek bed.

All had spirit now to face the discomforts of the 'wet'—the blowflies that came in droning battalions with the new green grass to infest every crease and cranny of the salt meat slabs, the small flies that carried infection from the blacks' to the children's eyes, the mildew that ruined stacks of clothing overnight, the fungi that spread over the wet timber of yards and buildings, the mud that clotted every boot and every hoof, the foot-rot that infested the few sheep and goats in the paddock.

The sea of water left behind a rising sea of sweet clover and grass—Flinders and spider-couch, Mitchell, wild sorghum, cane, pepper and button grass. Then came the wildflowers, brightening the drab plains with vivid splashes of colour. Melons, pumpkins and snake beans sprang to life in Grandfather's kitchen garden and he watched them, rejoicing and calculating the harvest. One morning he brought his wife to see how quickly the fruit was maturing, but the garden had vanished overnight with a strip of land half a mile wide swathed clean as though from the scythe of a giant reaper. Locusts had bred in the warm, damp soil, thriving on the new, green grass until the young hoppers had been strong enough to begin their forward march. Within a few days their wings had grown and they were flying in dense clouds across the sun, crackling like a bush fire as they stripped trees and shrubs to gaunt skeletal shapes.

Grandfather ploughed out through slosh and bog to repair yards that had been damaged or washed away. Climbing the sand dunes he surveyed the receding flood, saw drowned stock hung up in the branches of the trees or eddying with driftwood in swiftly running channels, his relief at the breaking drought mingled with apprehension of this land of extremes. Perhaps someday, somewhere, he would find surer, kinder country, but meantime he must secure himself here in the best way he knew, by spreading his net as far as human energy and the law of the land would permit. From the blacks and his own observations he had formed a theory of seasonal cycles on which he calculated that western Queensland was now due for a succession of good years. He was determined to run a race with the next drought.

'Sooner or later we'll all have to walk out of this country,' the pessimists predicted.

'When I walk out,' said Grandfather, 'I go in a four-in-hand, and I go a rich man. So help me God.'

14
TURN OF THE TIDE

The years 1873 to 1874. First sale of Thylungra cattle at Wilcannia. The marriage of 'Stumpy' Michael Durack and Catherine McInnes. The bride and groom return to western Queensland with Great-grandmother Bridget Durack and an Irish tutor, Mr John Healy. Life at Thylungra. Sale of land on Cooper's Creek. Blocks taken up by Duracks and Costello. Establishment of Charleville. The Tullys and Skeahans arrive in western Queensland. Death of Anne Redgrave and her child.

In April '73 Anne Redgrave wrote to her friend Kate McInnes:

Well my dear, it was a disappointment again about the mine but Mr Redgrave has got a machine to go out to Bumbo now so I will hope they will succeed after all their trouble and expense. I feel dreadfully lonely as I must still stay in Sydney. If he is to be long away I might go back to Goulburn and get into business of some sort for I am tired of waiting and doing nothing.

I had a letter from Patsy and one from Michael written on the 28th February and they were soon to start on the road with cattle which they tell me are rolling fat since the drought broke and should fetch a good price. I suppose you have heard of the dreadful floods they had out there. They all had a very narrow escape. Dear Michael and some other men were nine days on a sand hill, stranded on the way back from Charleville where there is a postal and lands office since last year so they do not have to ride so far as Tambo now. They got food by swimming three miles to a house for it. Fortunately Michael is a strong swimmer and does not mind tackling the flood except for some channels that are death traps they say. Patsy reckons the flood waters covered eighty miles and out on the open plains was six and ten feet deep measured on the tree trunks. When the river came down a second time stronger than the first Michael went to help a neighbour, a Mr Tozer, gather in his cattle and he and four others were five days cut off eating anything they could catch in the flood. Bush rats, snakes

> and frogs are very good, he tells me, if you are hungry enough. Do I see you shudder my dear Kate? There is worse even than this that they have eaten out there but I will spare your feelings.
>
> My brother Jerry who started for Goulburn in November did not reach home until the 28th February after a good deal of swimming, for the flood caught him up also. I will write when I hear when you might expect to see Michael again . . .

In June of the same year Anne reports to her friend of a letter from her brother Michael from Wilcannia, 500 miles south of Thylungra, where he had sold 200 fat cattle at £8 a head. She mentions also that her brother Patsy meanwhile had been on a 600-mile jaunt to Brisbane to interview the Colonial Treasurer about land matters and had there sold a lease he had taken up 'to a young gentleman from Melbourne' for £500. He was to return by Roma, 350 miles from Thylungra, with a mob of store cattle for fattening on the now incomparable Cooper pastures.

> When do you expect my dear brother down? [Anne asks her friend]. I hope you have not written to put him off coming down at Christmas as he planned. I shall be very angry if you do. I see what you are up to my lady! You don't want the hot weather for your wedding! Do not put it off dear Kate, for my poor old Mother's sake. I am sure it would break her heart if he does not come at Christmas. I do believe that all that keeps her alive is the thought of his coming then. You know she is by herself now at Scanlan's for my sister Sarah is starting to the Adelong this week, and my sister Mary is up near Lambing Flat. I often cry when I think how dreadfully lonely she must be. Write him immediately dearest Kate and say you will be ready and willing when he comes. Things are improving out there now and the brothers are partners in everything. My brother Patsy has taken up some property to which Mr Redgrave and I may go soon when he is through with this mining job. Patsy has called the property Bunginderry and has put some stock on it for us which he has branded with an 'R'. It is very likely we would be going out with you and that we will be up there together my dear *sister*. I wish from my heart it may be so.

Stumpy Michael, now twenty-seven years old, with his handsome, dark-bearded face and quiet manner, had been too diffident to make verbal proposal to the young lady his sister had long since picked out for him. Even his letters had been few and far between for he was, he insisted, 'a poor fist with the pen'. His request for Kate's hand he had contrived to write on the banks of the Darling so that the address might serve also as a term of endearment that might otherwise have seemed presumptuous. Truth to tell, he had been somewhat in awe of his sister's friend, an accomplished girl who was not only well versed in classical literature but who played the piano with distinction and produced faithful copies of seascapes which hung, elaborately framed, in the McInnes home at Tarlo River. Daughter of the inland, she had a great love for the sea, a throwback, her people said, to her seafaring Scottish ancestors from the Isle of Skye. She had little natural taste for rough bush life and the unlettered conversation of outback folk but Stumpy Michael had been her hero since their childhood days and Anne's earnest plea that she should not delay his coming had proved unnecessary. He reached Goulburn after all in September and they were married early in October by Father Michael Slattery in the Goulburn Cathedral, as a cutting from the *Goulburn Herald* makes ponderous note:

> Mr Michael Durack, formerly of this district, now of Cooper's Creek, Western Queensland, has contracted marriage with an amiable and respectably connected young lady to whom he has been long attached—Miss Catherine McInnes. This lady's father, Angus McInnes Esq., originally of Inverness, Scotland, is an old and respected resident of the Tarlo River, Middle Arm, N.S.W. His mother was a McLeod, niece of Captain Neil McLeod of the McLeods of Gesto, an ancient family, not unknown to history and able to prove a pedigree extending back into remote centuries . . .

Great-grandmother Bridget was now free to join her family in Queensland, for Pat Scanlan, widower of her daughter Bridget for whose four children she had been caring, had recently married another Irish girl named Mary O'Keefe. All Great-grandmother's children were now in the Cooper's Creek district except Anne Redgrave, then with her mining husband in Moruya, about 200 miles south of Sydney. Anne was then expecting a child and had not after all been able to get to the wedding she had dreamed of for so long but the bride and groom made a hurried trip to visit her before setting off from Goulburn on their long journey north. A sad little letter that caught her up on the road was the last Kate was ever to receive from her devoted friend:

> I cannot tell you how lonely and wretched I feel since I got your letter to say you were starting next day. I had made up my mind

to start for Goulburn next Monday to see you all before you left and stop until after my trouble would be over, but it would be no use going now that you are all gone. Do you think that Mother is quite willing to go? I wish now that I had decided for her to stay with me, for I am so very lonely. I hope and trust we will be able to follow you out there soon ... Write frequently while you are on the roads. I send you my portrait at last but was not at my best when it was done and should have waited except that if all should not go well for me I would like you to have a reminder for your prayers.

Your fond sister,
Anne.

The honeymoon of Stumpy Michael and his Kate was unorthodox to say the least. They had set out from Goulburn about two weeks after the wedding, Stumpy Michael, his bride and old mother travelling in a covered waggon packed with wedding presents and furniture. In a smaller waggon with the camp cook went an elderly Irishman by the name of John Healy who had at Grandfather's request been selected by friends in Ireland as tutor for the children at Thylungra. On what grounds this unlikely choice had been made other than his claim to have 'studied for the priesthood', was something of a mystery but there he was and having paid his fare from Kilkenny there seemed no option but to bring him out to Cooper's Creek. Considerably more than the years he owned and as broad as he was long, Mr Healy, irascible, talkative and devout, peered like some quaint bullfrog from behind thick-lensed spectacles at the Australian scene that he did not hesitate to declare was the devil's making. To the memorable disgust of his travelling companion, when not lecturing on the iniquities of local behaviour and customs, berating the heat, the dust, the bumps, the flies and the unholy landscape, Mr Healy told his beads aloud all the way to Cooper's Creek.

In charge of the horses were the bride's brother, Donald McInnes, and Stumpy Michael's devoted black boy, Willie.

Looking back through the years, it always seemed to Kate Durack to have been a happy and romantic trip, with her husband, now a personality of the Bogan River stock route, everywhere greeted with friendly words and congratulations, his wife and mother warmly welcomed.

After over three months on that thousand-mile track there had been at last the excitement of arrival at Thylungra where Grandfather had worked fanatically to have a new pisé house, a hundred yards from the original homestead, ready for the young couple. That arrival was remembered by my father mainly because his grandmama had brought in her trunk a few oranges which although pathetically shrivelled from those long weeks over the arid plains were the first fruit, other than wild berries, the bush-reared youngsters had seen.

The family at Thylungra now numbered three boys, Michael, John and Pat, and a daughter Mary, named after the first child who had died at Dixon's Creek. Grandmother's small figure was growing roundabout in its tightly fitting bodice and full skirts, her fine skin, once her mother's pride and joy, roughened by wind and weather, but her small hands, for all the work they did, still soft as a girl's.

Thylungra, now shaded with bush shrubs and wild creeper, the flagged floors daily washed and swept down, starched chintz at the shuttered windows, the rough bush furniture spread with crisp linen, everything smelling cleanly of strong caustic soap and river water, the dripping canvas water bags swinging from wire hooks, the big white station cups rattling in their saucers announcing the next cup of tea, was now a haven in the hard land. Grandmother made a creative art of her homely hospitality and had expended herself in preparing this welcome. There were exclamations of wonder and delight at the feast she produced—the kangaroo-tail soup demanded by Grandfather, fish from the now brimming Kyabra Creek, spiced and pickled beef, home cured bacon and ham from pigs that had mightily increased and were now running wild among the Cooper channels. She had mastered the delicate art of extracting rennet from the carcasses of calves for making cheeses which she kept in store with a variety of queer sausages that festooned the rafters between hanging bladders of lard while the greenhide shelves below groaned under rows of pickles and preserves, some from the produce of the kitchen garden, some from wild oranges and bright red rosellas that grew along the river bank. But although a woman of many parts she discounted any talent in herself and her respect for her 'clever' sister-in-law amounted almost to awe. Her brother's wife, Mary Costello, could discuss world affairs with the best of them while Kate Durack was always 'brilliant' in Grandmother's eyes. When some of the bride's seascapes were hung on the mud walls of her dining room Grandmother stood before them in speechless admiration, and she listened in rapture to Kate's patient practising on the piano that Grandfather had brought 600 miles from Brisbane as a wedding present. In all the years, although she helped deliver their babies, rejoiced and grieved with them in the ups and downs of their close-knit family life, Grandmother was never entirely at ease with either of these 'gifted' relatives.

The sight of their first tutor, Mr Healy, had sent the children into paroxysms of suppressed mirth, but Grandfather, though not himself without apprehensions of the old man's suitability, had insisted that he be treated with the respect due to a scholar and a member of the depressed Irish aristocracy and his rambling discourses 'attended to'. Only Great-grandmother Bridget found much in common with the quaint old Irishman and the two would talk together in their native Gael and weep for the wrongs and sorrows of their country. They even managed to trace, in the Irish way, some far distant form of relationship, and the kindly old lady was able to assure the sceptical of the validity of Mr Healy's claims to aristocratic lineage. Had she not herself, on a girlhood visit to cousins in Kilkenny, seen the stately grey battlements of Paulston Castle, his birthplace?

Dubiously the carefree bush youngsters had watched every stage in the erection of the school house with its mud walls and thatched roof. 'School' began shortly after breakfast in the morning and, in the absence of a clock, ended when the shadow of a gum tree in the yard reached the schoolroom door. Every day, at this sign of blessed relief, the cry went up:

'The shadow's at the door, Mr Healy! The shadow's at the door!'

In the warmth of afternoon the old man would doze over the lesson, to waken with a start when his heavy spectacles fell upon the desk. His pupils soon learned to catch the glasses as they fell, set them gently down and go about their own devices, returning in time to announce the end of the school day:

'The shadow's at the door!'

'Ach! God bless my heart and soul,' Mr Healy would exclaim, waking from a long, sound slumber, 'and I upon the point of dozing!'

The tutor's rule of three, his eternal pothooks and long prayers could hold no interest to compete with the activities of stockmen at the yard, the blacks at the waterhole. The children's toys were of their own and the blacks' devising—boomerangs, old waggon wheels, bows and arrows, shanghais, curved bullock horns filled with sand with which to stun small birds and butterflies on the wing. Born to a world of wonder and discovery, they learned the habits and haunts of bush creatures, sought out hidden clutches of duck eggs in nests of grey down, found where the grebes built and laid their spotted eggs upon fragile rafts.

Few days passed without excitement of some sort, from ordinary station happenings to extraordinary nine-day wonders that Great-grandma Bridget was inclined, like the blacks, to attribute to sorcery. There was the time when a deluge of tiny fish and frogs fell from heaven with the rain, and another occasion when a horseman galloped into Thylungra with news that a vast rodent army was on its way towards the homestead. The rats had come surging in a low-moving, grey wave, tumbling, struggling and squeaking into the lime-filled trenches that had been hurriedly prepared, the rearguard clambering over their fallen leaders, to be met on the other side by an onslaught of waddies, pikes, sticks and spears. Thousands of the creatures were destroyed, but many escaped to continue their blind, hungry march. No one knew where they came from or where they disappeared.

Then with the good season had come the big grass fires that could be heard from miles away, their centres marked by masses of soaring, smoke-blinded birds. The men would return from fighting the flames, blistered and blackened, with singed beards and the soles of their boots charred through.

After the breaking of the long drought life on Cooper's Creek became more lively every month. Grandfather and John Costello had no difficulty now in disposing of the land they had taken up 'on spec' and there was an animated coming and going of buyers and settlers. The saying that they had thrown open between them an area larger than the map of Ireland, or some 35,000 square miles of country, was taken with a grain of salt by this generation, until we found, on closer investigation, that it could not have been far from the truth. The combined area of registered holdings that can still be identified, and which I have sketched as accurately as I am able, amounts to over 17,000 square miles, or nearly eleven million acres. Of this, over 13,000 square miles was taken up by John Costello, whose son Michael listed and located most of the properties and their purchasers.

Moving about the countryside like the wandering Jew, Costello made tracks from the New South Wales border to Charleville, north and west to the head waters of the Diamantina, naming creeks and landmarks, even, unwittingly, a township, a remote outpost in the mulga scrub. One hundred miles west of Stoney Point, now the township of Windorah, he had one day carved his initials on a bauhinia under which he had struck camp and soon the tree became a landmark.

'Strike out 'til you hit the "J.C.",' men would say when giving directions to travellers. Later someone started a grog shanty on the site, a store followed, and soon a pub. It became a coaching stage, later officially named Canterbury, but even when the tree had disappeared it was never known locally as anything else but 'the J.C.'.

Farrar's Creek, a Diamantina tributary, he named after his head stockman, Jack Farrar, to whom he later presented the well-grassed property of Carawilla.

Out west on the Diamantina he had registered by this time the big holdings of Monkira and Davenport Downs and up along Farrar's Creek, Mt Leonard, Daru, Mooraberrie, Morney Plains, Currawilla, Congabulla, Connemara, as well as Keerongoola on the western side of Kyabra.

No such list was kept by Grandfather's family but his notebooks and cheque butts are full of scattered references to blocks of land taken up under many names no longer in use but which must have covered all told somewhere near the same area.

Random entries of land registered up to this time, often referring to blocks simply as 'country', and sometimes spelling the same place in a variety of ways, are jotted in this wise:

> *Thylungra* (sometimes spelt Thylyoungra). S. M. and N2 registered in Tambo 1st June '71.
> *Cornwall*, 1st June '71.
> Mt *Orthievan*, same time.
> *Cumbroo* E. and W. March '72
> Four big blocks *Cooper's Creek* country Nov. '72
> *Bunginderry* for the Redgraves
> *Bulgroo*, *Stoneleigh* and *Kaffir* to join Thylungra. '72.
> *Eucobodalla* block June '72.
> *Wathagurra* for P. and S. Tully. '72, in Tambo.
> *Rasmore* registered Charleville for Skeahan July '73.
> *Galway Downs* for brother Jerry 19th May '73 (this country stocked May 13th and taken up Tambo on 19th).
> *Worcannia* in Charleville Nov. '73.
> *Whynot*, *Mongalo* and *Count* blocks '73.
> Registered *Warrabin*, *Bodalla*, *Copai*, *Earlstoun* and *Markavilla* (no doubt the present station of Nickavilla).
> *Tallyabra*, *Wallyah*, *Yambutta* and *Old Kyra* now taken up.
> *Westbank* and *Sultan* blocks now registered Charleville.
> Country for Coman registered '73.
> Taken up for self and brother Jerry *Lough Isle*, *Lough Neagh*, *Lough Derg* and *Wallinderry* blocks.
> *Durack Downs* and *Durack Plains* adjoining *Galway* registered '74.
> *Kangaroo* country for brother Michael.
> *Maughereaugh*, *Middle Arm* and *Mount Shannon* for self and brother Michael '74.

As many of these blocks are now difficult to identify, measurement is not possible, but the original Thylungra holding, comprising the Bulgroo,

Stoneleigh, Kaffir and Westbank blocks, all taken up by the end of '72, covered an area of some 3,000 square miles.

The establishment of Charleville brought communication thirty miles closer than the nearest previous lands and telegraph office at Tambo, a 200-mile ride from Thylungra. The Cooper settlers had been jubilant at this evidence of approaching civilisation and the ride to Charleville to post letters and register country became a regular jaunt for Grandfather. One of my father's earliest memories was of his solitary mounted figure disappearing with a single pack into the scrub, to reappear some days later heralded by long-drawn cries from the blacks' camp.

'Ayeee! Boonari come up, Missus! Boonari come up now!'

Friends and branches of the family, mostly from the Goulburn area, were now constantly arriving in big parties to take up the selections picked out for them, and often the Thylungra and Kyabra homesteads were filled to overflowing. These were brisk, noisy days of men riding together to stock country and put up homesteads, women cooking, sewing, gossiping, scolding and warning their children against getting in the way of horses' hoofs, slipping in the waterhole, interfering with hornets' nests, falling out of trees or fondling the blacks' dogs.

Early in '74 Dinny and Poor Mary Skeahan and their three remaining boys had arrived with Sarah and Pat Tully and their surviving brood of six. Eager to cover the distance as quickly as possible, Sarah Tully had insisted that the birth of her third son, little Francis, at Parkes near the Bogan River Gates had held them up no more than four days. Their arrival at Thylungra had been celebrated in fine style with the green banner of Ireland's abundant welcome, 'Céad Míle Fáilte', fluttering from the homestead roof. Grandfather had offered the Rasmore run to the Skeahans but whether the prospect of a settled place was really anathema to Dinny, or whether he was genuine in stating that he would take on contracting jobs until he had built up enough capital to develop it, Poor Mary and her boys remained at Thylungra while Dinny went off on the roads with teams and fossicked about in the dry beds of lonely rivers. Betweentimes, when he took on the building of a yard or a pisé homestead, his wife went along with him, making a home of sorts in an open tent, her tired voice calling him back to work when he seemed to have downed tools for too long.

'Where's your sense, woman?' Dinny would expostulate. 'Can't ye see I'm looking to make your fortune?'

'Never mind the fortune,' his wife would protest. 'Just a steady living and a roof over our heads will be heaven to me.'

But Dinny had forsaken his deep shafts in the Adelong only when news spread south in '73 that fine opals had been dropped on around the Bulloo River in western Queensland and that these hitherto unpopular stones were now fetching a fair price. Obsessed with his search, it was not long before he was encouraged by finding a few good specimens.

'See there,' he said, holding them so that the light flashed from the shattered radiance of the rough gems. 'How's that for wasting time?'

But Poor Mary refused to look at the lovely stones.

'Take them away, Dinny. As if we have not had enough bad luck without you must tempt providence with the devil's toys.'

Her sister Sarah Tully shared this superstition of opals and when, not long afterwards, some prospector she had treated for sore eyes presented her with a bag of dazzling specimens she had tipped them into the running creek.

Now settled at Wathagurra, soon to be renamed Ray Station, Sarah was happier than she had been for many years.

'This is our home now no matter what lies in store,' she said. 'We'll live and die here, the lot of us.'

'And if Sarah says so,' her husband sighed resignedly, 'then that's an end of it.'

Sarah said their homestead should be built with a welcoming face to Thylungra so that she could watch from the front verandah for her brothers. Her husband argued that it should be built facing east to the morning sun rather than into the fierce heat of afternoon and the prevailing desert winds. Sarah said 'Stuff and nonsense' so the homestead faced west and the green flag fluttered high whenever the Thylungra horses were sighted at the turn of the creek.

Two of Great-grandmother Costello's sisters, Mrs Hammond and Mrs Moore, with their husbands and families were settled on adjoining properties while Great-grandmother Bridget at Thylungra now had all surviving members of her family around her except Anne Redgrave whose husband battled on, hoping his mine on Bumbo Creek would soon finance them into the Queensland property. In July '74 he wrote to Kate and Stumpy Michael at Thylungra of his wife's death at Moruya.

> . . . Poor Annie did not see the child for she died two hours after the little fellow was born. She had complained for three months before of a pain in her side and it gradually grew worse. The doctor said that no medical skill could have saved her, or that had she recovered from her confinement she would have gone out of her mind. So you can see God willed it for the best and she is happily

> free from this troublesome earth. But to write of her death is almost more than I can bear with still the picture of her living form before my mind. Father Garvey told me when I asked him to say Masses for her that she did not need them. She was already in Heaven he said. You two are the child's sponsor's. I christened him John Patrick. He is such a fine, big child and is in the care of the good woman who lived next door to us at Moruya—a Mrs Williams. She is so frightened anything would happen to him that he is constantly under her watchful eye.
>
> Annie spoke to me two months before she died about you taking the child if she was not to come through. I promised her I would send him to you, but tried to cast from her mind all thought of dying . . . Others would take him but he must go to you for poor Annie's sake, though I am quite at a loss how I am to get him up to you . . .
>
> I am still mining at Bumbo Creek, but am doing no good and would be ready to leave at any moment but for the child.
>
> I am trying all the most likely spots to see if they will pay us at all . . .

A little later he wrote again in reply to Kate's suggestion that he take the baby to her mother's home. One gathers that Redgrave was now quite broke and had at last lost all faith in his mining venture.

> I am sorry to say I am doing no good in the claim and what is more I never shall . . .
>
> But the little boy is a fine fellow and the pride of Moruya. He is just like poor Annie as you will say when you see him. Scores of people call to see him every week because he is the child of one they so much respected. The good woman he is with has paid great attention to him and will be heart broken to lose him now as her own little boy was drowned two months ago.
>
> I would start north with Coman, who very much wants me to go with him, if only I had the good fortune to sell my interest in this show, which I have so far failed to do.
>
> The measles are very prevalent in Sydney, with scores of young and old dying weekly and in Moruya they are very bad. I am afraid of my boy getting them and hope God will spare him to me, for he is all I have in the world . . .

But poor Redgrave was not spared his child; nor did he sell his interest in the mine. Grandfather, moved by his loneliness and grief, made arrangements for him to come to Thylungra with one of the northbound parties. Not long afterwards we find him figuring as storekeeper and horsebreaker on the Thylungra books.

15

Closer Settlement

The years 1874 to 1875. Community life on Cooper's Creek. Sale of land rights brings many settlers. Father Dunham visits his outback flock. Trouble with the blacks. Death of young Maloney on Wombinderry. The Native Police Force. Murder of Welford on Welford Downs. Patsy Durack's opposition to Police. P. Durack now a J.P.

The association of the Cooper people over the next decade would fill a volume in itself. Robustly independent though they were in having come to the wilderness at all, they were interdependent in a typically Irish way. I expect every station kept a tally similar to Grandfather's daybook for Thylungra which reveals the wholesale lendings and borrowings that went on all the time. Grandfather, like the rest, was both a borrower and a lender, though in these early years he was tiding many families over until they could pay their own way from sale of stock. For some years he paid rent on country for various relatives, settled their store bills and even wrote cheques for their stockmen's wages. Page after page of entries, scratched over as the debts were settled or cancelled, run like this:

> Lent to Tozer on the 18th Sept. '73 70 lbs flour and 270 lbs salt.
> Got from Tozer by brother Michael on his way down to Wilcannia 12 lbs flour and 7 pints of sugar. Also Tozer owes me £5.
> Coming home from Tenham I got 3 lbs flour, one box matches, 1 lb tobacco, a tin of mustard and 22 lbs rice off Edward Hammond.
> Jim Hammond owed me £3 which I paid for him to Rev. Father Dunham in Roma.
> 94 lbs of flour from Jim Scanlan, Springfield. Returned by Young.
> Borrowed from P. Tully, Wathagurra: 6 lbs tea, 66 lbs sugar and 142 lbs salt. Pat wants the bags back.
> Lent to Kyabra in May, fetched by Michael Costello, 200 lbs flour, 50 lbs salt, 14 lbs tea.
> Nov. '74. Paid for P. Tully for rent on country, for the four cows from Reed @ £4 each, for the duty on cattle and horses coming

> from New South Wales, also for goods from Wilcannia £395. To be paid back after first stock returns.
> Oct. '74. P. Hackett has now payed everything which I have lent to him up to date only the tea and sugar still dew.
> Supposed to be coming to me from D. Skeahan after settling his Murphy account and price of cattle sold in Sydney. Also *Fine* on Rasmore country—*Expect back*—as have now paid this *twice* for D. S. £5. 5. 0 each time. Also D. Skeahan owes John Horigan £5 borrowed from him on road to Charleville for to give to Father Galagher.

Most of this was paid back in cash or kind and noted with complicated detail. Dinny Skeahan, Poor Mary's husband, appears to have been the only unreliable borrower. At last, no doubt weary of his long-range promises of settlement, Grandfather marked the Skeahan entries either 'Lent to be forgotten' or 'Lent to be paid back'.

When cash or labour was short they worked for each other. It is a common thing in the Thylungra daybook to find Pat Tully sometimes owing wages to one of the Duracks and the Duracks sometimes owing wages to him. They drove each other's stock to market, sold horses for each other and purchased anniversary presents for each other's wives. Everyone's life appears to have been an open book to the community but they were bound by a strict code of family loyalty. The black sheep was protected and defended by the flock and his shortcomings kept as far as possible from outsiders, for a single bad reputation was a blot upon the name. Each kept his private tally of debts paid on another's behalf, and could hound him until he settled up if he liked, but beyond the family circle no one would know of it. To the outside world every member must appear solvent, trustworthy, and living in domestic bliss. They were as tribal as the Aborigines. Inevitably there were rows and occasional flare-ups of jealous antagonism, but the only record of long-range feuding was between the Hammonds of Tenham and the Scanlans of Springfield, who rather than have a common boundary ran a two-mile strip between their runs. On this no-man's-land someone eventually ran up a shanty pub which later became a coaching stage.

In these days of motor-cars, party lines and pedal transmitters people somehow visit each other less than when a call meant harnessing a buggy or saddling a horse. They seemed quite indifferent to distances or to the heat and dust of long journeys.

Although 1874 and '75 were light seasons and the Thylungra stock book shows a disappointing branding of only 332 calves, the general feeling of optimism is indicated by the purchase of 525 store cows at £2,488. The tide of depression in Queensland had turned. All over the new colony people were drifting back to the land and pushing out into the back country right into the furthermost south-west corner over to the Diamantina and down to the Barcoo. Nappamerri Station had now been established by the Conrick family whose stock grazed over the place where Burke and Wills had perished in '62. The country Grandfather had taken up on Cooper's Creek he sold in '74 to a Victorian investor for £5,000. John Costello's big, lightly stocked runs on the Cooper, Farrar's Creek and the Diamantina were all snapped up within two years of the breaking of the drought. Keerongoola, on a Cooper tributary, had been bought by John Hope of South Australia; Whichello, with its splendid six-mile waterhole, and Morney Plains on the Diamantina by Collins Brothers. The stations Gilppie and Tanbar, below Windorah, had gone to Armitage and Gillately, Monkira to Debney and Mooraberrie to Coman Brothers of New South Wales. Daru and Mt Leonard, Connemara and Clastnamuck were all sold, Congabulla given to De Burgh Persse, another tract of land on Farrar's Creek to Mike Tully and Sandy Abbey, relatives of Great-grandmother Costello and Pat Tully of Wathagurra, who shortly afterwards sold the land for a good price and returned to Goulburn. Thomas Webber took over Milka Lake near the South Australian border and Currawilla was given to John Costello's faithful head stockman Jack Farrar for whom he had named the creek on which it was established.

Of the Costello country there soon remained only the huge holding he had named Davenport Downs adjoining Monkira on the Diamantina which was soon afterwards purchased by Cobb and Co. whose coach service had pushed from New South Wales into Queensland after the Gympie gold strike in '69 and was now running between Bourke, Roma and the east coast. This company already owned Cunnamulla Station on the Cuttaburra 120 miles north of the border and saw further possibilities for horse raising on the Diamantina.

Members of the family, on their visits to Roma, had already become acquainted with a stalwart English parish priest named Father Dunham who, being informed of the increasing number of his flock around the Cooper, decided to pay them a visit. He was no bushman and had already caused much anxiety by getting himself lost in the vicinity of Roma, so he brought with him an experienced companion named Noonan.

No prince or potentate could have been accorded a more royal welcome than this pioneer clergyman who had braved the lonely track out west.

Cynics were later heard to remark that any minister undertaking such a journey must be either very devoted to the Gospel or very fond of money and in truth Father Dunham had hoped to combine the spiritual consolation of his far-flung flock with the furtherance of his dearest wish—the building of a church in Roma.

Sunday best, long packed away, was taken from tin trunks. Buggies were polished and harnessed and the Cooper's Creek community bore down on Thylungra to pay its respects and press invitations on the distinguished visitor.

When all were assembled young Michael, my father, nine years old, hair sleekly brushed from a centre parting, came forward nervously to read Mr Redgrave's carefully prepared address.

Children mustered for christening included baby Ambrose, the first-born of Michael and Kate, Sarah Tully's new-born Annie Amy Forde, three young Costellos, Grandmother's Thylungra-born offspring Pat and Mary, and Poor Mary Skeahan's seventh and fourth surviving son, baby Jerry, born at Thylungra not long before.

In later years my Uncle Pat claimed the distinction (in which he was not alone) of having inspired Banjo Paterson's, ballad 'The Bush Christening' and would quote the lines with relish:

> He was none of your dolts, he had seen them brand colts,
> And it seemed to his young understanding,
> If a man in the frock made him one of the flock
> It must mean something very like branding . . .

He recalled being ushered up to the improvised baptismal font where the awesome stranger stood in outlandish regalia, amid an unusually hushed gathering of relatives and friends. In a flash he was through the door and across the yard, to the protection of the blacks' camp. Pumpkin pushed the terrified child into his humpy and stood guard until the boy was at last coaxed forth with many reassurances and promises of rich reward.

So charmed were the settlers with this genial and cultured priest that they became competitive in their efforts on his behalf. John Costello presented him with a 100,000-acre holding, Dunham Towers, north of Davenport Downs on the Diamantina, which Grandfather and his brothers undertook to stock and others to equip with homestead and yards.

Father Dunham left Noonan in charge of the estate and set off back to Roma in high delight. Before long, however, the 'natural increase' of the 'holy herd', as it was called, became nothing short of miraculous, and so often were the cows of neighbouring stations seen running with calves that bore the Dunham Towers' brand that the settlers rose in protest. Noonan made counter-accusations declaring that he was doing no more than protect the interests of Holy Church against black-hearted marauders.

The outcome was a stiff letter from the Archbishop of the Diocese suggesting to his minister that the roles of property owner and parish priest were incompatible.

The matter as patched up when John Costello again took over Dunham Towers, sold it to a more satisfactory neighbour and presented Father Dunham with the cheque. No grudge was borne on either side. The priest continued his annual visit and as guide, philosopher and friend was honoured and well loved, his name to be immortalised in a river which Stumpy Michael later discovered in far-off Kimberley.

But this long-hoped-for closer settlement had another side. The blacks, finding their lands and waters dwindling with every influx of newcomers, took to the wholesale killing of stock—at first for what they considered their rightful compensation, later, as bitterness and misunderstanding spread, with deliberate wantonness.

Some of the early opal prospectors were responsible for much trouble and misunderstanding with the blacks. A man, whose name is still remembered in the district, got one native after another helping him with the promise of tucker and tobacco in exchange for opals. If the black produced a stone and demanded payment he would tell him to be off and shoot him in the back as he went.

What wonder that the white men's herds became scapegoats for the bewildered rage of the tribespeople? Tongues and tails were hacked from living animals, horses hamstrung, maimed and left to die. Every traveller brought rumours of increasing trouble and many settlers now openly declared that Western Queensland could only be habitable for whites when the last of the blacks had been killed out—'by bullet or by bait'.

The first white man killed by the blacks in these parts was a young stockman named Maloney at Wombinderry on the northern boundary of Jim Scanlan's Springfield. John Costello had shown the Wombinderry block to two men named Reid and Fraser who stocked the run with horses and left Maloney and an older man named Silletor in charge while they returned to New South Wales for further stock. Young Maloney, bored to distraction with life in this lonely outpost, made friends with the local blacks and then, hoping to impress and astonish them with his 'white man magic', began firing around them from behind trees. They took his teasing in good enough part until one day he playfully shot one of their dogs.

'You shouldn't of done that,' Silletor told him. 'The niggers are fond of them dogs.'

'That wasn't no dog,' Maloney replied. 'It was a mangy dingo cur.'

He then went off to fish by the river and when, a few hours later, his mate went to call him he had vanished. Some days after when Jack Farrar rode across from Kyabra to see how the two men were getting on he found Silletor almost demented with fear and loneliness, declaring that the blacks had kidnapped his mate.

'If he's missing they'll have killed him,' Farrar said.

When Farrar got Silletor back to Kyabra, Costello at once sent word to the newly proclaimed town of Thargomindah about 120 miles south where Inspector Gilmour was then stationed with a contingent of native police. This force, consisting, except for officers in charge, entirely of Aborigines, trained, smartly uniformed and well mounted, was at first supposed to patrol the countryside, have parley with encampments of bush natives, try to explain the white man's laws and arrest and imprison ringleaders of bad crimes, and as such it had been hailed as a humane and timely move to restore peace and security to the community.

Gilmour rode out with his troopers and quickly had the mystery solved. The body of Maloney, or what remained of it, weighted down with heavy stones, was now partly revealed by the receding level of the waterhole. Jim Scanlan, who knew young Maloney's family in Ireland, had come with the party from Springfield, equipped with a shroud, blessed candles and a bottle of holy water so that he could at least write home that the lad had been buried with all possible ceremony.

There were, however, no questions asked of the blacks as to who had committed the crime or why. No arrests were made and the bodies of those shot around a camp at dawn were left to the ravages of wild dogs and birds of prey.

When news of the affair reached Thylungra, Grandfather rode after the police party in a towering rage, demanding an explanation of their policy.

'What kind of a law is it that will train blacks to murder their own countrymen?'

'Nothing of the sort,' he was informed. 'We never recruit blacks for service in their own district. A Kalkadoon will shoot a Boontamurra at the drop of a hat, and vice versa. They've been at each other's throats for generations.'

Whether or not they ever made an honest attempt to reason with the now totally unpredictable tribespeople, it was soon clear to all that the black troopers rode to kill—to shatter the old tribes, the Boontamurra, the

Pita-Pita, the Murragon, the Waker-di, the Ngoa, the Murrawarri and the Kalkadoon, to leave men, women and children dead and dying on the plains, in the gullies and river beds.

Not long after the death of Maloney a terrified native stockboy rode into Thylungra with news of the killing of Welford, the young Englishman who had been the family's first neighbour on Kyabra Creek and whose property, Welford Downs, adjoined their northern boundary. Grandfather heard with deep distress how his friend had been teaching a native, newly arrived from another district, to use an adze, when the boy took up a heavy tool and brought it down on his master's head. The murderer had then seized a firearm, saddled a horse and ridden off.

Fearful of being implicated in the crime, the station natives had hidden the body in a tree, but Welford's head stockman had galloped with news of the murder into Charleville where a contingent of black police had recently been stationed.

Grandfather at once sent Pumpkin and Willie to Welford Downs to advise all natives in the vicinity to gather at Thylungra where they would be under his protection. The blacks, however, with only a few exceptions, now dared trust nobody and suspecting a plot to trap them at Thylungra made off into the surrounding bush. Only a handful who had sought the refuge offered escaped the raid that followed. Faithful station natives and bush blacks perished together, among them one Ngurrun, the Emu man, a kindly giant of the Boontamurra who could run down kangaroos. Years later when the drifting sand of the plains uncovered the bones of the massacred blacks, some among them were found to be of phenomenal size. The bone of a man's forearm brought into Thylungra was the size of an ordinary man's entire arm.

All through the outback the hunted natives grew wary and shrewd, moving like shadows over the land. For years the black police would ride, until the country could at last be declared safe from menace—safe and quiet and the songs of dreaming stilled for all time. The police would earn the praise and thanks of the settlers for their work and a few would die in the cause of duty.

Constable Urquart's ballad, telling of the vengeance wrought upon the Kalkadoons after the death of his friend Powell some time later, is still remembered by old hands in the districts he rode:

> Swiftly the messenger had sped
> O'er the rough mountain tracks,
> To tell the news, our friend was dead.
> Killed by the ruthless blacks . . .

And one spake out in deep, stern tones,
And raised his hand on high,
'For every one of these poor bones
A Kalkadoon shall die . . .'

See how the wretched traitors fly,
Smitten with abject fear,
They dare not stop to fight or die,
And soon the field is clear.

Unless just dotted here and there
A something on the ground,
A something black with matted hair
Lies without life or sound . . .

From this time on Grandfather's half-humorous contempt of the police grew to a thoroughly Irish antipathy that often caused his family keen embarrassment.

'I'd sooner have an outlaw put his feet under my table,' he would say when the patrol came on its rounds, 'than any of that murthering gang. They'll be getting no thanks out of me for their protection.'

Not many, even among his own relatives, saw eye to eye with him on this score and demanded whether he would see all their stock killed and their families constantly imperilled for his principles.

'Principles be damned,' he thundered, 'it's common sense. We'll all be singing out for labour in a few years and not a mother's son of them left alive. And where would any of us Christians be today if it wasn't for the help we've had from your heathen blacks?'

Despite his wife's entreaties, he now refused to take any form of lethal weapon on his long, solitary rides.

Just over forty and in the prime of life, Grandfather was a dynamo of restless energy. He would return from registering country, purchasing or delivering stock, and plunge straight back into the station activities. Sometimes he would dismount at the yard where they were branding cattle and would enter into the job before going to the house to greet the family or have a cup of tea. He had no patience with what he called 'lommicking about' or 'going to slape on the job'. Even the blacks moved briskly on Thylungra, for paternal though he was, Boonari's quick impatience was something to look out for. It is said that he once stamped an indelible 7PD brand on a slow-moving black rump, a distinguishing mark that the boy bore proudly to the day of his death!

Another time he was incensed at a stockman's cutting out cattle in the blistering noonday heat.

'Be arl the goats in Kerry,' he shouted to McCaully, 'what's that kippenhead think he's doing?'

'I told him he was a fool,' the Scot complained, 'but there's no stopping the mon.'

'Isn't there at all now,' Grandfather fumed, and riding over to the importunate stockman laid him out with a single blow of his stirrup iron.

Created JP for the district from '74, he assumed certain magisterial duties and settled local arguments with a despatch and logic that was seldom questioned. One of his methods of resolving differences was to light a fire between the disputing parties, who, at a word from the umpire (usually himself), would begin a pantomime of leaping and thrusting across the flames. The first to touch his opponent's nose with his hand was acclaimed the winner.

At one time a difference arose between Grandfather and Duncan McCaully over the naming of a hill. The Scot plumped for 'Mt Aberdeen', the Irishman for 'Mt Ortheven' but when Mr Healy decided in Grandfather's favour McCaully insisted on another contest with a Scottish referee. This time Grandfather made sure that his 'tap' on the nose was conclusive enough to draw blood and Mt Ortheven stands today in testimony of his sprightliness.

Only once, as far as memory goes, was his verdict seriously challenged, and this when, having condemned a fencing job as sub-standard, he was taken to court in Charleville. Grandfather, owing to a recent tirade against the force, stood none too well at the time with the local magistrate, which may or may not have had something to do with the decision. When judgement was given in favour of the contractor he gave vent to his indignation with an eloquence that went down in local history.

'Is it like the blacks ye would be having us, propping up bark humpies and the like for to be destroyed in a puff of wind? What's become of the country atall with everything done slipshod and falling down all roads?'

Grandmother, hating fuss, tugged imploringly at his coat tails, but he refused to be quietened.

'What ails ye, woman? What sort of a JP is it atall that can't be condemning a miserable fence?'

16

EYE WITNESS

The years 1875 to 1877. Prosperity and population come to Cooper's Creek. Arrival of Pat Scanlan and his family, Darby Durack's sons and others. Account of Thylungra personalities given by an old drover. Letters from John W. Durack and Jeremiah 'Dermot' Durack telling of these times. Folk-songs of the Cooper.

Here now were the times that are legend on Cooper's Creek. Good seasons, boom prices for cattle and horses and ready sales for rights of the country they had taken up brought quick prosperity to the pioneer settlers and encouraged to the district some of the keenest stock dealers and best horsemen in Australia. The combined Thylungra and Galway herds stood at no more than 6,000 in '76 and cattle sales totalled £3,200. The sale of sixty well-bred horses at an average of £35 a head brought in another £2,050 and land rights a further £4,500. By '77 the two stations reckoned between them 10,000 cattle. On 1,000 head marketed they netted about £7,500, made £3,000 on horses and £5,000 on land rights. Debts were long since paid off and the family balance sheet began to weigh well on the credit side.

From this time into the eighties the Thylungra books tally an average of fifteen white stockmen, including drovers, six to eight fencing, building and carrying contractors and a married couple as cook and handyman. The couples came and went in more or less six-monthly succession, the stockmen and contractors changed about, but old Mr Healy, the tutor, stuck fast.

In '76 Pat Scanlan, with his second wife, her two children, one born at Parkes on the way north, and the four children of his first marriage with Grandfather's sister Bridget, came north and made their headquarters with Jim and Susan Scanlan at Springfield. For a few years, however, Pat hired out his great strength for contracting jobs and was as often as not employed on Thylungra.

About the same time an English couple named Curtis with a grown family of two boys and two girls, formerly well-to-do squatters who had fallen on hard times in Victoria, came to make a fresh start in western Queensland. Grandfather, always pleased to have contact with people of refinement and education, started them off on a small adjoining block which he named Curta and helped them put up a house no more than a mile from his own. Planning to build up capital for a bigger property, the Curtis boys worked most of the time on Thylungra and Mrs Curtis and her girls were regarded as part of the family community.

The brothers Michael and Stephen Brogan who had come from Scariff, County Clare, to take up a block near Grandfather on Dixon's Creek in the early sixties both came to Thylungra early in '75. The payment of £19 for their coach fares from Goulburn to Bourke is the first mention in existing family records of negotiations with the firm of Cobb and Co. that was soon to play such a big part in all their lives.

Darby Durack's eldest boy, Big Johnnie, then aged twenty-five, had also come to Thylungra in '75 and the following year his three younger brothers, Black Pat, Long Michael and Jerry Brice, aged about twenty-three, twenty-one and seventeen, took over the management of Mooraberrie, between Farrar's Creek and the Diamantina, for Edward Coman who had purchased the property from John Costello not long before. Big Johnnie, between taking cattle and horses to Sydney, Wilcannia and as far as Adelaide, was stocking a block called Mt Shannon which Grandfather had registered in the name of Darby's widow. It may be remembered that her name was formerly Margaret Kilfoyle and her younger brother Tom was also on the Thylungra books at this time, with a carrying contract to bring loading up from Bourke or Wilcannia.

The community, although preponderantly Irish-Australian, included a leavening of English and Scottish and at this time numbered even one German named Adolph Steinbeck. The blacks had one day brought word to Thylungra that a solitary white man was wandering about in the bush shouting at the sky and obviously 'silly alonga head'. Grandfather rode out and found the poor fellow, almost perishing and certainly near crazy. He had come to Australia with little knowledge of English and less of Aboriginal to bring salvation to the natives, who after seeming to accept him had suddenly cleared out and left him stranded. Grandfather brought him in to the station and suggested he stayed for a while as carpenter and got to know something of the blacks and their country before taking on further missionary work. His name figured on the pay roll for two or three years, but whether he after that returned to his original calling is nowhere recorded.

Considering all the personalities either permanently at Thylungra or moving in and out over these years it is little wonder that an old-timer named Will Blake whom I met many years ago described it to me as 'a menagerie'.

'I could write a book about it only my sight's gone on me,' he said.

Fortunately I jotted down what he told me, for future reference, and am surprised to find in view of what I have since learned how accurate his memories were.

He arrived in Charleville with cattle from New South Wales towards the end of '75 when the Cooper settlers were buying breeders or mixed store cattle for fattening. Grandfather had come in to purchase a mob of 1,000 store cows and was evidently concerned by the condition of the sixteen-year-old drover's boy.

'I was a mess all right,' he told me, 'eyes bunged up with sandy blight, skin covered with Barcoo rot and scurvy and a whitlow on one hand.'

'Better come back with me, son,' Grandfather said. 'Give a hand with the cattle and have a rest up when you get there. The wife and the old mother will have ye right in no time atall.'

Thylungra had a big spread on it by this time, with two main homesteads and a number of other buildings, stockmen's quarters, blacksmith's 'shop', meat houses, saddle and buggy sheds, and blacks' wurlies along the bank of the creek.

'And what a crowd of characters,' my friend said. 'I can see them now, after sixty years, men, women, children and a big mob of blacks, all running out to meet the boss and see who he's picked up this time. There was your Grandma, Mrs Patsy, a wonderful little woman—always on the go but never flustered, making everyone feel happy and at home, but it was the old lady, your Grandpa's mother, who took me in hand. She was the sort of medicine woman of the tribe and had me smeared over and bandaged up before I could say "knife". "You've got to keep the light out of your eyes," she told me. "How'm I going to see?" I asked her. Then I found she had a nice little piccaninny trained for the job. I wasn't the first blind man he'd looked after. He'd been leading his old dad around by a stick since he was five years old. The eyes were pretty well cleared up inside a week, but I stayed on at Thylungra for over five years. It was the only real home I ever knew and it was home to plenty others as well, but I was away a lot of the time droving with Stumpy Michael and I got to know him better than any of them. He was a quieter man than your Grandpa, a different type, but I never saw brothers more devoted than those two. Stumpy was a natural bushman like Johnnie Costello. We used to say he carried his compass in his head and he could track as well as any blackfellow I ever knew. He never blew his own trumpet. He was stocky and shorter than most of the crack stockmen round the Cooper but he stood out among the flash, skiting young fellows and they looked up to him. He knew all the main routes and the back tracks from Western Queensland down to Sydney or into South Australia. He'd been over them time and again in drought and flood, with cattle or horses and with the teams, stood up to bushfires, and stampeding cattle and hostile blacks and came through the lot. He had more guts and less swagger than any man I ever knew, but he wasn't doing it just for the fun of the thing. His wife was never struck on the bush life and he wanted to make enough money to build her a good home in a settled district, where he could breed racehorses and settle down in the one place with his family.

'Come to think of it, I reckon that's what they all wanted then—even your Grandpa, Galway Jerry and John Costello.

'Now I want you to put down all the names of the chaps there at that time,' he said, 'because pretty soon no one will remember them and they deserve to go down in history. Barney Lamond, George Kermode, Duncan McCaully, Jack Horrigan, Bill Feeney, Jim Russell, Jack Storier, Fred Cavanagh and John Copley were all first-rate horsebreakers and stockriders and a pack of regular wild colonial boys and there was the Colonial Experience chap Ivor McIvor we used to call "The Toff", but who turned out as tough as the rest of us. Later on he married one of the Curtis girls and took up a property on the Bulloo. There were the Brogans, Mick and Steve from County Clare and John Redgrave, another Irishman, your Grandpa's brother-in-law who'd not long since lost his wife and kid. We used to try and cheer him up and Patsy Durack wanted him to take up a place called Bunginderry, but he never seemed to fit in very well up there. He left after a year or two and went back to the mining.

'And don't forget there were some mighty fine black stockmen there too. Maybe they didn't have the style of the whites but they could handle horses and cattle with the best of them. Pumpkin was your Grandpa's right-hand boy. He was quick and intelligent and could turn his hand to anything, horsebreaking, butchering, odd jobs, blacksmithing, gardening, but horses were his main interest like with the rest of us. And there were other wonderful young fellows—Pumpkin's brothers, Kangaroo and Melon Head, and Willie who offsided Stumpy Michael and old Cobby who shadowed the youngsters like a watch dog and little Waddi Mundoai hopping about on his wooden leg. There were plenty of black women too, but any young fellows who had ideas on those lines had to go elsewhere. There were no half-castes born on Thylungra in your Grandpa's time but there were a few fellows had the romance licked out of them with his stockwhip just the same.

'Your Grandpa thought the world of his blacks and they gave him some good laughs too. One day a new chum boy told him he'd lost his stirrup irons.

'"Now how in the name of Moses would ye be losing yere stirrups?" the old man asked.

'"You ask'm saddle," the boy said. "Him been lose'm—not me."

'Your Grandpa's cousin, Big Johnnie, who was droving for Thylungra and Galway Downs, was about twenty-five or six then—a fine-looking young chap and a nice, friendly way with him. The ladies all used to go for him and we had bets whether he'd get off with one of the Curtis girls or one of the Hammonds, but he kept them all guessing. "I've got to get half a dozen sisters married off and see a bunch of young brothers through college before I can think of settling down," he'd say, and he was genuine about that too. I often think how he planned for his family and how just when he might have started for himself there was that blackfellow's spear came out of the scrub with his number on it. But he had a long way to go still if you reckoned it in miles. His three younger brothers, Black Pat, Long Michael and Jerry Brice, used to come over from Mooraberrie sometimes and were always in on the Galway race meetings. They were handsome lads and fine stockmen—and they knew it too. Black Pat was the local boxing champ and Long Michael, six foot three and supple as a piece of whipcord, was about the best marksman on the Cooper. He used to come in for a lot of chiacking though, because he'd always stammer when he got wild and was never one to take too kindly to a joke against himself.

'Their mother's brother, Tom Kilfoyle, one of the best bushmen in Australia, was doing the carrying for Thylungra. He'd been through a few dry gullies in his time and he knew the ropes and all the tricks of the stockman's trade. Your Grandpa used to reckon he'd sooner have him on his books than his borders. Every time he'd pay him he'd say, "And here's a bonus, Tom, to keep ye from taking up the block next door."

'Some used to say that Jack Horrigan, who was head Thylungra stockman, was the best horseman in Queensland at that time and others used to reckon Bill Feeney was better. They were always challenging each other and your Grandpa would be called in to judge. Naturally it was a pretty hard job and the old man had a rhyme about it that wound up like this:

"And when I get to heaven feeling that I've earned a rest,
There'll be Horrigan and Feeney, at me yet to name the best,
In and out the choirs of angels, through the halo-waving crowd,
Bill upon a streak o' lightning, Jack upon a flying cloud."

'Horrigan was the toughest looking bloke you could imagine. He had long arms and bandy legs and he walked like a gorilla, but there was another side to him. He had a relative who was a nun in the convent in Bourke and she used to pin medals over him every time he came through. Wear them? My oath he did! Used to reckon no horse'd ever get the better of him while he had them on and no horse ever did as far as I know. He reckoned his motto was "Live hard, pray hard, swear hard and die hard" and he did all those things.

'Your Grandpa's youngest brother Galway Jerry used to take all the fellows off. He was a wonderful mimic, a natural born comedian and when the old man would get in one of his rages the young fellow could always bring him round.

'"Be off wid ye, Jerry ye kippenhead," old Patsy would say. "Ye'd have a man laugh on his death bed when he ought to be crying for his sins."

'The best act Jerry ever put on was taking off the old Irish tutor, Mr Healy, and the German carpenter, Adolph Steinbeck. They were both pretty strong on the praying, but Steinbeck was a Lutheran and he had a different style. Your Grandpa let them both take turns saying Grace but they wouldn't leave it at that. They'd take the opportunity to throw in all the prayers they could think up and when they ran out of ready-made ones they'd start inventing. Finally the old man said they'd have to cut it down to two or three each, but old Healy used to spin out the Hail Mary like nobody's business: "Pray for us sinners," he'd wind up, "what ails them heathen blacks, can't someone tell them to quieten down outside there 'til the prayers are over, and if there's somebody here thinks he can be converting them he could start be teaching them a bit of ordinary, decent respect . . . now and at the hour of our death . . . ye stop yere shinannakin there, young Johnnie, or ye'll be getting a butt over the ear . . . Amen."

'Young Galway Jerry had only to start doing that act and he'd have us all in stitches. They called him "The wild Irishman of the family", but he was the only one of them born in Australia. He was pretty wild all right at that time, but he was mighty popular with the crowd. He used to hit the grog a bit and then the game'd be on. Some chaps want to pick a fight when they've had a few in, and some want to cry and some get sentimental, but Galway Jerry always wanted to start a race meeting. Never mind what time of the day or night—out would come the horses and there'd be shouting and galloping all over the flat and your Grandpa usually enjoying it as much as anyone. Galway Jerry organised the first proper races on the Cooper and before Windorah was established there were picnic meetings on Galway Downs.

'Horses were the main thing in life for us all. We lived for horses and any spare time we had we were training and grooming our hacks for fancy stockwork and bush race meetings. We all minced around the Cooper with short, quick steps and spurs jingling on the high-heeled elastic-sides that were mostly a size too small. We suffered like hell, but it was the fashion to have small feet outback—supposed to be a sign of good horsemanship. It was stuff and nonsense of course. Duncan McCaully used to get a bad time about his size tens, but he could stick a horse with the best of us. Wriggling out of our boots was as hard as a snake getting out of its skin, and we used to cut U-shaped hollows in the timber frames of the bunks to help us lever them off . . . '

How vividly the old man brought the past to life for me as he talked on of these noisy extrovert days of the teasing—'chiacking' as they called it—the rivalry, the practical joking, nicknaming, bragging, swaggering, fighting and coming together on lively sprees. Scattered most of the time, they all tried to make back to Thylungra for Christmas and Saint Patrick's Day when Grandfather celebrated his birthday.

'I never knew anyone celebrate as hard as Patsy Durack,' I was told. 'You couldn't knock him up and he never expected anyone else to knock up either. We'd start early in the morning and carry right on through 'til late at night, horse races, foot races, jumping, boxing, tap dancing and stunts. Everyone had a special stunt of some sort, walking on his hands, balancing knives on his nose, lifting weights—that was Pat Scanlan's specialty—turning handsprings, or maybe just singing or reciting or giving a tune on a tin whistle or a gum leaf. Your Grandpa played the fiddle and the flute by ear and Stumpy Michael's wife was a first-rate pianist.

'After dark they'd always have the "Thylungra Championship" for the new chums. All the fellows would line up and at the word "go" they'd be off hell for leather but the new blokes always got out in front somehow—through the tape and splash into the waterhole five foot down the bank!'

There had been no objection to men taking their 'drop of the crathur' on Thylungra. Grandfather had little patience with drunkards but liked his men to enjoy a few drinks on high days and holidays and there was always a cask or two of rum or whisky with the Thylungra loading.

Often, when the crowd was in, there had been two and three sittings for meals, but there was no such thing as a 'men's table'. Grandfather regarded mealtimes as a chance to talk with the men, to ask them about their homes, their folks and their experiences.

'Your Grandpa never seemed bored listening to our yarns,' my friend said. 'He'd sit there nodding, or maybe plaiting a bit of greenhide for a stockwhip and saying "Go on now", or "You don't say", and sometimes he'd give an almighty yell and slap his knee. "Go on," he'd say. "So your great-aunt married a Hogan"—or whatever it might be—"well, I had a cousin back in County Clare married a Hogan in '45." And next thing he'd be claiming you as a relative, as if he didn't have enough of them as it was—Duracks, Costellos, Hammonds, Tullys, Moores, Skeahans, Scanlans, Hacketts, Dillons, Minogues, Brogans, Kellys, Roaches, Abbeys, Kilfoyles—all out there then and all related in some way. Those who weren't working on the place were always visiting. Your Grandma's first cousin, Frances Hammond, whose family had Tenham Station, stayed at Thylungra for weeks at a time, and her brothers were always in and out. There were five of them, I remember, Ned, Mick, Martin, John and Jim. Well, we all fancied ourselves as pretty smart fellows in those days but we had to hand it to the Hammond boys for social style. They were doing well then and beginning to spread out around the Cooper. They drove their own cattle to market like the rest but when they hit the cities they lived high. The yarns they'd spin when they got back—especially young Mick—about the beautiful actresses he'd taken around—had us green with envy. Some of them reckoned they were kidding us up a gum tree about their high times and conquests, but we'd find out later it was nothing but the truth. They had top hats and tails and walking-sticks in the city—had their photographs taken to prove it—and back home they rode some of the flashest horses on the Cooper. Ned was thrown and killed by one of them but the others lived to a good age and had families. They had four stations finally, Tenham, Hammond Downs, Munro and Ingella. You'd meet them one time and they'd be flat broke and the banks taken over, and next time they'd be back again on top of the world.

'Frances Hammond had been bridesmaid at your Grandma's wedding and they were like sisters. That was why she was there so much—independent too, used to ride over on her own from Tenham to Thylungra—forty-five miles in the day. She was a lovely figure in the saddle in those long, graceful riding skirts they used to wear, but she was too old for me. The one I was sweet on then was little Delia Scanlan, Big Pat's girl, who was living with her uncle Stumpy Michael and his missus at Thylungra.

'I can't say any of us got much chance with the girls out there though, what with the ragging we'd get from each other and the eagle eye we had kept on us by the older women. There was never the free and easy way between the boys and girls they have these days. Any fun we had was with the crowd—no cutting off in pairs.

We used to reckon some of the older women were tartars but looking back now I can see they had to be to keep that wild mob in hand. Every now and again your Grandpa used to count the women and girls on the place and the more there were the better he liked it, but sometimes they'd gang up on him about something the way they do and he'd blow his top.

'"Come on boys!" he'd say. "Let's get out of here while there's any manhood left in us. Wamen," he'd say, "they're the curse of the country. I'd like to ship the lot of them out to sea."

'Sometimes your Grandpa's sister Mrs Dinny Skeahan was there with her four boys. The two eldest, Michael and Patsy, were old enough for stockmen then and their Dad, Dinny, and his brother John were contracting on Thylungra most of the time. I was always sorry for Mrs Dinny. She looked like a woman who'd had a terrible hard life and I don't wonder with a man like hers.

'There was a time when Dinny and his missus had a bit of a selection called "Newcastle" which was the closest he ever got to having a permanent address. Being almost illiterate himself he got one of his sons—who wasn't much better—to do the station ordering. Once Dinny told him to write away for one hundred yards of a strong sort of material we called "bungaree". "How many noughts in a hundred, Dad?" he asked. Dinny thought over this for a while. "Put two," he said, "and another one for luck." That might make more," the boy suggested. "Nonsense," Dinny said. "Another nothing can be neither here nor there." In due course along came one thousand yards of material and everyone on the selection, black, white and brindle, wore bungaree until the white ants got into the roll and finished it off!

'Later they took up a little bush pub known as "Jack in the Rocks" but Dinny soon became his own best customer. When his wife had to go off somewhere one day she put a jar of rum on the counter with instructions that he had to put a shilling in the till for every nip he took. When she got back the jar was empty and so was the till—except for one shilling. "There was only but the one bob to hand," Dinny told her, "and I swear by all the saints in heaven that I put it in again for ivery nip taken."

'At Jack in the Rocks you got corn beef and spuds in their mud when the coach stopped for dinner and Dinny would entertain his clients with tales of his palmy days as a station owner. "Sure and when I uster droive in to Adavale wid me spankin' four-in-hand, the shout would go up ''Tis Mister Skeahan from Newcastle' and the people would come running out to welcome me, but a different story indade it is today when I come along in me old buckboard. 'Sure,' they say, ''tis only old Dinny o' the Rocks—to hell wid him!' As if I was to be held in any way responsible for the cruel blows of fate!"

'Another of your Grandfather's sisters, Mrs Pat Tully, used to ride over about once a week from Wathagurra, twenty-five miles away, with a kid in front and another hanging on behind . . .'

Will Blake was there when Sarah Tully came to Thylungra with her sick child, the two-year-old Francis who had been born on their journey north, hoping that her mother's skill might cure him. With no doctor nearer than Roma, the child's case was never diagnosed and he died in a spasm in his mother's arms. Again Thylungra and Kyabra were plunged in grief and the little body was buried beside the Durack baby Jeremiah who had died in the depths of the Cooper drought in '69.

My grandparents had five children by the end of '74—my father, Michael, my Uncles John and Pat and my Aunts Mary and little Birdie. Their last child, Jeremiah, my Uncle Dermot, was born in February '77. The oldtimer remembered the event quite clearly.

'It came as a sort of surprise to us, but we might have known when the old lady, Mrs Costello, your Grandma's mother, showed up from Kyabra. A typical pioneer woman she was—face like a nutcracker and a voice like a cross-cut saw, first thing in the morning, last thing at night, always laying down the law, but there was a lot of comon sense in what she said just the same. Well, there was Mrs Patsy looking after the crowd as usual, pouring out dozens of cups of tea, and next morning we hear a sort of bleating noise when we come in to breakfast and there's the boss on the verandah proud as Punch with a baby in his arms.

'He was proud of all his children and some people used to say he'd ruin them. Old Mrs Costello was darn sure of it and didn't mind telling him, but I reckon they were all right. Your two uncles, Johnnie and Pat, were young rips, into all sorts of mischief but your Dad was never the kind to get into scrapes. He was a rather serious, responsible sort of a boy and the fellows treated him pretty respectfully even then. Somebody once asked the old man what he was going to make of "young Mick", and he looked surprised as though he hadn't thought of it.

' "Make of him?" he said. "What do you mean—'make of him'? Michael comes down from a long line of eldest sons and after me he's head of the family."

'The boy had the makings of a good rider at eleven or twelve and his Dad had him well schooled in stock breeding but he never seemed to get into the life like most of the other kids. He mostly had his nose in a book, even when there was a mob of cows and calves bellowing out in the yard. "Aren't you going to watch the branding?" we'd ask him. "Not just now," he'd say. "I've seen it plenty times before."

'"He'll never make a stockman like his Dad," someone said once, but Jack Horrigan wouldn't hear a word against any of them.

'"He won't need to be," he told us. "The old man come up the hard way but his kids'll always have plenty others to do the hard yakka. Patsy Durack'll be a millionaire before he's through."

Others too have given verbal and written accounts of these crowded days at Thylungra. My Uncle John, one of the 'young rips' mentioned in the foregoing account, wrote from Perth during the 1920s to his Tully cousins at Ray Station, earlier known as Wathagurra, recalling memories of their youth. With typical family sentiment the letter was treasured and a copy given to me after my uncle's death in 1936:

> ... I still see all the nooks and corners of the dear old home. I see the flocks of wild birds, the placid waters, the butterflies on the perfumed wild oranges and the gooseberry bushes. I find myself in memory, chasing their elusive ways ...
>
> I remember the fearsome 'Tri-anti-wonti-gong' that devoured boys who did not do as their Mother told them. This monster poor Mother created in her anxiety to keep us from falling into the water from the slippery banks. It lived in our childish imaginations until time dispelled the illusion—and delusion, for we actually saw it, dressed in black, with great horns and monstrous shape. I remember too, it had the desired effect ...
>
> I see the old school house where Mr Healy taught us pot hooks and hangers, the rule of three and long prayers. I hear him reprimanding us because we did not 'do as he desired us'. I see the shadow of the big tree steal across the school room door that measured the termination of school for dinner hour. Even as I write I hear the rattle of the spoons in the tea cups as they always did rattle when the shadow crossed the door ...
>
> I see you all at Wathagurra, as you used to call the old place. There sits Uncle Pat Tully enjoying the sweet peace of his good, old heart. I see dear Aunt Sarah gauging my wistful face as she brought in the cakes and cream that only she could make. My cousins Pat, Joe, Sis, Clara, Maria, Sarah Ann and you all. We sit down at the feast together. After it is over we all make merry.
>
> Uncle Michael, Aunt Kate and cousins; poor Aunt Mary and cousins Skeahan and their old homes run through my memories. I hear Uncle Jerry's jovial laugh; and poor old Grandmother—

> Why! Today, Easter Sunday, is the day she used to ask us to get up and see the sun dance. Dear old loving soul . . . But too much retrospect does not fit in with the modern trend of life. It will not pull you through the drought nor help you crank your cars . . . God be with you all . . .
>
> J.W.D.

The baby Jerry, my Uncle Dermot, whose birth in February 1877 was another of my old friend's memories, became a Professor of Mathematics, was for a time Principal of the Allahabad University, India, and retired to Ireland where he died in 1956. I visited him there during the thirties and when he knew I was writing this book he helped me in many ways, particularly in delving into the family background. Although his memory can hardly have extended further back than 1880, much that he wrote adds to the general picture of life at Thylungra about this time and the characters of many of his relatives.

> Never in my life [he said], have I written such long letters as now, at the end of it, but you might as well have all I can remember of the family, of father and mother and the old life at Thylungra and at Maryview, our Brisbane home. Part of me belongs always to the Australian bush, and I still cry sometimes over Banjo Paterson's 'Man from Snowy River' as I did when you were here in '36, but I doubt I will go back now. Ireland holds me and will claim my bones. As well perhaps that one of the family returned to honour the land they left in the years of grief and famine and had forgotten how to love.
>
> 'You children do not know the meaning of hunger,' Father said to me. 'Please God you never will.'
>
> Being the youngest in the family I believe I was closer to him than the others. My first memories of him are at Thylungra, Cooper's Creek, when I was a very little chap and your father and Uncle John away at college. Later when we made our home in Brisbane the elder boys were again away. I went everywhere with Father, on horseback or by buggy. It was from him I first acquired a love of horses and had learned to ride well enough at three or four years old. He could talk of horses by the hour going right back to his first loves, the big Irish hunters of the Galway Blazers. He always bred from thoroughbred sires and produced some of the finest half breds in Australia. His two famous grey buggy horses, Banjo and Tarragon, often carried him, Mother and me from

Thylungra to Adavale, one hundred miles on a bush track in a single day.[1]

Would I could adequately describe the character and warm personality of your Grandmother. She was a simple, homely woman, very capable and calm and greatly loved by all. Everyone confided in her, knowing that her advice would be sound but that she would not censure them for their shortcomings. In this she more resembled Father's Mother than her own, our Grandmother Costello, who was somewhat stern as we remember her, probably in her anxiety that we should not degenerate into young bush scallywags. 'Grandma Bridget' as we called her would defend us no matter what we did. When a bad tempered governess soundly rapped my knuckles she would say 'That vixen' and would take me to her room and console me with a boiled turkey egg. I suppose it might be said that we were somewhat indulged in our youth, with Mother and Grandma Bridget always so gentle and poor Father so anxious for our happiness, as he was for everyone's, so eager to give us everything he had been denied in his own youth, especially education, and so proud of any little scholastic success we had. Although I followed an academic career, our Father and Uncle John were actually more 'bookish' by nature than myself and how proud Father was to tell his friends that they 'knew Latin and something of Greek and all the writers you could lay tongue to'.

Although firm in his own faith, remember that your grandfather had no bigotry in any form. No man was ever refused hospitality on account of race or creed in his house, nor did he ever utter a disparaging word on any religion that another held dear. Servants he always regarded and treated as members of the family, and if they left for any reason he kept in touch with them wherever they were, worried about them if he heard they had struck hard times and remembered their children's birthdays. This human attitude he had to all men may explain his wonderful tact and unusual success in dealing with the aborigines. Dear old Pumpkin always regarded himself as one of the family, referred to Father as his 'brother' and would have given his life for any one of us. Any

[1] Unless my uncle's memory failed him here, this could no doubt only have been done by staging the horses as my own father often did later in Kimberley. Native boys would be sent ahead a day or two before to camp with the buggy changes at stages along the road.

natives Father had with him from boys did not speak pidgin English, though some said they spoke with an Irish brogue. It did not strike us that Father spoke with a brogue, but I suppose he did as you will see from his letters that he sometimes spelt with one.

Yes, the verses you found in your Grandfather's handwriting were his own. Did you not realise that all Irishmen are poets at heart and that most of them, even I, have a go at it at some time? I had a number of poor old Father's efforts, but I burnt them some time ago. I understood the bush jingles that were so much a part of our lives in those times were rather scorned by your generation. I did not want them laughed at. His metre was not always the best no doubt, but to me they carried the unmistakable rattle of bridle and spurs that I always associate with him, and like him they are full of good, homely sentiment, sadness and humour and reflect a real love of the bush life he lived. Lawson, Paterson and Ogilvie did much the same thing better, but they came somewhat later.

I cannot remember that Father had any faults, except perhaps that he was somewhat mercenary. Or should I say 'acquisitive'? And is that a fault? It stemmed from his desire to give his family the advantages and security he had missed in his own youth. He reached out after great lands and great wealth and in his time held both. He would have done better to keep a firm grip on somewhat less. But that was not in his nature and who are we to criticise men like himself, his brother Uncle Michael, and Mother's brother Uncle John Costello, who rode through the mirage and found the rivers? . . .

It is a pity my uncle burned his father's verses, for the snippets that have come into my hands indicate that he had a ready flair for rhyme. Before the era of the more famous balladists rhyming had become the fashion of the bush and there was a wealth of folk-song among these Irish and Scottish Australians with their singing hearts and dancing feet. Fiddles, accordions, mouth-organs, flutes and gum-leaf bands accompanied the topical jingles with familiar tunes and sometimes original airs that were never set down. Grandfather's verses had titles like 'The Stockman's Sweetheart', 'When Duncan Rode the Winner', 'The Duffer's Luck' and 'The Drover's Song', the last being the only one that survives intact and which was no doubt inspired by his first, ill-fated expedition from Goulburn to the Barcoo.

The Drover's Song

Cheerily sings the drover
With his stock so fat and sleek
Up to the border and over
His fortune for to seek.

Merrily sings the drover
For with luck upon his side.
There'll be Mitchell grass and clover
And creeks ten miles wide.

Dismally sings the drover
For himself and his luck fell out
But still he rides on like a lover
Into the arms of the drought.

Mournfully sings the drover
As his stock die one by one.
Wild dogs and eagles hover
And bones turn white in the sun.

Wearily sighs the drover
As he lies him down on the plain
To sleep with his swag for a cover
Til the grass springs green again.

Eerily wails the drover
When the drought wind sweeps the sky
And men say 'Hear the plover!'
As he moves the ghost mob by.

Mick Skeahan, Poor Mary's eldest, then a boy of fourteen or fifteen, also composed trailing topical verses and songs. One, written later in his life, of which a single verse will serve, bespeaks the nostalgia of his generation for those horse-mad, enthusiastic days:

And where are the horses we took such delight in,
Old Sunshine, the reefer, that never would fall,
And Midnight, the rager, and Blantyre, the camp horse,
And the old chestnut Bally, the best of them all . . . ?
They have gone on the road down the River of Silence
They've crossed the long stage that we all have to cross:
They are going to stay on the Station of Silence,
Where Death is head-stockman and God is the Boss . . .

17

New Towns in the Wilderness

The years 1877 to 1879. Tragedy at Wathagurra. Mr Healy and his pupils are lost in the bush. The problem of education. Patsy Durack's increasing interests. The Costello family move out. Opal mining brings towns to the Cooper and Cobb and Co. comes west. Races at Windorah.

It was during one of Father Dunham's visits, when the family at Wathagurra was assembled at Mass, that the three-year-old Annie Amy Tully disappeared. Nobody, not even one of the blacks, had seen her go and when they found her little pannikin beside the creek they at once began dragging the waterhole.

Helpers, black and white, came over from Thylungra and Kyabra and for three days the search went on. Even Pumpkin, Willie and Scrammy Jimmy, notorious trackers though they were, could find no trace of footprints on that stony, windswept plain where the child had wandered in hopeless circles among the breakaways.

Young Michael, my father, riding with Pumpkin, found the little body at last lying in a gully with some bush flowers clutched in her hand as though she had died in sleep. They brought her to Thylungra and buried her with her baby brother Francis.

Father Dunham spoke of 'another angel in heaven' and of 'resignation to the will of God', but Sarah, acquainted with sorrow, keening in the tradition of her people, wanted no formal words of comfort.

'And who is any Englishman whatever to be telling an Irish mother how she must bear her cross? This is the fourth child He has taken from me, Father, and I shall thank Him in my own way and my own time but I shall have my grief out.'

Devoted as her brothers were to their robust pioneer priest, Sarah Tully never quite forgave him his English dislike of emotional display. Once when he rebuked some of his Irish parishioners for their hot-headedness she had turned on him in scorn.

'You may know something of our souls, Father, but it's little you know of our hearts.'

After the tragedy at Wathagurra, Grandmother had forbidden her children to go across the creek without Mr Healy or one of the blacks. The boys, bush-reared and quite capable of looking after themselves, resented the old tutor's forever trundling along behind, panting and perspiring, shouting for them to 'go no farther' and having no idea of his whereabouts. The two younger boys, John and Pat, enjoyed seeing how far they could lead him before he realised he was headed in the wrong direction. It was a joke they played once too often, for one afternoon, having been led for two miles out of his way, the old man grew irritable and obstinately refused to be put on the right track.

'D'ye think ye'll be knowing the way better than yer teacher! Come now, after me. Not another word!'

As evening drew in Grandmother sent old Cobby to call the wanderers home, but the native returned to say he had followed their tracks until after dark when they were still heading away from the house. Grandmother sent at once for her husband who was out after cattle with most of the station hands and despatched the young 'Colonial Experience' man McIvor to fetch her brother John from Kyabra.

Costello, the first to receive the news, galloped with his faithful tracker Scrammy Jimmy to Thylungra where fresh horses were ready saddled at the yard. Few bushmen had not at some time gone in search of a wanderer only to find him perished of thirst and they had no delusions about the difficulties of their task. Much of the country over the creek was hard and stony which made tracking difficult, while many of the gnamma holes that, according to the blacks, had held a steady level of water from time beyond memory, had gone dry during the last drought. When filled again by the rains they had quickly evaporated, probably because, since the coming of the white man, the natives had neglected the careful ritual of covering them.

Time and again Costello, McIvor and the natives, Jimmy and old Cobby, picked up the trail of the wanderers that sometimes crossed and recrossed their own steps in the manner of the hopelessly lost. When night fell again the searchers camped till dawn, followed the tracks for another day of increasing anxiety and camped again.

It was the following afternoon when Scrammy Jimmy stopped, put his ear to the ground and pointed confidently westward. They hurried towards a dry thicket from which rose the delirious tones of an Irish voice.

'Lost in the wild bush of Australee and related to the Duracks. Keep to the north-east, children! Keep to the north-east!'

The old man had stripped off all his clothes and was lying upon the ground exposed to the blistering heat. The two children were nowhere in sight but from marks upon the ground it was discovered that they had been lying nearby.

'Blackfella bin take'm away!' Scrammy Jimmy announced suddenly.

Having quickly put up a shade for the old tutor and left one of the natives to tend him, the search party hurried on to where the boys and a few blacks were seated in the shade beside a small concealed waterhole, enjoying a primitive meal of wild roots and wallaby.

The blacks explained how they had found the exhausted wanderers, had tried to carry all three to the waterhole, but the old man had fought them in terror and had been impossible to cope with.

The party returned to Thylungra with Mr Healy secured to a horse, still commanding at regular intervals: 'Keep to the north-east, children! Keep to the north-east!'

'Another hour and he'd have been finished,' John Costello said, giving over the demented old man to the care of his sister and her mother-in-law.

For a while it seemed Mr Healy could not survie the effects of his experience. His Irish voice, cracked and desperate, raved on night and day, while his blistered skin peeled off in great slabs and his eyesight, always poor, seemed quite gone. Slowly, with careful nursing they brought him round, but it was clear that his teaching days were over. A shadow of his former portly figure, he could no longer pretend to be other than an old man, hard of hearing and with failing sight, and sometimes he would cry like a child.

'Ah, but it's a cruel land, a cruel land, and what am I to be telling them at home in Ireland?'

It was realised then that he had misled his people about the position he held in Australia, indicating that the money he sent them, a good three-quarters of his modest salary, was a mere trifle. To ease the old man's mind Grandfather increased his wage and elevated him to the nominal position of bookkeeper.

Grandfather's boys had no regrets when it was realised that poor Mr Healy would never teach again. He had been a sore trial to them for three years although he could not have been quite impossible as a teacher. He had taught them to read, and instilled a certain respect for books. They had at least the rudiments of mathematics and already wrote a better hand than most children of the same age today. He had, moreover, so hammered in the prayers, litanies and Latin responses of their church that they would never forget a word of them. Thirty years later when my father met a priest travelling through the Northern Territory he surprised him by being able to serve Mass under a boab tree without the aid of a prayer book.

Their future education was a great worry to Grandfather and the often discussed project was again raised of sending them to St Patrick's College that had been established in Goulburn in 1875.

Poor Mary Skeahan had just then fought out the issue with her husband of sending her boy Patsy whose education had been so far neglected. Dinny saw no sense in it at all, but could hardly raise further objection when Grandfather undertook to pay the fees. Still, Grandmother was heartbroken at the thought of parting with her sons. She argued, practically enough, that if Grandfather wished them to follow in his footsteps he should engage another tutor and begin to train them in the many parts a station man was called upon to fill. People were already complaining of a shortage of labour outback, for although there were so many men on the Thylungra books, they were a restless crowd of fellows, always coming and going and changing about from station to station, while it was almost impossible to entice good tradesmen so far into the wilderness. Thylungra and Kyabra, having looked after their Aborigines, were better off than many places but few children were being born in the station camps since the shattering of the tribes and it seemed that there would be few to take the place of the faithful first retainers.

'How would you have got on,' Grandmother asked her husband, 'if you had not been able to turn your hand to anything—stockwork, building, blacksmithing, saddling, gardening and the rest? Think of all the things you could do when you were their age.'

'That is not to be compared,' Grandfather said. 'When I was their age it was a great struggle to keep alive from day to day, but how often I longed for the chance to read a book when I must be milking the cows or cutting the turf or digging in the fields. I would not wish that situation on my family.'

He took the optimistic attitude that the labour situation must improve with closer settlement and the establishment of outback towns and held that it was more important to educate his growing sons to the station of this new landed aristocracy. But for a while Grandmother, backed by her female relatives, had her way. No doubt that was one of the occasions when Grandfather wished the women to the bottom of the sea.

The elder Miss Curtis, who had been engaged to teach pot hooks and pretty manners to the two little girls, was at last put in charge of the schoolroom. Unfortunately for the reserved, rather prim girl, her pupils

John and Pat soon detected her romantic attachment to young Ivor McIvor and they proceeded, with the mischievous cunning common to small boys, to wreck her chances. Anonymous letters and traps calculated to make the girl look ridiculous in the eyes of her hero eventually reduced her to a state of near breakdown. Relations with the Curtis family became somewhat strained and they decided at last to give up the idea of cattle raising on Kyabra Creek. They packed up and moved to Roma where Mrs Curtis and her girls opened a small school while Mr Curtis and the boys worked on surrounding stations.

A man of reputedly aristocratic lineage, who received occasional remittances from his family in England and had come to Thylungra as bookkeeper, next took over the task of tutor. Since he was seldom quite sober, however, and regarded his task of instructing the young as an amusing turn of fate, his regime suited the boys all too well.

Grandfather, now thoroughly preoccupied by the increasing tempo of his life, unwilling to start another argument with the women, let the situation run on. By '77, along with his two brothers and John Costello, Grandfather realised that he was now well on the way to becoming a rich man but far from relaxing he became more active than ever before. He was now seldom at Thylungra for more than a few days at a time, for his interests were becoming more widely spread every month. It seemed that as his bank balance increased so also did his sense of insecurity, for he knew well enough that money amassed through the sale of land and stock could be as quickly lost in a succession of bad seasons. His aim was to secure himself and his family against disaster by having enough outside interests to keep his Cooper properties going over a drought period.

He had no thought of sale at this time, for he realised well enough that there could hardly have been any richer fattening country in the world than those Cooper channels in good seasons. Still, he was mindful always that the land was not freehold. They had no more than a tentative right to the grass on which they pastured their herds and in law had no right to the soil or any minerals it might yield and even to plant a kitchen garden, unless within the bounds of a limited 'homestead area grant', could have been held illegal. It was a clause of the Pastoral Leases Act of '69 that they must be prepared to give up the land on demand for cultivation or closer settlement and certain small resumptions were already going on. Although these did not much trouble the settlers since they were compensated for improvements and pioneering work, there was no guarantee that government demands might not at any time force them out of the country. They were not then to realise that the hardships and isolation were a certain security in themselves, that none but an occasional voice crying in the wilderness would contest these million-acre holdings or prove over-anxious to try them out for 'other purposes'. In the seventies they did not yet speak of their pastoral empires as though they were empires indeed. ' "Cattle kings" you call us,' Grandfather wrote in answer to a newspaper correspondent complaining of the big landholders. 'Then we are kings in grass castles that may be blown away upon a puff of wind.'

And so he rode on and on, hungry for land and more land and the security that seemed always just out of reach. Land hunger was a disease of his time, leading many besides himself on pastoral trails that ran out as often as not into sand and ruin. Will Landsborough, Nat Buchanan, John Costello, the brothers Prout, Patsy Durack ... riding, riding ... Cattle, horses, country ...

'And now,' Pat Tully told Grandfather one day, 'Sarah says we must all be going in for sheep.'

'Nonsense,' said Grandfather. 'Haven't we told her already the country's not suitable for woolgrowing? It'll do no good out here.'

'But Sarah says it will,' Pat sighed. 'She declares she knows it in her bones that the Cooper will grow wool fit for to make a garment for the Pope.'

'Take no notice of the poor girl,' Grandfather advised him. 'What would a woman be knowing about such things?'

'It's too late,' Pat told him. 'We've got five hundred head on the road out now. They'll be here in a week or two.'

Grandfather left him in disgust with a 'Glory be to God' and a vow that no sheep, other than a few for home consumption, would ever sully Thylungra soil. But how many today, knowing Thylungra as the most valuable property in the Commonwealth, shearing 100,000 sheep a year, have ever heard that it started as a cattle run? And who, outside her family, knows that it was an Irish woman, sensing the future 'in her bones', who nagged the first sheep to the Cooper Plains and lived to realise her ambition of presenting His Holiness with a garment made from Cooper wool?

Grandfather had scarcely recovered from this shock when John Costello rode to Thylungra with another.

'Patsy,' he said, 'we're getting out.'

Grandfather turned on him in surprise.

'What's that ye're telling me?'

'Peppin and Webber have offered me £60,000 for Kyabra and I'm going while the going's good.'

'And what would ye mean by that?'

'We've had a wonderful run of good luck but it can't last forever. Besides, I've promised the family to take them to the coast. Here's young Mary, the eldest, ten years old and never set eyes on the sea.'

'But you couldn't be going 'til after the wet!' Grandfather exclaimed.

'Why not?' Costello asked. 'I've made up my mind and it's no use hanging around. We're getting out next week.'

'And what has poor mother to say to it?' Grandmother asked.

'She's delighted of course,' Costello said. 'You know she never liked this country, but she'll be out every year to visit you, you can bet your life on that.'

John Costello had now disposed of all his Cooper properties except a small block adjoining Thylungra which Grandfather immediately purchased from him for £2,000.

'And what does that make ye worth now, John?' he asked. 'Just as a point of interest?'

Costello and Grandfather took delight in ragging each other about their prosperity. The well-worn jokes cropped up whenever there was a collection being raised, maybe for a sporting trophy or the convent at Bourke in which they all took a special interest or for one of Father Dunham's priestly schemes.

'Ye're the rich man of the family now, John. We'll be expecting to see your name right at the top of the list.'

John Costello would counter: 'What! After the deal you made with Jimmy Tyson last week?'

Costello was undoubtedly richer than the Durack brothers at this time but he never conceded the point.

'There's just enough put by to retire on, Patsy. I'll get a little property where I can raise some chooks and maybe a few stud bulls and a horse or two and stay at home with my family. You'll do the same if you've got any sense.'

'I've been thinking of it,' Grandfather admitted, 'but I'll never sell out of the Cooper. I'd always be coming back to Thylungra once or twice a year and the boys will be carrying on out here.'

'You can afford to set them up in more dependable country now,' Costello argued.

'You tell me where I'll find it, and I might consider it,' Grandfather said. 'But what about the poor blacks—old Cobby and Pumpkin? They'd be breaking their hearts.'

'Take them with you,' Costello said. 'I'm bringing any of mine who want to come along.'

Another point of rivalry between the two men was their understanding of Aboriginal psychology.

'I'd never take a blackfellow away from his country,' Grandfather said. 'They get too homesick.'

'Nonsense! What about old Cobby and the rest of them we brought from Waroo Springs and the Bulloo?'

But Grandfather would not be talked down.

'That's nothing but a step and a jump. I tell ye no inland born black will ever settle on the coast.'

Still Costello maintained, rightly enough as it proved, that his old retainers would grieve less for their country than for the family they had served and loved, and when they moved out of Kyabra a week or so later old one-eyed Jimmy, his gin Susan and two or three others went along with them.

The families from Thylungra and Wathagurra rode out to see them on their way with their waggons piled high, Great-grandmother Costello and her umbrella beside her old husband in the self-same buggy they had driven over the long miles from Goulburn to the 'back o' Bourke' twelve years before. Although there was sadness at the parting of these people who had faced the unknown together and depended so much upon each other in their empty land the leave-taking had its brighter side. After all the years of struggle and uncertainty, of hardships and sorrows shared, of building and expanding and watching the tide of settlement flow out across the Cooper to the Diamantina and beyond, Costello was getting out as a rich and successful man and there was nothing to prevent his relatives doing likewise when they pleased.

'But good and all as it is to be going,' Great-grandmother Costello said, 'how like John to be moving us in the mud and slosh. I tell ye it's rivers we'll be swimming before we get to Brisbane and poor old Father with his rheumatism.'

She was right about the rivers, for rains that meant fat cheques for the settlers made hard travelling for wayfarers. They wallowed and bogged through glassy heat haze over those 350 watery miles to Roma, camping for days, plagued by mosquitoes and sandflies, waiting for flooded channels to subside.

Near Roma they met Father Dunham, coming out by buggy to his congregation in the west. The priest showered the family with blessings and good advice, celebrated Mass under a tree by the roadside and before parting handed over the key of his presbytery in Roma.

This was haven for the weary and weather-beaten family. Great-grandmother Costello sank into an easy chair on the latticed verandah with a sigh of profound relief.

'We'll go no farther, John,' she said firmly, 'until ye've a home for us to come to. Your father and I can count every bone in our old bodies for the ache of it.'

Costello rode on alone a further 250 miles to Rockhampton where he found that a lovely coastal property named Cawarral was for sale. He purchased it on sight, with its 4,000 splendid shorthorn cattle, hundreds of wellbred horses of racing stock and rambling old homestead built up, Queensland fashion, on high blocks and topped with a shingled roof. There were outhouses, training stables, paddocks, orchard and flower garden and—most wonderful of all—several miles of ocean frontage!

On the way south to Brisbane to finalise his purchase he was met at Gladstone by his old friend Pat Drynan, early settler of the Wilson River, who told him that his coastal property, Annondale, was also for sale. Elated no doubt with the heady smell of the sea air, Costello clinched the purchase of this estate as well before rejoining his family.

Meanwhile, in Roma, the Costello children had their first experience of formal schooling at the little academy run by Mrs Curtis and her daughters. On Costello's return Curtis gladly accepted the position of manager of Annondale and the two families joined in an excited procession to Rockhampton.

Their going had brought a wave of restlessness to Cooper's Creek.

'Our children have never seen the ocean either.' Stumpy Michael's wife reminded him. 'You know how I love the sea and not in the whole of Australia could you have found a place farther away from it.'

Little wonder that Kate Durack, a woman of strong character and independent views, should often have chafed at the family habit of living more or less on each other's doorsteps and making mutual decisions, which nearly always meant doing as Grandfather suggested. In all their married life her husband had rarely been home for more than three weeks at a time and was frequently away with cattle or supply teams for over six months on end.

'Patsy says cattle are bringing seven to eight pounds in Adelaide and only fetching five in New South Wales, so we shall have to poke them along down.'

'But that's over a thousand miles again—and another thousand back! Can't you go the shorter route?'

'It doesn't pay unless they've had an exceptional season down the Birdsville track. They'll lose no condition at all this year down the Darling-Murray route. Well turn them in rolling fat like they leave the Cooper.'

'What about Big Johnnie and the others? Can't this mob wait 'til they get back from Goulburn?'

'No chance. They'll have to start straight back to the Darling with those horses for Sidney Kidman.'

'Tom Kilfoyle?'

'He'll be taking the teams to Bourke. Patsy and brother Jerry will be fetching the store cows across from Roma and Dinny Skeahan's given up everything for his opal show at Mount Margaret.'

'You're nothing but a slave,' Kate said. 'They called you "Handsome Michael" a few years ago but they'd hardly know you for the same man now, and still only thirty-two! Isn't it time we got away—lived our own lives? Surely we can afford it now?'

'Soon, Kate,' her husband promised. 'We've all been thinking for some time of getting into city property, settling down nearer the coast, but we want to get a few more stations going out here first. The west is going ahead fast now and we'll get boom prices for Cooper properties in a year or two. We've got to be thinking of the future, my dear.'

'The future,' Kate sighed. 'You Duracks talk of nothing but the future and life slips by.'

After '77 with the sudden rush of opalers to the Grey Range the country opened at an exciting pace. Cobb and Co. with 6,000 horses on the roads in three States, following the rivers and the prospectors, quickly swung their coaches west from Charleville with miners for the opal fields and speculators to view the land. Coaching stages were proclaimed town sites before names were found for them—'The Blackwater, Gumbard Junction', 'The crossing of the Mt Margaret and Kyabra roads'.

By the middle of '78 the storekeepers had come out from Roma and Charleville, the shanties had gone up and the dusty little centres of Adavale and Eromanga—the most inland town on the continent—were there to stay. 'Civilisation' was sweeping west and south into the forgotten corner—Thargomindah, Eulo, Hungerford, Tinnenburra, Barringun and back to the Darling at Bourke, the busy coaches forging intricate chains of communication in the wilderness, linking the rivers, bogging through the sandy channels, flashing and bumping over the big grass plains, conquering the loneliness. Their drivers were personalities of the bush roads, men of experience and resource, proud of their spanking turnouts with from six to twenty-two horses in a team, coaches brilliant red, jingling harness polished bright, coloured saddlecloths, rosettes on the ear buckles.

'It's a wonder someone hasn't put up a pub at Adavale,' it was remarked at Thylungra a month or two after the coaches came through.

'I've been thinking the same way meself,' said Grandfather, and a few days later was pacing out the fairly generous proportions of his 'Hotel

Imperial' which was open to business, complete with billiard table brought out express from Brisbane, within two months.

By the end of '78 the opalers were out among the stony ridges on Galway Downs. A man named Jack Cummings who had been prospecting for some time without much success put up a shanty pub for the miners who would ask the coach driver to take them out to 'old Jack in the rocks'. So the first licensed premises on Cooper's Creek, that was to be the last bid to elusive fortune for Dinny and Poor Mary Skeahan, acquired its name.

The opal fever spread west across the channels and out to Canterbury—'The J. C.' A hawker, ploughing west with goods in his waggon for the Diamantina settlers, had struck the heavy wet of '78 and made for the highest land in sight just as the Cooper flood roared down, spreading its watery mantle over the countryside. A party of drovers had taken refuge in the same spot and some blacks had pitched their wet weather wurlies there among the stones and spinifex.

'Blackfella all day come here flood time,' they said. 'This one Windorah—high, stony place.'

When all the rum on the waggon was gone there was nothing to do but fossick for potch and colour until the flood went down. The whisper of opal spread as the waters shrank back into the channels, the prospectors pushed out with Cobb and Co. and the teamster's waggon became a store.

When Costello had first taken up the site in the early seventies he had called it 'Stoney Point', but the native name Windorah was now officially bestowed.

Grandfather, elated to hear of a town and some 200 opalers less than seventy miles north-west of Thylungra, a mere thirty from Galway Downs, rode out to inspect. Encouraged by the success of his Imperial at Adavale he had The Western Star run up at Windorah within six weeks. McPhellamy, the local butcher, put up the Cosmopolitan next door and business was brisk. Both hotels had *adobe* walls made from hard baked mud and spinifex with antbed floors and roofs of scrub thatch but on Cooper's Creek in '79 they were shining examples of progress and confidence.

Grandfather and Galway Jerry organised a racing carnival to follow through from the annual meeting at Thargomindah, on to a picnic meet at Galway Downs and out to the new town. Bough shelters and stalls were hustled up, the horses began to arrive and the crowd flocked in.

Teamsters' outfits became 'bumboats' overnight, hurriedly stocked with flash shirts, riding pants and hard liquor. Some traders charged exorbitant prices for the clothing and gave the 'snake juice' in with the purchases to encourage further spending. One enterprising hawker brought bolts of material for the ladies, heavy silks and tarlatans, dainty muslins protected by canvas covers from the insidious dust. The 'city prices' he advertised were a fiction, but his stock was ridiculously cheap on present-day standards and it had quality. A heavy grey silk, made up by Grandmother for her cousin Fanny Hammond—a creation of bouffant skirts and ruffles of fine Irish lace—is treasured still by Fanny's grandchildren on Mayfield, their Cooper's Creek property.

When the first meeting started, the pioneers delightedly counted 400 heads in a land where a few years before they would have been hard put to make a score. Events were quickly organised, handicaps, hurdles, ladies' bracelets, blacks' races, donkey races and the jealously contested Cooper Cup. Sarah Tully on her Arab stallion won the ladies' race and Grandfather's grey Panic carried off the bracelet for his wife.

There were inevitably some fights and split heads and as no police constable was present Grandfather and John Costello, both JP's, assumed magisterial duties. When Ned Hammond and Dinny Skeahan took to one another with the stirrup irons it was Grandfather who finally intervened, laying Dinny clean out 'to save further bloodshed'.

It seems to have been a poor show for Dinny all round. His horse ran a close finish with one of Horrigan's and after some discussion Father Dunham, who had nicely timed his annual visit with the Cooper carnival, gave a decision in favour of Horrigan. Dinny, primed with hard liquor and no great respecter of persons at the best of times, challenged the priest to a fight, whereupon Father Dunham, to the surprise and joy of the community, not only took on the hot-headed Irishman but promptly laid him flat. Dinny, scrambling from the dust amid the jeers of the onlookers, came adroitly to his own defence:

'And what sort of a man is it atall would be hitting a praist?'

'Fifty yards around a post', a favourite novelty race, had man on horseback matched against man on foot, the latter on the inside, racing around the post and back to the starting point. A champion could run one hundred yards in eleven seconds and leave the horseman looking foolish, but the average good runner was hard put to beat a trained camp horse.

Groups under every shade entered into noisy games of two-up, mumble-the-peg and stag-knife. Agile stockmen, the braver for rum, tap danced, turned catherine wheels and walked on their hands. At night they thronged the gambling tables lit with slush lamps down the centre of the town. Accordions wheezed with flute and mouth organ and irrepressible bush songsters rendered numbers one to one hundred from *The Australian Melodist*, with a leavening of Moody and Sankey hymns. Ladies picked up their skirts and joined in Scottish and Irish reels on the dusty street but any man whose tongue ran loose with grog was thrown into the 'dog house' overnight.

After five days the crowd gathered for parting words and reconciliations. The winners shouted for the crowd in a jostle of buggies and loaded packs, men leaning from horseback to shake hands and distraught parents searching for straying offspring. Most of the stockmen had empty pockets and sore heads and were content enough to return to work and save for the next meeting. Grandfather, upbraiding them for their spendthrift ways, knew that they would settle to the job better for being broke.

18

ONE THOUSAND MILES TO SCHOOL

The years 1879 to 1880. Opal mania on the Cooper. Patsy Durack's many journeys. He takes his sons to college in Goulburn. Reunion with the Costellos and Solomon Emanuel. College life for the bush boys. Letters from Patsy Durack to his sons concerning his return to Thylungra.

Grandfather's hope that the new townships would bring more labour to the Cooper stations was not realised, for opal no less than gold brought restlessness to the countryside. Even the blacks were smitten with the opal fever and walked with eyes on the ground looking out for the 'pretty fulla stone' for which the unpredictable white man was willing to pay in tea, sugar and tobacco. Grandfather and his brothers, however, though readily excited by any other form of mining, were little interested in opal fossicking. Although they did not share their sister Sarah's superstitious dread of these multi-coloured gems of their arid land, they came, as their good men drifted off and undesirables flocked in, to see the opaling as a great nuisance.

'If this is the population we are getting,' Grandfather fumed, 'we could have done better without it.'

'But you do all right with those pubs of yours,' people reminded him.

Grandfather liked to think of his hotels as 'public amenities' and resented such references to their flourishing bar trade.

'To hell with the pubs and the good-for-nothings that hang around them,' he fumed. 'I'll burn them down!'

But he continued to tot up the returns along with his other assets.

In '79, from an estimated 10,000 cattle on Thylungra and 2,000 on Galway Downs, Durack brothers marketed 2,000 head and netted £12,000. Horses brought in £6,000 and land rights £4,500. 'Incidentals', which included the hotels at Adavale and Windorah and now a third in Thargomindah, a butchery business and three houses in Roma, returned a further £4,500. Grandfather's cheque butts are a permanent record of the travelling required to keep up with his ever-expanding interests.

Jan. 3rd '79 Men on building at Adavale, £700.
Jan. 18th '79 Paid land rentals in Charleville, £2000.
Jan. 30th " Paid in Roma for houses repairs, £200.
Feb. 7th " For swap of horses or road Thargomindah, one saddle (old) thrown in, £8.0.0.
Feb. 16th " Paid for bulls bought in Thargomindah, less price of horse brought from me – £90.
Feb. 30th " For the sheep I got in Bourke – £500.

From this it will be seen that he covered well over a thousand miles by buggy in this fairly typical two months. It will also be noted that he had soon changed his mind about the sheep. The Tullys had done well with their wool clip and classers had expressed enthusiasm for its quality.

'So it seems we must have the silly cratures,' Grandfatler admitted reluctantly.

Cattle, horses, country, hotels, butchery, houses—and now wool.

Fond of travelling though he was, Grandfather missed the company of his wife and family and sometimes on shorter trips persuaded Grandmother to accompany him with the youngest boy Jerry—or 'Sunny' as they called him then. On one of these many journeys between Adavale and Thylungra Grandmother had one day become alarmed at the illness and pallor of the child in her arms.

'Stop the buggy, Patsy,' she said. 'I think the boy has fainted with the heat.'

Grandfather pulled in the horses, protesting as always in moments of anxiety. 'Why should a child faint? I've never beard of it.'

When they could find no stir of life in the limp little body they held a mirror to his lips.

'We have lost him,' Grandmother said, incredulously.

Grandfather whipped up the horses and galloped into Thylungra while his wife sat, holding her baby, numb with grief and shock.

The family, joyfully rushing to meet them as usual, stopped short at sight of the two gaunt, stricken faces.

'Little Sunny has gone,' Grandfather said as his mother took the baby and carried him to the house. It was in moments such as this that the gentle old Irish woman assumed command. Wordlessly she laid him on the verandah flags, took down the water bag and dashed the contents over the lifeless body.

'Dead, is he?' she said, gazing down at him. 'Then what is he doing with his eyes open and the smile of an angel for his Grandmama?'

Later there would be 'natural' explanations of the child's coma but for years it remained the miracle of Cooper's Creek with each member of the community attributing it to the intervention of his or her particular patron saint.

There was much talk now of finding 'nice little properties' closer to civilisation. Stumpy Michael had promised his wife that he would get her to the sea before the end of '79 and was constantly enquiring about holdings fairly near the coast. Grandfather agreed with Kate that the time had come when they might all think of establishing a base near the city. It was only Grandmother who now demurred.

'Not that I was for coming here in the first place, Patsy,' she said in her quiet, sensible way, 'but we have made a home at Thylungra. What would become of the place if we were not here to look after it?'

'Nowadays, with the coaches running,' Grandfather argued, 'I can be out two or three times a year until the boys are old enough to take over. We'll get a good couple to look after the place.'

Grandmother, after much experience, was sceptical of 'good couples'.

'Still,' Grandfather said, 'the place is well established now, everything running smoothly and comfortably and the blacks well trained. A woman would have to do very little and any capable man could attend the stockwork.'

Galway Jerry who had not long since returned with his gay, red-haired bride, Fanny Neal, was all for putting on a manager as soon as possible and starting a racing stud near his wife's people in the Ipswich district.

'But with three of you out of the country and labour already so short—' Grandmother ventured.

'This opal mania will soon pass and all the boys will be wanting station jobs again,' her husband assured her.

In fact there were already signs of waning enthusiasm among the opalers, for it was hard, tedious work digging shafts and cracking stones among the sunbaked rocks. Unlike gold mining there was no chance of bringing machinery to work on the opal fields. It remained a pick and shovel game since blasting shattered the gems more readily than the surrounding rock. The family regarded it as a hopeful sign when Dinny Skeahan gave up his claim at Eromanga, returned to contract work at Thylungra and displayed fresh enthusiasm for the Rasmore property which Grandfather, weary of paying fines for his brother-in-law's noncompliance with the terms of occupation, had divided between Pat Tully and Big Johnnie Durack.

'It's an outrage,' Dinny stormed. 'The block belongs to me and only wait until all the country hears how the great Patsy Durack has robbed his own poor sister of her heritage.'

'And when have ye ever paid the rent or done a hand's turn to improve the place?' Grandfather demanded, but for his sister's sake he agreed that Dinny should once more have a share in it.

How this complicated arrangement worked out is a mystery, but for at least four years from this time Pat Tully and Big Johnnie continued to agist stock and pay part rent on Rasmore while Grandfather paid the remaining third for the Skeahans. Dinny at last built a shack there that was home of a sort for Poor Mary and her boys.

By '79 Grandfather realised that he must take a firm stand about the education of his two elder sons and booked them in at St Patrick's College, Goulburn, for the following year. My father was then fourteen and his brother John twelve and Grandfather was determined they should have three years at boarding school. Grandmother was broken-hearted at the prospect of so long a separation, for unless the family moved to Brisbane meanwhile there would be no chance of their returning home for holidays.

'You can go down with me to visit them whenever you like,' Grandfather consoled her.

'And leave the place for four or five months at a time! Whatever would become of it?'

'There's always Kate here and Grandma to look after things and the younger ones. Why not come down now and see them settled in?'

A letter from Great-grandmother Costello in Goulburn finally decided her to go. The old couple had gone south from Cawarral some time before to visit their friends and relatives and in Goulburn Great-grandfather had been taken seriously ill. John Costello and his wife, already on their way to see him, wrote inviting Kate Durack to Cawarral with her children to enjoy a seaside holiday and also keep an eye on their own family. Kate was delighted and her husband, soon to leave again with a mob of cattle for South Australia, heaved a sigh of relief, but a new problem of what to do with Great-grandma Bridget and the other children had now to be faced. When she caught the coach at last from Adavale, poor Kate had with her not only her own three and her niece Delia Scanlan, but Grandmother's three youngest, Mary, Birdie and little Sunny as well. The third boy, Pat, with Great-grandmother Bridget and old Mr Healy, went off to stay with Galway Jerry and his young wife at Galway Downs while a newly-appointed 'married couple', the aristocratic bookkeeper, three white stockmen and the blacks carried on at Thylungra.

Grandfather's spirits rode high at the prospect of going with his wife and sons on a journey they had not taken together since they came north in '67.

'It's not many boys will be able to say they've ridden one thousand miles to school,' he enthused. 'Ye'll be heroes to them all down there.'

The party set out early in November, the two boys and the native stockman Willie riding with the fifteen packs and buggy changes while Grandmother and Grandfather rode in the station vehicle. Of all the journeys in his hard travelling life, none stood out more clearly for my father than this when he and his brother saw the great world south of the border for the first time in their memory. The country had been dry when they crossed the Bulloo, Paroo and Warrego but as they neared the little town of Barringun the wet set in and they were warned of flooded rivers further south.

'But we'll get there in time for the opening day if we've got to swim,' their father said. And swim they did.

They found the Culgoa in roaring flood, sweeping down to the Darling with the driftwood and grass of Queensland prairies. The boys waited with their mother on the insect-ridden banks while their father and Willie forced the horses into the turgid water and each clinging to a horse's tail, had been swept by the current, to come out on the opposite bank over a niile downstream.

A rough and ready pontoon bridge was made out of casks supplied from the nearest station. This was attached to an overhead rope slung across the river, and packs, buggy and family mounted and hauled over. It had been splendid fun especially when Grandfather, trying to secure the buggy, had toppled off and narrowly escaped drowning by clutching a rope flung by the resourceful Willie.

The going had been tough to Brewarrina at the Bogan head, horses plodding through shaking quagmire and the buggy bogging all the way. The straining horses, sunk deep in mud and maddened by sandflies, kicked and plunged until their harness broke. Sometimes smoke fires were lit to ward off the stinging pests, but it was not always easy to find timber on the big, bare plains and when they did it was frequently sodden with rain. It had not been such fun riding in wet clothes through steaming heat. The boys' bites itched and swelled and their mother had cried at the sight of their bung eyes. But when they reached Ridge's Monagee Station everything had been wonderful. The owners were old friends of the family and had welcomed them lavishly, introducing the bush boys to the wonders of their orchard—pink bloom of peaches, gold of apricots, hanging bunches of purple grapes—such marvels as they had never seen before. They had gone on their way with brimming baskets.

From here the course had lain through more settled districts, down the Macquarie and on to Dubbo, their mother exclaiming all the way at changes and progress since her northward journey twelve years before. This had been a crowded and exciting stage on which they talked with fellow travellers, stockmen with cattle and packs, station people in buggies or waggonettes, sometimes a dashing Cobb and Co. outfit clopping and jingling on its way. When Grandmother grew conscious that her bonnets were outmoded and her dresses shrieked of the backblocks, her husband laughed and promised her the finest clothes in all Goulburn.

At Molong they put up at the Court Hotel, the lease of which had been taken on a year before by Darby's widow, Margaret, and her bevy of much courted daughters. The bewildered Irish girl who had arrived in the colony with her husband and sea-born baby thirty years before was now a buxom capable soul with a jolly, hospitable manner combined with a keen business sense. The hotel was thriving under her direction and with some help from her sons in Queensland her younger children were already receiving the best education available.

'A pity the others had not the same advantages,' she said.

Grandfather who felt strongly himself on the subject of education was sincere enough in his consoling words:

'But they will do well, my dear. They take their place among the best stockmen in Queensland and for looks there are none can hold a candle to them.'

Travelling down the Lachlan Grandfather had been in great form, telling tales of the gold rush days and the mad rides after brumby horses and wild cattle in his youth. To his boys the sight of the ever-changing landscape was a wonder and delight. Having known nothing higher than the red sandhills of the Cooper or the eroded summits of the Grey Range it seemed to them there could be no higher mountains in the world than the Abercrombies where their horses slipped and trembled on steep declines and the buggy made perilous descent with logs hitched on behind.

Then at last the roofs of Goulburn—the big town, all the bewildering bustle of metropolis and the excited embraces of a horde of relatives and family friends. There awaiting them were Great-grandmother Costello, her son John, his wife and the four children they were leaving at school in Goulburn. Old Mr Costello had died while Grandmother was on the road but her brother had been in time to see him before the end and to register his last wish that they should on no account dispose of their old home, Tea-tree Station, near Grabben Gullen, now in the hands of tenants.

Patrick Durack, about 1880.

'Great-grandmother Bridget' (Mrs Michael Durack) with her grand-daughter Mary Anne Bennet.

'Great-grandmother Costello' (Mrs Michael Costello).

Thylungra homestead, built of mud-brick by Patsy Durack in 1868. The first roof was thatched.

Outer buildings at Thylungra station.

The Durack boys, John (left) and Michael, on their arrival in Goulburn to attend St Patrick's College.

Father Dunham, pioneer priest in Western Queensland.

John Costello (Grandmother's brother), brother-in-law of Patsy Durack and Queensland pioneer.

Tom Kilfoyle, member of both the exploratory expedition and the overland droving trek.

Sydney Emanuel, son of Solomon Emanuel of Goulburn and a member of Stumpy Michael's pioneering expedition.

Big Johnnie Durack, son of Darby and a member of the overland party.

Patrick Durack (back, left) with his brothers, Stumpy Michael (back, right) and 'Galway Jerry' (front, right), and his cousin Long Michael.

Mustering cattle at Argyle Station.

Cattle drinking at the river.

Photographs by A. J. Campbell

Michael Joseph Durack ('Long Michael'), third of Darby Durack's eight sons.

Jerry Brice Durack, Darby Durack's fifth son.

Argyle Station homestead

Ivanhoe Station homestead

Patsy Durack's sons (left to right): Patrick, John, Jerry (later known as Dermot) and Michael.

Patrick Durack ('Black Pat'), also known as 'Mantineau Pat' after the land he temporarily held.

Crossing a creek by buggy.

'Old Pumpkin', member of the Boontamurra tribe. Photographed on Argyle Station.

Mary Durack Davidson (Mrs James Davidson)

Bridget 'Birdie' Durack

Patsy Durack's favourite sister, Sarah.

Anne Durack (Mrs John Redgrave)

Camels carting corrugated iron from Wyndham to outlying stations.

Camel team, East Kimberley, c. 1920.

Horse teams leaving Wyndham for outlying stations. The Wyndham Hotel is in the background. The Connor, Doherty and Durack store is on the right.

Grandfather Patsy towards the end of his life.

'Ye may be glad of it yet, son,' he said, 'though a thousand acres is small indeed to ye now.'

So the devoted old man who, when nearly seventy, had so cheerfully faced a new life with his children slipped peacefully away at the age of eighty-three.

'There's nothing left in life for me now,' his wife mourned. 'Ye'll see how soon I shall be following him to the grave.'

'Stuff and nonsense,' Grandfather told her. 'I'll guarantee you'll see the rest of us out.'

He spoke more truly than he realised, for when the news of his death reached Goulburn in '98 his mother-in-law, over ninety years old, demanded that the remains of the man with whom she had never exchanged a cross word be sent to rest where they 'rightly belonged'.

John Costello spoke enthusiastically of his Rockhampton property.

'A lovely home for us,' he enthused, 'especially Mary and the children.'

'And how much will they be seeing of ye,' his mother demanded, 'when after all yere fine talk of getting into the settled areas they tell me ye have now taken up another Godforsaken place out west?'

'It's a beautiful property,' her son said, and proceeded with a glowing account of this tract of virgin and unstocked country somewhere on the unsurveyed boundary between Queensland and the Territory, still part of the colony of South Australia. A good thousand miles west of his Rockhampton station, the Lake Nash lease had been taken up by a man named Frank Scarr who had given Costello first option of its purchase.

'And why would he not be wanting it himself if it's all that he tells ye?' his mother asked.

'Scarr went out to explore the country—not to settle. He's moved on since into the centre to God knows where,' Costello reasoned.

'So ye'll soon be out to have a look at it?' Grandfather asked.

'I've bought it already,' Costello said. 'Cash down, sight unseen. I'll ride out and mark a boundary when I get back and bring the stock on later in the year.'

'You must be letting me know more of the country out that way,' Grandfather said wistfully.

Great-grandmother Costello left them in disgust:

'It's the mad craving on them for the land like the poor fellows that are possessed of the gold or the drink.'

As always on his visits to Goulburn, Grandfather visited the Emanuels. Samuel Emanuel had died in 1868 and his son, now a member of parliament, was running the business.

'They tell me John Costello and the Duracks are rich men now, Patsy,' Solomon Emanuel beamed, 'on the way to your first half million if reports are to be believed.'

'They exaggerate of course,' Grandfather said. 'We have done well enough since the first hard years but we need some reliable city property behind us for security.'

He expanded to his friend on the progress and prosperity of Queensland since confidence was restored with the discovery of gold. Brisbane had gone ahead by leaps and bounds during the past ten years, the little weatherboard bush-style houses and buildings pulled down to be supplanted by fine new places of stone, brick or well-seasoned timber. That the colony was still existing largely on the 'golden stream' of outside capital was of little concern to Grandfather, for the faith seemed well justified in the prosperity of her cattle, wool and sugar and further boosted by new gold strikes. Investment companies from Victoria and New South Wales were now eager to compete with the banks in extension of credit on overseas finance and land was booming. Every day columns of the *Brisbane Courier* were devoted to the advertisement of land sales, many with the added enticement of 'champagne lunches', while the fantastic prices obtained for city blocks were quoted as further proof of progress.

Emanuel was well in touch with the Queensland boom.

'They have a fine aquarium in Brisbane, I hear,' he said.

'I had not yet heard of it,' Grandfather said.

Emanuel smiled.

'A great pool for little fish and big land sharks. I would go carefully if I were you.'

Grandfather was surprised.

'And was it not yere own father first taught a timid Irish boy to tread more boldly in the world, telling me in this very room that credit properly used was a good friend?'

Emanuel nodded. 'And so is fire.'

St Pat's College, still austerely new, sent a chill of loneliness through the two young Queenslanders who stood about, awkwardly dangling bowler hats, in suits and matching waistcoats over-large to allow for growth. Here time was to be measured by clocks and clanging bells, their hours marshalled into precise compartments, no longer to ramble through warm, carefree days with Mr Healy as eager as they to see the shadow at the door. Their father had said it would be three years before they could go home again, even for a holiday, but tears must wait until 'lights out' in the big dormitory.

'What's it like here?' they asked their cousin, Patsy Skeahan.

'Like hell,' they were told, 'but you get used to it.'

The Reverend Dr Gallagher, as plain as his revered Socrates and seeming to his pupils incredibly old at thirty-two, regarded the newcomers quizzically.

'It will be a fine task now, plumbing the depths of your ignorance.'

He found the depths no doubt profound, but he discovered also two eagerly receptive minds and he warmed to the task of unfolding for them the mysteries of syntax, mathematics, Latin and Greek.

Many years later my Uncle John wrote in memory of this scholarly man:

> He was a born teacher, a most profound and erudite scholar . . . His influence on the boys of his time was wonderful and years after his exhortations were recalled. He was a great believer in 'Do what you are doing', and his favourite motto was 'Age Quod Agis'. There was a 'sursum corda' in his Excelsiors, his 'man to know thyself', and his never forgotten slogans. He kindled from the lamp of his own enthusiasm a lasting love for classical literature and opened windows upon mountain peaks that were remote indeed from the rolling plains of Cooper's Creek.

Their companions, some from as far afield as New Zealand and Tasmania, to whom they were known as 'the Queenslanders', regarded them with curiosity and not a little awe, for 'down south' the northern State was still regarded as a wild and woolly land, refuge of long-horned cattle, outlaw brumby horses, wild blacks and escaped bushrangers.

'Tell us about the blacks,' they would say. 'How many men have you seen speared? Ever see Darkie Gardiner? He escaped up your way, didn't he? Tell us how you crossed the flooded rivers coming down!'

The Thylungra boys elaborated shamelessly on their adventures with wild blacks, demonstrated the arts of spear and boomerang throwing and of catching duck, Boontamurra fashion, by grabbing their feet and pulling them under water.

Still, it was many weeks before the nagging pain of homesickness was eased by new friendships and interests.

A graveyard, in a corner of the spacious grounds, became a secret meeting place to which the homesick boys escaped in odd, breathless moments. All their lives they would remember this retreat, the scent of jonquils and freesias that clambered over the untidy graves, the awesome epitaphs, one of a boy who had died at the age of fourteen:

> He was taken away lest wickedness should alter his understanding or deceit beguile his soul.

It was here they brought letters from their father to be read and re-read and carefully preserved. Some of this correspondence, quoted as written and spelt, has historical interest and throws some light on the writer's character and activities at this time. Although the lack of formal education is obvious, his handwriting would put many a scholar to shame.

The first letter was written from Blackney Creek, near Yass, NSW, on January 20, 1880, while staying with Grandmother's Aunt Mrs Moore before leaving on the return trip to Thylungra:

> My dear Michael and Johnny,
>
> I wish to tell ye that on tomorrow we are bound for home with the help of God and as soon as I reach I shall write to ye again ... Be sure and write to Uncle Michael and Uncle Jerry. I should rather ye would write to them than to myself for when ye write to them it will be as good as if youd ritten to me and be sure and make all enquiries about all at all the places and especially about Grandmother and Mr Healy. Uncle Martin Tully is sending for ye at Easter and when ye are leaving his place after the holiday let both of ye go to him and Mrs Tully and thank them for there hospitality to ye and do the same with Mrs Roach and Mr Roach and any place ye go ye are to do the same. Ye are to go to see Paddy Tully and Michael Tully also. Dear Michael Mr Mcguinnes will lend ye and Patsy (Skeahan) his violin until he buys you a new one ...
>
> Dear children ye are to write every fortnight regular ... I am sending ye 5 shillings worth of stamps. I thought I would see ye the day after I left ye as I was going past the college about ½ past 8 o'clock, but could not see ye.
>
> Whereiver ye are be always mannerly and manly and dutiful to yere masters especially Rev. Father Gallagher.

The next letter, dated February 16, was sent from Moonagee Station on the return journey.

> My dear boys, Michael and Johnnie,
>
> ... We reached Mr Ridges on the 12th, and we are here since on account of the Bogun being flooded so that we cannot cross. From what we can hear every river and creek between here and home is flooded, but we will try to cross tomorrow as this river is falling fast ... Mr Ridge has treated us all very kind and as for grapes and other fruits there are no end to what is here. Half of

the grapes will not be used before they go to hops. Pat Moore and Donald Maguiness is with us and also Martha the servant girl. When we came to Molong we stopped two days and the young horse we bought from Mr Lee is a beauty, we call him Starling and the Sydney horse we call him Exhibition . . . Any amount of good grass and too much water, all the horses, including the new ones we purchased, are looking well. The Taffey Filly foaled and I left her at Mr Boards until I come down next time to see ye my dear children . . . Your mamma and me will be very anxious to hear from ye, and let ye be writing every second week the longest. Let me know how ye like the College and also let me know how are your cousins, Patsy Skeahan and Michael Costello, and let me know are ye all in the one class and are ye sleeping in the one room.

Did Mr MacGuiness buy the violin for ye, dear Michael, and also let me know how is the Rev. Father Gallagher and how are ye're teachers and are ye both in the one class. I do not understand why I have had no word from home since we left. I am hoping for some word when we get to Bourke . . .

And from Thylungra some two months later:

. . . We reached home on the 18th inst. after a long and wairesome journey. Since we parted from ye in Goulburn we could scarcely travel twenty miles a day and not that some days on account of the heavy rain.

We stopped at Bourke for a few days and there lost the Taffey colt, so Willie gave a circle round and got on his track for nearly sixty miles, where he overtook him, or we would never have seen him again before he reached home. After leaving Bourke we got on very well until we came to the Warrego where we were detained again for five days, but at last Mr Chambers, at the boundary, brought up three casks to the crossing place and we made a raft again and crossed and from there to home we did well. We thought to be home for St Patrick's day—my 'birthday' but only got as far as Bunginderry.

My dear boys I cannot explain it to ye how it was when we got home only Uncle Jerry will tell ye as he has left here two day ago for Goulburn and he will tell ye about the stallion Hard Times and the nice little bay colt that was off the Forester bay mare Count's mother and nothing looked after since the day we left

> here. Dear children I hope in God I shall see the day ye will be able to stop here while we take a trip to our friends in Goulburn. I do not intend for yere mama and me to leave here again until you are able to look after the place dear Michael and Johnnie the overseer and Pat the stockman. All the horses got home alright we had. Dear Michael I think it is better ye learn to practise the violin as Johnnie is learning the piano but please yereself. Tell cousin Patsy Skeahan to take care of my saddle and bridle and tell him to bring it to Blackshaw and he will stuff it for him and remember me kindly to him and Michael Costello . . .

All the way home Grandfather had tried to cheer his wife by saying how they would soon buy a fine home in Brisbane from where she could take ship to Sydney and go by train to Goulburn to visit the boys. Passing derelict homesteads kept going by a handful of men and a few blacks, he had drawn comparisons with their comfortable home at Thylungra, recalling what joy he had always had in returning to the warm welcome of his orderly and well-kept establishment.

'It was always my idea,' he said, 'that a good home and proper living must come first. How can they expect a place to get on where the men live little better than the blacks—often living with them in fact from what we see of the unfortunate progeny.'

The gate of the Thylungra homestead paddock was open when they arrived. Puzzled, Grandfather closed it but as the road swung past the kitchen garden and the chicken run on the river bank the truth began to dawn. Only a few dusty feathers blowing in the wind betokened Grandmother's fine Leghorns and prized Muscovy ducks. The goats were pulling at the rank weeds in the otherwise denuded garden and Grandmother's pot plants and creepers were long since dead. The place seemed quite deserted, the stone flags of the verandah hidden under inches of mud, the rooms dusty and derelict, everything blown about by the wind and stained with rain. Grandfather gave a shout of rage and presently a few old natives came straggling up to the house.

'Where is everybody? What has happened to the place?'

They explained as best they could. The bookkeeper had eloped with the female unit of the 'good couple'. The man was somewhere out on the run trying to carry on with the help of a few blacks. He had fought with the other stockmen for going on the grog and making trouble with the black women. They had thereupon given notice, one clearing out with two of Grandfather's most prized horses. Big Johnnie and Stumpy Michael had not yet returned from their long droving trip to Adelaide. The other blacks had heard that the police were coming out to 'investigate' a murder and all but a few had got frightened and cleared out. This meant that Pumpkin had had to go with Dinny Skeahan who had taken the teams to Bourke. Old Cobby was sick, 'close up finish', and a piccaninny had been fatally burnt some weeks before.

Grandfather sank into a broken verandah chair and hid his face in his hands.

'Oh Mary, Mary, heaven help the country when the women go.'

19
WESTERN HORIZONS

The years 1880 to 1881. Patsy Durack's letters to his sons at college. A lawsuit. Will Ogilvie and his Thylungra horse. Growing interest in the Northern Territory. Further adventures of John Costello and his expanding Territory interests. Patsy Durack reads report of Alexander Forrest on the Kimberley district, discusses it with Solomon Emanuel and goes to Perth with his brother to interview Alexander Forrest.

Grandfather's letters to his sons show his life in some detail over this period and also indicate the way in which he was training his eldest boy for the position of head of the family.

> Dear Michael,
>
> Now I am sending ye £6. 10. cheque and you are to go to the bank and get a draft for £6 to send it to John Quirk Esq., White Gate County Galway Ireland. You will have discount to pay also and the very day ye receive this letter send this money home . . . Send him a nice letter and send me a copy. Tell Mr Quirk that you hear from me every week and that I send them all kind love and I hope his children are on the way to Australia and this £6 is to fit the girls out he is to send to me and £1 to be kept by his youngest son from yourself . . .
>
> Father Gallagher now gives a fine character of ye and Patsy Skeahan and Michael Costello to everyone and there is not one he talks to about ye but lets us know and not one from Goulburn to here but is expecting they will hear ye taking a prize at Xmas next . . . Mr Hopson says he is quite shure he will see yere name in the papers for a prize and so does Mr Fitzwalter and Mrs Baird and Mr Webb on the Macquarie is on the look out for ye also.

My father accepted such commissions conscientiously and began to enjoy a sense of importance as the son of a big squatter who 'brought people out' from Ireland and whose name stood high in the community.

On August 3, 1880, Grandfather wrote from Brisbane:

Dear Michael and Johnny,

Ye will be surprised to get a letter from me here. I had to come down concerning the country I sold to Pollak and Hogan. They summonsed me for one of the blocks of country I sold them being differently situated to what they expected. My solicitor tells me that he never heard of such a case before. He thinks they only want to friken me, and that they will not do very easy—to see what they could get out of me. The case is to come off in November next when your Uncle Michael and me are to come to Brisbane again. If God spares me I shall go down to see ye then. If I was to go now I would not be home for the races next month . . . I have Jerve Storier training for me and another man with him which rides Whynot over the jumps . . .

I took up a lot more country since ye left. For Thylungra 148½ sq. miles on the Bargo Bargey and 100 sq. miles adjoining Sultan on the head of Thunda Creek and I took up for Galway Downs about 200 square miles. When your Uncle Jerry came home I bought in with him in Galway Downs again and am to put on 1000 head of cattle and 5000 sheep and we are to be halves in everything on the station. I have the sheep partly bought on my way down and am to inspect them on my way home.

I hope in God ye will devote your whole time to yere study while ye are in school for you know I badly need yere help as soon as ye have yere education received. Uncle Jerry is in a great way to have Michael back to go with him and I suppose I will require Johnny. I do not intend to take either of ye from school until ye have received a good education. If God spares me, and Pat we will manage with Sunnie's help until such time as ye are home . . .

Your mama was very lonely when I was leaving. When ye are writing cheer her up by telling her ye will be home soon again with the help of God.

Tell Patsy (Skeahan) Woods has Gaslight and he is to run in a big race at Thargomindah 10 days after Galway Downs races. Tell him his father is going to get some sheep with mine. I am to start for home after tomorrow . . .

James Pollak and Thomas Hogan were partners in Comeongin Station about eighty miles south-west of Thylungra and adjoining the original land taken up by the Duracks and John Costello on Mobel Creek. The dispute ran on for some time with an exchange of enraged claims and counterclaims which, reduced from their colourful original wording to bald legal summary, ran as follows:

> *The Plaintiffs* . . . claim £5000 damages from Patrick Durack for the reason that the land he sold them having Mobile (or Mobel Creek) as a boundary not being what he represented it and they having lost through this misrepresentation buildings and stock they had put upon it.
>
> *Defendant* denies misrepresentation of country in dispute. He alleges that Pollak and Hogan inspected it themselves and pronounced themselves satisfied with the situation at the time of the sale. *Defendant* further alleges that Pollak and Hogan having mustered cattle on this country over a period of years could not have been ignorant of the nature of the property disputed. *Defendant* moreover *counter-claims* and charges the plaintiffs with unpaid debts and the loss of a horse lent to them by the defendant during formal inspection of the country in question.
>
> *The Plaintiffs* file in rejoinder to above complete denial of debts and loss of borrowed horse. They allege that only that part of the land inspected by them was properly represented by the boundaries stated the remainder of the land purchased being useless.
>
> *Defendant* files in rejoinder to above that if Pollak and Hogan are not satisfied with the country he will refund purchase money being the sum of £800 and again take over the rights of the disputed area. He states that the disputed land was a gift at this price.
>
> *Plaintiffs* allege that on discovery of misrepresentation they had asked Patrick Durack for return of purchase money which he had refused since when they have sustained losses to the extent of the £5000 claimed. They did not wish to surrender rights to the whole area only that which was misrepresented.

Eventually the matter was settled out of court, the bold strokes with which Grandfather recorded the payment of £900 to Pollak and Hogan and £300 to his solicitors betokening his moral indignation.

Having unearthed this account of a long-forgotten quarrel I wrote to my cousin Francis Tully of Ray Station (earlier known as Wathagurra) asking him about the country in question.

> The disputed property, [he wrote], would, from the locality indicated, be part of the original Mobel run, a block now known as Whynot

which was resumed from Pinkilla. Whynot and Mobel are both beautiful properties and the country on both excellent so I can well understand Uncle Patsy's being indignant when they said the land he had sold them was no good.

Grandfather and Stumpy Michael, finding themselves in Brisbane with time on their hands between legal engagements, had made their first ventures in the purchase of city properties. Grandfather purchased the Bowen Hotel in South Brisbane and he and his brother between them some blocks of city land at already inflated values that they were not wrong in supposing would shortly be doubled.

The temptation, while in the city, to take ship a mere 510 miles south to Sydney and thence by rail to visit his sons in Goulburn, proved too strong for Grandfather, as is seen from the following letter written after his return to Thylungra at the end of August.

Dear Children,

The day I left ye on that day fortnight I reached home and spent one day out of that in Sydney and two clear days where I bought the sheep inspecting them. So you see I lost no time . . .

On tomorrow I am to go out to Galway Downs. The horses are all out there . . . The races . . . are to come off on the 1st and 2nd September. You know the grey colt that John Horigan broke in before ye left—He called him Tarigan. He has beat mostly everything here and has got only a fiew gallops yet. He beat Silvery and Bachelor over 100 yds. hard held . . . The four that was in to train before I left is out at Uncle Jerry's. John H. is gathering the horses. There is about 250 head gathered now and all look very well . . .

I had a letter from yere Uncle Michael since he left Wilcannia with the cattle. They are all well and by this time very near Adelaide. All here at Thylungra and Wathagurra are well and were very glad to hear from ye . . . Grandmother wishes to tell ye she prays for ye night and morning and I hope ye shall pray for her. Do not be forgetting to write to yere Grandmother Costello at Blackney Creek . . .

An account of the races followed ten days later.

Dear Michael and Johnny,

I am just after coming home from the races on yesterday . . . Whynot did not stand training well. He was rather weak when they started for the hurdle race. Going over the second jump Whynot and Colman's horse cannoned and my rider fell. Whynot could not be cot until he went to the camp about one mile from the coarse. He was brought back again and went over the jumps 4 feet high like a bird they all say. He is the best jumping horse in Queensland, and then he came in second and only got £8. Colman's horse came first. Shamrogue won the maiden plate and the big handy cap. Curnell won the ladies purse. Saladden another race and Silvery another. All the horses we ran was either first or second, and we beat all Redford's cracks and won the most part of the money. We won £151. The only big money we lost was the Steeple race.

We had three days racing and everything went off well only Tom Kilfoyle and Edward Hammand had a bit of a fite. Ned came off second best. James Hammond and Simpson had a smawl row—only one nock down and all was over. James was no match for Simpson. Any amount of all other sports and dancing . . .

Mr Hambleton asked me why you did not rite to him. I told him you wrote to him and sent him yere portrait, dear Michael and Johnny. Now let both of ye send Mr Hambleton and tell him ye wrote to him and I will send him one of yere portraits. He is going to buy the house at Corongla. Direct youre letter to Himself. He is living at Corongla station, Cooper's Creek, near Thargomindah, and enquire for his Mrs and also Mr Colman and Mrs Colman. Make it a nice letter and let him know what ye are learning . . .

Pat was at the races. John and Michael Skeahan rode all the races for us. Gaslight is to run in a few days time at Thargomindah . . .

Letters later in the year indicate the rapid increase of sheep on Thylungra and the state of the beef market in 1880, which was a fairly poor year on the Cooper.

Thylungra 10th Nov. 1880.

Dear Children,

You did not let me know where are ye going to at Xmas and did anyone ask ye yet and if not ye can go to Sydney with Patsy Skeahan for a week or two and if ye want some money ask a few pounds from Father Gallagher and I shall send it to him at once. I never had so much to do in all my life as I have now with the sheep. They are commencing to lamb on today. There is 2050 to lamb now and the remainder 5759 to lamb in the middle of January next. I shall have more peace when ye are home again and can relieve me of so much writing also that grows all the time more pressing for that I have not the learning for to make light of it . . .

Uncle Michael came home last Saturday. He sold the cattle for about £6 a head. We have about 3700 calves branded now in this year and are to commence branding next week again as there are any amount of calves now. We expect to be able to brand 1200 more this year. All the cattle are in on the creeks now as the weather is very dry and hot. We got over 300 calves on one camp and are branding them on today. I have the sheep all on the Conna Conna above the three sandhills. Pat Scanlan has put up a splendid dam here. We have heard nothing of Pannick since he was taken, only what the blacks tell us. They told us who took him but we cannot believe them.

A generation later, correspondence between Sarah Tully's youngest son, Frank, and the Scottish-Australian balladist Will Ogilvie revealed that the poet, while working on Belalie Station in his youth, had purchased a grey horse from a pound. Later a traveller identified its 7PD brand and recognised the fine animal as one that had been stolen from Thylungra in 1880. It was probably the horse named Pannick to which Grandfather refers in this letter and which, renamed Loyal Heart, was to inspire the dedication of Ogilvie's best known book of verse.

To all grey horses fill up again
For the sake of a grey horse dear to me . . .

From Scotland Ogilvie wrote in his latter years:

I have ridden many hundreds of horses in Australia, America and over here hunting and in the Remount Department in the Great War, but there was never a horse like Loyal Heart. His old grey tail is here as I write, memento of many a glorious ride. I begin to think that when I am dead they will find 7PD engraven on my heart . . .

From a letter written on December 20, we gather that the boys were to spend Christmas with Great-grandmother Bridget, who was then visiting friends in Goulburn. After that they were to go to Blackney Creek Station near Yass where their Grandmother Mrs Costello was staying with her sister.

The simple details of these letters, not of much interest in themselves, give some idea of the family's constant movement and shuffling about as though Sydney, Brisbane, Goulburn, Adelaide or Wilcannia were the merest step from Thylungra. Now that times had improved and coaches were linking western Queensland with New South Wales the women took these journeys, if not as often, certainly as lightly as the men, the formidable distances and difficult travelling serving only to strengthen their determination to keep in touch with their widely separated friends and relatives. This is the more remarkable when we consider that a coach trip from Thylungra to Goulburn in those days often took about the same time as a sea voyage from Australia to England today.

> Dear Children,
>
> I and your mama were more satisfied that ye are to have Xmas with yere Grandmother and Mrs Kelly, and ye are going out to Blackney Creek after to spend yere holidays. While ye are there ye must be doing anything said for ye to do by yere Grandmother Costello and Mrs Roach . . . [Here follows further general instructions on behaviour and remembrances to friends and relatives.]
>
> We got a letter last mail from youre Aunt Margaret at Molong. She said she was going round to see ye all. Give her and Cousin Big Johnnie our kind love . . . Let me know which of ye three done the best at the Examinations . . .
>
> If young Mr Quirk comes out he is to come straight out to Goulburn to see ye. If ye can get a horse for him bring him out to see all the friends at Blackney Creek and Grabben Gullen. Give him my kind love and his sister also if she is out. Tell Mr Cleary if he possibly can to get him into some billet in Goulburn and he will ever oblige yere affectionate Father until death,
>
> PATRICK DURACK.

So on the surface life continued much as usual on Cooper's Creek, except that the shearers had moved out and the supply teams that once bumped empty down to Bourke now swayed away under bales of wool. Mustering, branding and droving followed the seasonal cycle and a few men drifted back from opal prospecting to station work. It was obvious, however, that most of the young fellows who had sought adventure in what had been the farthest outpost of settlement were now looking to an even more distant west, referred to still rather vaguely as 'The Northern Territory', 'The

Centre' or in journalistic phrasing 'This Terra Incognita'. Its 523,620 square miles of largely unoccupied and only partly explored country were then under the jurisdiction of the colony of South Australia that for years had been trying to solve the problem of this top-heavy and controversial burden on her young shoulders. The Territory was a desert of gibber plains and shimmering salt pans. The Territory was a paradise of splendid rivers, rich soil and sweeping pastures. The Territory was an incredible potential asset. The Territory was a hopeless liability. Raffles Bay and Port Essington, those early outposts of trade and military strategy, has long since returned to the jungle. Port Darwin, or Palmerston as it was then generally called, was established in 1870 and two years later the Overland Telegraph had been rushed through from Port Augusta at the head of Spencer Gulf 2,000 miles to the little frontier port on the Timor Sea, overcoming the seemingly insuperable obstacle of communication in an eighteen months' epic of human achievement.

Meanwhile, through much confusion of opinion, bubble pastoral companies were floated and dispersed, gold was being mined at Pine Creek, plantations were established and some thousands of Chinese coolies and hundreds of Manila men introduced to provide cheap labour. For two decades Australian investors had looked with speculative interest at this mighty tract of country where so many promising schemes had been stillborn and as many others died in infancy. Conditions of land tenure at 12s 6d an acre on a twenty-five year lease seemed attractive enough at first glance but distance from markets, the climate and natural hazards of the country cast shadows of doubt.

In 1870, not long after the formation of the port, a tough pioneer drover D'Arcy Uhr had pushed a mob of cattle 1,500 miles from Charters Towers to the beef-hungry settlers but it was eight years before anyone travelled that route with stock again. In '76 the Prout brothers, Sydney and Alfred, whom John Costello had piloted to Kangi Station in the Cooper district some years earlier, forged north and west across the border hoping to stake the first claim on the Barkly Tableland. The well-known verses of Mary Hannay Foott commemorate the story of these men:

The creek at the ford was but fetlock deep
When we watched them crossing there;
The rains have replenished it twice since then,
And twice has the rock lain bare.
But the waters of Hope have flowed and fled
And never from blue hill's breast

Come back—by the sun and the sands devoured
Where the pelican builds her nest.

Both brothers perished of thirst on the Tableland but a year later Nat Buchanan, then a partner in Landsborough's Pastoral Company near Longreach, with that 'man of wire and whipcord', 'Greenhide' Sam Croaker, who appears in later stages of this story, rode right across the Tableland to the Overland Telegraph. There, wiring away for pastoral rights to the best of the land they had explored, they were speedily informed that city speculators, blind stabbing at blank spaces on the map, had taken up all the most likely areas. Most of these 'spec leases' changed hands many times during the three-year period allowed for stocking and men secure in city offices made money from a country which Buchanan and his mate had traversed at their peril, gaining only hard experience. But the Territory had got into Buchanan's blood and in '78 he undertook to pilot 12,000 cattle from Aramac in Queensland to form Glencoe on Adelaide River, the first Territory station, thereby opening a stock route for the big overland cattle drives of the eighties.

John Costello had taken up the Lake Nash lease in '79 as a first foothold in the Territory. It is hard to believe that he ever seriously entertained the idea of retiring in comfort to the coast at the age of forty-two. Not only would he have found it extremely hard to change his lifetime habit of constant movement but the sense of insecurity and its resultant land hunger that was obsessional with them all would hardly have allowed him to relax and invest his money in other ways. The process of taking up virgin country, stocking, improving, selling it and moving out and on was something he understood but he displayed little touch in handling business ventures of other kinds. The reputed quarter-million with which he left the Cooper was quickly eaten into when, not long after his arrival at Rockhampton, a bad drought hit the east coast. A tobacco plantation and factory which he had heavily financed went broke while stock losses on his two coastal places, Cawarral and Annondale, and his practical sympathy with the plight of neighbouring smallholders, made a further hole in his pocket. As in the hard times out west he was again pulling bogged cattle out of dwindling waterholes, sinking wells and shifting stock. Rain had no sooner relieved the situation on the coast than a dry year set in out west. News came from Lake Nash that dingoes were hunting in packs like hungry wolves, killing calves and even venturing into the men's huts. Costello hurried out and rode the countryside, dropping strychnine baits, riding always wider and wider afield, magnetically drawn up the western waterbeds of the Milne and Sandover Rivers, on into the Hart Range, not far east of the Telegraph—300 miles south-west of his border property. Here he took up another 2,000 square miles which he planned to stock with heifers from Lake Nash. Not long afterwards, riding back to his family on the coast, he met up with Nat Buchanan whom he told about his latest acquisitions:

'You might do all right in there,' Buchanan said, but you're getting into the chancy, low rainfall belt again. Now, I've passed through some country on that gulf route with cattle—splendid grass flats ard rivers that hold the year round—never miss out on the monsoon. A man would need a stout heart of course—there's a lot of it jungle country and the blacks are bad. We lost a man out there—had his head chopped clean off from behind while he was mixing the bread. There's a fair bit of fever too, and plenty 'gators in the waterholes. Don't know that I'd advise a man to take it on, but when I think of those rivers and the big grass plains . . .'

'Might ride over and take a look at it some day,' Costello said.

> . . . It is now three months since John left for the gulf country, and no word of him yet [Mary Costello wrote to the family at Thylungra in '81]. He said he would let you know if it comes up to his expectations and is more reliable than anything he has struck yet, for you may want to come in with him . . .

But Grandfather had just then received the report of an expedition made in '79 through the northern part of Western Australia and his attention was focused in this direction. Larger, by about one-third, than even the giant Queensland, Western Australia's 975,000 square miles stretched from the grey skies and giant timbers of the south, through arid kingdoms of saltbush and spinifex to the wild ranges and palm-fringed rivers of her monsoonal north, her coastline curving for 4,350 miles. Vast desert wastes and 2,000 miles of ocean cut her off from the other colonies so that she had been from the beginning a land apart, little known to the rest of Australia, more in touch with London than the eastern capitals. Established forty years later than New South Wales, she had remained correspondingly forty years behind in her development, numbering, by the year 1879, slightly less than 29,000 of Australia's two million inhabitants.

Established as a colony of free English and Scottish settlers, for the most part families of gentle breeding, who had come with their servants and all the appendages of upper class Victorian life, the western colony had, for the first twenty years of her existence, little in common with the raw, convict-built prosperity of her sister States. All these, excepting Tasmania, had already done with transportation before the West succumbed to the temptation of convict labour in 1850, but the system, carried on for eighteen years, had brought little of the hoped-for prosperity and caused many headaches. The gold discoveries in New South Wales and Victoria so drained her already limited free population that by the time some 16,000 convicts had arrived and been in due course emancipated, Western Australia, in fear of being overwhelmed by the riff-raff of British jails, had brought further transportation to an end.

Fighting against labour problems, limited population, distance from market and the inevitable difficulties of adapting old methods to a new environment, farming in the temperate south had met with only mild success and pioneer sheep men were spreading north of the capital of Perth into the Murchison district. Tentative efforts at settlement of the Kimberley division, that extended north from about latitude 19, had been made during the sixties at Camden Harbour, between Prince Regent and Glenelg Rivers, at Roebuck Bay and also at Sturt Creek near the Territory border. All three attempts had ended disastrously but although the district remained unessayed throughout the seventies, pressure of settlement in the eastern States was creeping steadily north and west, sheep pushing the cattle further out, wheatgrowers edging on the sheep. Cattle men, chafing at fences and the restrictions of closer settlement, grown nostalgic for the good old semi-nomadic days of the open range, had moved north to Queensland and were spreading now over the borders into the Territory. By the latter seventies men like Nat Buchanan, with his relatives the Gordons and the Cahills, 'Greenhide' Sam Croaker, Bob Button, John Costello and D'Arcy Uhr were already goading stock beyond the furthest outposts of western settlement, their eyes on horizons still further west.

Big rivers were now known to flow north into Cambridge Gulf and others to the western coast, but none knew in what ranges they rose or what type of country they watered. Queensland cattle men, battling with their land of extremes, were interested to find out. Sheep farmers in the backward south of the backward colony, troubled by scab-infested stock, were interested. Prosperous investors in the big cities were interested. Little men, since sheep-farming had become a game for the capitalists, looked to a possible field for expansion on limited outlay. Big men sought a wide new field of limitless monopoly.

In '79 it was decided that a party be sent to find an answer to these questions. Alexander Forrest, the leader of the expedition, was a member of an early Western Australian family whose brother John was later to become the first Premier of his State and ultimately elevated to the peerage. The younger man, however, was no less devoted to his home State and as surveyor and explorer played an equal part in its development. It was the report he wrote on his return from this journey from the De Grey River on the west coast to the Overland Telegraph in the Territory that caused Grandfather such excitement when it came into his hands early in '81. Here, it seemed, was the type of country he most desired—a land of splendid rivers, fine pastures and reliable rainfall.

'But Patsy!' his wife protested, 'It's every bit of 2,500 miles away. However would you get stock to it?'

'How else but the way we have got stock to anywhere? By droving it, of course! Buchanan got stock to the Victoria River, and what are a few hundred miles more?'

'But you always said you would not sell Thylungra!'

'And neither I shall, but what sort of a father is it would hear of country like this for the taking and not be securing it for his boys? How could I expect them to settle down here knowing of this pastoral paradise out west?'

Grandmother knew too well the futility of argument.

'Of course, you will do as you decide, Patsy. I only ask that you speak about it to Mr Emanuel when you are next in Goulburn.'

If Grandmother had hoped that Solomon Emanuel would dissuade her husband from his folly she had underestimated Grandfather's powers of infectious enthusiasm.

'Read this!' he said, flourishing the report at his friend's door. 'Can you picture a country where ye would not be haunted by the fear of long, ruinous drought or terrible floods? Can you see the deep rivers and the plains of sweeping Mitchell and Flinders grass?'

Emanuel read. He had two growing sons of his own, Sydney and Isadore, both of whom showed a taste for the land and already talked of the limitations of their sheep property Lansdowne near Goulburn. The Kimberley district looked promising, he agreed, but he thought it unwise to start cattle on the long and hazardous track without further investigation. There was a tendency with surveyor-explorers to fall in love on sight with country they discovered if it was in any way fertile and the fact that Mr Forrest had since set himself up as agent for Kimberley pastoral leases might have added something to the enthusiasn of his report. If Patsy Durack and his brothers could organise a private exploration of the country, Emanuel himself would share in financing it and might even feel disposed to select Kimberley country for his own family.

'But meantime—what happens?' Grandfather demurred. 'The map graziers get in first just as they did with Nat Buchanan. Look at the way he battled out and discovered that wonderful Barkly Tableland only to find it had been taken up by city investors who had never set foot outback in their lives.'

Emanuel agreed blandly.

'It seems then,' he said, 'we must become map graziers ourselves.'

A week later Grandfather and his brother Michael set sail from Sydney for the western State to interview Alexander Forrest.

Finding 2,520 cold sea miles more than enough for their land-lubbing tastes, they disembarked at the port of Albany, site of the first West Australian settlement of '27, now connected by coach service with the capital of Perth. The 250-mile journey was full of interest and unexpected charm. Here was a softer facet of the Australian scene than any they had known—a land of towering forests that filtered soft sunlight on bracken-covered slopes. The people at the coaching stages were quiet-spoken, slow-moving; the sleepy townships, unlike the crude, dusty settlements of Queensland and New South Wales, were respectable as English villages. Even the coachman had no sense of urgency. He covered the distance in a leisurely fifty-six hours, clattering at last down the main thoroughfare of Perth with a curved post-horn to his lips. People came out of their houses, some to wave, others to follow to the post office and await the sorting of the mail. Flocks of sheep and little herds of cattle moved quietly through the streets, their shepherds clad in the blue smocks of old England. People stopped to talk in the thoroughfares while carriages moved out of their way.

Perth, set on the dreaming blue waters of the Swan River, was patterned on an English country town. There seemed less here of what had come to be known as 'the Australian twang', nothing of the hurly-burly of Sydney, Melbourne or Brisbane, those vigorous, jostling cities of opulence and poverty. Secure behind her desert barrier, pretty little Perth, like a staid Victorian damsel, sighed for the progress she at once envied and despised.

People looked curiously at the two bearded Irishmen in their stout moleskins and broad-brimmed hats but were not, on introduction, slow to extend the warmest hospitality.

Alexander Forrest, continuing in the comfort of his own home discussions begun in his office, enlarged on the conservative outline of his official report. Kimberley was, he declared, without doubt the coming pastoral land of the continent.

'I can hardly describe,' he said, tracing on an outspread map the route he had taken from Beagle Bay on the west coast, 'the grandeur of that northern scenery—vast open plains heavy with pasture, cut across by creeks and rivers, girded by ranges of unbelievable colouring.

'This Fitzroy country should prove an extremely rich pastoral area, suitable for all kinds of stock, but it is clearly subject to inundation in certain seasons. Farther over here to the east would be, I should say, a cattleman's paradise with vast plains of splendid pasture, much of it well watered and not subject to flooding since the land is higher and the rivers contained between deep banks. This river, which I have named the Ord in honour of our Governor, may yet prove to be the Queen of Australian rivers and is probably the same observed by Phillip King to enter Cambridge Gulf a little to the western side of its head. I have sketched here its most probable course since sickness and shortage of rations prevented our following it farther.'

The Queenslanders were already acquainted with many details of that expedition, the sufferings of some members of the party from fever, sunstroke, and sore eyes, of how with dwindling rations they were reduced to killing some of their precious horses for meat, of how grateful they had been for an occasional meal of snake or kangaroo, and how when Forrest and one companion had forged ahead of the rest on a thirsty trek to the Overland Telegraph they had shot a hawk for its blood with their last ammunition.

The visitors enquired how Forrest's companions had fared since their return.

'My brother Matthew and James Carey quite recovered,' they were told, 'but poor Tommy Pierre, the faithful aboriginal, whom we were forced to tie to his horse in his delirium, lived only long enough to die back here in his country and among friends.'

Forrest did not think the Kimberley natives would prove hostile to settlers, although no doubt they would have to learn that sheep and cattle were not to be regarded as the huntsman's quarry. Those encountered by his party had been surprisingly friendly, except a few so frightened and surprised as to be deprived of their power of speech.

'I should think them decidedly less warlike, probably more backward, than the Queenslanders,' he said.

He was enthusiastic about the suggestion that a private expedition be organised to trace the course of the Ord southward from Cambridge Gulf and carry out more detailed exploration of the country than had been possible in his hurried cross-country trek. Meanwhile, it was wise, he agreed, to secure tentative holdings on the map as others were already doing. Some of the Fitzroy country had already been selected, while two speculators, O'Neill and O'Connor, had marked themselves off about a million acres each along the supposed course of the Ord on the understanding that when the river was eventually mapped the same areas would be transferred as accurately as possible to the true course.

In the name of Durack, Emanuel and one or two other interested associates, including Tom Kilfoyle they reserved, therefore, eight adjoining 50,000-acre blocks along the conjectured banks of the Ord, 150,000 acres around the Negri Junction, further blocks along the upper Ord, on the Nicholson Plains and Margaret River, and large chunks on either side of the Fitzroy. Some of these blocks adjoined those of the Kimberley Pastoral Company and other interests to remain closely associated with the development of the district, and those of various outside speculators, including the Duke of Manchester, whose names would fade from the map with their dreams of quickly flourishing pastoral empires. In all, the tentative Durack-Emanuel selections covered about two and a half million acres, a comparatively small area to that over which their respective interests would extend in the years to come.

There was every indication, Forrest said, that occupation of west Kimberley had already begun. The King Sound Pastoral Company had not long before sent a man to inspect their blocks on the Lennard River, while rumour had it that young George Julius Brockman had already taken sheep by lugger from the north-west to a landing point used by the pearlers at Beagle Bay.

'So your expedition may find a station or two by the time it gets to the lower Fitzroy,' Forrest predicted. 'Many of these whose names you see here, however, will be unable to stock their country within the required time, so that soon you should have the chance of selecting from their land as well. City investors in the eastern colonies are finding it almost impossible to obtain experienced drovers for such a trek, whereas you are fortunate in numbering many competent to undertake it in your own family.'

Grandfather agreed.

'But my brother and I have given enough of our lives to pioneering. We can organise and finance, but the conquest of this new country is for the younger generation. They shall make a pastoral empire of their own.'

20

TO FIND A RIVER

The years 1881 to 1882. Organising for the expedition to inspect the Kimberley district. Leavetaking of Stumpy Michael Durack and party from Brisbane. A disastrous beginning and a second start. Arrival at Port Darwin and hiring of the schooner Levuka *to Cambridge Gulf. Rough passage. Arrival in a strange land. Letter from Cambridge Gulf. Hard travelling and hostile natives. Deep rivers and open plains.*

It was agreed on the return of the travellers from the western State that the proposed journey of inspection called for a party of expert bushmen of proved toughness and resource, including at least one scientist, and that their horses must be the best procurable. A supply of rations and equipment must be selected with an eye to weight and with foresight to any possible emergency and arrangements made for the chartering of three vessels—one to take men, horses and gear from Brisbane to Port Darwin, another to convey them from there to Cambridge Gulf and a third to pick them up when they had battled through to the west coast. Distances and travelling times had to be nicely calculated, for once in the unknown wilds of Kimberley they would be cut off from all means of communication until their journey's end. The estimated cost of the expedition was £4,000 which Grandfather and Emanuel agreed to share equally.

That Stumpy Michael was to be leader of the party was already a foregone conclusion since he combined all the necessary qualities of bushcraft, leadership and sure judgement of country with a reputation, amounting almost to a local superstition, of always 'getting through'. There remained only the difficulty of breaking the news to his wife, who with their three children was then awaiting his return in Brisbane. Kate Durack had already said goodbye to the home at Thylungra and she and her husband had been inspecting small properties within reasonable distance of the coast when Grandfather had wired from Sydney suggesting the interview with Forrest in Western Australia. Leaving his family comfortably enough accommodated at his brother's recently acquired hotel in South Brisbane, Stumpy Michael had obeyed the call with his wife's words ringing in his ears:

'Go to Perth if you must, but remember, Michael, your pioneering days are over. We are settling down in a comfortable home as you promised, where the children can go to school and you can have a rest from all this travelling.'

Even with the support of his elder brother, Stumpy Michael found the interview with his wife one of the hardest hurdles to sumount.

'It's an imposition, Patsy!' Kate gasped when they broke the news. 'Hasn't it ever occurred to you that poor Michael has a right to live his own life?'

Grandfather was astonished.

'But my dear sister, Michael has always led his own life!'

'If I *was* your sister, Patsy, I would probably agree with you, but I am a McInnes and a Scot. We never lived each other's lives like you Duracks. Besides, Michael hasn't the strength any more. There's that chest trouble of his and the doctor said . . .'

'Nonsense!' Grandfather scoffed, irritated as always by any suggestion of ill health in his family. 'Anyone'd think he was an old man to hear ye and what is he?—thirty-five and never fitter in his life!'

'Just this last time, Kate,' her husband promised. 'I'll select the finest piece of country in Kimberley for young Ambrose and get someone to manage it until he's old enough to take over.'

'And by that time my boys and probably Uncle Darby's too, will be there,' Grandfather enthused, 'all making their fortunes. What would your son be saying if he knew ye had spoiled his chances?'

Kate made a final bid to reason.

'Tell me, Michael, do you really *want* to go?'

Stumpy Michael hesitated. How explain to a loving and commonsense woman the lure of new country, good, bad or indifferent? How find words to say that for all his passionate devotion to his family the thought of leading this expedition to find the course of a mysterious river was the breath of life to him?

'Yes, Kate. Yes, my dear. In a sense, I do want to go.'

The intended leisurely inspection of 'likely little properties' went by the board. A 14,000-acre estate near Darra, a few miles out of Brisbane, of which Kate and her husband had been doubtful on first sight, suddenly appeared to Stumpy Michael as having endless possibilities and on June 6 he purchased Archerfield from one Mary Elizabeth Murphy for £15,000.

Grandfather, assessing his brother's new acquisition, inspected the stock and scratched about for mineral possibilities.

'Some fine horses there all right, Michael. The land's not up to much but ye might find ye've got a coal mine here.'

'I'll put down a drill when I get back,' his brother said.

While Kate moved in with the family, her husband's attention was fully occupied organising the Kimberley expedition. There had been no need to advertise for men. Emanuel had enlisted the services of one John Pentacost, surveyor and geologist who had been for some time tutor to his boys, and had asked that his eldest son, Sydney, be another member of the party. The remaining three, Tom Kilfoyle (Darby Durack's brother-in-law), James Josey and Tom Horan, all tried and experienced men, had been contacted by wire in various parts of Queensland:

> WILL YOU JOIN EXPEDITION KIMBERLEY DISTRICT W A STOP AWAY ABOUT FOUR MONTHS STOP WIRE IMMEDIATELY IF INTERESTED AND MEET US BRISBANE EARLIEST DURACK

In a week all three had materialised at Grandfather's Bowen Hotel.

'How soon do you want to start?'

'Two or three weeks from now. Time to see your folks and cancel your commitments for a few months.'

'We're on!'

'You haven't asked about the pay.'

'I thought we might be paying you to let us come,' Horan said.

Kilfoyle, bluff and down to earth, dismissed this suggestion, though he too had probably not given much thought to the financial side of it before. 'And them with all the money in the world! Not on yer life!'

'It'll be a hard trip,' Grandfather said, 'and we're prepared to pay handsome for the best men. What do you say to three pound a week—all found?'

'Three pound ten,' Kilfoyle said.

'It's a deal!'

Twenty-three tried and well-bred horses were purchased for an average of £30 a head from breeders around Brisbane, while Emanuel busied himself with the selection of fifteen hundredweight of rations and equipment from Sydney stores. The items ran as follows:

800 lbs flour (16 bags.)	1 box caps
30 lbs tea	6 pint pots
140 lbs sugar	6 each knives, forks, spoons
10 lbs rice	6 tin plates
250 lbs salt meat	1 camp oven
10 lbs currants	1 gun
15 lbs tobacco	2 cwt horse shoes
50 lbs salt	1 axe, and sundry tools
20 lbs soap	2 billies

6 tins pepper	60 doz. matches
4 tins mustard	14 lbs horse nails
6 tins curry powder	Saddler's tools
12 tins jam	12 blankets
5 lbs shot	10 pack saddles
1 can gunpowder	6 riding saddles

The list, by reason of its rigorous simplicity, makes interesting comparison with the cumbersome equipment of other exploring parties that set forth with waggons, drays and herds of sheep for killing on the way. Stumpy Michael, like Nat Buchanan and John Costello, had a simple formula for such expeditions: 'Travel light and ride good horses.'

On July 6, 1882, friends and family farewelled the travellers on the chartered steamship *Volmer*. Kate Durack's apprehensions for her husband's safety increased to near frenzy when two days after the departure fierce storms lashed the Queensland coast. Several wrecks were reported during the next few days but no word of the *Volmer* until a wire came from Rockhampton, 350 miles north of Brisbane:

> VOLMER AGROUND ALL ASHORE SAFE AND WELL RETURNING COACH BRISBANE IMMEDIATELY DURACK

Gathered again at Archerfield the travellers told their tale of seemingly miraculous escape from the fury of the hurricane. Half the precious horses had been battered to death in the hold, most of the provisions washed overboard or ruined by salt water. The remaining horses had been swum ashore and left at John Costello's Rockhampton property, Cawarral, since it had seemed impractical to return them to Brisbane in their shocked condition to begin the voyage anew.

This misfortune increased the cost of the expedition by well over £1,000 but the organisers considered themselves fortunate in being able to charter another steamship almost immediately. A second start, with a fresh supply of provisions and horses, assembled with astonishing speed, was made by the 900-ton steamship *Vortigen* on July 19. Stumpy Michael, starting his diary from that day, commented blithely on

> our colourful crew, skippered by Captain Brown, pilot Captain Dark, first mate Jack Green! . . . Passage between Brisbane and Townsville extremely rough. Spend most of my time in the hold with the horses, at one stage fearing another disaster . . . Smooth waters Townsville to Torres Strait. We have now named all the

> horses and selected our respective favourites for the journey. Mine, a piebald of the circus kind which I have named Doughboy. Thursday Island . . . One thousand, two hundred and thirty-five sea miles from our dear ones . . .

Another 730 miles of tropic calm and colour brought them around the tip of Arnhem Land to the little Territory port on the red cliff above the mangroves where everything upwards from the jetty, indicated at high tide by tins stuck up on sticks, bore the mark of makeshift and lassitude. Ramshackle tin sheds, Chinese huts and Malay shanties hugged the edges of the steaming mud alive with hermit crabs and scavenging seabirds.

A white-clad Customs official in tropical topee and sandals, waving a palm-leaf fan, enquired their business and directed them up the rough roadway to the straggling town on the jungle's rim above. As the port of a new land boom, Darwin would hardly have inspired confidence, with her few Chinese stores and government offices, private houses built on stilts and straggling tumbledown shanties, all partly obscured by long rank grass and fighting a losing battle against white ants. The population was preponderantly Chinese with a sprinkling of European, Malay and Aboriginal. Blacks and Asiatics dozed in the shade of trees or lounged in narrow doorways, while white men in a state of chronic ennui reclined in cane chairs on latticed verandahs, syphoning soda water into whisky, rum or 'square face' gin.

Sight of strangers in the port caused a stir of interest and the newcomers were pressed for confirmation of rumours that cattle were soon to start overland from Queensland into Kimberley. Armchair politicians under every verandah in the rambling streets propounded upon what should be done with the Territory, half a million square miles, then boasting hardly more than a thousand white inhabitants, four or five thousand Asiatics and a few thousand Aborigines. The Asiatics, encouraged to supply cheap labour for the seventies, had guickly graduated from work on the plantations or on the railway project between Darwin to Pine Creek and had either gone prospecting or set up as shopkeepers in the port.

The newcomers listened with some bewilderment to a variety of opinions. It seemed generally agreed that the land was rich and that rice, cotton, sugar, tobacco and tropical fruits could be grown in abundance. Some contended, however, that transport must come first, that a railway run up from Port Augusta along the route of the OT would transform Darwin from an obscure tropical port to 'the Singapore of the southern hemisphere'. Some said the country's first need was more white women, others more amenities, or a strong-minded Vermin Board to deal with dingoes, tick, buffalo fly and troublesome blacks. Some held that the natives should be gathered into compounds and trained for service, others that it was impossible to train or educate them for anything since as a race they were mentally backward and congenitally treacherous. Another faction held that success could only come from the organised development of mining, beginning with the immediate despatch of 'the bloody Celestials' at present engaged in systematically smuggling Territory gold to their home land. Others argued that this was primarily a pastoral country, that the cattle industry should be developed, with meat works in Darwin to ship away frozen and tinned beef to the world's markets. 'A great place for talking,' Stumpy Michael wrote to his family, 'but very little done.'

Enquiries for a ship to take them to Cambridge Gulf brought forward one of the few really energetic inhabitants of the sleepy port—Captain Murray of the 120-ton schooner *Levuka*, who bustled about arrangements with every show of zest for the adventure. It was on his suggestion that they engaged two Aborigines of the local Larakia tribe—reputedly reliable fellows and good trackers revelling in the white man names of Pannikin and Pintpot.

A combined farewell and twenty-first birthday party for young Syd Emanuel was organised at the Palmerston Club, and ended uproariously when an improvised band, marching to the tattoo of kettle drums, escorted the wayfarers to their ship to catch the midnight tide.

All through the Timor Sea adverse winds lashed blue walls of water against the *Levuka*'s frail hulk. The horses, whinnying in terror, were thrown from side to side in the narrow hold and the native boys, huddled together, too sick and frightened to eat, seemed likely to die before they could touch land. When Stumpy Michael spoke to them encouragingly they rolled hopeless eyes.

'Finish, Boss! Finish.'

On the seventh day out two of the horses were so severely injured that Stumpy Michael was forced to shoot them. While hauling the carcasses up, the pole on which he was balancing rolled in a sudden pitching of the ship and he was hurled ten feet into the hold, badly spraining his shoulder and injuring his back. After eight miserable days, when the ship swayed towards Cambridge Gulf, he was just able to limp about again with his arm in a sling.

As the schooner rounded a small island, rugged and cleft with gullies and ravines, its beaches criss-crossed with turtle tracks, the Gulf channel could be seen swinging away between broken sandstone ranges.

'The last man in here, as far as I know, was Phillip King, in the *Mermaid*, about sixty years ago,' Captain Murray said. 'I wouldn't care to be navigating these shoals and reefs and tidal rips without his charts.'

Stumpy Michael, comparing these with the map of later years, picked up what he judged to be the mouth of the Ord River, but Captain Murray was doubtful.

'It might be any one of a number of streams coming in from either side and this is hardly an inviting country to be lost in.'

Evening closed in over the lonely gulf. A dark cloud of vampire shapes, wheeling and squeaking, rose from the mangrove thicket and white cockatoos went screeching off into ranges whose fortress shapes, rising 1,000 feet sheer above salt marsh, King had well named The Bastions.

By morning, on a swiftly receding tide, the ship lay careened in mud. Flat-topped ranges, touched by the opal colours of sunrise, glowed like the mountains of dreams, lending false colour to the tide-churned waters of the Gulf.

Getting the horses ashore before the turn of the tide was an anxious business. The animals had finished all the water and hay aboard the day before and stood dejectedly in the hold with hollow flanks and drooping heads. They seemed scarcely fit to walk ashore, let alone carry men and packs more than 600 miles over rough country. Michael was confident that they would pick up after a few days' spell on fresh feed and water but Captain Murray, now thoroughly sceptical about the whole venture, reminded him that King had failed to find drinking water thereabouts and had remarked even dingoes and kangaroos lapping from salt pits.

Stumpy Michael and his men, however, were already over the side with helpers from the ship's crew, ploughing through the reeking mud to cut mangroves for a rough landing-stage to the shore. When all was ready the horses were hoisted from the hold and coaxed across the branches. They floundered and sank in mud and, as the tide turned, jibbed, weak and trembling, on the edge of deepening channels. Water was swirling over the mangrove bridge before all horses and equipment were ashore.

At once the search for fresh water was begun. Stumpy Michael and Captain Murray climbed a steep point to look across a vast expanse of marsh, shimmering like a hoar frost under a layer of salt, patterned with the tracks of wild creatures, scattered with the branches of trees washed down by rivers from far inland. Isolated ranges with the buttes and talus slopes of African table mountains rose from the level plain, intensely blue and purple in the hard light of afternoon, some seeming to float above the horizon on shimmering drifts of mirage. Captain Murray said he could hardly bring himself to leave his friends with their near-spent horses in so fantastic and desolate place and urged that, failing to find fresh water, they would abandon their project. Stumpy Michael informed him that he had many a time found water in more unlikely and barren spots than this, and pointed to where the others on the plain below were cooeeing and waving their hats.

A recent storm had filled a number of holes and shallow billabongs, and brought on isolated pockets of good grass to which the horses were led and hobbled out to graze.

A camp was made and a tree marked 'D1.', the first of twenty-four marked trees denoting stages between Cambridge Gulf and the Negri River. Nightfall found them in a circle of blacks' fires, glowing in pinpoints of spinifex from range and pinnacle like a chain of festive lanterns. Faintly, from the darkness, came the sharp tapping of hardwood sticks, the hollow far-carrying throb of a didgeridoo, the wailing notes of Aboriginal chanting.

> A homely sound [Stumpy Michael recorded], bringing me back in memory to our people at Thylungra. The boys, Pintpot and Pannikin, very much afraid and huddled in their blankets at the fire, for always with the blacks it is the same old story of the terrible tribes next-door, but after meeting them in many parts of the continent I must say I have found them everywhere much the same.

Having entered the day's events in his journal he wrote his wife a letter to be cherished and preserved for the grandchildren he would never see.

> Cambridge Gulf,
> 17th August 1882.
>
> My dearest Kate,
>
> I hope these few lines will find you and all my poor little children in good health as this leaves all of us at present . . . This is the 4th letter I have written you since I left home. Oh, how I would love to hear now how you all are . . .
>
> Well, since we left Port Darwin till we came here we were eight days. Bad weather all the time so we could not sail and we had two of our best horses died on the voyage. I had a fall into the hold myself while hoisting one of the poor creatures overboard and have come ashore here with my arm in a sling. We have only twenty-one horses now.
>
> We got goods and horses off on shore today and pitched our

camp. We will have to give the animals a week's spell here before we start. They are very poor, in fact it is a marvel they did not all die on the little schooner. The day we got here we gave them the last drink of water we had on board and the last bit of hay, so you see they had a narrow escape. Now they have plenty of grass and water, thank God. Although the country on the coast along here is very rough there seems to be plenty of fresh water in every gully. We had a great job landing the horses and were very lucky we did not drown any of them.

My dearest Kate, I think we will be much longer over this trip than I expected on account of the horses being so poor so I don't think you need expect to hear from me now for about four months at least. The day I get to a telegraph office I will send you a wire and as soon as you get it send Patsy a wire that same day and let him know how we got on. The day you hear from me, wherever I am, you may depend I will travel as fast as the mail till I get home, if God spares me. Don't forget to write every fortnight to Perth for the next three months and please God I will get your letters all together when I get there. Give me all the news of the children and how they are geting on . . . and has the baby begun to walk yet? Don't forget to kiss them every morning and night for me till I get back to them.

My kindest regards to all the friends and a thousand kisses to you and all my poor little children and believe me, my dearest Kate,

Your fond and loving husband til death,
MICHAEL DURACK.

Three days later the travellers watched the departing vessel out of sight and resigned themselves to camp for another ten days while the spent horses recovered from their sea journey. John Pentacost became absorbed in examining rocks and looking for the colours of gold while others amused themselves fishing and shooting at the big man-eating crocodiles that dozed in the mud or floated on the turbulent brown waters. Some of the party waded to the gulf islands at low tide, returning with hawk-beaked turtles and hats filled with turtle eggs. Stumpy Michael and Tom Kilfoyle, his second in command, walked for miles surveying their situation and became increasingly confident of having landed at the mouth of the Ord River. The stream ran west from the gulf but they had no doubt it would presently turn south and lead them to Forrest's marked tree at its junction with the Negri.

They broke camp at dawn on August 24 and, saddling packs and riding horses, set off along the mangrove-bordered river. Four miles of rough country opened on to good grass prairies, ribbed with sandstone ridges and cleft with a bewildering network of nameless streams among which the original watercourse was lost. They ran up what seemed the largest of these many creeks until the jagged arms of cliffs dropped down to hold it to an impenetrable northward course.

Unlike the sprawling Queensland rivers that spread far and wide after the rains to disappear sometimes completely when the floods had run their course, the larger of these Kimberley streams had bitten deep, tortuous channels in the plains and worn towering gorges through the ranges. Expanses of dry bed alternated with deep green reaches where waters were held between high banks, creviced by centuries of wind and water, luxuriant with trees, creepers and trailing palms.

Disappointed, they crossed where the waters ran between heavy cedars, Leichhardt pines and drooping pandanus palms and where the horses, bending to drink, stiffened and drew back. The cause of their fear was not far to find—a party of natives on the bank above, standing solemn and withdrawn with their long barbed fishing spears. They appeared strong and well-made, like a people who lived well, their naked bodies heavily decorated with tribal scars, the men with hair pulled stiffly from broad foreheads and bound at the back in peculiar elongated knobs. A woman screamed and ran for hiding, dragging her child by the hand, but the men remained standing. Stumpy Michael stretched out a hand to them in a friendly gesture, whereupon they turned stolid backs and sat down, as though determined to show neither interest nor fear, hoping perhaps that when they turned again the apparitions would have passed on their way, out of sight and out of time, a thing for wonder and memory, a daydream to record in corroboree.

The white men rode on, through spreading eucalypts with trunks smooth and clean as though freshly white-washed, to where another river entered the channel from the north. They struck uneasy camp, for the water was salt here, the horses thirsty and nervous and the two native boys apprehensive of a night attack. They were not disturbed, but in the morning they found a maze of footprints encircling their camp.

Following the course of this new river they were cheered by the sight of open plains and abundant grasses—a wonderland of pasture and fine trees. Huge bottle-shaped boabs—friendly giants of the plains—dangled big velvet brown nuts from their dropsical branches silver-grey and leafless in the dry season. The slender stems of wild cotton bore a dazzle of saffron blooms and red-brown pods spilling a froth of white down. Bauhinia branches were heavy with the scarlet blossoms whose pistils swelled to gleaming seed pods that rattle on the wind. Cork-woods spurted fierce flames of flower from leafless branches. Between the trees the even spread of golden grass gave an impression of park land, artistically planned, a reserve of wild life where bustards strutted in stately families, pausing to regard the strangers with haughty surprise. Wallabies and kangaroos stopped in their tracks to turn soft bibbed fronts in curiosity. Brolgas rose in great flocks and with them many bright birds familiar to the Queenslanders, with some others that were new to them.

Stumpy Michael recalled how his wife had lamented the lack of colour and variety in the western Queensland scene and longed to tell her of this country—an artist's paradise of scenery in the grand manner.

> If one were to paint this country in its true colours [he wrote], I doubt it would be believed. It would be said at least that the artist exaggerated greatly, for never have I seen such richness and variety of hue as in these ranges and in the vivid flowers of this northern spring.

21

PROMISED LAND

The year 1882. A crocodile attacks. Durack River found and named. Hostile natives on Pentacost. Splendid grass country. Naming of Dunham and Bow Rivers. Marooned on a precipice. Loss of horses and worn boots. Shortage of provisions. Auriferous country. Failure to short-cut Leopold Range. Fever. Arrival at Minnie Station. Long wait at Beagle Bay. Arrival at Fremantle in the Mary Smith.

The river swung north, south and west on a tortuous route through plain and range, cutting through dense pandanus thickets and tattered cajuputs, cascading over rocky falls and into still reaches of pale blue lotus where jabiru and ibis preened and fished. When the water ran fresh they rode in to drink and leaning forward in their saddles dipped down their pannikins. The sudden, terrified scream of a horse, a wild lashing of water, sent the packs scattering up the bank and set the riders instantly on guard. One of the horses, seized by the nose between the teeth of a twelve-foot crocodile, was pulling and scrambling for a foothold on the slippery bed. Kilfoyle fired quickly, the monster unlocked its jaws and disappeared and the horse, shaken and bleeding, stumbled from the water and up the bank.

In an instant the quiet scene became pandemonium. Cockatoos and flying foxes rose in noisy alarm and what had seemed a forest of small charred trees on the opposite bank turned to running, gesticulating black figures, streaking off with terrified cries into the long grass.

The horse, caught half a mile across the plain, relieved of its packs, and the severe wounds on its nose, neck and shoulders treated with coal tar, was soon moving quietly along with its mates.

When the river turned north to be joined by a large creek junctioning from the west, it was realised that this too was not the Ord. Pentacost, sketching its course on the empty map, named it the Durack.

Now plains and parklands faded into rugged country where they rode in weird cities of termite strongholds. Scarcely a shape that human sculptors might devise had not been wrought by these myriad white ant builders, working in the dark, conjuring fantastic biblical images, hooded and cloaked, squat Buddhas, gorillas, and madman's castles with domes, turrets and minarets. Each took its colour from the surrounding earth—red, ochre, dun-grey—some so small and fine as to crumble under the horses' hoofs, others looming fifteen feet above the spinifex.

The party made camp on the Durack tributary and Stumpy Michael, Kilfoyle and Emanuel climbed a nearby vantage point to survey the lay of the land. Far and away to the north and west, ranges fell from flat tops or rugged pinnacles in folds like sculptured drapes of pallid gold studded with emeralds of spinifex.

Trapped in hills, there was no choice but to proceed on foot to the south-east, leading and driving the horses over dangerous ravines and sheer rock crevasses, with nothing to be seen from every summit but spinifex ranges and jagged rocks clutched by the talon roots of stunted eucalypts.

Anxiously they watched the horses falter, too tired to pull at the scattered grass, some casting their shoes and limping on bleeding hoofs.

When lower country opened at last they made painful progress downward to a good camp, resolved upon a two days' spell to renew shoes and gather energy for a south-eastern march—time at last to shoot a wild turkey and cook it, feathers and all, in an earthen oven covered with coals

A river, running swiftly to the gulf's head, gave every promise of being the Ord at last. They ran it up for eight miles through rough country and rank kerosene grass towering high above their heads, where Pintpot and Pannikin, fearing ambush, rode warily, their eyes keen as hawks on every movement of grass and foliage.

'Look out! Blackfellow come up behind!'

The riders turned to see over one hundred naked warriors, painted, befeathered and armed, stamping down the grass, springing with flourish of spears and boomerangs from behind trees and boulders. Every man had his hand upon his firearm, but Stumpy Michael ordered restraint. He had faced angry blacks before but had never found them over-anxious to hurl the spears they brandished so bravely. Most genuine attacks took place under cover of darkness or from behind rocks or trees, when men least suspected their danger.

A cry of savage rage went up as he rode forward slowly with hand outstretched. Spears quivering in throwing sticks were sullenly lowered as a dervish dance of old men leapt from behind, waving branches of leaping flame. In seconds the rank, resinous grass along the river bank was blazing to the tree tops, fanned by an east wind. The frightened horses reared and baulked but the fire was blowing the other way.

'Hold steady,' Stumpy Michael told his men. 'Don't fire and don't run.'

They remained as quietly as rearing horses would allow while the blacks, trapped between river and fire, turned in disorder, plunged into the water and disappeared.

The party followed the river until it dwindled into ranges to the south-east, whereupon they named it the Pentacost and camped to consider their situation.

While scouts went out to survey the countryside others caught barramundi, cat-fish and turtles in the newly named river. Sentinel tribesmen, perched at safe distances, watched quietly, ignoring peace messages shouted and mimed by the Territory boys who disdainfully pronounced them 'myalls' ignorant of a superior language.

The boys were less nervous now and found merriment in simple incidents, delighting in the discovery of familiar birds, animals and edible roots in this alien country.

Inspection showed that days of hard travelling had been in vain. Cut off by ranges to the south-east, they were forced to retrace their tracks and strike camp under the shadow of Mt Cockburn south. From here Stumpy Michael and Kilfoyle followed fertile valleys and fitful streams in anxious search of the lost river, camped on beds of grass without nets and with saddles for pillows, slept soundly within a circle of native fires. Their joy of beautiful country, the discovery of many of Queensland's best grasses and remarkable landmarks such as the strange, bald hills they named the 'Sugar-loaves' was shadowed with grave concern. Coming on another good stream, they returned to bring on their companions, but seven miles up their hopes were shattered again when the river veered west. Here a horse died of a restless wandering disease and others were sickening. Stumpy Michael named this sturdy stream the Dunham, after the pioneer priest of western Queensland.

Anxiety deepened when a mare broke its hobbles and was lost and when Michael's favourite horse, Doughboy, fell in a rocky pass and broke its leg. Forced to shoot his faithful mount, he named a hill nearby to its memory. Next day a mare they had been carefully nursing along died foaling and with other horses sickly and weak the situation began to look grim indeed. Winding and turning for over one hundred miles over range and plain and river they had still come no more than fifty—in a straight line—from their starting place. They were forced to abandon precious pack saddles and to cut down on rations. The salt beef ran out and tinned foods were low, but there was kangaroo and wild game and fish in yet another river which led them south on rising hopes that were rudely shattered when it turned in a capricious hairpin bend to the north-west. This stream they named the Bow, after the Irish river that marked the old boundary between Counties Galway and Clare.

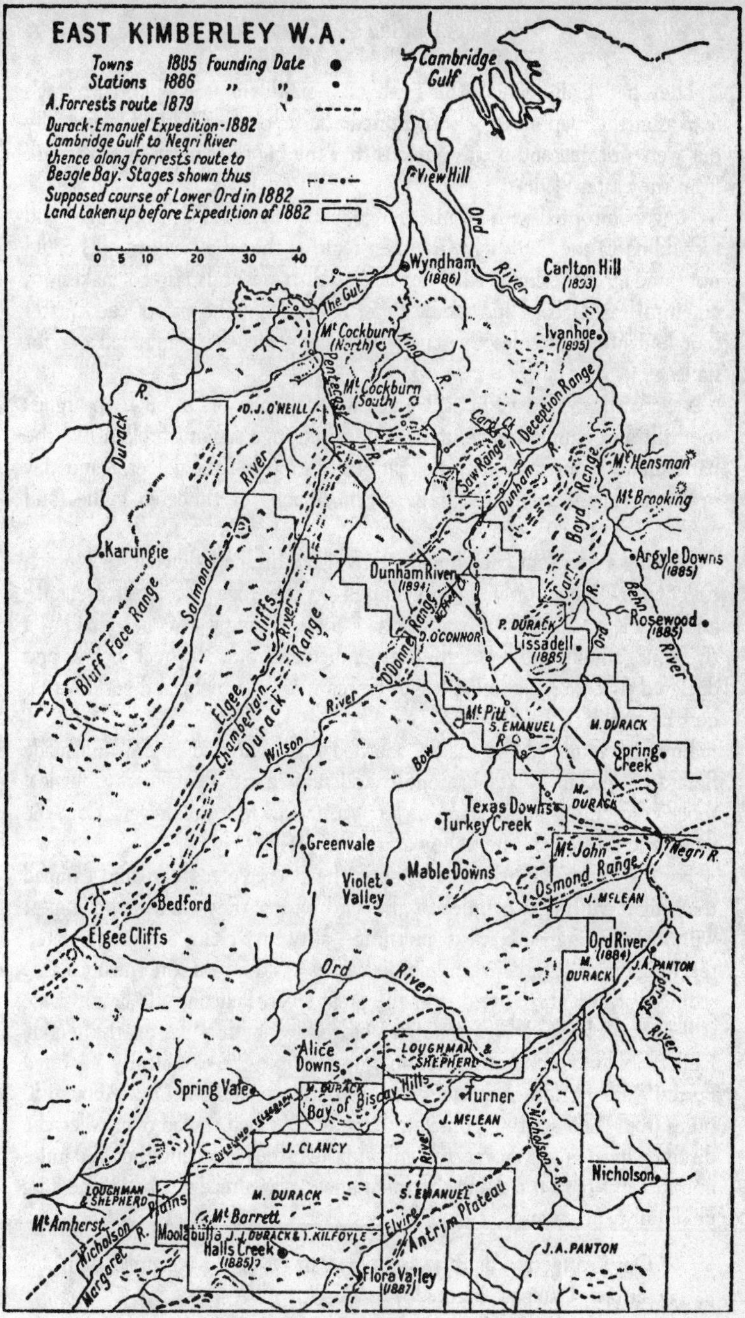
EAST KIMBERLEY W.A.
Towns 1885 Founding Date
Stations 1886
A. Forrest's route 1879
Durack-Emanuel Expedition-1882 Cambridge Gulf to Negri River thence along Forrests route to Beagle Bay. Stages shown thus
Supposed course of Lower Ord in 1882
Land taken up before Expedition of 1882
0 5 10 20 30 40
Cambridge Gulf
View Hill
Ord River
Wyndham (1886)
Carlton Hill (1893)
The Gut
Mt Cockburn (North)
Mt Cockburn (South)
King R.
Pentecost River
Ivanhoe (1895)
Deception Range
Card Ck
Saw Range
Dunham R.
Boyd Range
Mt Hensman
Mt Brooking
Durack R.
D. J. O'NEILL
Karungie
Argyle Downs (1885)
Dunham River (1894)
Carr Range
Ord R.
Behn River
Rosewood (1885)
Bluff Face Range
Salmond River
Elgee Cliffs
Chamberlain River
Durack Range
O'Donnell Range
D. O'CONNOR
P. DURACK
Lissadell (1885)
Wilson River
Mt Pitt
S. EMANUEL
M. DURACK
Spring Creek
Bow R.
Texas Downs
Turkey Creek
Negri R.
Mt John
Osmond Range
J. McLEAN
Greenvale
Violet Valley
Mable Downs
Bedford
Elgee Cliffs
Ord River (1884)
J. A. PANTON
Forrest River
Alice Downs
LOUGHMAN & SHEPHERD
Spring Vale
Bay of Biscay Hills
Turner
Overland Telegraph
J. CLANCY
Nicholson R.
Nicholson
Mt Amherst
Plains
Moolabulla
Mt Barrett
J. J. DURACK & T. KILFOYLE
Halls Creek (1885)
Elvire River
Antrim Plateau
Flora Valley (1887)
Margaret R.
Nicholson

They had realised now the truth of their dilemma. Captain Murray's fears that the map maker's 'conjectured course' of the Ord had been badly out were justified and it was obvious that the big river must enter the gulf from the eastern side.

Now, confronted with another range whose sheer slopes rose rugged and forbidding in the hard light, the men realised that their worn boots could not stand up to the climb. Kilfoyle, Jack-of-all-trades and master of makeshift, cut into leather bags and saddle flaps, marked out the size of each man's foot and attached soles to uppers with copper rivets hammered out for nails.

Meanwhile Stumpy Michael and Emanuel rode on through speargrass foothills and climbed ridge upon ridge to a range summit broken like the battlements of an ancient castle. Far below stretched the golden Kimberley savannah lands, cut through by green ribbons of timbered gullies and creeks.

Seeking a short cut back Emanuel inveigled his mare down a steep pinch to a narrow ledge, only to find himself on the edge of a sheer precipice and unable to return the way he had come. Stumpy Michael, making a two-mile circuit, surveyed the perpendicular from 300 feet below and declared that Emanuel must leave the mare for the night and get down as best he could.

Emanuel removed the saddle, soothed his frightened mount and made hazardous descent. Next morning all hands, armed with Pentacost's geological tools, cold chisels and tomahawks, cut a narrow footway upward from the ledge and coaxed the trembling animal to safety.

Fortified with Kilfoyle's new boots, the party veered east and camped that night within two miles of the Ord which they came upon almost without warning early next morning—a twenty-chain width of water, reaching out of sight between luxurious trees. As they rode on, the unearthly stillness of noonday settled over the great river. Pelicans and cranes were still as though carved in stone and crocodiles lay log-like on the muddy banks. Six miles up another stream entering from the east clearly answered Forrest's description of the junction of the Negri and the Ord. About 130 miles from their starting point on the gulf, they had trailed over twice the distance in their anxious search and although they faced another 500 miles and more of hard travelling the route ahead was already mapped, the long uncertainty at an end.

> Our satisfaction at this discovery can be better imagined than described. Camped. Marked tree 'D24'.

Here was the pioneer landseeker's dream-come-true. High-water level marked by grass and brushwood caught up in river trees thirty or forty feet above the bed indicated the mighty volumes of water that swept the channels during monsoonal rains, but there was no evidence of inundation on the plains above and the vegetation was nowhere that of a country subject to long, rainless periods. Here the trees spread broad trunks and luxuriant foliage in marked contrast to western Queensland's stunted mulga scrub, and the meagre outlines of lignum and boree. Only the remoteness of the district was against it, but the landseeker of the last century knew that where one man dared others had not been slow to follow. Men found more time and heart for long and hazardous ventures then than in the age of speed.

Already the travellers knew that Thylungra stock, with all the chances of the continent between, would graze on Kimberley pastures and drink the waters of the Ord. Riding along, they discussed ways and means of getting the stock across. Water was undependable on the direct route from the central Queensland border and through the Territory. They must take a roundabout route—up to the gulf and out west across the northern rivers. They might make it in eighteen months with luck, but what was a year or two here or there?

'Finding the country everything that could be desired, suitable for all kinds of stock,' they followed the Ord sixty miles towards its head. They would abandon a great deal of useless range and spinifex—already taken up 'sight unseen' on the map and concentrate on the open plains, though inevitably their holdings would include a good deal of rough and inferior country.

There was little time to linger, for flour and sugar were already very low and they were still 300 hard miles from Beagle Bay. Pentacost gathered specimens under protest from the others who declared he would soon have them all staggering under loads of stones and all else abandoned. He found his companions unappreciative of rock records of millenniums past while some, riding the sun-scorched landscape, were frankly sceptical when he displayed a fragment of sandstone grooved by a moving glacier. The down-to-earth bushmen had little time for reflections upon a geological past when rocky outcrops were reefs of a forgotten sea, when the table tops of eroded mountains formed the plateau level of a lost landscape, devastated by seething floods grinding and tearing at rock and soil, racked by convulsions of nature that mingled rocky strata in violent confusion. Interest quickened only when he drew attention to the auriferous quartz picked up from the dry beds of creeks that wound through the billowing Bay of Biscay hills—a range that in four years' time would awaken to the roar and turmoil of a gold rush shanty town.

The weary horses had dwindled now to fourteen and the travellers were making most of their way on foot. When their boots wore through again Kilfoyle did what he could by cutting into the remaining saddle flaps, but the rough going ground them quickly into gaping holes. Cut and blistered feet were tied about at last with bags and pieces of clothing. Only Pannikin and Pintpot, swinging along on horny pads, suffered no hardship.

Today, looking down from the mail plane on the furrowed unshaven face of Kimberley, it seems incredible that men walked through those stony spinifex ranges, over sandy river beds, through ant-hill plateaux, and bald clay-pans, and across the undulating pastures of Nicholson Plains.

About thirty-five miles above the junction of the Margaret and Fitzroy Rivers the party was excited to come upon its first indication of white man's penetration in this lonely land—a large white gum marked 'WF 22, PA 9, '81'. Curiously enough their subsequent enquiries both on the lower Fitzroy and later from Alexander Forrest in Perth failed to identify the initials. There can be little doubt, however, that they belonged to William Forrester and his companion who had been sent by the King Sound Pastoral Company to inspect blocks they had taken up on the Lennard River.

Their first sign of Forrest's expedition was a tree marked 'F137', where Tommy Pierre, the faithful black companion of Forrest's many exploring trips, had been so close to death that the mountain named after him might well have been his headstone.

From here on the party camped a few days at a time to rest the horses and examine the country to the south, since all to the north was hidden by the forbidding slopes and sheer rock faces of the King Leopold Range. Michael knew that Forrest had tried in vain to cross this barrier but where the Margaret, emerging from its gorge, lapped the canyon wall, he was tempted to see whether chance would reveal a pass on the other side. Crocodiles nosing the surface among cobblers, turtles and banded rifle-fish were of the long-nosed fish-eating variety, and, assured by the native boys that they were harmless and timid, Michael swam across and climbed the blackened 500 feet of precipice. Beyond lay range upon range, down-tumbling and upward-sweeping among scattered boulders, wild gorges and sapphire mountain pools. He followed the gorge for some miles, cutting his blistered feet on razor-sharp rock edges, but the range was unrelenting to any but the nomad tribespeople who came there to bury their dead in hidden caves, and to hunt rock python and porcupine. In a deserted camp he picked up some part-finished and broken spearheads, fashioned from the flint and agate of the rocks around, like relics of the stone age found in the drifts and caves of Europe. The camp had been left hurriedly, probably on his coming, and embers still glowed on a small cairn of stones. Hoping to find a bird or goanna, ready cooked in skin or feathers, to appease his hunger, he moved the hot stones to uncover in horror the part-cooked body of a child. He stumbled on, with darkness closing on the savage range, and slept in a cave among the droppings of bats and kangaroos. Next morning he retraced his steps to the precipice and swam to rejoin his company.

Fever broke out within 280 miles of Beagle Bay, but already behind schedule, there was no choice but to trudge doggedly in near delirium, with splitting heads and tortured feet. Only the two boys were little the worse for their journey and worked hard and faithfully to bring the white men through.

The Fitzroy, mighty river of the western plains, abounded in fish and game and the sight of its splendid reaches and pastoral country heartened them for 150 miles. A grey sea of stunted pindan and minnerichi scrub broke at last into red ridges, which the blacks climbed, hoping to find an easy route for the sick men. They returned excitedly with broad smiles and a gabble of good news.

'Station that-a-way! House, yard, everysing. True-fella we bin find'm!'

Their surprise and joy was no greater than that of Will McLarty, manager of Minnie, an out-station of Yeeda, who made the little homestead of bush timber with its bark roof a palace of comfort and respite to the exhausted travellers.

While the Durack-Emanuel party had been organising in the east, sheep men from the south-west, also stimulated by Forrest's report, had joined forces with Victorian investors, and the first pioneers had come with their sheep by lugger to settle in around the west Kimberley rivers. George Julius Brockman had brought sheep from the Nicol Bay area to Beagle Bay and had established Yeeda Station in 1880, long before news of his intention had reached civilisation. Soon other isolated stations were cropping up along the Fitzroy—Mundoona, Meda, Lulugai, with flocks of from two to four thousand sheep. Here too the first-footers were of sturdy pioneer stock, but mostly descendants of English and Scots landed gentry brought up in the tradition of fences and careful paddocking, vastly different in background from the rugged cattle men soon to press in from the east, tough overlanders schooled in the rough-and-ready New South Wales style of the open range.

Will McLarty, whose people were early settlers of the south-western Pinjarra district, related the story of west Kimberley development. Already, it seemed, a shadow of despondency, not yet touching the bright dreams of city investors, had fallen on the pioneers. After the first wild flush of enthusiasm it was evident that this was after all a hard land. Early reports of its fertility and abundance had deceived many that pioneering settlement would be a simple matter here. Terms of land tenure were more severe than were warranted for a remote and lonely land of long, dry winters and wet tropical summers. A port was needed desperately, a jetty for shipping and local stores.

'Don't exaggerate the value of the country or underestimate the hardships,' McLarty advised his guests. 'They talk down south as if we live in a sort of Eden here—everything handed us on a silver platter, but it's a tough battle every inch of the way, as pioneering has always been, and little romance in it that I can see.'

McLarty took over the party's sadly reduced outfit and the eleven remaining horses and saw them off on their eighty-mile journey to the coast at Beagle Bay, where, according to plan, the schooner *Mary Smith* should have been awaiting their arrival. There was, however, no sign of the ship and the party made camp in the bush above the tide-swept beach. Three weeks of speculation and worry dragged by, during which time a pearling lugger put in for water. The owner of the outfit, an Englishman with a crew of Aboriginal 'skin divers', men and women, invited the party on board, displaying a deck strewn with giant oyster shells—*Pinctada maxima*, the world's finest mother-of-pearl. In a box lined with green felt and with a double lock was what seemed to the travellers a fortune in pearls—hard-earned, the skipper said, for there were many hardships and hazards in the game. Cyclones had already destroyed luggers, all hands on board. Sometimes divers were smitten with paralysis, attacked by sharks, giant gropers, rays or devil fish.

Stumpy Michael, fascinated by this new aspect of northern industry, recorded that the pearler seemed a 'colourful but somewhat callous customer' who maintained that the black women were gamer and could stay down longer than the men. Trouble-makers, he said, had now begun to talk of 'exploitation', and he was afraid they would soon have to import divers from overseas at great expense, no doubt causing the ruin of a budding industry.

The *Mary Smith*, a sailing vessel of 650 tons, turned up at last with a tale of accident and bad weather that had caused long delay.

In his diary Stumpy Michael made a brief concluding entry:

> 1st. Jan. 1883. Arrived Fremantle after a rough passage – 1400 miles from Beagle Bay, and half a year since our departure from

> Queensland. Received with the greatest kindness by everybody, especially Mr Alexander Forrest, whose warm hearted welcome we shall never forget.

The party still faced a 3,400-mile sea journey around the south coast and north back to Brisbane, another two to three weeks' travelling, but Kate Durack, at Archerfield, had already received news of their safe arrival over the telegraph that had linked Western Australia with the east five years before.

> COUNTRY FINE BEYOND EXPECTATIONS NO CAUSE REGRET COST.

The final cost, owing to delays and mishaps, was actually about £2,000 over their original estimate of £4,000 but neither Duracks nor Emanuels ever considered it misspent.

The two boys, Pannikin and Pintpot, returned to their country on the first ship Darwin bound and were later to share the honours of leading Queensland cattle into Kimberley.

22

START OF THE BIG TREK

The year 1883. Duracks and Emanuels divide their Kimberley holdings and plan to stock them. Organisation at Thylungra for overland cattle trek. Partnerships and agreements. Stores and equipment. Departure from Thylungra and Galway Downs. The cattle rush. Galway Jerry Durack and family retire to Ipswich. Patsy Durack's eldest son Michael returns from college.

Mr Solomon Emanuel and Grandfather were both in Sydney to welcome the exploring party on its return from Western Australia and big decisions were made with surprising speed. Stumpy Michael summarised the situation:

'Part of the area we took up previously on the map we found to be inferior and abandoned in favour of what seemed more likely the pick of the Ord and Fitzroy country. You understand they want only genuine settlers over there—not speculators. Lord Kimberley, the Secretary of State for the Colonies, is standing firm in England against the locking up of undeveloped blocks. He has set the rental very high at ten shillings per thousand acres and rules that any who have not stocked their country to the extent of twenty sheep or two head of cattle to the thousand acres within two years will forfeit their leases. At present over fifty-one million acres are held in lease in various interests but few of them will be able to meet the conditions and a lot of land now taken up will soon be available if we want it. I have taken up with Mr Forrest no more than we should be able to pay for and stock within the required time or thereabouts. This covers roughly one and a half million acres in west Kimberley in the Fitzroy region and about the same on either side of the Ord River near the Northern Territory border. Both areas are untried but seem on the face of it to be equally promising, although west Kimberley is at present thought to be rather more suitable for sheep-raising both because of the type of country and because sheep can be got to the west coast by ship. The cattle will have to come overland, but since mobs have already been driven from Queensland into the Territory as far as Victoria River it should be simple enough to bring them a couple of hundred miles farther to the Ord.'

'The question is, gentlemen,' Emanuel summed up, 'which of us, at the present juncture, is more interested in sheep and which in cattle?'

It would seem that the decision was already made, for the Emanuels preferred the safer and quicker project of bringing sheep by sea to that of droving cattle overland, and saw brighter immediate prospects in shipping bales of wool to market than in droving or shipping beef on the hoof. On the other hand, although Grandfather and his brothers had been for some time experimenting with sheep on Thylungra, they had never been really interested in the 'woolly-backs'. Men accustomed to working cattle found the handling of sheep a tame occupation, while the fences that patterned the sheep men's properties were traditionally anathema to them. They knew all the risks connected with droving big mobs over what was probably a greater distance and a harder track than men, even in the time of Moses, had ever succeeded in taking livestock before, nor were they unacquainted with the fact that at least two parties had already lost all their cattle in the attempt. They had, however, supreme faith in their own experience and organisation. They were not out to break records. They would, if needs be, camp for months on end, even at risk of overstepping the time limit, rather than push doggedly on through hopeless drought. Better, they reasoned, to save the stock and argue the case out afterwards, for even the august Lord Kimberley could hardly prove impersonal enough to foreclose on an overlanding party making so epic an effort to stock the new country.

More cautious men might well have been daunted by the lack of existing markets at the end of the long trail, for the population potential of the north was limited, and the Kimberley district was after all the last outpost of the sparsely settled Cinderella colony whose resources were too small to develop even its more fertile and temperate south. Grandfather and his associates, however, readily dismissed such worries. If they had waited until the way was safe and the markets assured, they argued, they would still have been on their cocky-runs around Goulburn.

So, in a few strokes of the pen, the Emanuels became heirs to the vast flood plains of the Fitzroy and to the spinifex and pindan of the desert margins, and the Duracks to the rolling basalt downs and rugged quartzite ranges of the Ord.

Grandfather could hardly contain his excitement at this new acquisition and found hard to understand the lack of enthusiasm displayed by some of his relatives for this new promised land or neither drought nor flood.

'It's not a property I'm offering you,' he told Sarah Tully and her husband. 'It's a Principality!'

'But as if the Cooper wasn't far enough out already!' his sister protested.

'Sure and the Ord seems a long way from anywhere now,' Grandfather agreed, 'but the towns will be moving out there soon as they have moved out here and there'll be coaches running and railways in no time atall.'

'But we've made our homes and buried our children here, Patsy,' Sarah reminded him. 'Why should we be wanting to start again just as we all begin to do so well where we are?'

'Because I've a feeling we're in for a run of bad seasons,' Grandfather told her. 'Michael, Jerry and I have our interests widespread enough to tide us over a bad spell but smaller holders have been wiped out here before and they'll be wiped out again.'

Sarah set her lips in the determined line that hard years had drawn on her weatherbeaten face:

'We'll not leave the Cooper, Patsy, not though the drought wipes every beast off the Wathagurra run. We'll hang on and see it through until the good Lord sends us rain.'

Dinny Skeahan, at the first whisper of 'auriferous country', had pencilled his name across an area of rock and spinifex in the vicinity of Hall's Creek but Poor Mary, having at last got a roof over her head on the Rasmore block, refused to consider it.

So eager was Grandfather to see the Kimberley country for himself that he toyed for a while with the idea of taking ship to Cambridge Gulf, burying there a quantity of iron rations for the droving party on arrival, riding down the Ord to the Negri Junction, mapping as he went, and surveying a stock route from there to the Victoria River. No one besides Grandfather, however, seems to have considered that the journey would fulfil any useful purpose. The rations, even if buried in tanks, would probably be discovered and disposed of by the blacks long before the overlanders arrived, and the West Australian Government was supposed already to have sent out a party to survey the Ord. The scheme died a natural death not so much because Grandfather was talked out of it as for the fact that he had too much else to do.

The surviving records, lists of equipment, memos, odd agreements with one and another, incomplete as they are, often ungrammatical and clumsily worded, may well convey a general impression of muddle but there was actually nothing of the kind about Grandfather's activities over this period. In fact he was now operating at the height of his powers as a man of vision combined with extraordinary organising ability. He felt confident, by everything he had learned over the years, that Kimberley offered the greatest possible security for the future. Here was the land of permanent water, regular rainfall and abundant pasture where they need not live in constant fear of pending ruin. He was planning now not for himself but for his sons, nephews, cousins and any other of his friends and relatives who shared his confidence. He was planning broadly but with minute attention to detail.

Volunteers for the big trek had not been hard to find, but the organisers realised that the success of the project depended largely on the skill and personality of the leaders. They would need to be not only trained stockmen and experienced bushmen but should have the ability to hold a party together and a reputation for reasonable temperance. It was decided that, since they might well be two years or more on the road, the task must lie with the single men and that the cattle should travel in four mobs under separate leaders representing the different combinations of interests.

Galway Jerry had undertaken to see a mob of Thylungra breeding cattle, jointly owned by himself and Grandfather, over the first stages of the journey, when he would give over to Grandmother's cousin Patsy Moore.

The same Jerry was also in partnership with Tom Kilfoyle and Tom Hayes who were to tail 2,000 head of cattle to stock a jointly owned holding near the Territory border.

Darby Durack's eldest son, Big Johnnie, was to lead a mob of 2,000 head to a property tentatively named Forrest Vale around Spring Creek, an Ord River tributary. He was to be partner with Grandfather in this piece of country, and owned a third share of the 2,000 head of cattle, half of which were to stock an adjoining property which Grandfather had taken up for his sons.

Grandfather's affairs were by this time so widespread and complicated that the old free and easy style of business 'understandings' and home-made agreements had given place to a new order of legal deeds. These were drawn up on tough parchment and consisted of page on page of redundant clauses and provisos written in finest copperplate and costing eight guineas apiece. They were, as Grandfather said, 'pretty well everlasting' but few of the legal documents so well preserved in his fire-resisting waterproof tin box were applicable to the future and served as nothing more than an illustration of the fate of so many of man's best laid schemes.

Big Johnnie probably never had time to study the ponderous agreement drawn up just before the cattle left, stating that

> . . . the said Patrick Durack and John Durack, of Thylungra Station in the colony of Queensland, graziers, shall carry on the business of partnership on those leasehold lands known as Forrest Vale situated in the district of Kimberley in the colony of Western

> Australia comprising several blocks containing three hundred thousand acres or thereabouts and that the said John Durack shall devote his whole time and attention to the said partnership business and shall conduct and carry on the same with all due diligence, attention and sobriety . . .

At all events, Forrest Vale proved to be one of the less fortunate blind stabs made at the map of Kimberley and Big Johnnie, after a brief glimpse at its rock and spinifex expanses, was content to leave it to the blacks.

The following letter shown me after the death of Stumpy Michael's eldest son Ambrose in 1955 indicates that Grandfather promised him a share of the cattle then on the way to Kimberley:

> Thylungra,
> 30th August 1883.
>
> This is to certify that I, Patrick Durack, has gave Half of 1270, twelve hundred and seventy head of cattle now started for Western Australia in charge of my brother Jeremiah to Patrick Angus Ambrose Durack my Nephew and the said Patrick Angus Ambrose Durack now minor his Father is to look after the above mentioned twelve hundred and seventy half of them which I now give to the above mentioned Patrick Angus Ambrose Durack. His Father Michael Durack or his trustees will give the above mentioned half to his son with increase added as soon as he is 21 years of age.
>
> PATRICK DURACK.

Ambrose's father, Stumpy Michael, had taken up for himself and his family a big section of the country traversed between the Dunham and Bow Rivers. The wealth of Lissadell, however, was not for the first white man who laid claim to it. Stumpy Michael was at this time arranging for his cousin Long Michael to drove 2,000 head of cattle to its rich river frontages.

Long Michael and his two brothers, Black Pat and Jerry Brice, had been for some years managing Mooraberrie Station on the Diamantina, a property Edward Coman had acquired from John Costello. Hard years and many setbacks lay behind these young men who as children on Dixon's Creek had spent a deal more time at scrub bashing and fencing than at schoolwork. As boys they had knocked about the country with teams and droving plants, gaining experience but gathering little moss, while their first bid for a holding of their own on the Castlereagh had petered out in the terrible drought of the early seventies. In western Queensland they had made names for themselves as tough, resourceful stockmen, often bringing cattle down the arid Birdsville track into South Australia and they had set their hearts on one day purchasing Mooraberrie for themselves. Two light seasons on the Cooper, however, and a drought on the Diamantina brought their schemes to an abrupt end with a blank foreclosure on the property early in '83. The brothers, having handed over stock and property on behalf of their employer, prepared to ride off when the bank inspector challenged their possession of a few head of horses.

'These happen to be our own private property,' Long Michael told him.

'You can prove that in Court,' the inspector snapped.

It was the last straw for Long Michael.

'Never mind about the Court. I'll prove it to you right here.'

A backward glance as he and his brother rode off revealed the infuriated bank official shaking a vengeful fist as he rose from the dust.

'Well boys,' Long Michael said, as they turned their horses' heads towards Thylungra, 'it looks as though it's cousin Patsy's Principality for us after all.'

At Thylungra he accepted the position of head drover for his cousin Stumpy Michael who offered him, by way of incentive, one-third of 2,000 head of cattle. Having engaged his drovers, including his brother Black Pat, he then led off along the Barcoo River to collect the cattle Stumpy Michael had purchased from Mount Marlowe Station, about 100 miles north of Kyabra Creek. From here they planned to cut across to the Thompson River to meet up with the other parties then also about to set out from Thylungra and Galway Downs.

I knew Long Michael and Black Pat only as old men, but even in their eighties they were upright, lean and tall with the fine aquiline features and distinction of bearing that marked all the thirteen children of Darby Durack and his wife Margaret. Long Michael was still subject to attacks of malaria first picked up on the Territory track and he attributed his deafness to the quinine he had taken in regular doses ever since. His stammer and the fist poundings that went with it gave emphasis to his statements and as the family acceded him the longest memory as well as the longest legs he usually had the last word in arguments about the 'early days'. Towards the end of his life he returned to Kimberley, a rich and lonely old man, to visit the scenes of his youth and it was only then, sitting with him on the river bank at Argyle, while he taught me to smoke the porous root of a cajuput, that I really listened to the story of the now legendary trek and to please him set down certain details that he considered important. 'Never trust hearsay,' he told me. 'They always get it wrong. And never mind the adventure. The hardest part about the trip was the *b. .lasted monotony*!'

There was a fever of excitement and activity around the Cooper as the big mobs were mustered, the droving plants and equipment made ready for the track and the stockmen's roles assigned. Many would-be overlanders had ridden hundreds of miles to present themselves at Thylungra while others turned up at Archerfield, Stumpy Michael's place outside Brisbane, asking to be put on. For the most part only relatives or stockmen of known reputation were recruited but a few more or less new to the droving game somehow got in. Among these were George Rae, a runaway seaman, Bertie Belcher, son of the headmaster of the Goulburn Grammar School and his mate Frank Cooper from Tarago. A nephew of Belcher, to whom I wrote for information, told me that his uncle had joined the trek after learning that his fiancée had eloped with a naval officer. 'The tradition in such cases, of going out to shoot lions in Africa,' he wrote, 'being beyond Uncle Bertie's means, he simply downed tools and went to Queensland to go with the Duracks.'

It has not been possible to list all members of the overlanding party, since some who started dropped out along the way to be replaced by others. The following extracts from Grandfather's notebook, however, sets out the four parties, the stock in hand and at least some of the men who started out with them.

> June 12 1883. Cousin Big Johnnie leaves Thylungra on today with two thousand head of breeding cattle, brand 7PD in which he holds with me one third share according to our partnership. With them is starting:
>
> Johnnie Durack, (drover in charge.)
> Bertie Belcher,
> Frankie Cooper,
> Harry Barnes
> Will Blake (for part of way.)
> J. Storier (to the Thompson river)
> In hand......2000 head.
>
> June 14th 1883. My brother Jerry leaving from Galway Downs with one thousand, two hundred and seventy head of Thylungra breeding cattle, brand 7PD, held in partnership between himself and me. With this party is starting the following men, (Mick Skeahan and Dick, black boy, to return with him in about six weeks and Patsy Moore is to take charge).
>
> Jerry Durack
> Patsy Moore

Mick Skeahan
George Rae
Charlie Gaunt
Dick (black boy).
In hand. . . . . .1270 head.

Tom Kilfoyle and Tom Hayes is starting from Galway Downs with two thousand head held in partnership with brother Jerry to stock country also in partnership. With them to date, to go as far as the Thompson or thereabouts is:

Mick Brogan
Steve Brogan
Jim Minogue
Two others (?)
In hand. . . . . .2000 head.

On July 29th 1883 cousins Long Michael and Black Pat started from Mt Marlowe on the Barcoo where they have purchased two thousand two hundred head of cattle for brother Michael, one third in partnership with Long Michael. They took on with them the fifty young bulls I had bought from Pollak and Hogan of Comeongin and they are to catch up with the other cattle on the way. With them is travelling so far as I now know:

Cousin Long Michael
" Black Pat
John Urquart
Bob Perry
Jack Sherringham
In hand (with bulls). . . . . .2250.

Total cattle left on road for Western Australia in
these four mobs .... 7,250 head
Horses with all four parties............................(approx) 200 "
Working bullocks with teams .... 60 "

On May 16th 1883 Cousin Jerry Brice Durack left for Sydney with a mob of five hundred bullocks from Thylungra and Galway Downs in fair condition. Expects return about six months time.

The last entry reminds us that while young breeding cattle were being set on the road for Western Australia bullocks were being despatched as usual to southern markets. It will be noted also that young Jerry Brice undertook this droving contract while his three elder brothers were on the road to Kimberley where he was later to join them.

The detail connected with the organisation of the big trek is indicated by lists of equipment and random memos in these old Thylungra notebooks. The following items were purchased for Big Johnnie's party:

GOODS PURCHASED FOR GOING ON ROAD TO WESTERN AUSTRALIA

	£	s	d
5 lbs shot		3	9
1 box caps		1	–
1 handsaw		6	–
Carried Forward		10	9
Brought Forward		10	9
1 doz. pint pots		5	6
1 doz. knives and forks		12	–
Files		2	6
1 doz. tin plates, 1 doz. spoons		10	6
4 lbs tobacco	1	4	–
Auger		5	–
1 bottle turps		2	6
2 dishes, tub and bucket		10	–
1 camp oven	1	10	–
1 gun	1	5	–
1 hammer and pinchers		12	–
1 cross cut saw		10	–
1 bag flour	2	10	–
156 lbs flour	3	5	9
Steel bar	1	10	–
4 bars	5	–	–
Shovels and axes (old)	1	10	–
Adze and handle		15	–
3 braces	3	15	–
Tongs and wire slit plugs		10	–
Billies and anvil and ten irons	8	11	2
2 doz. augers	3	16	–
6 shovels	2	11	–
2 shafts	1	–	–

One tin paint	1	–	–
Soap	1	2	–
1 case raisins	2	12	–
1 case currants	2	12	–
60 doz. matches (7d a doz.)	1	15	–
1 gal. boiled oil		9	6
1 grinding stone	1	6	8
1 tin blue paint		2	–
6 lbs mustard		9	–
2 tins pepper		3	6
45 lbs sugar		18	9
Punch, awl and hemp for saddler		4	6
14 lbs horse nails	1	1	–
1 doz. links		12	–
Plus carriage on goods per cwt.	6	10	–
Driving team from Adavale	2	5	–
Beef and accommodation for man	1	2	6
Extra man with team	2	9	–
Blacksmith	1	10	–
6 pack saddles @ £3. 10. 0 each	21	–	–
6 saddles @ £5 each	30	–	–
10 horse bells (Condamines @ 10/– each)	5	–	–
2 spurs at 5/– each		10	–
Harry for breaking horse for Johnnie D.	1	10	–
	£128	18	1

Further Expenses

One team bullocks purchased from Thos. Hefferman July 14th, '83, also his waggon, tackling and goods	289	5	7
Bulls from Comeongin Station	236	10	–
Deed of partnership between cousin John D. and me	8	8	–
A/c paid Skinner Adavale further rations, blankets, mosquito nets, saddle serge, canvas, medicines and gear going with waggons	248	9	1
Bills drawn by brother Jerry and Ashley's bill and blacksmith	53	16	–
Cash for guns to Cobb and Co.	4	15	–
Cash paid to Dick that started with Jerry to W.A.	5	–	–

To Duncan McCaully at Windorah before he started	4	1	4
Wages for men for mustering cattle for overland, also taking cattle in hand before starting, also for one man going as far as required. In all 60 weeks wages @ 30/– per week	90	–	–
Two sets of brands, 7PD for self and OMU for brother Michael for taking on road	3	–	–
TOTAL	£1072	18	7
Plus exes. listed in other book making present total of	£1551	8	8

(Horseshoes not counted here.)

A first-hand account of how he rode into Galway Downs as the party was packing up for departure was given us by an old man who as a boy of eighteen had joined the overlanding party. There were horses in the yard, he said, a big mob of cattle in hand on the flat and everyone moving briskly with a clinking of harness and spurs. While making his way to the homestead for the usual traveller's handout of bread and beef, the young stockman met Galway Jerry bustling from the yard in answer to the urgent clanging of the breakfast bell. Thirty years old, slim and agile with his merry blue eyes and cheery whistle, the youngest of the three Thylungra brothers had the reputation for being a keen sport, a bush wit, an expert tap dancer and altogether—in the old man's words—'a bit of a lad.'

'Hello kid!' he said, 'Come in and have some grub. You look as if you could do with a square meal, whoever you are.'

'Me name's Gaunt,' the boy told him.

'Suits you pretty well too,' the boss laughed. 'How did you manage to get so poor?'

'I been droving in the Territory with Buchanan,' Gaunt said. 'Nine months' hard tucker and hard riding. A bloke was a fool to take it on.'

'What about a droving trip to Kimberley, two quid a week and plenty of good, clean fun?' he was asked.

'If you're not joking,' the boy said, 'I'm game.'

And so the Galway cattle, closely followed by the two mobs in charge of Big Johnnie, Tom Kilfoyle and Tom Hayes, headed north to the Thompson River. The cattle were harder to hold in the early stages for being of quiet station stock and, however tenuously the route wound, kept stopping in their tracks to stare back towards the familiar waters and well-worn cattle pads of Kyabra Creek. At night they would start at shadows, at a movement in the dark bush or a sudden flare-up of the camp fire and the sentinel stockmen rode quietly alert, mechanically turning the persistent stragglers back into the uneasy herd that rumbled monotonously with the long, low bellowings of nostalgia. Creatures of habit, the cattle would take time to settle to the rhythm of the road to become adjusted to a meaningless moving-on through slow weeks dissolving into months and years.

The ill fortune that was to haunt Galway Jerry in all his Kimberley ventures struck within two weeks of his departure. Who could say what started that terrible night rush? A sudden noise from some bush creature in the scrub? The frightened starting of a beast from sleep? On an instant the cattle were away, plunging through the camp fire, over the waggonette, while stockmen, startled from their swags, rode frantically to turn the lead of the fear-crazed herd.

Grandfather arrived on the scene a few days later with my father who had returned from college to help him over this busy period. They found the scrub flattened as though it had lain in the path of a hurricane, the ground littered with branches, crushed carcasses and scattered horns. Where the camp had been lay the splintered ruins of the waggonette, scraps of canvas and blankets from the trammelled swags. Two hundred head of cattle had been irretrievably lost in the scrub, another hundred crushed to pulp. The cook, who had managed in the nick of time to flatten himself behind a tree, had departed the following day and one of the stockmen had been taken into the nearest station with a broken leg.

Galway Jerry reorganised his party, replaced the lost cattle, the cook and the injured stockman and was on the road again when news reached him of the illness of his three-year-old daughter Janie. Patsy Moore took control of the cattle while the anxious father hurried home only in time to see his little girl before she died.

The second child, Bridget, seemed now to show symptoms of the same mysterious sickness that had taken her sister and the distracted young parents felt they must get her and their little son at once to a more settled area. Within a few weeks they had packed up and, accompanied by Great-grandmother Bridget who would not have the delicate child out of her sight, left for Ipswich, near Brisbane. In this flourishing district Galway Jerry purchased his dream property, a place named Moorlands, near the little town of Rosewood, where he at once built training stables and began breeding racehorses. He and his brother Stumpy Michael, now within easy visiting distance, became foundation members of the newly established

Tattersall's Club in Brisbane and the gay young couple's home soon became a centre of social activity. The change, however, had come too late to bring strength to the frail child who died not long after the family settled in their new home. Of the three children born within three years of their married life there now remained only the little boy who bore my Grandfather's name. He was that same Patsy who, in my own youth, was the much-battered, drink-forsworn and well-loved manager of Argyle and who, when people cast aspersions on his hard-bitten countenance, would inform them wryly that he had been, at least in his mother's opinion, 'a very pretty little boy'.

My father Michael, young though he was, now took over much of the management of both Galway Downs and Thylungra while Grandfather grappled with the problems of his unwieldy estate, trying to devise some scheme by which he could build a city home for his family, deal with a chain of hotels, butchers' shops and houses strung from Brisbane to Windorah, visit Kimberley and at the same time keep faith with Cooper's Creek. That he actually succeeded in doing all these things, even for a time, is surely remarkable.

23

The Rule of the Road

The years 1883 to 1884. Stock converging on Kimberley. MacDonalds leave from Goulburn district. Nat Buchanan leaves from Flinders River. Durack cattle head for the gulf. Life in the cattle camps. Too many calves. Dry stage to the Hamilton. Drought camp on the Georgina. Long Michael returns to Brisbane for horses. Sickness in the camp. The drought breaks.

A bird's-eye view of the continent in the middle of 1883—'the overlanders' year'—would have shown thin trails of stock converging on the big northern rivers from east to west. Sheep, to be driven inland along the Fitzroy and its tributaries, were being landed in thousands on the west coast at the newly established port of Derby where the first bales of Kimberley wool already awaited shipment to southern markets. Meanwhile droving parties with thousands of cattle were making from Queensland and New South Wales for scattered destinations in the Territory and Kimberley.

In May, while the Durack parties were still mustering and organising, the MacDonalds and their MacKensie cousins, originally hailing from the Isle of Skye and some of whom had been guests at my grandparents' wedding, were already on the trail north from Tuena in the Goulburn district with cattle bound for the junction of the Fitzroy and Margaret Rivers, some 3,500 miles from their starting point. By the time the Durack cattle got under way the MacDonalds had already run into drought conditions in New South Wales and were suffering heavy stock losses.

John Costello, meanwhile, was negotiating the sale of his coastal properties near Rockhampton and planning to establish a chain of Territory stations on the Limmen River that ran a wild course into the Gulf of Carpentaria.

At much the same time Nat Buchanan and his relatives the Gordons and the Cahills had taken delivery of a mob of cattle on the Flinders River, about 350 miles north of Thylungra, to stock country on the upper Ord for the Melbourne firm of Osmond and Panton. During an exchange of reminiscences in later years old Tom Cahill, a member of this party, told how the redoubtable Nat—or 'Bluey' as he was generally called—had been sent to take over this mob from an incompetent head drover:

> One of the first things he did [Cahill wrote] was to sack the man who was being paid seven pounds per week as Pilot to the cattle along a main road. The next thing Nat did was to go to each camp and empty the demijohns of rum that was on the drays out on to the black soil . . .

One can well picture the dismayed faces of the drovers watching their precious liquor disappear into the thirsty ground, but controlling the drink problem was one of the head drover's greatest headaches. Whether there was grog in their camps or not the theme song of all the overlanding parties was the much parodied drinking chorus:

> Oh, Shenandoah, I love your daughter,
> Hurray, the rolling river,
> We love Three Star with a little water,
> Ah, ha, we're bound awa', across the Western border.

The route from Thylungra stretched north to the Gulf and swung west to no-man's-land. On the map it looked simple enough and measured a fairly neat 2,500 miles. In fact it veered to every compass point from water to water, from grass to grass, and nobody knew how far they must travel in 'drover's miles'.

Half-way up the Thompson River Long Michael's party had caught up with the other mobs and from here they were to travel more or less together, but keeping the four mobs apart as far as possible. Which lot 'went lead' for the day seems to have depended upon which got the earliest start in the morning.

Each party had its waggonette containing supplies, water drums and drovers' swags. This was driven by the cook who liked to strike camp ahead of the drovers and have the billy boiling and the johnnie cakes roasting in the ashes when the men rode in off watch. A good camp cook took a tremendous pride in his speed and efficiency. He was traditionally a touchy customer, but the sight of his busy figure, moving briskly among the neat rows of packbags and cooking utensils, was a welcome one to a band of hungry men after a long day in the saddle. They judiciously praised the lightness of his dampers and brownies, the succulence of his salt beef and stews.

There were conventions to be observed, small points that marked the experienced stockman from the 'newchum'. Nattiness was one of them, for untidiness meant muddle and delay. It was against all the unwritten laws of the road to waste time looking for one's personal effects. Hat, boots, pannikin and stockwhip must always be to hand, while matches, revolver and pocket knife were carried in neat leather pouches in their belts. It was 'not done' to linger over meals or get in the cook's way between the packs and the fire, and no one but the cook was ever permitted to meddle with the impedimenta in the waggonette.

Tough customers as many of the old-time stockmen were, some so illiterate that they signed their names with a cross, there was a certain code of etiquette in the cattle camps. Unless he volunteered information, a man was never questioned about his past and the name he gave himself was good enough. Nothing he said in drink was held against him and he was not reminded of his indiscretions at a later date. A man could skite as much as he liked, he could leg-pull and lie, but he must on no account be 'flash', though what was considered 'flash' in one district often passed in another.

Letting the cattle spread out over good grass, the drovers 'poked' their mobs quietly north-west up the Darra and over the rugged dividing range to the head of Western River. At Longreach they had taken on as many stores as the packs would carry to avoid bothering station people with their needs. Some settlers resented the passing of big herds through their properties, for in the words of the old ballad:

When the Overlanders gather
In the wide and dusty plain,
When tomorrow's never mentioned,
And they never speak of rain,
When the blazing sun is setting
Like a disc of shining brass,
They wouldn't steal a copper,
But they all steal grass.

Some station owners, however, went out of their way to show hospitality to the overlanders. They never forgot how, on their way down Western River, stockmen from Vindex Station had ridden after them with a tribute of fresh vegetables and wished them luck as they moved on.

'They could b . . . ally well see we'd be n . . . eedin' it,' Long Michael would observe whenever he came to this stage of his story.

Already watering places along the route were dwindling fast and if rain did not fall soon they could well be trapped in the dreaded western Queensland drought.

No mother fended for her family more diligently than these drovers for their cattle. They battled and thought for their mobs as they nursed them along, aware of the slightest tenderness of hoof and hollowness of flank, grieving for a perishing beast, calling halt for a cow to calve.

Long Michael and his brothers would have considered war well justified against men who cracked their stockwhips at the wrong moment or did anything to excite a mob in hand. They had certain pet theories and prejudices against other methods of working cattle that they would uphold to a point of fanaticism. The fourth brother, Jerry Brice, who lived to the age of ninety-four, gloried to his dying day in having slashed a man's shirt down the back with his whip for having put cattle dogs on to a mob he had nursed down the Birdsville track to the Burra in '81. Charged with assault and battery and fined ten pounds by the acting magistrate, stock dealer Jenkin Coles, his feelings were bitter indeed, especially since he had previously held Coles' stock knowledge in high regard. Later in the day he met the dealer in the pub and was shaken warmly by the hand:

'Put it here, young fellow,' Coles said (or so the old man's story went), 'I'd have done the same to the so-and-so myself.'

New-born calves were slung into canvas hammocks underneath the waggonettes and when the cattle caught them up were taken into the mob to be claimed by their mothers, but as the weeks passed the new arrivals far exceeded the capacity of the slender hammocks. When as many as thirteen calves would be born in a single dinner camp there was no alternative than to destroy them. It was one of the drovers' saddest reflections that they had been forced to dispose of no less than thirteen hundred new-born calves during the trip. It was a complete waste, for stockmen were oddly squeamish about eating veal or 'staggering Bob' as it was known in the cattle camps.

Keeping the bereft mothers on camp at night was an all-time job. They used every wile of their kind to escape the mob and make back along the route in desperate search of their young. Those that managed to break travelled quickly and sometimes returned three or four day stages before they could be overtaken and brought back. Often they went plodding on, far past the camp where their calves had been born, until the drought closed in on them and they perished on their tracks. This maternal instinct meant extra work for men and horses and the waste of precious time while waters along the route were sinking perilously low.

Dust driven on hot desert winds blew in the face of the mobs as they trailed over bare plains and dry creek beds.

When the drovers hit a township it was not easy to get them out.

'Give us time to wash the dust down,' they said, but they had collected a lot of dust and there were 'old cobbers' in every outback bar.

At Winton one of the waggon drivers found romance with a full-blown beauty behind the bar of the local pub and became so lovelorn at the Diamantina River that he asked for his cheque and returned to the township as fast as horse and packs would carry him. A bagman camped beside the track was glad enough to take on the job and the party continued downriver to the Diamantina gates.

The stock route lay over country flat to horizon's end, meandering through a maze of claypan channels edged with tea-tree, salt-bush and wild cotton. Red bare sandhills, beaten by desert winds, broke the skyline as the stock veered west to Parker Springs, where round wells, warm and bubbling with soda and magnesia, overflowed into a shallow creek. Here, while the drovers enjoyed a plunge in the buoyant, effervescing waters, the cattle were allowed to browse and refresh themselves in preparation for a dreaded fifty-miles' dry stage.

At the end of a three-days' spell the stockmen filled their water bags, a small tank and some barrels, gave the cattle a last long drink and headed them into the setting sun. Forcing the pace, they pushed on to daylight, took five minutes for a pannikin of tea and a johnnie cake and were off again until noon. They camped for the hours of intensest heat, to press urgently on at sundown into another waterless night.

Towards dawn the leading cattle were stretching out their heads, eyes and nostrils dilated until the whole thirsty mob had broken into an urgent trot, bellowing what the drovers knew as 'the water call'. It was still a full day's stage to the Hamilton River, but knowing how thirsty cattle were quick to smell water on the wind the drovers hoped they might be nearing a billabong. When advance riders discovered that the water scent was being wafted from a private tank, all the steadying tactics of the stockman's craft were used to force the cattle in a detour past the tantalising spot to which they continued to turn and strain for miles.

One big three-year-old bull managed to break from the mob and gallop back. Duncan McCaully turned his mare after it in the moonlight, his long whip flashing out to cut its flank. The beast turned, head down, to charge, but the rider, already off his horse, seized the bewildered animal by the horns, brought it to the ground, and flung sand into its eyes. It was an old trick, cruel but effective, for an angry, half-blinded animal will always charge the nearest moving object—invariably, unless the stockman is extremely unlucky or inexperienced, the travelling herd which quickly envelops the outlaw and carries him along with it.

The mob strung on sullenly, bellowing its misery, through another sunrise, another dinner camp, too thirsty now to pull at the tufty, dry remnants of

Mitchell grass along the way. A few hours' uneasy spell and off again, the stronger beasts stringing ahead, the weaker lagging painfully.

Towards evening a dull green line of timber marked the winding course of the Hamilton but advance riders brought news that there was not enough water for the great, dry mob at the nearest hole. The drovers knew too well how the cattle would charge the water in their frenzy of thirst until it was churned to an undrinkable slough in which the weaker animals would hopelessly bog or be smothered in the crush. Grim tragedies of the droving track were known to them all, when perishing herds had stampeded to total destruction in boggy river beds.

The stronger cattle were now drafted from the various mobs and taken fifteen miles downstream to a big reach of water while the weaker animals were steadied on to the nearer hole. Only a little water, thick and foul-smelling, floated on the slimy mud, but the cattle drained it frantically and then nuzzled and sucked at the evil slime.

Late that night the sturdier mob, breaking at last from the weary drovers, plunged so precipitously into the big hole that when the mighty thirst was slaked dozens of smothered fish were found floating in the muddy waters. These provided a rare feast for the tired, hungry men, able at last to relax while the exhausted cattle fed quietly out over the river flat.

By the time they reached the big Parapitcherie waterhole on the Georgina everyone in western Queensland was talking drought and the drovers knew they must camp and wait for rain. Optimists in the party attached hopeful significance to 'the ring around the moon', the 'pinky haze' in the sky at sunset or the antics of insects and birds, but Long Michael at least had no illusions. As the horses had suffered badly over the dry stages and some had died from eating poison weed, he resolved to ride back to Brisbane for a fresh supply. Maybe a 960-mile ride to the capital with an extra mount and pack was no worse than holding cattle on a waterhole and waiting for the drought to break. At all events he seems to have taken it very much as a matter of course. Grandfather had news of his cousin's coming while in Brisbane and at once busied himself to have suitable stock horses ready in hand. Through letter and when possible by telegram he had kept in close touch with the movements of the cattle and paid wages and running expenses into the accounts of his head drovers. He was at the same time looking after the affairs of his cousins, Big Johnnie and Long Michael, selling stock they had left on the Rasmore and Shannon runs and keeping accounts after his fashion.

WEST AUSTRALIAN ACCOUNT

	£	s	d
1st Jan. 1884 paid for exes and wagon on road W.A.	100	–	–
12th Feb. " paid in Brisbane for T. Kilfoyle	202	5	–
10th Sept. " cash paid	303	11	–
19th Oct. " order drawn by Cousin Pat Moore on me which I have not down in orders paid by brother Michael to me when with him last	135	12	6
Also Bertie Belcher's order when going on road, which I forgot to note with brother Michael	30	–	–
1st Dec. 1884 cash sent to credit of Cousin Johnnie D's account at Thargomindah	100	–	–
17th July 1885 " "	150	–	–
Paid rent on country in W.A. for cousin J.D. and myself for years 1884 and 1885	100	–	–
Paid rent for same years for part of the W.A. country held by myself	200	–	–
Plus commission and exchange on all country	5	5	–
6th March 1886 paid to Thargomindah account for cousin Johnnie D.	200	–	–
	£1526	13	6

On behalf cousins John Durack and Long Michael while on road with cattle by me P.D.

John Durack sold 21 bullocks to George Ellms and my brother Jerry on the 15th of June 1885. Also 12 on the 12th June to above all at £5 per head.

I have sold altogether to F. Cavangh 9 head of bullocks for £53 cash.

Sold a mare and filly for Long Michael on the 21st June 1885 for £17 and received cash. (Have not paid Long Michael as yet.)

The three brothers, Grandfather, Stumpy Michael and Galway Jerry, assembled in Brisbane to meet their cousin and hear first-hand details of the droving trip, found Long Michael somewhat low-spirited.

'We should have got away six months earlier,' he said. 'We'd have been at the gulf then instead of in the middle of this God-awful drought. If you ask me, we'll be lucky to get half the cattle through now.'

In an effort to cheer him they took him to inspect their properties at Archerfield and Moorlands, and Grandfather showed him a block of land he had purchased for a home on the high bank of the Brisbane River, but it is doubtful whether these activities had the desired effect. Long Michael, well deserved as was his reputation for stockmanship and devotion to his job, had never regarded the bush life as his chosen calling. He had, as he confessed in later life, always hoped to work himself out of it before he was too old and establish himself in some less rigorous form of business. He was inclined to resent the turn of fate that had set him toiling on into the wilderness at much the same age that his cousin Galway Jerry had retired from the bush life to become a figure in the fashionable racing world. Long Michael's branch of the family, although in Australia three years before the other and as hard-working as anyone in the colony, did not seem to have been favoured by fortune like their relatives. Darby Durack had never made money and had dropped dead slogging in the sun, while his sons had walked, penniless, out of the drought in New South Wales into another on the Diamantina and were still more or less broke. On the other hand everything their cousin Patsy touched had turned to gold since he dug up his first nugget on the Ovens in '53.

'I was born either too soon or too late,' Long Michael said. 'A bit earlier I'd have been in on the gold rushes and a bit later I would have come in on the college education we're giving the younger boys.'

'As it is,' Grandfather consoled him, 'you'll be the first in on some of the richest country in Australia. You won't regret taking on this trip.'

Back on camp the drovers now had time to kill. Men off watch sat about whittling stockwhip handles from lengths of ironbark that had the pliability of whalebone and was known for some reason as 'dead finish'. They spent hours patiently working bits of greenhide into their favourite types of whip, making rounded 'snake belly' plaits that would cut like knives in a straight thrust.

Young Charlie Gaunt started a two-up school and Jack Sherringham played the concertina and sang the '101 bush melodies' and a few of his own all to the same tune.

Then there was 'mumble-the-peg', so much in vogue among stockmen of the day. Like knuckle bones but played with an open penknife, it kept the players amused for hours on end. Wild applause greeted feats of digital dexterity, with shouts of mirth for the loser who must worry a buried penknife out of the dust with his teeth. So great a grip had the game taken outback that James Tyson when advertising for stockmen added the curt advice: 'No mumble-the-peggers need apply.'

Still, the weeks dragged wearily. The cattle, forced to wander miles to grass, were falling away and the stockmen began to suffer from a mysterious skin affliction like scurvy. Other symptoms followed until, overcome by weakness and lethargy, they lay about in the shade of the scraggy coolibahs, some too weak to ride after the cattle and others too ill even to sit up. The boss drovers, sick themselves, doled out the nostrums of the bush – quinine, Epsom salts and Holloway's mixture – but without avail. The nearest doctor was at Cloncurry, 200 miles away, but sicknesses such as fever, dysentery and Barcoo rot were regarded as part of a stockman's lot. This seemed like all these common ailments in one, but only when two men died within a day of each other was its seriousness realised.

Two black stockmen whose assistance had been called in to hold the cattle provided a clue to the problem by pointing out that the far end of the Parapitcherie waterhole had always been held taboo as a tribal camping-place.

'That belong long time,' they said. 'Must be some reason. Might be poison.'

Acting on tribal custom they dug sand soaks in the dry bed of the Burke and carried water each day in canteens and water bags to the sick men, who began to recover at once. Realising that the cattle and horses were also being affected by the water, they fenced off the death trap and sank large dry wells, hollowed troughs from tree trunks and filled them with whip and bucket for the perishing stock. Many beasts, however, were already dead or dying and although attempts were made to burn the carcasses the reek of carrion hung horribly about the waterhole.

Later it was discovered that the Parapitcherie hole was fed by alkaline springs which attained a near lethal concentration as the freshwater-level fell.

Light rain fell about the end of April '84, just enough to make a little water and give fresh hope, but it caused the cattle to spread out, feeding over a wide range which made hard work for the weak horses.

About a week later a rider from the nearest station came galloping at dawn.

'Get moving, you fellows. The river's down!'

The drovers knew droughts and they knew floods—those sudden avalanches of water pouring from some distant part of the river into country where perhaps no rain had fallen for many months, filling the long dry channels of creeks and rivers, lifting timber and carcasses to go surging downstream, turning the parched landscape into an inland sea.

'The river's down!'

Expertly the cooks had their equipment into the waggonettes and the stockmen were in their saddles and away. They were always competing over the time they took in catching and saddling a horse, getting a fire alight and a billy boiling, rolling a swag and hitching it to a pack—little things, seemingly unimportant, but on which at certain times might hang the fate of an entire mob and of men and horses too.

The cattle but for the inevitable stragglers were taken at a run to higher ground where, minutes later, drovers watched the waters surging down, swirling into the topmost branches of the river trees under which they had camped for weary months . . . death-dealing, life-giving water, changing the face of the land.

24

On to the Territory

The year 1884. Dividing the mobs. Long Michael rejoins party at Cloncurry. Pleuro camp on the Nicholson. Reunion with John Costello at Burketown. Blacks and crocodiles in the Territory. Fever camp on Roper River. The death of Jack Sherringham and John Urquart.

The rain brought on a green haze of pig weed and 'scurvy grass' that the stockmen mixed with vinegar into a vile green mess and ate in great quantities. They swore by its curative effects and showed each other how their Barcoo sores were healing day by day. Horses and cattle too began to pick up, but over the long camp the four mobs had become in the stockman's term 'boxed up'. Six thousand head of stock, for they were now down over 1,000 head, must be mustered and redivided.

Each boss drover had the task of cutting his own cattle from the big mob and cleanskins were held to be the property of whichever party ran them into his lot.

This part of the story is Charlie Gaunt's version. I had no chance of checking it with Long Michael or Black Pat but neither ever mentioned it to my knowledge. Perhaps they felt it reflected little credit on those who had since become heroes in the eyes of a younger generation. Perhaps Gaunt drew the long bow.

Sometimes, he said, two or three men would get on the tail of a single unbranded beast, each trying to edge it out of the main mob and run it into his own. With nerves and tempers frayed through long waiting, sickness and tedium, personal antagonisms had arisen and what might have been a merry sport turned to angry disputes. The drover's weapon was his stirrup iron and swung on the end of a leather in the manner of a mace could be extremely effective.

When a fight looked like starting a shout would go up. The men would gather, barracking and taking sides, until, as Charlie Gaunt had it, 'a Connemara Fair was a piccaninny to the Parapitcherie cattle camp.'

When Duncan McCaully and Big Johnnie Durack got into holds, Gaunt said he had to 'holler' for Duncan as they were both Kilfoyle's men. Hopping around he saw a chance to 'deal Johnnie a welt' but Johnnie's stirrup iron swung round in a flash and laid him low. He claimed to be as proud of that gash on the forehead as a Heidelberg student of his slash from a sword.

'Every man jack of us had a brand of some sort out of it,' Gaunt declared, 'all except Tom Kilfoyle who somehow came out of the mêlée unscathed and with the most cleanskins to his credit.'

With green feed and good water the cattle soon looked like the fine animals that had started from Mt Marlowe and Thylungra. They strung along up the Burke to Boulia, the same ones always in the lead of each mob, all taking their accepted positions with their particular cronies.

The bar at the Drover's Rest in Cloncurry overflowed with lanky, sunbronzed, bearded overlanders, swapping yarns, sketching maps on the bar counter or on the floor, forefingers wetted in whisky or rum. Among them was Long Michael, back from Brisbane with his plant of fresh horses and news of the big city. Before they moved on two of his drovers pulled out and he was forced to engage a young stockman who was eager for adventure but who looked too 'flash' in jodhpurs and sombrero to be any good. He hailed from Carrandotta on the Georgina, one of the young 'Colonial Experience' jackeroos from England who had erected a steeplechase course with stone wall jumps near the homestead, and he assuredly did not belong in that outfit of tough, efficient stockmen.

From 'the Curry' the route ran over a deep crossing where the cattle were forced to swim. Half-way across, the leaders of Long Michael's mob began to turn. So far the new hand had been given little chance to use his 'flash' outsize stockwhip but he chose this moment to wield it on the backs of the cattle. At once the panicked animals made a frenzied circle.

'Straighten 'em there!' Long Michael shouted, at which the newchum's stockwhip swung again. In the swirling circus of heaving backs and panting heads some of the weaker animals had already been pushed under and drowned. Black Pat wrested the mischievous stockwhip from the newchum's fist and set to work with the rest to force the cattle out of the mill by turning the horns and heading a lead for the far bank.

Once on the other side Long Michael rounded on the new hand:

'You in the b—— f . . . ancy pants . . .'

Words failing him, he wrote off his rage with a cheque. At least that was his version. Charlie Gaunt's was rather more picturesque.

Short-handed, and with now only two waggonettes between the four parties, they veered north-west into the teeth of biting south-westerlies that whipped up long clouds of red 'Leichhardt dust', famous even before the shadow of man-made erosion had fallen on a misused land. The route wound through bold outcrops of copper-coloured hills, over stony, treeless vistas—hard country, unfolding into open plains with welcome belts of messmate and shady silver box.

Dawn upon dawn awoke to the rattle of hobble chains as the goaded mob slouched on across tenuous gulf streams. Spring followed on the heels of the rainless northern winter, trees blossomed and put forth new foliage. Palms, ferns and luxuriant creepers flourished along the water courses and Leichhardt pines gave deep shade to the cattle camps, but as the clouds banked up the raging heat pressed down. This time the optimists read their signs of an early wet aright. Storms broke in October of '84 and the cattle strung out contentedly as lush grass sprang thick and fast on the broad plains.

It was at a camp on the Nicholson that the first dread symptoms of disease appeared. John Urquart called attention to a sick-looking cow in Kilfoyle's mob.

'It's when the grass is fresh like this we can expect trouble,' he said and was laughed at for a Job's comforter.

Soon animals in the other mobs began to lag, their eyes glazed and sunken and nostrils streaming. This was a blow they had not bargained for. A skilled stockman could pull his mob through drought or flood, wheel it in a rush or turn it in a ring, but pleuro was a hazard against which they stood defenceless.

Sick animals were quickly isolated and carcasses burned as they died, but the drovers knew the damage was done.

John Urquart, whose veterinary knowledge was advanced for his day, had been laughed at for his 'new-fangled' kit that included an inoculating outfit. Now the overlanders' only hope of saving their herd hung on its efficiency. A broken-down yard and cattle crush on the Nicholson was hastily repaired. Urquart obtained serum from cattle slightly affected and setting himself at the head of the crush inoculated each beast as it filed past.

During the next three days a few more animals died but most got through with only a slight attack. In a week or more, to the frank astonishment of the sceptical drovers, all traces of the sickness had disappeared, but before moving on they nailed up a sign as a warning of possible infection to further droving parties.

PLEURO CAMP. OCTOBER '84. BEWARE!

While here Long Michael and Patsy Moore took the waggons into Burketown, supply centre for the spearheads of northern settlement and then a little metropolis of the lonely gulf. To their great delight they found in the animated gathering of stockmen, teamsters and drovers, John Costello and his son Michael, who had been at St Pat's with my father, on their way to Roper River with 1,700 head of cattle. Costello had recently sold his Rockhampton property, Cawarral, and his Gladstone interests—Emu Park, Tanby and Annondale—sent his wife and family on a trip to Ireland and set off with his eldest boy to carve a station out of a piece of country that then seemed to promise everything his former holdings lacked.

Other old acquaintances, from Cooper's Creek turned up and they could think of no better way to celebrate than to run a race meeting and yarn on into the night of the good old days and the fortunes they would make in Kimberley and the Territory.

'We'll get together every year,' they promised. 'We'll have meetings with fooling and dancing all night like we used at Galway Downs and Windorah, women and kids and all.'

A drover who had been with Buchanan to stock Wave Hill in the Territory smiled in his beard.

'If it's women and kids you want,' he said, 'you better head back the way you come—unless of course you prefer 'em black.'

Settlement Creek, near the Territory border, was regarded at that time as the drovers' point of no return. Those whose aim was to leave the past behind or to avoid the police breathed a sigh of relief when they reached the border camp. Those who had left families or sweethearts or who looked to the protection of the law thought twice before starting on the next stage. The boss drovers put the situation to their men in plain terms:

'If you want to pull out this is your last chance. If you've decided to carry on you'll have to take the rough with the smooth and no whingeing.'

'That was how Big Johnnie summed it up,' Charlie Gaunt told us. 'Only thing was, I been in there before and I known there wasn't gonna be no smooth. I don't think they knew just where the border was in those times but after we passed Settlement Camp we sort of *knew* we had crossed it. There was always a special feeling about the Territory.'

As they had talked of the dreaded drought and the pleuro scourge they now talked of the blacks. A day would come when men would visit the Territory for no other purpose than to meet the people of myth and dream, to learn what they could of their ancient way of life and the unwritten story of their past. To these first-comers, however, bound to the context of their times, they were simply 'niggers', another hazard to be overcome with the rest. If it was to be a battle for survival there would be no question of sentiment or the black man's rights.

'Look out for yourselves past Settlement Creek. The blacks are bad.'

Punitive parties, meting out stern retribution for the death of Jack Travers, the cook in Nat Buchanan's party who had had his head chopped off while bent over his baking dish, had done nothing to intimidate them. Lately they had taken to mutilating horses, skulking on the outskirts of the mobs and sometimes causing a stampede.

One night Black Pat had heard stealthy footsteps approaching his swag and had let go the full contents of his revolver without further enquiries. There had been a wild shriek and in the morning they followed a blood trail to the river bank where it disappeared.

Another night Long Michael, riding round the cattle, spotted a dozen natives rounding up some horses. Not wanting to fire his revolver so close to the drowsing mob he galloped towards them full tilt and they dispersed like shadows. Sometimes there were 'nigger tracks' around the camp in the morning and marks showing that the blacks had been dragging spears along in their feet as they often did to disguise the fact that they were carrying weapons.

But even though they kept for the most part discreetly out of sight, the blacks were always there, a danger skulking in pandanus or tea-tree thickets, crouching on the ant-hill plains. Horses smelt them at the waterholes and riders sat alert in their saddles as the cattle drank.

For four months the steaming wet held the gulf country in the grip of bog and 'bankers'. Sometimes the party was held up for weeks on end waiting for the rivers to go down. Tempers grew frayed and personal idiosyncrasies strained taut nerves to breaking point. It was little wonder that seasoned drovers became known as men of few words and iron self-discipline.

After tropical downpours great clods of sticky mud on the hoofs of cattle and horses made the going heavy and slow through rank, wet-weather grass often high above the backs of the moving herd. The cattle, which fed always against the driving wind and rain, had often to be pushed into the weather and forced along until they sometimes turned irritably and charged the drovers.

After the intense heat of the day the night wind would blow cold and strong off rain-drenched country, and men on shift, holding the restless herd, would shiver in their saddles and coming off watch throw themselves down under their nets in their wet clothes and muddy boots. Bad colds and attacks of fever followed and they began to look back nostalgically to the good old dry stages of the Queensland track. But slowly they were ticking off the miles as river after river dropped behind them—Calvert, Robinson, Foelsche, Wierien.

On McArthur River they found a station under the management of one Tom Lynott. He had almost completed a fine homestead from timber that had been shipped around the coast by the optimistic owners but he pointed out how before the roof was on the white ants were in the rafters and the blacks were chasing the cattle into the ranges.

'Where are you making for?' Lynott asked.

'The Ord.'

'Do you reckon you'll get on any better over there?'

'God knows.'

A man known as Black Jack Reid had brought a schooner up the McArthur to form a shanty store at a spot the blacks called Borroloola—place of the paperbarks. With a stock of provisions and a tank of rum he hoped to make his fortune from overlanding drovers and prospectors making across to Pine Creek, and maybe soon, it was already whispered, into Kimberley.

'A man ought to do well here on the stock route,' he said and the drovers agreed, though so far 'the route' was more or less a figure of speech.

Sometimes they crossed the trail of a previous party—probably that of Nat Buchanan—but they lost no time looking for tracks. Their compass course lay due west and one man's guess was as good as another's which way to deviate in looking for a river crossing or skirting a range.

Sharks and crocodiles abounded in these swiftly running tidal streams. Four horses had been taken on the Robinson and while camped at the Limmen several beasts, wading belly deep as cattle love to do, had been lost. One cow had managed to shake herself free and struggle out, badly torn by hungry teeth and claws, and was afterwards known affectionately as the 'alligator cow', for in these times, before it was established that only species of crocodile are found in Australian waters, the blunt-nosed, man-eating kind were always referred to as 'alligators'.

At the Limmen John Costello's party, held up by pleuro and other setbacks, caught up with the Kimberley-bound expedition. Sending their cattle on so they would not become mixed with Costello's herd, Big Johnnie and Long Michael remained at the river for a day or two while Costello picked the site for his homestead. He had leased all the rivers of the Limmen Bight, he told them, and planned to form several stations.

'Look at it,' he enthused, with a sweeping gesture. 'Did you ever see such country?'

As they were now well into the wet season both pasture and water were plentiful and the homestead site Costello quickly chose was magnificent. Backed by ranges and with a foreground of lily-covered water, it was close to a remarkable valley, laced with streamlets, overgrown with tropical palms and creepers and the haunt of wild birds.

'You will not get better country than this by going farther,' he said. 'If you feel like coming back at any time, just let me know.'

Once he had the homestead up he planned to leave his men in charge and set off to meet his wife and family at Rockhampton on their return from the old country. There he would charter a ship and bring his family around to their new home, 'The Valley of Springs'.

'How will you get them all this way up from the coast?' Long Michael asked.

'They can ride,' Costello said cheerfully. 'I reckon the river should be navigable to Leichhardt's Crossing and we can have the horses waiting there.'

'You've got a nerve bringing women and kids out here,' Long Michael told him dourly. 'The Cooper was bad enough, but the Limmen . . . G . . . od Almighty!'

'Well, if you think you'll do any good over there without the women you're making a big mistake,' Costello said.

Long Michael shrugged and rode off with his brother on their lonely trail. Big Johnnie, a tough man with a tender spot for family life, spoke yearningly:

'How long will it be, I wonder, before we can bring our women to the Ord?'

Long Michael had his own views on that subject.

'I'm going to Kimberley to make money. Not to make a home.'

Christmas '84 was celebrated on the Rosey River where the party was held up again by heavy storms. A Christmas morning surprise in Black Pat's swag was a death adder, twenty inches long with a tapering tail from which projected a silky yellow tassel. Everyone carried a snake-bite cure in his pocket but for all the hair-raising snake stories they all loved to tell, no one seems to have required the antidote.

Here, horse tracks coming into water recalled the story of an unsuccessful venture of some years before when horses had been brought to the Territory to breed remounts for the Indian Army. On the journey inland from Darwin some of the escort died of fever and the rest, sick and dispirited, abandoned the project and turned their horses loose.

By the time the drovers came across, hundreds of brumbies of good stock ranged the countryside, and almost every party from Nat Buchanan onwards had organised a brumby muster hereabouts with little or no success.

Renovating one of Buchanan's ingenious traps, the drovers hoped to be able to add a few good horses to their plant, but the swift-footed animals, quick and shrewd enough to have eluded blacks and crocodiles, were more than a match for such clumsy tricks. The sum total of the muster was a single stallion, a fine well-bred animal which continued with the cattle on the journey west.

During ten weeks' enforced spell, plagued by sandflies and with gear going mouldy in the packs, repairs were made to the two waggonettes which had become badly damaged on the rough track. Long Michael and Black Pat never tired of telling how they contrived and improvised, even making a new thread for a broken axle with a three-cornered file. Long Michael made an eight-strand stockwhip from the hide of a wallaroo, while others fished and shot game for the pot.

Stockmen studied the bird life closely during the enforced camps. Here they watched the antics of native companions, jabirus with seven-foot wing span, glorious white cranes with flowing plumage. Game was plentiful, magpie geese, whistling duck, Burdekin duck went wheeling and calling in dense clouds over the lush wet-weather landscape. There were millions of painted finches, pigeons, bright parrots. Crows and wedgetailed eaglehawks gathered in great flocks around the camps to pick the bones of butchered or perished beasts. Bower birds filched spoons, spectacles or pieces of broken glass for their playgrounds in the scrub. Squall birds, mallee hens, wild turkeys and cuckoos provided the drovers with endless interest.

The party came on to the Hodgeson River about where Nutwood Downs Station stands today. The cattle were brought across and camp struck on the other side, but the provision waggon could not be got over. The stockmen began swimming back and forth with rations tied to their heads until the knobby nose of an outsize crocodile appeared and the rest of the goods came by packhorse via a rocky bar some miles downstream. Here the waggon too was at last trundled across and a start made for the Leichhardt bar on the Roper where pioneer storekeeper Matt Kirwan was then running a depot.

Here now was the lush, tropical north that returning drovers spoke of with mixed repugnance and fascination, the deep, oily green waters of the Roper with thickly bordering pandanus palms, bamboos, banyans and paperbarks. Some blacks passed them in a dugout canoe, the flood waters carrying them swiftly downstream while they poled dexterously to keep free of the banks, floating debris or overhanging limbs. At this stage anything with a black skin was a potential enemy to the drovers and they viewed with apprehension the strong, sinuous fellows with their raised tribal markings, bamboo belts and bracelets, woven neck charms and finely tapered nose bones. They judged them bigger, stronger and more savage looking—almost another race to the familiar Queenslanders—and read their seeming indifference to themselves as 'audacity'.

The Roper depot among thick tropical trees and creepers on the river bank had the unreal quality of a stage setting. A supply schooner was anchored among the mangroves waiting for the tide and the crew, Chinese, Aboriginal and Malay, was lounging about the little timber and angle iron shanty. The skipper, in tropical topee and whites, sat fanning himself in a hammock, drinking 'square face' with the storekeeper and some drovers from somewhere inland. A few sporting types were shooting at bottles and crocodiles, playing poker or mumble-the-peg and singing snatches of bawdy Territory songs, while black women hung about and cast sheep's eyes at the newcomers. Two or three of these wore moleskin trousers and shirts and carried themselves with an air of importance. The newcomers learned that they were attached to various overland droving parties and were reputed to be splendid horsewomen.

'You're in the land of Black Velvet now,' one of the loungers remarked. 'Unless you go round to Darwin you'll not find a white woman in the north between Burketown and Broome.'

The storekeeper tossed them a bundle of mail and pointed from a bottle of whisky to the water bag.

'Help yourselves—no measuring nips in this country. Just pay what you reckon's a fair thing when it's time to make tracks.'

The system evidently paid in the long run as most helped themselves so lavishly that 'time to make tracks' was often when their cheque cut out. Long Michael and Tom Kilfoyle resolved to make their stay within reach of the depot as short as possible.

They had pitched camp at McMinn's Bluff seven miles upstream, but the heavily loaded waggons were blocked by flood waters on the way back and had to be left while the men made rafts from tent flies and got emergency rations across to their hungry men. It was a miserable camp, for the intolerable muggy heat, ceaseless rain, mud, mildew and plagues of every pest that crawled and flew had a bad effect on the men's morale. A rule of the road that a stockman could drink what he liked in town but nothing must be brought into camp somehow broke down at this stage. Rum, smuggled in from the depot, increased the boss drovers' work and anxiety and did nothing to alleviate the fever that had laid siege to the party.

Desperate to get away, the four leaders decided to make a supreme effort to move the waggons over what now seemed a possible crossing. The blacks, however, had got in first. Bags of sugar, cases of tea, tobacco, rice and dried fruit had disappeared from the vehicles and the ground about was strewn with battered tins which they had not succeeded in opening and flour for which they did not then know the use.

Cursing niggers, purveyors of rum and their ill-fortune in general, they made back to the camp before returning to the depot for fresh supplies.

John Urquart was by this time so ill with malaria and the effects of 30 OPR that they hurried him in with them, hoping he could catch the schooner for Darwin and medical aid. By the time the boat arrived, however, the good old bushman had shot himself in delirium.

When they returned to the camp they found that young Sherringham, likewise maddened by malaria and rum, had put an end to his misery in the same way.

25
End of an Epic

The year 1885. The Overland Telegraph to Victoria River. Black Pat and Tom Hayes leave the party for Cambridge Gulf. Last stage. Life stirring in Kimberley. The overlanders ride to Cambridge Gulf where Black Pat has set up a store. Early arrivals on the gulf. Tom Kilfoyle, Big Johnnie and Long Michael Durack ride back to Queensland.

The Roper ran west to Red Lily Lagoon, a place of fantastic beauty with its massed water lilies, crimson and blue, green reeds and drooping paperbarks, haunt of wild duck, and, judging by the bark canoes floating on the water, of wild blacks.

They pushed on to the Overland Telegraph line and the little post office at Elsey Station—symbol of hope and progress in the never-never. Palmer, the manager, welcomed them warmly and filled their depleted tucker bags when they rode in to send wires to their Queensland relatives. Telegrams and letters, advising of the deaths of Urquart and Sherringham and the loss of about 3,500 head of stock all told between Thylungra and the Roper camp, had gone off by the schooner from the depot to Darwin. These had been received when the following telegram reached Thylungra about May '85:

> PARTY NOW OVERLAND TELEGRAPH AND TRAVELLING WELL CONDITION REMAINING STOCK REASONABLY GOOD EXPECT REACH ORD FOUR TO FIVE MONTHS TIME REGARDS AND LOVE FAMILY AND FRIENDS DURACK KILFOYLE HAYES MOORE.

A sixty-mile stretch west of the Telegraph was heavy going through rough, heavily timbered but almost waterless country. The long wet was over and the grass quickly turning yellow. The smaller waggon broke down completely and had to be abandoned and around Dry River the cattle began to lag and show symptoms of red water fever. The decision to push on rather than rest the cattle was fortunate as they lost only a few head, whereas later expeditions, lingering in what proved to be a badly infected area, were to lose hundreds.

It would be some ten years before the cause of this dread disease was finally traced to a small bug-like parasite that had come into the Territory with a shipment of cattle from Batavia. The drovers were not then to know the grip that cattle tick was already taking of the north, how the travelling mobs were spreading it across the Territory into Queensland and over to Kimberley. Their deadliest enemies were not after all to be the blacks but two species of insect smaller than a man's fingernail—*Ixodes bovis* and the Anopheles mosquito.

Hurried down the Dry River for about twenty miles, the cattle were again turned due west.

Basalt ridges, swampy flats of tangled cajuput and gutta-percha trees, tantalising rivers that turned their tracks to north and south, led on at last to the Victoria. This river around which Nat Buchanan had stocked a vast holding comprising many millions of acres for the city investors Fischer and Lyons in '83 was a major landmark in the journey. 'Wait 'til we're eating johnnie cakes on the Victoria,' they had said to cheer themselves back on the Georgina.

'Call this a river?' said a returning drover they had met on the McArthur. 'Wait 'til you see the Victoria!'

And here she was—queen of the north, sweeping majestically between the bending ranks of river trees with exultant escorts of wild birds.

Long Michael, when telling me the story many years later on the Behn River, paused significantly at this stage.

'Now here's something you may never have heard before,' he said. 'Except for a bit of luck I might have gone down in history as "the man who shot Willie MacDonald".'

All the way along they had kept in touch with the MacDonald party that had at times been only a stage or two behind, and they already knew the story of their many misfortunes. Every beast of their original herd had perished in the drought of '83. Most of their men and their MacKensie cousins had pulled out and gone home, but Willie and Charlie had taken up this land in west Kimberley and were determined to get stock to it somehow. Short of money, they had taken jobs here and there to help build up another mob and had battled on into the Territory against pleuro, fever and shortage of hands. On the Roper Charlie MacDonald became so ill with malaria that he was forced to leave the cattle and ride to Darwin with a party of prospectors. Alone with his little mob and a Chinese cook, Willie managed to engage two stockmen, Charlie and George Hall, from another party. Past the Telegraph their stores were rifled by blacks and they were for three weeks on salt beef and ship's biscuits. Coming on the fresh tracks of a big mob, Willie inferred that the Durack party must be close to the Victoria and had ridden ahead to try to borrow a few provisions. It was late at night when he saw the fire by the river bank and not wishing to create a disturbance had tied his horse to a tree some distance away and walked up to the camp. He had long since worn out his last pair of stockman's boots and was barefooted so it was little wonder that Long Michael had mistaken the quietly moving figure for a native.

'I had my finger on the trigger,' he told me, 'before he had the sense to speak up. Willie had eyes like a cat in the dark and he must have spotted me under my net. "Put that rifle away there, Durack," he said. "It's only another poor bloody drover like yourself, and a hungry one at that." We weren't too flush with the tucker ourselves, but we gave him enough to carry them on to the Ord.'

Next day they passed the station on the west side and followed up the big river to its junction with the Wickham. About here they met up with Edward Weldon, an experienced drover who had overlanded with Buchanan, taking cattle for Osmond and Panton to stock the first cattle station in east Kimberley. That Weldon turned up at the Wickham junction was opportune for he agreed to continue with the party into Kimberley. This allowed Black Pat and Tom Hayes to return to the Roper depot and take the schooner to Darwin, from where they planned somehow to make their way by sea to Cambridge Gulf with stores for the party after its arrival.

'I've got a couple of offsiders,' Weldon said. 'Territory boys and making back for their country, but I think they'd come if you want them.'

And there were the inseparables Pintpot and Pannikin who, after their return from Perth, had constituted themselves authorities in chief on the Kimberleys and had already been across to the Ord a second time with Buchanan and Bob Button. The idea of leading the Durack cattle on to the country they had helped select three years before must have appealed to them for they cheerfully headed their horses west again.

The route swung south up the Wickham and turned west.

This was strange country to the Queenslanders, for although the lush tropical growth of the coastal route modified as they turned south and west it nowhere reverted to the flat prairie lands of the other side. Vast plains there were, but broken by flat-topped ranges, folded and creviced and bathed in wild, strong colour. Open, park-like vistas of white gums, boabs, bauhinias, nutwoods and cork trees gave place to tea-tree thickets and bulwaddie scrub. Creeks and rivers, fringed with palms and spreading wild fig and Leichhardt pines, twisted through rugged hills and ridges and broad volcanic valleys where the lava flows of ages past had left sandstone outcrops jutting like ancient ruins, or straight-topped, sheer-sloping island masses of spinifex-covered rock above shining seas of grass. The bird life, for the most part, was common to that of western Queensland and the north coast, the flashing shrill parrot flocks, cockatoos and wild duck, finches, jewel-bright, wild turkeys, brolgas, eaglehawks and crows. Oddly, however, kangaroos and wallabies were not as numerous as in later years, for the new order was to suit them well.

Of all the weird, wild stages they had travelled none was more fearful or memorable than that through the canyon cliffs of Wickham Gorge where rocks rose sheer from the winding river, leaving a narrow pass for the complaining herds. Hardened as the cattle were to rough going, they were soon footsore fom the broken stones on which they slipped and stumbled through the echoing ravine. They bellowed their misery while the drovers' steadying voices and cracking whips made such a confusion of sound that only the utmost skill could prevent disaster.

Through the nightmare pass and over the Rudolph Range the route was more than ever confused with meandering waterways and scrubby patches where cattle and horses became lost, sometimes irretrievably. All signs of a previous mob had vanished under the quick, rank growth of a wet season, and even though Weldon and the two native boys had been through before the going was slow.

Grandfather's notes record that £20 was paid at this stage for services rendered by one Jock McPhee. Like many another whose name crops up in every journal and memoir of the time, the threads of this hardy bushman's story cross and recross the paths of better documented pioneers and here he was opportunely to pilot the cattle over a difficult pinch across the Victoria–Ord River divide.

From Black Gin Creek the route ran on to the Ord River fall, down the Stirling to the Negri, through the beautiful limestone spring country later to form the Vestey property of Mistake Creek.

Yarns swopped along the way were of McPhee's adventures droving cattle, exploring, prospecting about the tumbled hills and river beds, of Ned Weldon's trip through with Nat Buchanan's party twelve months before, and how they had left Bob Button in charge of the vast raw holding with the gentle English name of Plympton St Mary, later more appropriately 'The Ord'.

There were stirrings of life around Kimberley apart from the arrival of the sheep men in the west and the cattle men in the east. During the year a government party had been sent up to report on the possibility of gold, and was said to have been favourably impressed.

About the same time William O'Donnell and William Carr Boyd had surveyed the lower Ord for the Cambridge Downs Pastoral Association that planned to start a sheep station on the gulf—while surveyor Johnston had a party blazing trees and driving in pegs around the upper reaches of the big river. In fact, although Weldon and McPhee could hardly have known it then, Johnston's party was at that time camped near the Behn River, as one of their number had slipped on a mountain slope and broken his leg. They had put up a timber barricade as protection against the blacks and named Stockade Creek and Mount Misery after their long, uncomfortable camp, besieged by blacks, plagued by mosquitoes and flies. Years later one of the entertainments to which we subjected visitors to Argyle was to take them to the top of Mt Misery to see Johnston's peg and to point out the charred stumps of his stockade on the creek below. From the dome-shaped mount, the vista of sweeping Mitchell grass plains, dotted with grazing cattle, and the misty blue of the O'Donnell Ranges tumbling into the Ord River gorge has always seemed to me one of the loveliest on earth.

The drovers were cheered to hear that there were now some ten other white men in east Kimberley, that there was talk of gold and more stock coming in. Their spirits needed a lift like this, for the last stores procured at the Roper depot had almost gone. Flour, dried fruit, jams and condiments had cut out on the Victoria, sugar and tea had been rationed for weeks. They scrounged the bush, like the blacks, for wild honey and armed with yam sticks dug for edible roots which they boiled in beef water or roasted on the ashes. They chewed pig weed and lily roots as they rode along, hoping to cure the Barcoo rot which harassed them as persistently as bouts of fever that made every mile's ride an agony and sometimes halted the party for days at a time.

But what delight there was when the Negri junctioned into another broader stream and Tom Kilfoyle pointed out a tree marked 'D24'!

'In case it means nothing to you fullas,' he said, 'Stumpy Michael Durack marked that tree in September '82 when we'd been a whole month looking for this ruddy river.'

It was three years later almost to the day when Long Michael carved his initials 'M.J.D.' and the date 'Sept. 25, '85' on the gnarled, broad trunk of a boab at Red Butt above the Ord to mark the end of the long road. Others of the party followed suit and the historic tree became a favourite landmark and camping site on Argyle until it was razed to the ground by lightning in 1937, the year Long Michael died.

The 7,520 head that left the Cooper had dwindled to less than half, only the hardiest and luckiest animals having survived the ordeals of the track to drink Ord River water and fatten on Kimberley grass. Their zig-zag trail had covered a good 3,000 miles over which the estimated droving cost was £20 a head. This figure, which included wages, provisions, equipment and stock losses, brought the total cost of the trek to something over £70,000.

The mobs would move off now to their different runs, Long Michael's lot across the river to Lissadell, Kilfoyle's to Rosewood on the Territory border, Pat Moore's and Big Johnnie Durack's remaining on Patsy Durack's country along the east side of the Ord.

Long Michael told how he then rode thirty miles downriver to find a crossing and a station site, camped without a fire and hobbled his horses without bells in fear of the blacks whose fires blazed on every range. Next day blacks appeared on the high red banks above the river and sent a shower of spears into the sandy bed where the cattle were drinking at the waterhole. A shot or two dispersed them and no harm was done, though Ned Weldon claimed a hair's-breadth escape and the incident put the settlers on their guard.

The months to follow were a helter-skelter of chasing and trailing stock, trying to keep the mobs apart, branding calves, running up temporary yards and bough shelters to serve until permanent homestead sites had been selected. The first need, however, was supplies and a few days after arrival Patsy Moore and Duncan McCaully rode off downriver and over the white salt marsh hoping to find Black Pat's provision depot on the gulf.

Black Pat, hammering away at the mangrove rafters of his store, saw the riders and packhorses half a mile off, threw down his tools and hurried to put the billy on to boil.

'Well, Pat, we got here.'

'How many head came through? Everyone all right? Did you save the alligator cow?'

Over strong tea and damper thickly spread with jam they exchanged experiences since parting at the Wickham two months before.

Pat told how he, Tom Hayes and Jack Brown had chartered the barque *Lorinda Borstil* at Darwin, and come to the gulf with three Chinese cooks, one for the store and two 'on order' to Kilfoyle and Long Michael. Anticipation of a gold rush following the promising report of geologist Hardman had prompted them to bring not only stores, but mining equipment, which they unloaded at the gulf two days after the drovers rode onto the Ord.

The Captain of the barque had looked pityingly at the men, surrounded by their goods on the desolate mangrove-skirted gulf.

'Pat,' he said, 'you look heartbroken.'

'And that was how I felt,' Black Pat admitted, for all their rosy hopes had seemed suddenly absurd. Not only was their situation intolerably lonely and remote but their camp seemed actually besieged, with native fires dotted for miles along the gulf's edge and surrounding hills. After all, they had come purely 'on spec'. What if the overlanders had met disaster on the last stage of the journey, for indeed they had hoped to see one or two members of the party already waiting at the gulf when they arrived? What if all the predictions of prospectors and settlers soon to pour into Kimberley had been foolish optimism?

The immediate need for finding fresh water, however, allowed no time to brood. About three miles away they located a small pandanus spring from which they carted water in buckets, coolie-fashion. They made a canoe from the scooped-out trunk of a boab tree which they used in bringing mangrove timber from one of the gulf's islands. In this unique craft they had also made short voyages of exploration. They had caught turtles and dug their round, soft-shelled eggs from the warm sands, and from these the Chinese had concocted strange and delectable dishes.

But they had not, after all, been more than two days at the gulf when the steamer *Otway* arrived to pick up surveyor Johnston and his men, who trailed in about the same time from their miserable sojourn at Stockade Creek.

Thought of hungry mates upriver allowed the drovers no more than a night's spell and they were off again with Tom Hayes who was anxious to join his partner Tom Kilfoyle.

Shortly after his arrival at his partner's camp on the Ord, Hayes returned to the gulf in company with Long Michael, Big Johnnie and Willie MacDonald who, arrived at the Ord shortly after the Durack party, was riding in for stores.

By this time another store had gone up on the gulf, the proprietor, one August Lucanus, a colourful character, ex-Territory trooper with tales to tell of rough justice dealt out to murdering or cattle-spearing blacks, of the Territory gold rushes and the crude little mining towns that followed them. Now, tales of a new and bigger gold rush to Kimberley had inspired him with the idea of getting in first with a store for the prospectors, and he had gone into business with W. K. Griffiths of Darwin who sent stores around by the schooner *Ellerton* while Lucanus rode overland from Katherine to the gulf. In later years Lucanus in fact claimed to have been first to put a store up in east Kimberley, but his memory failed him here as is seen by comparison with contemporary records.

Odd prospectors had begun to make inland and in November the steamer

Catherton brought Billy O'Donnell, his black companion Pompey, who had been to England in the black cricketers' eleven, and one Jamison to join William Carr Boyd in pioneering a track through the unnamed Ord River ranges in case of a sudden influx of gold-seekers.

Letters from home had arrived for the overlanders, among them one from a sister of Big Johnnie, Long Michael and Black Pat. Their mother, normally so robust and optimistic had, it seemed, worried herself almost to death over her sons and her brother, Tom Kilfoyle. She had lately become obsessed with the idea that some terrible misfortune had befallen them and said she would not believe they were all alive and well until she saw them again with her own eyes. Surely, the girl begged, once they had reached their destination, they could come home, if only for a few weeks?

It was obvious that Black Pat could not abandon the store on which not only his future but the incoming settlers were dependent, but Big Johnnie and Long Michael determined to leave for New South Wales as soon as possible. Returning to the Ord they consulted their Uncle Tom Kilfoyle and the three decided to return overland by a short cut through Newcastle Waters to the border town of Camooweal and down through Cloncurry and Longreach to Roma, a mere 1,600 miles. At Roma they could leave their horses and take coach for Molong in New South Wales.

'With a bit of luck and hard riding we could be there in ten to fourteen weeks,' Kilfoyle reckoned.

So early in January '86 the three men left the Ord to prove to the folks at home that they were alive and well.

26
MEANWHILE IN QUEENSLAND

The years 1884 to 1886. Young Michael Durack returns to Thylungra. Patsy and Stumpy Michael Durack form the Queensland Co-operative Pastoral Company. Land purchased for a Brisbane home. Michael returns to college with cousin Jack Skeahan. Payment deferred. Goodbye to Thylungra. Sarah Tully takes a stand. The new house completed. Mr Healy leaves for Ireland. Rumours of gold in Kimberley. Tom Kilfoyle, Long Michael and Big Johnnie Durack meet their cousin Patsy in Charleville. The Rajputana *sails for Cambridge Gulf with young Michael and John Durack, their uncle Stumpy Michael and others.*

Grandfather's decision to take his eldest son from college early in '83 had caused him much heart-searching, especially in the light of Dr Gallagher's regret. Back at Thylungra after meeting his brother Stumpy Michael on his return from Kimberley he had written to his sons:

Thylungra.
Feb. 1883.

Dear Children,

I cannot tell ye how much there has been to do since my return more even than I thought of before and I have had to reconsider my decision to leave ye at school another year dear Michael as The Rev. Dr Gallagher has suggested. I am sorry I will have to ask ye to come home on the next coach north after ye receive this letter and that ye will not compleat yere examination that would fit ye for the University. I had not in mind for either of ye the law or the classics for a career of which Dr Gallagher has spoken to me but would have yere names associated with pioneering of new country as is in the blood dear children, and yere people always on the land as others are associated with professions such as doctoring and the Law which is not in yere blood.

I should acquaint ye that I have gone into partnership with Cousin Johnnie in 300,000 acres and stock in Kimberley and this is to be a separate property to the one which I have taken for ye both and also Pat and Sunny when they are older. There is a limit of about 1,000,000 acres to what one holder can take up in W.A. and also a limit to what ye may hold of river frontages but we can later take up pretty well any area we desire and divide into different properties in the name of a company as has been done in Queensland and within the law. This country I would have for yereselves and in yere own names for to run in yere own way as ye will be men soon and must be standing on yere own feet. We shall come to a business agreament for the purchase of the Kimberley property from me upon certain terms so that it will not be said ye have been pampered and everything come to ye for nothing, the aisy way.

This is as I would have it, dear children, but if it is the will of God and the considered judgement of yere teachers that ye go for the professions then I will be standing down but at this time with all the arrangements to be made for getting the cattle on the road and running the stations at the same time as my other business I must have Michael at the first chance.

Your loving father,
P.D.

The learned headmaster of St Pat's had been prepared to admit that the boys had made good progress in those three years but refused to concede that they had, in their father's words, their 'education completed'.

'The boys stand only on the threshold of learning,' he had pointed out, 'but they show a great aptitude for study and it is my opinion they are both more suited to the professions than to station life.'

Father himself, like many youths of the same age, had no singleness of purpose at this time. His years at college, after the first agonising months of homesickness, had been happy and rewarding. His studies interested without entirely absorbing him and as the son of a wealthy pioneer squatter he had enjoyed a certain schoolboy prestige. As time went on he and his younger brother had not lacked for holiday invitations to the homes of well-to-do schoolmates in Sydney and Melbourne and on prosperous country estates. The little mud-brick homestead at Thylungra, for all its homely charm, was a mere hovel to the fine mansions they visited. People were impressed by the area of the Durack holdings on Cooper's Creek but the boys felt that they would no doubt be sadly disillusioned to see the flat, grey plains of that arid west. The rivers too sounded splendid enough in terms of length and of breadth in flood, but what of the drought years when the isolated waterholes dwindled to reeking puddles that trapped and held the dead and dying stock?

Brief glimpses of city life had shown them a world in which people attended theatres and fashionable race meetings, discussed books and music and made seemingly easy money in comfortable offices. By comparison the social life of the bush had begun to seem something of an uncultured rough and tumble and stock rearing in the far outback a crude means of livelihood. On the other hand my father's inherited energy and zest for life and movement found outlet in the hard riding, open air station life and he was happy enough to return to the excitement of the big musters and all the plans for the overland drive. Naturally the romance of numbering in that expedition appealed to him strongly but his father's need of help was more urgent than the party's need of men. Although more reserved than most of his relatives, my father was, like them all, happiest when with his own. He was deeply devoted to his mother and to the two little sisters who now regarded him with the awe they would never really lose for him. Although he berated his brother Pat as 'an ignorant young hooligan' he was proud of the lad's precocious stockmanship and the good looks he promised, and he believed as fervently as his parents that the baby Jeremiah—'little Sunny'—was a budding genius. His brother John, probably his only really intimate associate, remained at St Pat's and the two exchanged letters over this period. In September '83 my father wrote from Thylungra:

> Cher Frère,
>
> Writing in great haste as you can imagine from my last. The parties have all got off now but all here still pretty busy. Father trying to be in two or three places at once as usual and nearly the whole management of this place and Galway has fallen to me pro tem. It is no easy job especially as the water position on both places pretty poor this season. Only hope we are not in for another bad drought and that the cattle get to the gulf without delay. We are shifting cattle onto the big hole up the creek already and some of them beginning to look poorly, but the sheep look all right and we turned off a good clip.
>
> I have put up a yard on Galway since Uncle Jerry left—Pumpkin and Kangaroo offsiding. Did I hear you say 'Doing most of the work, I bet?' Well, I have taken the skin off both hands and they have now hardened up.
>
> It looks as though it will be 'goodbye' for me as far as the studies are concerned. Have been reading Goldsmith and thinking of the

old school, and shall I say, not without a sense of nostalgia. Sometimes I would like to think I was going back. I have not mentioned it to Father as he does not seem to want to talk too much of the immediate future just now. I don't think he knows what to do for the best. Dear mother says that whatever happens she will not be parted from her Muscovy ducks and the best of her pot plants which will be left to die in any other hands. I often play the piano to her and the girls and Sunny and they do not notice the mistakes nor that I make up most of the bass myself.

Old Mr Healy continues dotty as ever but pretty well and sometimes think we will probably have him with us for the rest of our lives even though he feels convinced the Irish question will never be solved until he gets back to set them on the right road. His conversation is much of the Phoenix Park murders of last year. Father keeps his fund going for the Irish Land League and will have nothing said against Parnell. He is much distressed by the news he gets from home though from what I can read of it the Irish are not helping the situation by their behaviour. Tell me all the news when you write and have you seen any more of Jim's pretty sister? No need to envy me the girls' Governess Miss Quirk. She is all prunes and prisms.

Your fond brother,
MICHAEL P. D.

No doubt the responsibilities with which be was entrusted at this early age developed in my father the habit of authority that formed much of the background of his personality. From that time onwards no one besides Pumpkin ever appears to have disputed his decisions. The faithful Aboriginal recognised only one master and although his attitude to the boys he claimed to have 'grown up' was protective, respectful and affectionate, they remained always 'the young fellows' who still had plenty to learn. It would be some years before my father came to realise the degree of his dependence upon this stalwart and capable retainer, and longer still before he could recount with amusement the brush they had soon after his return from college to Thylungra. Very much the young laird in well-fitting breeches, polished leggings and spurs, he had devised a series of signals on the iron triangle that served as a station dinner gong—three for Pumpkin, four for Willie, five for Kangaroo and a sustained clanging for general assembly. Pumpkin disliked the innovation and feigned deafness. He never argued. He simply failed to co-operate when his own ideas differed from those of his young master.

'Fetch me that black stallion, like a good fellow,' Father told him one day. 'I'll give him a try-out on the bullock muster today.'

Pumpkin disapproved of a small sharp type of spur Father effected at this stage and had no intention of letting him ride the stallion that was his pride and joy. He brought up another horse on the pretext that the one wanted could not be found and when sent back with instructions not to return without it finally reappeared leading the stallion which had developed an unaccountable limp. When this disability recurred each time he elected to ride the horse Father became suspicious and found on examination that the limp was caused by a few strands of hair passed under the shoe and wedged tightly in the cleft of the hoof. He turned on the black man indignantly.

'What's the meaning of this? Don't you reckon I can handle this horse?'

'You can handle him all right, young fulla,' Pumpkin said. 'I'm only thinking about the horse—that's all.'

Later the youth complained to his father: 'Seems to me you've let old Pumpkin have too much of his own way all these years. He'll be telling us how to run the station soon.'

'He's been doing that ever since we came to Thylungra,' Grandfather chuckled. 'Maybe that's the reason we got on here so well.'

When the cattle were about nine months along the road to Kimberley Grandfather believed he had hit upon the solution to the problem of how to have his cake and eat it too. While on a business trip to Brisbane the inspiration had come in the form of a half-jocular enquiry from a business acquaintance who had previously asked for first option on Thylungra if he ever decided to sell out.

'Well, you old beef baron, I hear you're going to build yourself a mansion in the city at last and you'll be sending your sons over to the Ord River. Isn't it time you decided to let somebody relieve you of a few of your burdens?'

'I'll admit the whole thing's getting a bit much for me,' Grandfather replied, 'but as far as the Cooper's concerned it's a matter of sentiment. I cannot bring myself to sell my interest in this country that I brought to life as though it were no more than a matter of cash.'

'Then why not a syndicate?' his friend suggested. 'There are plenty others, besides myself, interested in getting a foothold out there. If we were, perhaps, to combine forces . . . ?'

In less than a month the deal was finalised and the Queensland Co-operative Pastoral Co Ltd formed. It was to be a powerful combine 'to carry on in Queensland and elsewhere in Australia the businesses of stock and station holders, sheep, cattle and horse farmers, breeders and graziers'. The company was to 'purchase the stations known as Thylungra, Galway Downs and Sultan in the district of Gregory South; of Tongy in the Maranoa district, of Buckingham Downs in the district of Gregory North . . . of a butchering business and certain freehold lands situated in or near Roma; and also of the Forrest Vale run situated in the district of Kimberley, W.A., together with the cattle, sheep and horses depasturing on the said station runs.'

The estimated number of cattle on Thylungra in January 1884 is stated as being 30,987—an astonishing increase on the pathetic 100 head that first came to Kyabra Creek in '68!

The agreement was drawn up between 'Patrick Durack of the first part, Michael Durack of the second part, Richard Wingfield Stuart, Henry Benjamin, Cyril Selby, David Benjamin, Reginald Arthur Whipham and Richard Newton of the third part' by which those of 'the said third part' were to pay 'those of the first and second parts' the sum of £160,000 for coming in on the spoils of their pastoral empire.

This seemed to Grandfather the ideal compromise, for by maintaining his share in the syndicate he was keeping faith with the Cooper district while being relieved of the full burden of its responsibility. He could visit Thylungra with a proprietary interest any time he wished without being tied down to dates and obligations. Losses sustained over the seemingly inevitable drought periods would be shared while he should continue to receive handsome dividends from good seasons. His agreement with his cousin Big Johnnie had left him free to make any business arrangements deemed advisable for the land they held in partnership in Kimberley, so he had thrown in the untried Forrest Vale run on Spring Creek for good measure, his other Kimberley holdings having already been signed away in favour of his four sons.

Galway Jerry had preferred to be bought out by his brothers rather than join the syndicate and was promptly paid £20,000 of the down payment of £30,000 made by the incoming shareholders, who, despite the company's declared half million capital had asked for a year's grace in which to make final payment. The remaining £10,000 Grandfather paid at the same time to his brother, Stumpy Michael, who had been appointed as a director of the Queensland Co-operative Company.

Reluctant still to sever his close relationship with Cooper's Creek, Grandfather lingered on, dallying over plans for his Brisbane house, 'putting things in order', waiting for messages about the progress of the cattle. It would seem that having travelled so far with such undeviating clarity of purpose he now hesitated, on the brink of a new phase, wondering 'Where next?'

In July 1884 my father wrote again to his brother in Goulburn:

> I do not think Father seems so well lately. I think the sooner he leaves Thylungra now the better but he appears irritable when I ask him whether he has quite made up his mind when he will go or what he wants me to do when they have all gone. Whether I am to stay here, go to Kimberley at once or return to college I do not know and am in a state of uncertainty as to the future. Somehow a lot of the life seems to have gone out of this place since the cattle got away and so many of the old hands left for Kimberley. There is not the same excitement about sports and race meetings since Uncle Michael and Uncle Jerry left and I miss old Duncan McCaully and all the others who have gone. I hear cousin Mick Costello has gone to the Territory with Uncle John and they have some splendid country on the Limmen River. Aunt Mary and the children will be back from Ireland soon and are going out there and Aunt and the girls will be the first white women ever in those parts.
>
> Well John, I was nineteen last week so time is getting on and I would not like to think the years would drift by in this undecided way. I wish Father would make a clean break now and be done, for although there will be some regrets at leaving the old home where we all grew up I sometimes think the Cooper is going back now rather than forward. We need rain badly and the blacks say there is to be a real drought though please God they are wrong. Poor Pumpkin professes great sorrow at the thought of the family leaving and Father has promised him the black stallion, Ebony, and the bay mare, Forest Maid and another colt that he was supposed to be sending to Kimberley. I don't know what Pumpkin would want with horses of his own as he rides anything he likes on the station and seems to have an idea he owns the lot. He may not enjoy such freedom in the future, but no doubt he will get used to it . . .

Pumpkin had asked most earnestly to be allowed to accompany the family to their new Brisbane home but Grandfather held to his belief that even so exceptional a native would fret and sicken away from his own country. The case, he explained, was not to be compared with John Costello taking blacks from Kyabra to his station on the coast, for the town property they were going to was little bigger than the Thylungra kitchen garden. It would be just a big house on a small piece of land with other houses all around it. There would be no more than a few buggy horses and no cattle or sheep whatever. Pumpkin, whose wife had died a few years before, returned sadly to his lonely humpy and Grandfather believed the matter finalised. In this, however, he had not truly estimated a devotion that was stronger than the ageless ties of race and country and a determination equal to his own.

For his beautiful block on the high bank of the Brisbane River at Albion Grandfather had paid £8,000, a price indicating the inflated land values of that time. Grandfather considered it a bargain, however, since inferior blocks had been selling for as much as £10,000 at auctions in Brisbane. Eventually, having great faith in a Jewish name, he engaged an architect by the name of Cohen and building began on the spacious colonial home with its wide verandahs and elaborately balustraded balconies. A grand mansion in its day, it appears from existing records to have cost little more than £2,600 furnished, which further indicates the lack of balance between land values and other contemporary costs.

At the end of '84 Grandfather made a sudden, rather unexpected decision. His son Michael must return to college for another year.

'But Father,' the boy protested, 'I'll soon be twenty! Surely it's too late to go back now?'

Grandfather, however, had made up his mind.

'No, son. I was reluctant to take you away when I did and it has been troubling my conscience since. You might after all have wanted to go on to the University as Dr Gallagher suggested. Now you must go back, get your final exam and make up your own mind what you really want to do.'

No doubt, since his son's return from college, Grandfather had wondered at times how this rather reserved and bookish boy who had little in common with the romping, 'chiacking' young fellows of the Cooper would settle to life in a possibly even tougher community. Grandfather might have felt more at ease had his son been given to youthful peccadilloes, if he had had to warn him off the drink or censure him for hard swearing, but this was never necessary. The boy was not a prude but his attitude to the cruder or lustier side of life about him was that of spectator rather than participator. As later becomes apparent from his letters and journals he had the capacity, even when actively involved, of regarding the drama of life rather as a member of the audience. Hardy and not easily tired, he was by no means afraid of work but his fine-boned hands somehow lacked a natural aptitude for handling tools and working timber and Grandfather teased him that his 'fingers were all thumbs' with a saddler's needle.

So, to the delight of Dr Gallagher, Father returned to his Alma Mater at the beginning of '85 and settled back into college life with remarkable ease. With him had gone Poor Mary Skeahan's boy, the thirteen-year-old Jack, whose education had so far consisted of occasional shared lessons with his Thylungra cousins. Young Jack himself saw no purpose in education at that time and his only ambition was to get across to Kimberley as soon as possible. After a month or two of inward rebellion he decamped one night via the dormitory window and made his way back to his father who was then runnng the mail for Cobb and Co. between Charleville and Adavale. Dinny chastised his son for throwing away his golden opportunity, consoled himself in traditional style for having fathered a waster, then gave the reins into the boy's considerably more capable hands and settled down to sleep the long miles away on top of Her Majesty's Mail.

At Thylungra the season continued drier than the last and the promised date for final payment from his associates in the Queensland Co-operative slipped past. It was a further six months before Grandfather could bring himself to press for settlement and his reply from the Acting Managing Director ran as follows:

> Brisbane,
> Sept. 1885.
>
> . . . I beg to acknowledge receipt of your account for disbursements since the 1st Jan. 1884.
>
> Owing to the continued dry season it is still inconvenient to make final settlement and I trust you will again let it stand over for a short time when I shall have the pleasure of giving you a cheque for the amount of £130,000 to which you are entitled . . .

Grandfather returned the letter carefully to its envelope and placed it among the other documents in his little tin box.

In October the Thylungra children with old Mr Healy and the prim little Irish governess Miss Frances Quirk went off to stay with their Uncle Galway Jerry and his family at Moorlands while Grandmother and Grandfather finalised their long-drawn-out packing up.

In November, after receiving news of the arrival of the cattle on the Ord some eight weeks previously, there was no further excuse to hold Grandfather to Cooper's Creek. Managers had been engaged long since for both Galway and Thylungra and the 'heavy stuff', including the piano, the big trunks of household goods, the iron safes in which Grandfather locked his money and his best Scotch whisky, Grandmother's cheese presses and a few pieces of treasured furniture made by Great-great-grandfather Michael, had already gone ahead. The place seemed deathly quiet since the children had left and most of the rowdy young stockmen were either in Kimberley, on the way there or making hell for leather to a new gold strike at Croydon. Earlier in the month Grandfather had watched the last of the old hands, Mick Byrne, Tom Connors and Jas Livingstone, ride off with forty head of Thylungra horses for his holdings on the Ord. Noticing the sadness of his eyes, Grandmother had exclaimed:

'Why, Patsy, I believe you'd like to be off with them yourself!'

'Maybe if I was sixteen years younger, Mary,' Grandfather replied, 'as I was when I first came into this country—with the best of my life in front of me.'

'But you got where you wanted, my dear,' Grandmother reminded him. 'You've made money.'

'Was it for the money then?' Grandfather asked. 'Now that it has come I cannot be sure.'

It puzzled his wife how a man who had done so much with such speed and efficiency seemed almost incapable, at this stage, of any action whatever. Often she would find him sitting quite still, not even pretending to read a newspaper or plait some strands of greenhide as he had liked to do when not otherwise employed.

Occasionally he would rouse himself as though in sudden decision and would stride purposefully down to the stock yard. Pumpkin would see him coming and be there before him.

'You want the buggy horses, Boonari, sir? You go to Brisbane now?'

'I have been thinking I may first have to see how they are getting along over on the Ord.'

'You can't go by meself, sir. I got my swag ready any time. Tomorrow might be?'

'I don't know, Pumpkin. I'm just wondering. Do you think they can get along all right on their own?'

'I dunno. I s'pose they got to learn just like me and you.'

'You reckon they wouldn't thank us for meddling, eh?'

The accusation of interfering with other people's lives, so often levelled at him by his mother-in-law and sometimes by Dinny Skeahan, in his cups, had never much troubled Grandfather before. He had shaken off their remarks with an impatient shrug.

'And where would they be now if I had left them to make a mess of things? I tell ye I'll be happy the day they are all on their own feet and making a success of their own affairs.'

'But it is a matter of opinion whether yere own ideas are always the best,' Mrs Costello would retort.

Grandfather would not let her have the last word on this point.

'If it is no more than a matter of opinion, then another man's ideas may be as sound as my own, but when it is something I have carefully worked out and to which they have given no more than a passing thought, then why should I not be telling them?'

At times he would shake his head over the Australian-born generation of his family, unable to express himself clearly on where the difference lay between their attitude and his own.

'I will not criticise them in their stockwork or their bushmanship, for they were born to it and I was not, but in other things they do not seem to think beyond a day or a year. They will act upon impulse and make the law for themselves as they go along and hang what shall be the end result of it. They have been brought up in the faith but they do not return to it for advice. They look only to themselves as though they were Almighty God Himself, which they are not.'

To this 'the young fellows' in questions would reply with some scorn.

'We have been brought up in a country where a man has to rely on his own judgement. We have no time to be riding a thousand miles to find a priest and besides, we don't carry our religion on our sleeves like you Irishmen.'

'You do not understand me,' Grandfather would protest. 'Ye must carry the faith in yere hearts and yere work will be blessed.'

And who could say that he had not been blessed when he rode into the lonely land with his hand in the hand of God? He had loved the country and its wild people and both had served him well. His family had grown up about him with strong bodies and good minds, his flocks and herds had increased and multiplied. He had brought people and life to the wilderness. There were homes now on the inland rivers and roads criss-crossed the vast, grass plains. He had been self-reliant, hard-working, purposeful, but every day he had acknowledged the help of God and his need of it. Some of the young people, like his own son Michael, could run rings around him in a theological argument, but their religion had become a formal thing and the saints who were so close and real to an Irish generation were far away from them—high and strange upon their heavenly thrones.

Would these young fellows, riding a new wilderness, be equally blessed? Had he done right to set them upon this adventure without wives and families to soften the harshness and loneliness of their pioneering work? Many may have considered John Costello and himself imprudent in bringing women and children to Cooper's Creek and yet it would never have occurred to them to have left their families behind. Nor would they have considered postponing their marriages until life seemed plain sailing. It had seemed to them that little worth while could be achieved alone. How could the country have come to life without the families—the women he had sometimes wished to the bottom of the sea, the children who had not all been spared to them?

Without the inventive of family life, would these young men put up decent homes for themselves and live up to the standards in which they had been reared? How would they handle the blacks? Would they ride rough-shod, insensitive, or would they bear in mind, as he and Costello had done, that these too were the children of God? Had he been right after all in encouraging them to leave the Cooper country? Was he right in leaving it himself or should he, like his sister Sarah, have decided to remain and weather another drought?

Somehow talking to Pumpkin helped him to cast aside his doubts. He saw it as a sign of age to lose faith in youth, and remembered that after all they were fine, practical fellows, good-hearted enough and braver than the average. Big Johnnie had a nice girl in Molong—Irish-born, whom he would no doubt marry in a year or two and they would make a home on the Ord. Black Pat and Long Michael had a string of girls to choose from and meanwhile they had their Uncle Tom Kilfoyle also still unmarried, but a solid fellow, to keep an eye on them. Young Duncan McCaully should be all right too, for although simpler and more sentimental than the Durack brothers he had been one of the toughest fellows on Cooper's Creek. Once there was a woman or two in the country others would come and soon there would be normal social life. It was a wonderful opportunity for them and they had one and all been keen to go. No one could ever say he had coerced them into it and in case that should be said of his own sons he was keeping them at college and equipping them for professional careers if such should be their choice.

Meanwhile Grandmother was quietly performing the final tasks, for however her husband might vacillate she knew with her woman's realism that the die was cast. Their time at Thylungra had come to an end and for better or worse they must enter this new phase. She consoled herself that whereas she had not felt well-cast at first in the role of pioneer woman of the lonely west others now came to her for advice and called her 'the Mother of Cooper's Creek'. Perhaps in time she would come to feel at home in this new role as wife of a prosperous retired squatter in a city mansion.

When the buggy was packed at last and her pot plants and crate of precious ducks carefully settled in, Grandfather still sat on, his gaze wandering down the bank into the near-dry bed of Kyabra Creek where the white cockatoos and crows flapped and cried among the cajuputs and wild oranges.

'We came into the drought, Mary, and we leave a drought behind.'

'But you always said you would go in a four-in-hand and a rich man, so we must thank God for the good years between.'

'The happy years, Mary.'

'The happy years.'

Pumpkin was making a last adjustment to the buggy harness as old Cobby, now nearly blind and weeping unrestrainedly, held open the gate.

'I'll be back to see they're treating you right,' Grandfather said. 'The manager has it in writing that those horses belong to you now, Pumpkin, and he knows you're a free man and as long as ye wear that medal I gave you St Patrick will look after you.'

'I've got that travelling man too—that St Christopher,' Pumpkin said.

Grandmother looked down at the scraggy old man beside the gate, the 'guardian angel' she had once taken for a crafty savage.

'Good old Cobby,' she said. 'I will always remember . . . ' and let down her gossamer veil.

There now remained only the leave-taking with Sarah Tully and Poor Mary Skeahan who, since Dinny had finally given over the Rasmore run, was living with her sister at Wathagurra.

Grandfather, at sight of his sisters' stricken faces, forced a heartiness he did not feel.

'Whenever any of you want a trip to town there's a home for you to come to and all expenses paid, and I'll be back of course—I should say two or three times a year at the least.'

'But it's only I will see you, Patsy,' Sarah said, 'as I see my own lost little ones.'

Grandfather disliked what he called his sister's 'morbid prophecies'.

'I don't understand why you should be so fixed on staying on here,' he chided her. 'If it's the graves you're worried about why not send the poor little ones to lie with the others in the Goulburn cemetery—as Mary and I have done with our first little Jeremiah?'

'And have them wandering lonely about the empty house and crying for us along the creek? No, never while there's a Tully left.'

Not long after the family went away Sarah heard that stockmen were tying their horses to the railings of the Thylungra graveyard where her babies were buried. Grimly she set off in her buggy, dug up the crumbling bones with her own hands and reburied them at Wathagurra.

'It is here your father and I will be lying,' she told her children, 'and each of you according to your place in the family.'

And so Sarah established her dynasty that would draw from the Cooper all those things for which her brothers sought so far afield.

Long after her death a fine modern homestead replaced the wattle and daub shack that was made in '74, but it faces, like the first, into the prevailing wind of the west. That was as Sarah had wanted it—so that she could watch down the road to Thylungra for the brothers who never came back . . .

In Brisbane while settling into the new home came the happy news that both boys—Michael and John—had passed their matriculation and were returning home. Grandfather had cast off his depression in a fresh burst of enthusiasm. He called the new home Maryview, and early in '86 threw it open for a housewarming party that lasted for several days. Friends and relations flocked in to exclaim at so much splendour, at the view from the balcony and the newly planted lawns and gardens descending almost to the river's edge, at the modern stables where Grandfather's famous buggy horses that had carried him over so many thousand outback miles now munched and champed luxuriously.

Old Mr Healy, slightly tipsy with champagne, wandered among the guests announcing his decision to return to his sister in Kilkenny. Up to this time, he said, as tutor to the children and business adviser to their father, he had been indispensable. Now with the elder boys grown up and a credit to his teaching, the younger ones, Pat and Jerry, starting at Christian Brothers' College near Brisbane and Mr Durack's affairs at this satisfactory conclusion, he felt he had earned his retirement. It was his duty now, he felt, to put all his weight behind the Home Rule Bill for Ireland. Grandfather saw him on to his ship with mingled feelings of relief and sorrow, and to ease the old man's grief at the final parting said that he and his wife would try to visit him in Ireland 'in a year or two'. Mr Healy nodded through his tears:

'I will wait for you.'

At home the old man told everyone of the rich relations in Australia who were soon to visit him and waiting, he held on to life:

'Oh yes, they will come for sure. My cousin, Mr Patsy Durack, is a man of his word, you know.'

Items about the possibility of gold in Kimberley had now begun to appear in the Queensland press. It was revealed that as far back as '82 three prospectors, Phil Saunders, Adam John and John Quinn, had found colours among ranges south of Nicholson Plains. John had taken ill at the time of the discovery and, tied to his horse, had been led back to the Territory by his mates, but word of the find had caused a government party, led by geologist Edward Hardman, to be sent to the site.

In his report, which appeared in August '85, Hardman wrote of 'a large area of country which I believe will prove to be auriferous to a payable degree ... good colours of gold ... distributed over about 140 miles along the Elvire, Panton and Ord Rivers as well as on the Mary and Margaret Rivers where indications are very good ... sufficient to justify the expenditure of a reasonable sum of money in fitting out a party to thoroughly test the country ... '

It needed no more to touch off the easily roused optimism of a gold-minded community. The more responsible papers published warning articles, pointing out the costs and risks involved in prospecting in this remote and still unsettled area but already a party had chartered a ship from Brisbane to Cambridge Gulf. Grandfather, as easily excited by rumours of gold as the rest of them but with more caution than some, tried to discuss the possibilities calmly with his sons.

'It may prove another blue duck, of course, but if there's to be a rush it means an immediate local market for the cattle. It would give us time to look around for other avenues. If you decide to go, the country is yours for the taking. If not ...'

By this, as might be imagined, wild horses could hardly have kept the boys from their Ord River heritage. Grandfather booked their passages on the *Rajputana*, Cambridge Gulf bound, with the prospecting party, in a month's time.

While preparations for departure were in progress a telegram from Longreach made known that Long Michael, Big Johnnie and their uncle Tom Kilfoyle had returned overland from Kimberley and planned to take the coach from Charleville to visit their family in Molong. Grandfather was on the next coach west and arrived at Charleville at the same time as the three overlanders rode in. He knew more about the news of gold than they.

'It looks as though there may be more than has been published,' he said, 'for the South Australian Government proposed setting up a port just inside the Territory border to capture the new gold trade but the West Australian

Premier decided to get in first. He is supposed to be already on his way up the coast to open a port on Cambridge Gulf.'

The travellers were greatly excited at this news.

'Then Black Pat should be in the money with his store and there will be some people in the country after all.'

Big Johnnie reported his disappointment in the Forrest Vale run but declared the Ord River country taken up in the boys' names to be the best he had seen anywhere in Australia.

'If they have decided to take it on,' he said, 'I will help them start the place when I get back and we can select another block later when you get across yourself. Meanwhile I have left all the cattle in charge of Duncan McCaully on the Ord.'

Decisions for momentous journeys were made with the usual speed. Long Michael and Tom Kilfoyle, having seen the family at Molong, were to hurry back to catch the *Rajputana* with the boys, Big Johnnie was to return overland, this time with his younger brother Jerry Brice who had been running Grandfather's hotel at Adavale and they would try to purchase a few hundred head of cattle on their way through the Territory.

'If ye get married in Molong,' Grandfather said, 'the girls could go around to Wyndham on the *Rajputana*. There'd not be much time but ye'd have only to wire and I'd get anything they'd be needing put on board.'

Long Michael answered vehemently for them all.

'It's no country for white women, Patsy.'

'If it's no country for the women, then what use is it to the men?' Grandfather demanded.

'When the markets open up we'll make our fortunes there,' Long Michael said. 'Time enough then to think about marrying. Just now women and kids would be nothing but a handicap.'

This was a new outlook to Grandfather.

'And where is it any different to Cooper's Creek in the early days?'

'The isolation, the fever, the blacks. The women'd want company, get sick—maybe worse.'

'But the fever should go when the living improves. Ye get it anywhere living in the open and no vegetables. As for the isolation and the blacks . . .'

'I want to get married,' Big Johnnie confessed, 'but I'll give it another year or two. It would hardly be fair to ask a girl just yet.'

Grandfather shook his head.

'But a country without women, I cannot picture it! It will be a sad, barren place until they come.'

After the departure of the cattle Stumpy Michael had gone into partnership with a wealthy friend, Mr Lumley Hill of Brisbane, and had given Long Michael a third share in the stock he had driven for them into Kimberley. A few days before the *Rajputana* was due to sail, Stumpy Michael came up to interview his cousin but the sight of the preparations, the horses ready for shipment, the talk of gold, of the country he had taken up and the tremendous work of settling in, sent him hurrying back to Archerfield to pack his own bags.

'It is all more than Long Michael and a couple of men can handle on their own,' he told his distraught wife, now the mother of seven children. 'There is so much to be decided and gone into that can only be done on the spot and it seems ridiculous that I should be taking it easy here. I should not be more than two or three months at the outside.'

So when the ship sailed at last Stumpy Michael's name figured on the passenger list, with his two nephews, his cousin Long Michael, Tom Kilfoyle, Jim Byrne (whose brother Mick was on his way overland with Thylungra horses for the Ord) and Mr Stockdale's prospecting party which included several women. It was not realised at the time that young Jack Skeahan, Poor Mary's son, was stowed away below with the horses. Determined on a desperate action to break the maddening monotony of the featureless miles beside his drowsing father, he had one day picked up a bag of mail and flung it off the moving coach. When the loss was discovered he had taken his punishment, told his father where to find the missing bag and made off on foot for the nearest town. Hearing that his cousins were leaving for Kimberley he presented himself at Maryview asking to be allowed to go along but his request was refused on account of his youth. The ship was three days out before they discovered him.

'All right,' he was told. 'You've chosen a man's life and you'll have to do a man's work.'

'That suits me,' the boy said. 'I never did anything else but a man's work anyway—except when they sent me to that confounded school'

As the *Rajputana* steamed through tropic seas to Cambridge Gulf my father and his brother broached the riches of their library. On the fly leaf of the journal he was resolved to start at Cambridge Gulf my father scribbled:

> April 25/86. At sea. John quotes sonorous passages on the Creation from 'Paradise Lost'. Myself much taken up with Shelley's translation of Homer's 'Hymn to Mercury'. Magnificent stuff:

The herd went wandering o'er the divine mead,
Whilst these most beautiful Sons of Jupiter
Won their swift way up to the snowy head
Of white Olympus, with the joyous lyre
Soothing their journey . . .

27
THE GOLDEN YEAR

The year 1886. Thc port of Wyndham proclaimed. Ride from the gulf to the Ord. Settling in. Gold rush to Hall's Creek. Growth of a mushroom port. Sale of cattle for the fields. Picture of a gold rush town. The fabulous William Carr Boyd.

'Welcome to Wyndham!' Black Pat called up from his boab canoe when the *Rajputana* anchored off View Hill.

In a few hours low tide would deposit the vessel quietly on the mud so that stock and goods could be brought ashore, but Black Pat's news was too hot to wait. The Premier, Mr John Forrest, had left by the SS *Albany* only the day before after proclaiming the port of Wyndham.

'They called it after some toff in England,' Pat explained, producing a sketch plan drawn up by Mr Ranford, the government surveyor. 'It's going to be a fine modern town, with public parks and terraces and streets named after the pioneers. You see the Duracks and the Emanuels both get a mention.'

The survey party, including Mr Ranford and Mr Nyulasy, had remained and were making a thorough inspection of the locality. A few prospecting parties had already arrived and Jock McPhee, who had piloted the cattle over the last stage, had ridden in and paid for his stores with a nugget his blackboy had picked up in the bed of the Mary River. Pat had put it in a tin and had it under his bed for safe keeping. He had intended keeping quiet about it he told them but of course the news had leaked out and by the time it reached the cities thc golf ball nugget would probably have swelled to the size of a cricket ball.

All this was great news to Stockdale's prospecting party and Mrs Wilkes, one of the miner's wives, insisted on jumping ashore to be put on record as the first white woman to set foot on the site of the big gold town.

But the gold was mostly talk yet, Pat cautioned, and the field a good 200 rough, trackless, nigger-infested miles inland, so the women had best go back with the ship and await further developments. There was as yet no accommodation at the gulf and the mosquitoes and sandflies were 'something cruel'. One of the three Chinese he had brought around from Darwin had become ill with fever, resulting it seemed from infected bites, and Black Pat had conscientiously dosed him three times a day with a patent mixture of his own which he called 'The Kill or Cure'. This was a dark purple concoction of quinine, spirits of nitre, tincture of iron and laudanum with a dash of strychnine and water, but for all his tender ministrations, he told the new arrivals, the fellow had died—and Chinamen were tough. In later years Black Pat never failed to mention, as a remarkable phenomenon, due he thought to certain qualities of the salt marsh, that when the remains were dug up twelve months later to be returned to China they were completely fossilised.

A day or two yarning and loading up and the inland party, including my father and Uncle John, Stumpy Michael, Long Michael, Tom Kilfoyle, young Jack Skeahan, Jim Byrne, two native boys and a prospector named Robert Wolfe who with his squat build, moustache and imperial looked for all the World like Prince Edward jogging along to a point to point, set off up the Ord River with twenty head of Thylungra horses.

Father, in his journal of May '86, recorded in some detail that 160-mile journey when he saw for the first time the white salt marsh vanishing in blue mirage, wild birds and pale cluster of lilies at the Twelve Mile lagoon, shadow-blue of House Roof Hill where the Ord swung out east, grass plains, stony creeks and a pass already known for its discoverer as 'Button's Gap'. From the billabong near the stony red hill where the Ivanhoe homestead was later to stand, thousands of wild whistling duck rose from among the reeds and lilies, and wheeled away, in serpent coils against the sunset sky. Half a mile on they camped among spreading wild figs, Leichhardt pines, pandanus and white flowering caesbania on the river that had swung in a great curve from the hills. Smooth grey rocks humped up like prehistoric animals above the still, green water where floating crocodiles presented irresistible targets.

Morning brought them over grass plains and grey ant hills into the scrubby sands where queer, rock outcrops jutted among the twisted eucalypts, squat boabs and quinine trees with clusters of astringently bitter yellow berries that Long Michael, who had been there before, persuaded the newcomers were good to eat. Father could never afterwards resist playing the same joke on anyone who travelled with him through 'the sands' for the first time, chuckling at sight of their revolted splutterings. Cockatoo Spring was a green oasis among cajuput and palms, like other pools among the red ochre spinifex hills. Scream of galahs and black cockatoos, spear grass high above the horses' backs and 'look out for niggers!' Snowdrift of white wings above the brooding dome of Mount Misery and 'ran down a wallaby for supper'.

Next morning they joined Duncan McCaully, Tom Hayes, Bob Perry, Harry Barnes and others of the overland party who had been left with the cattle and celebrated their reunion with the killing of a 7PD steer. It was at their meeting place on the Behn, across the river from the Argyle homestead, that Father in the last year of his life set up a memorial to his companions of that first ride, and to the pioneer associates who with him carved their stations from the wilderness.

The wording of the plaque, as I well remember, was a project that occupied several months and on which the advice of the family, collectively and individually, was sought and discarded. The legend now stands as follows:

> This plaque is to commemorate those departed who first camped here on May 8th 1886. The party included my Uncle Michael Durack, my brother John, my cousins Michael J. Durack and Jack Skeahan, also Tom Hayes, Jim Byrne, Theodore Wolf and myself. Later in the same year my brother and I selected the site for the Argyle homestead. Here my Mother died and my Father spent the last years of his pioneering life.
>
> Erected in the year 1950 by Michael Patrick Durack, born N.S.W. 1865.

Stumpy Michael, more impressed than ever with the country he had selected in '82, set off with Long Michael to ride their boundaries. Tom Kilfoyle and Tom Hayes rode up the Behn to what they called the Rosewood camp after the town near Galway Jerry's Queensland home, and the rest went tailing cattle and horses that had spread over a wide range and must needs be trained to keep within their lawful pastures.

My uncle John, nineteen years old, was rather preoccupied with duck-shooting during this period and recorded no more of his first inland journey than having brought down twenty-four Whistlers with one shot. His attempts at keeping a pioneering diary were spasmodic and apt to trail off into odd rhymes, conundrums and notes on 'How to astonish your friends', while Father's ran on consistently for over sixty years. In time these journals may have something of the historical value of Pepys' for they cover not only his life in Kimberley but his many journeys all over Australia and the outside world—in search of markets or simply travelling. His style seldom lapses from a formality more in keeping with the Victorian drawing-room than the full-blooded life of the outback cattle camps. There is, however, a certain charm in its incongruity, its quaint circumlocution and careful avoidance of calling a spade a spade. In Father's language a man is never drunk; he is 'suffering from over-indulgence with the God of wine—Bacchus'. The Aborigines are his 'sable brethren'. Sundown is 'the hour when majestic Sol declines to the western horizon', and women as 'fair representatives of their divine sex'. His notes are liberally interspersed with Latin quotations, proverbs, excerpts and reflections on his current reading but the comments, although somewhat laboured, are seldom pompous. Father was a modest man and although sensitive of criticism never boasted of personal prowess or talked, in the manner of the bush, of how he had got the better of this one or that. He was conventional but not hide-bound. He dearly loved what he termed 'discussion on a loftier or more intellectual plane' of 'man's place in the scheme of things', the nature of God and the views of rival philosophers. A firm believer in self-discipline, he observed the tenets of his Church, though hardly with the simple, unenquiring faith of his forebears. He had, as he often impressed upon us, seen many a good man 'slip' in the bush and observed that education and breeding were no guarantee against loss of self-respect under isolated conditions. For this reason he insisted on certain formalities in station life that he was prepared to relax in the city. Often an embarrassed and perspiring visitor at Argyle made a hurried exit from the pre-dinner gathering to borrow a coat and tie, or made the mistake of appearing late and dishevelled at breakfast. For a man of mild tongue Father had a peculiar power of inspiring respect and awe, though he lacked Grandfather's sympathetic human touch and ability to make other men's sorrows and problems his own. He neither gave nor encouraged simple confidences and his emotions, outwardly at least, did not range like those of the extrovert Irishman between exuberance and tears, but he inherited much of his father's infectious enthusiasm, his optimism and his energy.

I find it hard to place my father positively for the reader, nor is this solely because I am too close, for people found him hard to place in life. Abroad, he was not easily picked as an Australian for although obviously of the outdoors, neither his brisk, rather formal manner nor his crisp almost accentless speech betrayed him.

Although an indefatigable chronicler and a good raconteur, he was usually reticent in his personal comments so that our picture of most of his early associates is limited to what they would have 'gone' on the scales. Tom Kilfoyle was a 'bluff sort of character with no time for humbug' and would have 'gone about thirteen stone'. Duncan McCaully, generally known as 'the scrub bull', 'went every bit of eighteen' and was a very tough customer indeed. In fact when Father and his companions joined him on the Ord after their week's ride from the gulf, he was recovering from a spear wound in the chest that he had received while riding after cattle. He had wrenched out the weapon on the spot, broken off the jagged stone head, put it in his pocket and ridden back to camp. There he had filled the gaping wound with coal tar on the principle that what would cure a horse would likewise cure McCaully and the wound had healed over within three weeks. Later it was found that this display of white man *sang froid* had so impressed the blacks that Duncan went down as a hero in tribal legend.

Tom Hayes, partner in Rosewood with Tom Kilfoyle and Galway Jerry—one of the 'wire and whipcord' variety—had also narrowly escaped death during this time when his blackboy Ned Kelly intercepted a spear intended for his boss. From the scattered comments in Father's journals we gather that the relationship between these two was somewhat turbulent. The boy quickly recovered and was never far away from Hayes although they fought most of the time 'in a somewhat unseemly manner'.

In the six or seven months since their arrival in Kimberley the overlanders had somehow acquired a few native boys between eight and fourteen years old. How they got hold of them was nobody's business, but whether by fair means or foul they were to stand a better chance of survival in the years to come than their bush tribespeople. Long Michael had three boys, Cherry, Davey and Billy, Kilfoyle an inseparable named Sultan, while Duncan McCaully had 'secured' two likely youngsters named Tommy and Charlie, who were to live their lives out at Argyle in positions of respect and authority.

These first-footers had made no pretence of coming to 'an understanding' or forming a sort of 'treaty' with the Aborigines like the early governors. They had not even attempted to establish friendly terms like the early pioneers of Cooper's Creek. They had simply ridden in with their cattle and settled on the river banks. Sooner or later the blacks would learn that if they wished to survive their choice lay between working for the white man on his own terms or keeping out of his way among the hills.

Father, writing his journal under the tarpaulin camp by the river, told of 'knocking up bunks and rough furniture'—and very rough it would have been from what I remember of his skill with hammer and nails—visiting Tom Kilfoyle, welcoming Billy O'Donnell and the prodigious native Pompey who sang popular songs hot from the London music halls, farewelling his Uncle Stumpy Michael off back to Queensland after inspecting his property, and at the end of June riding to the gulf with Long Michael and Duncan McCaully for supplies and news of the outside world. There were two tracks to Wyndham, one, the way they had first come, along the Ord and through Button's Gap, the other over the Ord near Lissadell, across to the Dunham and into the gulf on a north-west line.

On this occasion they had chosen the latter route and it was when dipping his billy into a hole on the Dunham that Long Michael had been startled to see fresh boot tracks in the mud.

'Might be some poor blighter got lost,' he said and they climbed a ridge to scout around.

They had all heard of scenes like this from old hands who remembered the Turon in '51, Ballarat, Bendigo, Ovens, Gympie. Skirting the ridges, dipping into gullies and creek-beds and out across the plain, trailed the ant-like procession of urgent men, the riders goading their packs, the horse-drawn waggons and caravans, the buggies and spring carts, the camel-men and the men on foot, pushing barrows, or packing cases on wheels piled high with gear, men plugging on, swags on their backs, swinging water bags and billy cans, one with a tin whistle, another with a concertina wheezing 'John Brown's Body' and 'The Wearin' of the Green'. There were big fair-bearded fellows, Germans, Russians, Scandinavians, men with the dark features of the southern European, a few Chinese in coolie hats and dungaree blues trotting barefoot and carrying their boots, all raising between them a sound like a hive of angry bees.

The settlers cantered to the track and shouted excited questions to the prospectors.

'When did the rush start?'

''Bout two weeks back.'

'Where are you heading for?'

'Place called Hall's Creek.'

'Move on there! Move on! No time for gossiping.'

All afternoon they rode downstream of the rush, and only after sundown, when the diggers stopped to camp, did they get any coherent news of recent events. A well-equipped party of adventurous young Victorians with a smart horse-drawn caravan invited them to join their picnic meal. The leader, one Hogan, spoke as though the whole thing was a splendid lark.

'Some of them throw off at us—call us "the slap-up party", as though prospecting and comfort should never mix. Name your poison—rum, whisky, gin or wine!'

Then came the story of the rush. Prospectors were coming in from all directions, some landing at Derby on the west coast and making up the Fitzroy, others overlanding from Queensland and the Territory—some even footing it from Burketown, poor as church mice and living off the country.

Heaven only knew how many of these hatters would make the distance. Most of all were streaming into Cambridge Gulf, making a line of travellers 200 miles long, for rumour had it that there were not just reefs but mountains of gold in Kimberley, nuggets the size of footballs waiting to be picked up in the creek beds, 'jeweller's shops' sparkling in the sun.

'Who told you all this?'

'Oh, it's common knowledge. Carr Boyd seems to have been about first in with the really big news and he and Billy O'Donnell and that flash abo Pompey piloted some parties through for a pound a head. Must have made a small fortune. The rest of us are following their tracks.'

Another surprise awaited them at the gulf, for a willy-nilly settlement had sprung to life a few miles up from Black Pat's store, and steamers, sailing ships, barques, schooners and launches lay at anchor in the muddy stream. Seven shanties, hastily thrown together from mangrove saplings, brushwood and slabs of tin, claiming to be 'hotels' were doing a roaring trade amid a mushroom growth of stores and private shacks. A rough landing stage had been put up on to which newcomers were still streaming ashore with their goods into the quaint little township that sweltered and palpitated with excitement at the foot of the stony Bastions.

'This is just a makeshift place until the government men come to lay out the proper port farther round,' his cousin Pat explained as Father helped him move the last of his original store from View Hill to the new site.

Letters from home awaiting them in the township told of the completion of Maryview, of Grandfather's latest speculations and of land still booming on the coast. It seemed altogether a time of great progress and prosperity and the inlanders returned from the gulf with stirring tales of the big rush and the crazy makeshift port that had sprung up overnight.

If they had wondered at first where to start on the task of founding a station in this empty land the gold rush now dictated their immediate activities. For months they would be occupied mustering cattle and droving them to this fortuitous local market, riding back and forth to the fields in a state of constant excitement where otherwise they might have been quietly 'pioneering' in the slow, steady, usual way.

Bob Button, kindly pioneer of the overland tracks to Kimberley, then manager of Ord River for Osmond & Panton, rode in to Argyle with further tales. Yes, they were finding the alluvial all right, but the 'jeweller's shops' and the outsize nuggets were probably a myth.

'If the big stuff's there we're all made, and the country will shoot ahead, if not the crowd will soon move out and our local market's gone west, so make hay while the sun shines.'

A few days later Father, watching a man leading his horse to the little Behn River camp, remarked to his brother:

'I could almost have sworn that was old Jack Horrigan with his bandy legs and the big stockman's hat strapped under his chin.'

Uncle John went one better.

'And I could have sworn the fellow behind him was Georgie Lamond.'

And so they turned out to be, Horrigan, lately head stockman on Thylungra and Kyabra, Lamond who had ridden at the Cooper race meetings and been for a while horsebreaker on Kyabra. They introduced their mate Jock McPhee and told how with another man named McKensie, they had gone into partnership in a butchering business on the fields, and had come to offer gold as spot cash for beef. Horrigan and Lamond, squatting on their heels for a 'drink of tea and a yarn', said they had joined up shortly after the cattle moved off from the Cooper, bought some horses and started with the idea of getting into land in Kimberley. At Boulia, Horrigan saw a news sheet on a bar-room door telling of the gold strike at Croydon. He had gold in his blood, like most of the stockmen of the times, if not from New South Wales or Victoria, from Gympie or Palmer River.

'Come on,' he had said to his mate, 'let's go!'

Lamond, a younger man and not yet bitten with the mining bug, still hankered after Kimberley, but what Jack said usually went. A notice on the other side of the door attracted his attention as they were leaving the pub:

> W.A. Government geologist Hardman and party report good possibilities for gold in Kimberley.

So the die was cast and they pushed on into the Territory. Around the Overland Telegraph they had teamed up with two Englishmen named Marriott and Johnson and together they had come across to the fields. The Englishmen had gone into a show with old Billy Keelan and they were doing pretty well in Spear Gully until a few weeks before when a pack of niggers had crept up on them while they were peering together at the gold in their dish. Marriott was pierced through the heart, Johnson wounded in the head and Keelan escaped with a spear through his hat. Lamond told how he and his boy Friday had followed the murderers and in a dawn raid on their camp killed four and wounded as many more as they could hit, then silenced police enquiries by signing a statement that the blacks had shown fight and they fired in self defence. That satisfied everyone especially Lamond who felt he had struck a blow for justice in avenging a good mate.

It was July 22, 1886, Father's twenty-first birthday, when, the cattle mustered and handed over, he helped weigh out £1,200 in raw Kimberley gold for 7PD bullocks at £17 a head, and cows at £15. He never forgot the thrill of it.

What wonder there was little building or organising in that wild year of gold when one never knew who next was to turn up with a string of packs from the Queensland side. The three young stockmen, Mick Byrne, Tom Connors and Jas Livingstone, whom Grandfather had started from Thylungra with horses seven months before, arrived at the Behn claiming to have 'duffed' a tankard from every pub on the route and to have vowed to drain one for every ten miles travelled when they got to the gulf. They were still celebrating when Father met them in Wyndham some weeks later, 'its having taken them but a short time to see both the miles and the mugs in duplicate.'

By August, Cousin Big Johnnie Durack had turned up again with his brother Jerry Brice, a string of horses and some cattle purchased in the Territory, and the two set off at once with my father behind a mob of bullocks for the fields. The track was still peopled with prospectors coming and going between Wyndham and Hall's Creek but the first headlong race was over and travellers had time for a yarn. Father asked the same questions of everyone they met, presumably for the amusement of recording their varied answers.

'How many diggers would you reckon, all told?'

Romanticists hazarded 10,000, others nearer 5,000. 'Officials' had made tally of 3,000 but laid no claim to accuracy, for the miners had quickly spread over a 300-mile radius, coming from all directions, and getting out whichever way the Customs were least likely to catch up with them.

How much gold had been found? Nobody knew. How many prospectors had died or been speared on the track? Who could say?

At one stage, noticing an abandoned pack and tracks leading off towards the hills, they followed and found the scattered remnants of a man that the wild dogs had got to first. How many like him? God only knew.

They passed men dollying madly in the creek beds while their mates lay crazed with fever under rough bough shades. One of them told the drovers:

'We take it in shifts. Maybe we'll be down tomorrow and some of the others will be up, if they're not dead. The fever's like that—if you live through the worst of the attack you'll be down one day and up the next.'

Jock McPhee's camp was on the outskirts of the shanty town at Hall's Creek where the main body of diggers had pitched their tents or brushwood shelters among the stunted trees and spinifex of the turbulent hills. The sight of beef on the hoof caused a stir of excitement among the meat-hungry men who had made short shrift of the first consignment of 'killers'. The beasts were slaughtered and butchered in the open field while the diggers crowded round, took their meat warm from the vendor's hand and crossed his gory palm with gold or the rough and ready 'shin-plasters' of the bush.

The cattle men, reared in a tradition in which certain appearances were kept up under all circumstances, were surprised that so many, even those of educated and aristocratic background, should have thrown all conventions of dress to the wind, 'many going shirtless in the blazing sun, their tattered trousers more resembling kilts being in rags about the knees.' But there was no clothing then to be bought at the fields and the stoutest moleskins were soon in tatters from the sharp rocks and prickly scrub.

'Many living like niggers,' Father wrote but that was merely a current figure of speech, for no blacks ever existed in such a litter of empty tins, filthy rubbish and feverishly upturned earth.

> It is hard to ascertain, [he continued] what quantity of gold has been found to date or how many have struck it rich as most of the gold discovered is said to have been smuggled out to avoid duty. Most I have spoken to seem none so cheerful of their prospects. Many have never been in the bush before and had no idea of the conditions they would meet with. It was a surprise to them, on arrival in Wyndham to find they must track so far overland to the fields and few had any means of conveyance save their legs. They complain most bitterly of the heat, flies, bad water, fever and dysentery. Some believe the alluvial to be petering out already, others that they have not started upon the real gold as yet. I could hazard no statement except that I never thought to encounter so great a collection of mixed humanity as have gathered here from the four ends of the earth.

On their return journey Father and his cousins camped on the Bow River with a party of sadly disillusioned prospectors. 'What wouldn't we do to that misleading liar Carr Boyd if we could lay hands on him!' they grumbled.

Their chance for vengeance came that night when into the camp rode the big Carr Boyd himself, hailed the party breezily and produced a bottle of rum from his packs.

'It's all very well to offer us rum now,' one of the sullen men remarked, 'when we nearly perished for water on the way out.'

But no one ever got the better of Carr Boyd. Only ignorant fools perished of thirst in this country, he declared, for wherever you went there were crows hoping for some bones to pick and where there were crows there must be water. You had only to feed them a piece of salt bacon and they'd lead you in a beeline to the nearest rock hole.

Father, always fascinated with a flamboyant character, used up four pages describing Carr Boyd.

> Never, [wrote Father] have I heard such a string of tall stories as he regaled us with, and yet told in such a manner that only on reflection did one doubt their veracity.

Already, under the name of 'Pot-jostler', Carr Boyd's Munchausen Kimberley tales were appearing in Queensland papers and although he staunchly denied authorship his style was unmistakable.

Soon the bitter complaints had given way to good fellowship and Carr Boyd, on his haunches in the firelight, was charming the company with 'Queen of My Heart' and 'Come into the Garden Maud' in his melting baritone. When the cattle men left in the morning he had convinced the diggers of a splendid new reef near the Elvire River and they were rolling their swags in excited haste.

28

Settling In

The years 1886 to 1887. Lively times in Kimberley. Big Johnnie Durack is speared by the blacks. A punitive expedition. 'The wet'. Letter from home. Fever. Patsy Durack arrives and begins to build. White labour versus black. A new recruit. Patsy Durack visits the goldfields. First Wyndham race meeting.

Never, in all the years since, was there so much life and so much death on the rough bush tracks, so many callers at the station shacks. Even Father's brief comments on daily happenings reflect the excitement, variety and general disorganisation of the times, for no 'pattern of life' had yet been established in Kimberley.

'Tailing' horses and cattle occupied a great deal of time and in the process they were becoming familiar with their country. They rounded up and branded the new-born calves and expressed keen satisfaction at the rate of increase on the rich Ord river pasture. They put up a few 'rough yards' on their run, pegged out horse and bullock paddocks for the future, but as yet made no attempt to fence and for the rest were in and out from the gulf and across to the goldfields.

As long as Father was in the saddle going from one place to another, whether or not there was any practical necessity for the journey, he felt his time was being well spent. He was 'pioneering', 'empire building'. He had begun to cultivate an auburn beard and had, to his surprise, grown another inch in his twenty-first year, making him just six feet. Young John was shorter and still quite beardless and looked to his elder brother to make all the decisions. The two were devoted companions and at night sat together with their books, fighting off the insects that flocked to the light of their flickering kerosene lamp, while outside the still, warm bush pulsed with its unseen life and sometimes, throbbing from the hills like a muffled drum, came the sound of the black man's didgeridoo.

To and fro from their tent and bough shelter on the Behn River rode stockmen and prospectors, police and government officials from the fields, these last confident bearded men in tropical topees and riding togs like the *pukka sahibs* of India that some in fact had been.

> A delightful evening in company with C. D. Price, R. Wolfe. E. Baynes and Arthur Forbes. A lively flow of conversation and some wit . . . Forbes quite a brilliant artist causing much amusement with his sketches of gold-fields personalities—undoubtedly a rum lot . . .

Arthur Forbes, then warden of the goldfields, was the son of a British colonel who had retired to Western Australia with his large family. The water-colour sketches and cut-outs which he scattered throughout the North-West from Roebourne to Wyndham provide some of the most vivid impressions we have of these colourful times.

A party of Afghans came through with a camel team en route to the fields and travelling with them a woman:

> . . . presumably quite young, though could not see much for her copious veil. Remarked that as she was the first woman ever passed through this part and the first ever on the Ord I should put her name on record, but she would not give it, saying airily to put her down as 'The Mountain Maid'. Much regretted she would not wait for a meal or even a cup of tea.

'The Mountain Maid' threw up a shanty hotel on the fields and later followed the diggers' trail to the Nullagine to fade from sight with a string of camels headed south for the Nullarbor—one of the countless, lonely pilgrims to each new shrine of the great God Gold. Hall's Creek in these times was no place for women, except a few such intrepid characters as old 'Mother Kelly' with her scurrilous tongue and her heart of gold and 'Mother Dead Finish' with her noxious brew, lurking in her Dunham shanty to waylay returning prospectors. Legends grew up about the ill-gotten nuggets that rattled in her bulky corsage and she was found one day with a knife in her back and the clothing stripped to her waist.

Wyndham became gayer and wilder as the year went on. Gold was in brisk circulation and champagne flowed freely among the diggers, stockmen and business people of the town. Father, on his visits to collect mail and stores, wrote brief understatements of the lively scene.

> Oct. 30/86. Strolling through town reading ancient history. Plenty of 'hurrah' fights going on. Too much champagne. Got life insured by Mr Hamilton. Deposited gold in Mr Baynes' safe. Auctions two in a day . . .
>
> 31st. Town land sold today by Mr Stone, Govt. Resident, having realised £3600 odd, £2000 worth of Wyndham town blocks

> purchased by an English syndicate. Mr Ranford today presented with two nuggets of gold value about £120 . . .

Ranford, returning from his survey of the gulf rivers, was piqued to find that so many shanty hotels, stores and shacks had been set up at what he had intended as a temporary landing place. He suggested that the inhabitants now began putting up more seemly and permanent structures on the official site, but the makeshift port was voted 'good enough' until the future of the fields was established. In fact few of the inhabitants cared a fig for the future of Kimberley. They had come to make as much money as possible in the shortest possible time and thereupon to leave the sweltering, mosquito-infested little town with its feet in the mangrove mud for good and all.

Not yet the days when a flock of charming young women with 'honeyed tones and beguiling smiles' would draw the station boys to town on the flimsiest excuse. Father was relieved to turn his back on the gulf in November '86 and to make back upriver to the camp on the Behn. He found the place deserted with a note from the two Johns, brother and cousin, informing him they had gone after straying horses and that the others were mustering towards Lissadell. For the first time since his arrival in Kimberley, perhaps for the first time in his life, Father found himself alone except for the blackboy Tommy. Even in later years, accustomed to long, lonely days and nights in the bush, he hated to find himself the sole occupant of a lonely station.

> Nov. 17. There is an uncanny and desolate atmosphere about the camp, [he wrote]. I set to work to mend some packs but do not know when I have felt the hours hang so heavily, with no sound but the melancholy note of a few crows and the wild cries of the cockatoos . . .
>
> Nov. 18. Still anxiously expecting someone to relieve this monotony and do not relish the thought of camping alone again tonight. Last evening Tommy drew my attention to a chain of fires all along the range as far as the eye could see. He appears disturbed and says it is a signal of some sort, though I think more likely a bush fire having caught a long line of spinifex, giving a weird illusion of mountain villages lit up for some festivity. Do not know what can be keeping Duncan, the two Johnnys and Charlie away so long . . .
>
> Nov. 19. Passed a very lonesome day anxiously expecting somebody home . . . Just dark and could hear the occasional knock of a bell

> coming from upriver, did not know who they were until, to my surprise, I saw it to be M. J. Durack (Long Michael), Jerry (Brice), brother Johney, Duncan and Charley. Asked me did I hear the dreadful news—cousin Big Johney has been speared by the blacks and they had just come from burying him yesterday—a horrible affair . . .

The two Johns had been riding after horses near the Rosewood boundary on the fateful day. The spear had flashed out of the long cane grass on the riverbank but the doomed man had galloped on 300 yards before he slumped and fell to the ground.

Behind them a group of blacks stood as though deliberating among themselves, then began moving forward slowly, spears set in their throwing boards. Uncle John drew the small Colt revolver from his belt but the dying man restrained him.

'Don't fire, Johnny. If you lose your horse you're a goner too.'

'You'll be all right. I'll take the spear out and get you up in front.'

'No—I'm done for, son. Ride for your life.'

With the dead man limp in his arms the boy glanced again to where the blacks stood, straight and stiff, bodies slashed with white paint, heads bedecked with feathers and fur ornaments, spectres of inhuman vengeance. He laid the body on the ground and mounted the horse that stood quivering in terror, with its rein over his arm. It was dark when he reached the musterers' camp on the Ord and gasped out his terrible tale.

Back in New South Wales, an Irish mother, polishing up the silver in her country hotel, put her hands to her head.

'Something has happened to Johnnie. It is no use keeping it away from me. We will never see him again.'

Three weeks later the news, sent by ship to be telegraphed from Darwin, reached Molong, but it had swept through Kimberley like wild fire:

'Big Johnnie Durack's been speared by the blacks!'

From the gulf and the goldfields, mates—Barney Lamond, Jack Horrigan, Connors, Livingstone and the brothers Byrne—came riding to Argyle to show their respect in the only way they knew. Big Johnnie had been a hero to stockmen of Cooper's Creek and the overland trail and the shock of his death hardened their hearts to steel against the blacks.

The avenging party, police, 'special constables' and black trackers, rode to the scene of the murder where the dead man's brothers had buried him the following day. The body had been disinterred, pounded with heavy stones and the crushed remains pinned down with spears.

Angry men rode the ranges and the plains, following tracks that led to a deserted camp strewn with broken weapons, flint spear-heads and the bones of wild game and kangaroo. Mockingly, the blacks had left a clear trail to follow with spears stuck into tree trunks and kylie sticks thrown down where the trail might be lost to poor trackers over stony ground. Down into steep creek beds, over stony ranges, clay-pans, spear-grass plains, the tracks wound on until footprints mingled with the half-moon impressions of horses' hoofs. The young trackers pointed, shamefaced:

'This same way where we been before.'

They had been brought in a circle on an exhausting four-day ride, but still the tracks led on enticingly only to vanish at last under a thirty-foot perpendicular of limestone cliff.

The party broke up in disgust and whether further more successful reprisal measures were taken for this deed can never be known. The conspiracy of silence that sealed the lips of the pioneers added colour to the rumours that spread abroad so that whereas we know they took much rough justice into their own hands they were no doubt less devastating to the local tribes than was sometimes said. 'Punitive expeditions', like brumby musters, took a great deal of time and organisation and in that wild land where ranges and impenetrable gorges formed so ideal a refuge for fugitives they returned from such projects, as often as not, completely defeated. One lesson they learned from this chase, however, was that 'treachery' on the part of the blacks must be met with 'strategy' by the whites. The straight-out 'nigger hunt' would get them nowhere, for even with the help of trackers no white party was a match for the nimble-footed tribespeople who as surely as their dogs could smell the 'cuddjabah' and his horses on the wind. Nor could white men then be confident which side of the fence their trackers were on.

Towards Christmas the wet came in with blue flicker and forked dazzle of lightning, a rumble and cymbal clash of thunder that shook the plains and echoed back from the hills. Heavy rain fell on a labyrinth of creeks and gullies that sent the rivers roaring to the gulf. Kimberley changed in a week from gold and red of sun-bleached grass and scalded plain to a steaming, green land, splashed with the sudden colour of wet-weather flowers and white swamp lilies, quivering with heat haze, screaming, buzzing and droning with its multifarious wild life. Fragrant, creamy blossoms broke among the luxuriant foliage of the boabs and small, sweet flower clusters foamed on the cajuputs. Ranges, opalescent blue and rose in 'the dry', glowered indigo dark against tumbled skies and the grey tree trunks turned bold black as though splashed with tar.

A tangy, wild smell of rain-wet spinifex and eucalyptus swept down from the hills, bringing a sense of mingled excitement and resignation. The wet had set in and men's movements were subject to the caprice of the rivers, the bog and the quicksand swamps.

Still a police constable with some thanks to good luck and his black trackers managed to bog through to Argyle with the mail including a letter from Grandfather:

> My dear boys,
>
> When ye receive this letter I should soon be on the way to ye and all the news can wait until I come, except I should tell ye that I will have Pumpkin with me, for that he turned up here of his own accord with the horses I gave him when we left Thylungra.
>
> I was at first for surprising ye, but he says ye might be thinking to see a ghost and it is better that ye know to expect him. He would not have it otherwise but that he should come to you, dear boys, and does not know how ye will be getting on before he is there to help ye and to look after the horses. It has been a great concern to him about the Thylungra horses and since the sad news reached us of poor cousin Johney's death, I do not think that he has slept sound for the worry . . . Ye're mama is delighted that the good faithful fellow is to come to ye afterall and we have been having Masses said for ye along with our poor cousin, God rest his soul . . .

Speculation, as always after unspecific letters or telegrams in the bush, ran rife at the camp on the Behn. What did Grandfather mean by this vague statement that he should 'soon' be on the way? How soon and by what ship? Could he be so ignorant of the nature of a Kimberley wet season as to assume they could ride in and out of Wyndham for further news?

In March the Ord still rode high and mighty between its banks, cutting the settlers' world into 'gulf side' and 't'other side'. Father was looking for lost horses around the Behn Junction when Bob Perry came to hurry him back to the station camp.

'That crazy old man of yours turned up with his black offsider.'

And who, asked Grandfather, would be expecting any man to wait around in a hole like Wyndham when he had brought five good Thylungra horses on the ship with him? There was no mistaking the track since the diggers had strewn it with a litter of dead horses, tins and broken-down vehicles. They had got through to Lissadell without trouble and from there Long Michael and Jerry Brice got them across on a tarpaulin raft with the two strongest mounts swimming behind. It was like old times to be crossing a river in flood and fine fun had been had by all.

Grandfather had brought with him one of his innumerable parchment 'Agreements', signifying that his Kimberley interests, including those he had shared with his deceased cousin Big Johnnie, were to be sold to his sons on terms payable over a period of ten years.

'So that if things go smash in Queensland you children will be all right, except that ye will have to be keeping your parents in their old age.'

He spoke jokingly, for even though a run of bad seasons on the Cooper since the formation of the Queensland Co-operative had so far prevented the company from paying him any of his £130,000, he did not for a moment believe that ruin could actually befall so solid a combine in a boom State. In '87 he was concerned about minor difficulties but not greatly worried for the future.

From the time he appeared on the scene things began to take shape around the Behn. To start with he tossed out the pegs the boys had driven in on their homestead site.

'Just as well ye were a bit slow off the mark getting the place up,' he said. 'Ye'd have had it too close to the bank.'

He made quick 'flood calculations' and paced and pegged higher up. The place became a hive of purposeful activity as loads of grass and spinifex were carted in, horse-churned into the boggy, wet-weather soil and rammed between wooden stays. Timber was felled, carted and sawn to size, rafters, doors and window frames shaped and set in place.

'What! Call that a yard?' Grandfather exclaimed, examining his sons' handiwork. 'Ye ought to be ashamed of yereselves!'

'It was only a temporary structure,' Father explained.

The excuse was swept aside.

'Nonsense! Ye might as well do the job properly to start with. I know places where they've been propping up these "temporary" yards for twenty years.'

He and Pumpkin worked together in the simmering heat from daylight to dark, as they had done in the early days on Thylungra. Mustering and branding continued meanwhile and the erratic journals began to read more like the day books of life at Thylungra.

By August the house, outbuildings and yards were finished and the camp on Behn River could justifiably claim the title of a 'station'. They called it Argyle after the county in New South Wales where Grandmother was born and where the family had its first holding on Dixon's Creek. The main building was like the first Thylungra, verandahs shading its red mud walls and crazy paving of grey river flags, its roof a cunning thatch of grass, pandanus and spinifex. Inside the floors were a hardened preparation of ant-hill mud. Bullock and kangaroo hides served as floor mats, as table tops stretched over old cart and buggy wheels, were nailed to timber frames for the seats of chairs and window shutters, cut into strips for a criss-cross open weave that formed the 'spring mattresses' of the rough bush beds. Greenhide water bags swung on greenhide ropes from the verandah posts, riding and pack saddles, harness and leather or greenhide whips hung from the beams.

Store and kitchen were one, with broad shelves for the provisions, a big, rough-hewn table for the cook and outside an open fireplace, mud oven at one side and 'range' on the other with its impedimenta of pots and billy-cans, a bucket of salt beef on the boil or cooling off with a deep scum of cooking fat forming on top. The meat house was a bough shade and timber trestle where the beef was salted and left to dry while 'the fresh' dangled on iron hooks, quickly forming a hard skin Nothing could prevent the flies finding the moist crevices, but no one was squeamish about blown meat in the bush. You cut out the infested areas in 'the fresh' and threw the blown pieces of 'salt' on the wood heap for the ants to clean.

But all the time fever haunted the station camps on the rivers like the malignant spirit of a country that would repel the trespasser. The daily small doses of quinine were increased until the ears of the settlers buzzed and their heads swam. 'A touch of fever' was general lethargy and aching limbs, 'an attack' anything from uncontrollable ague, migraine and high temperature, to various stages of delirium.

All over the country men rode after stock in an aching daze or lay on the creek banks with their hats pulled over their eyes, praying for the night to bring remission from the cruel light and the blazing heat of the sun.

In April Pumpkin, out after horses, found a traveller camped across the Behn too sick to walk a few miles to the station camp or bury the native boy who had died a week before and lay rotting under the dark massed wings of eagle-hawks and crows. Pumpkin had hurried back for the dray and brought the stranger to Argyle where he was cared for until well enough to move on to Hall's Creek.

'Was it always like this here?' they asked the blacks, but gathered little sense from their reply. Everyone knew there were 'debbil-debbils' around the waterholes in the wet and when a man got sick the tribe would sneak off under cover of darkness, dodging about and trailing branches to obliterate their tracks and so confuse the evil ones as to which way they had gone, while the sick man was left to recover or die as the case might be. In this there was no doubt much sound, primitive sense for the white men's stations rapidly became hot-beds of infection, and if the blacks were reassured that their evil spirits were nothing more or less than the sprightly Anopheles, they sickened and suffered as never before.

Work progressed, however, since there were plenty of hands in those months when a feeling of disillusionment with the goldfields had brought many ex-stockmen back to station work. It seemed in fact that with so much white labour available there would be little need to recruit further Aborigines. Grandfather's idea of providing the blacks with regular beef to discourage cattle-spearing, establish mutual confidence and gradually absorb the younger people into station work was dismissed as impractical for Kimberley. The settlers declared they might soon find themselves impoverished by big native encampments demanding as their right not only beef but other provisions which, when withheld, would cause the blacks to become more of a menace than before. Most Queenslanders came west with a fixed idea of the inferiority of the Territory and Kimberley blacks to those of the decimated tribes of the other side, who were now seen to have had many admirable qualities. The Queensland Aborigines they declared could be quickly trained as loyal and efficient helpers whereas these, for all their cunning and treachery, were dunderheads in the stock camp. It was pointed out that their weapons were relatively clumsy, that they made no attempt to trap or net fish, and that in short they were best left as far as possible to their own devices since the more they learned of the white man's ways the more crafty they became.

My father's attitude to the native question was somewhere between that of Grandfather and those of his associates who thought that any sort of human consideration for the blacks was sentimental and ridiculous. I find it easier to imagine Grandfather, with his quick, Irish temper, taking a stockwhip to a native than I can my father who was not impulsive or quickly roused to anger, and I can imagine neither of them shooting a man in cold blood or using a gun at all except when necessary. Both disliked anything in the nature of blood sports and in later years when Member for the Kimberley district, my father, appalled by the wanton destruction of the bird life he loved, brought in a bill for its protection north of the 20th parallel. Nonetheless he would have been embarrassed, in these early years, to have been thought 'unrealistic' about the blacks, and had many a brush with 'the pater' on the stand they should take.

'Maybe if the government would subsidise us for feeding them there would be something in your policy of encouraging them about the place,' he told his father. Later he became so attached to this idea that he wrote suggesting it, by way of reply to a storm of criticism that had broken out against the northern settlers in the southern press:

> I would like to ask our critics how else they would have us deal with the situation in which we find ourselves, other than by remaining out of the country altogether, a course rather late to decide upon, for when Australia was taken over in the name of the British Empire its purpose was surely that of populating and developing it? My father, a pioneer of western Queensland, held it as an ideal to absorb the aborigines into the white man's economy and trained many natives successfully to this purpose. Others in the district pursued the same policy and the fact that so few aborigines now remain in those parts was in spite of their efforts. Had they been encouraged and subsidised to bring in and train many more natives the situation might be very different today for it was the behaviour of the outside or bush blacks who, in failing to co-operate with the new regime, in killing cattle, horses and sheep and committing a number of unprovoked murders that led to the settlers having to call in the protection of the police. I speak therefore from some experience and would regret to see the situation in Kimberley reach a point where the wholesale extermination of the aborigines would become inevitable.

Grandfather, however, sniffed at the idea of government subsidy for feeding blacks whose younger relatives were employed on the station.

'I don't know what's got into the younger generation,' he stormed, 'forever wanting to be spoonfed by the government. In my day we were glad enough for the opportunity to strike out for ourselves and make good. We never expected anything for nothing—not even native labour. We provided meat and rations up to a point for the black families as a matter of course. It was our part of the bargain. We lived up to it and they lived up to theirs.'

'They must have been a very different type of people,' Father argued. 'Where would you ever see a man like Pumpkin over here?'

'Pumpkin was just an ordinary, average blackfellow who was properly trained and treated from the start and the boys you've got here now will grow up the same way if you go the right way about it.'

Pumpkin, while agreeing in general principle about the inferiority of the Kimberley blacks, regarded the boys Charlie and Tommy as exceptions to the general rule and was a 'proper father' to them as they told us in later years. Like Grandfather he discouraged the careless 'pidgin' form of English and taught his apprentices good manners and good stockmanship.

When he had been only a few weeks at Argyle he met a traveller coming through to the fields from Queensland with a black woman and a boy of about eight or nine years old. The child had a roguish face and a confident seat in the saddle and Pumpkin asked the traveller if he would care to exchange him for a tin of jam. The fellow considered the proposition:

'I've trained him for a horse tailer, and he's pretty reliable,' he said, 'but I could do with some jam and that nice little mare you're riding as well.'

Pumpkin consulted my father, the bargain was struck, and Boxer came into service at Argyle, a companion for the other two boys Charlie and Tommy who camped on the river bank a short distance from the house. Pumpkin himself camped on the homestead verandah, being convinced that the 'myall' blacks were planning a night raid and that Father and Uncle John, being sound sleepers, would undoubtedly be taken unawares.

The house completed, Grandfather set off for Hall's Creek. The first excitement of the '86 rush had passed and half the early diggers had already moved on to try their luck elsewhere but Grandfather was still impressed with the possibilities of the Kimberley fields. He thought it a great pity that the miners should be moving out after merely skimming the surface for the alluvial and he was determined to investigate further prospects with the aid of heavy crushing machinery. In this decision he was personally less interested in becoming a successful miner than in encouraging population to Kimberley and establishing a firm local market for the beef industry. Having pegged out a claim he rode back to Argyle and arranged with his son John, cousin Jerry Brice and two other ex-Queensland relatives, John Dillon and Jim Minogue, to leave the station for a while and work the claim until he came back with up-to-date equipment.

He then packed up for his return and rode down to the gulf with most of the white population which was making in for the first annual Wyndham race meeting. For a week all cares, ills and anxieties were forgotten. Grandfather was happy in the company of so many fellows who had started their careers around Cooper's Creek and who carried with them the traditions and characteristics of the Queensland cattle camps. Listening to the lively talk of cattle, horses, stock routes, country and prospecting he felt a resurgence of the optimism that had faded somewhat in the fever-stricken months at Argyle when it had seemed that the young fellows might be right in believing that Kimberley, for all its potential, was less suitable for white habitation than western Queensland. With a race meeting in progress and a few women and children in the offing, a sense of normality returned and he again foresaw the day when home life would come to the lonely hinterland. Again he saw the roads pushing out to the little bush towns and station settlements on the rivers. He heard the rattle and rumble of the coaches, the noise of the big house parties, the sound of music and dancing and the merry laughter that he had missed in this great, quiet land. Soon the boys would marry and the time would come when he could bring his wife and daughters to visit them and the vast distances that now divided the family would seem less than they had covered so often between Goulburn and Cooper's Creek.

29

THE GOLD AND THE GRASS

The years 1887 to 1888. John W. Durack writes of prospecting at Hall's Creek. Visitors to the fields. Flood in the Behn River. Wyndham personalities. Voyage to Darwin. The brothers Patrick, Stumpy Michael and Galway Jerry Durack return to Kimberley. Black versus white.

Uncle John and his three prospecting companions set up their tents and a bough shed for meals on Butcher's Creek, took out miner's rights and got to work with cradle and dolly pan with plenty of time off for yarning with fellow prospectors and enoying themselves at the local hostelries.

'A wonderful lot of fellows they were,' my uncle would say with his crooked reminiscent smile, 'all with their local nicknames and likeable ways.'

Then would come stories of the Irish publican 'Paddy the Flat', who, unable to read or write, kept a pictorial ledger; of 'The Bower-bird', a quaint old kleptomaniac with corks around his hat who filched odds and ends from the miners' tents that would be tactfully retrieved when he was not at home. Another old favourite was 'The Tea and Tobacco Bushranger', ex-squatter ruined by the drought who ranged the goldfields with his string of ageing horses and his hunchbacked gin, and best of all that incorrigible band of scallywags known as 'The Ragged Thirteen'. To listen to them, my uncle said, you would have thought them the greatest band of desperadoes unhung, but they were very amateur bushrangers and never succeeded in terrorising the countryside as they dreamed of doing. One day Uncle John met their leader 'The Orphan' on the road and to draw him out remarked on the good breeding of his mount.

'Yes,' said the rascal, 'her original brand was 7PD, belonged to old Patsy Durack of Cooper's Creek.'

'That's a coincidence now,' said Uncle John. 'I got away with a few of his horses too,' and indicated the brand on his own mount and packs.

'You want to get to work on those quick,' 'The Orphan' advised, 'the bloody Duracks are thick as thieves in this country now, and a lousy lot they are too—clap a chap in jug for pinching a horse quick as you can say "knife".'

Nat Buchanan ('Old Bluey') and his son Gordon, then establishing the Sturt Creek and Flora Valley runs, were frequent visitors to the camp on Butcher's Creek.

'What a bushman!' Uncle John would say of 'Old Bluey', as he remembered him, his incurably sensitive skin well muffled against the sun, his famous green umbrella always part of his saddle gear, a gaunt old fellow with an uncanny bump of locality and a stock-in-trade of amusing anecdotes and kindly banter.

Uncle John had a profound admiration for bushmanship in which, having come straight from college to Kimberley, he had had little actual experience and for which he certainly had no natural aptitude.

'Greenhide' Sam Croaker was another of his bushman heroes whom he declared had senses of sight and hearing as keen as an Aboriginal's. He had come to the fields on behalf of the manager of Wave Hill, who, desperate for an outlet for the cattle, determined to set up a butchery at Hall's Creek. McPhee, Lamond and MacKensie, unable to withstand the competition, thereupon packed up and went a-droving to the Murchison.

Others, however, who had previously talked of getting out now hung on awaiting the return of Patsy Durack with his heavy machinery. The station men, one and all, pinned their hopes on the new venture believing, like Grandfather, that it needed only faith and capital to establish Hall's Creek as another Ballarat. They talked of him as a man of vision, sometimes, half jokingly as a man with 'the Midas touch' for whom nothing ever went wrong.

Bob Button from Ord River rode in and out for stores, bringing cattle for the butchery and lingering to fossick about always in the hope of 'dropping on a good thing' by happy accident. Carr Boyd still breezed about the fields, keeping alive the flame of enthusiasm and talking big of what should be done to encourage settlement to Kimberley.

By '88 it looked as if things had begun to stir at last when a party came through to survey the route for a telegraph line, bringing rumours of proper cattle shipping yards and jetties to be established at Wyndham and Derby.

Jim Durack, a young brother of Long Michael, Black Pat and Jerry Brice turned up from New South Wales and joined the camp at Butcher's Creek. A clever rhymester, musically inclined and inventive in the subtle art of practical joking, he was a welcome addition to the sun-loving goldfields community.

There were of course the inevitable tragedies and cases of 'sandy blight' and 'fever' which covered a multitude of ills. The diggers prescribed for each other and called on anyone who knew a prayer or two to preside at the burials. This task fell frequently to Uncle John and he told how when reciting The Lord's Prayer over the grave of old Robert Owens, one of the diggers interrupted:

'Spout it in Latin, Johnnie. The old b—— would appreciate that!'

The war between black and white continued intermittently, but it was now being whispered about that some of the natives had changed their tactics and instead of spearing a man for his tucker bags were offering their women in exchange. A few 'low down' types whose names were never permitted to defile the pages of a journal were said to have accepted the bargain.

Antagonisms flared up between 'the sandgropers' of the western State and 'the cornstalks', 'banana eaters' and 'crow eaters' of 'the other side'. Friendly allusions to 'rough-neck convict stock' hunted out of their own States by the police were countered by equally charming references to the 'Nullarbor rats' who knew more about kangaroos than horses and cattle. Europeans looked on while Australians of different colonies shed blood in the cause of 'patriotism'.

Typical of this spirit of interstate rivalry are the following verses found in the pocket of Uncle John's goldfields notebook:

AS OTHERS SEE US
(By Sydney 'Truth')

Land of Forrests, Fleas and Flies,
Blighted hopes and blighted eyes,
Art thou hell in earth's disguise,
Westralia?

Land of politicians silly
Home of wind and willy-nilly,
Land of blanket, tent and billy,
Westralia.

Home of brokers, poor paid clerks,
Nest of sharpers, mining sharks,
Dried up lakes and desert parks,
Westralia.

Land of humpies, cabins, inns,
Old bag huts and empty tins,
Land of blackest, grievous sins,
Westralia.

AS WE SEE OURSELVES
(A Reply)

Land of Fortunes, easily made;
The land where t'othersiders strayed,
To grab the dividends that are paid—
Westralia.

Thou art to us a chosen land:
We hold your gold at our command,
Your riches are not in the sand—
Westralia.

The home to be of Dukes and Lords,
In the near future—mark my words—
This land shall beat all best records,
Westralia.

You are but in your infancy,
The time is near when you shall be,
The strongest, richest colony,
Westralia.

They plugged on into '88, finding 'some stone with gold showing pretty freely', 'stone with no colours in that showed gold when crushed' and 'nice little pieces on the surface'. In December 'Jim Minogue cashed two hundred dwt. in gold, being his share of the takings so far', but that is the first and last mention of any division of spoil.

Before Christmas Jim Dillon had decided he would make his fortune quicker by setting up as a pub keeper, a shrewd move, as Uncle John remarks afterwards that 'Dillon is doing better in the spirituous than we in our more material pursuits'. A crowd gathered at Dillon's shanty for Christmas when there was music on fiddle and tin whistle, recitation, song and sporting events in which the redoubtable Barney Lamond carried the day with '38 ft. in the hop, step and jump and 4' 9" in the running high'. It was a memorable celebration with an exciting finish for news came through of fresh reefs struck in Jackson's claim and a great quartz find in the Mary River.

Father meanwhile managed at Argyle with only Pumpkin, the younger native boys and a German cook, for the stockmen who had animated the station scene during the dry season had been attracted back to the fields by reports of the fresh gold strikes.

Minor incidents had enlivened the monotony of the hot, wet days and nights, the drumming of rain and the constant hubbub of frogs:

> Roused out of bed just at daylight this morning [Father records] when I felt something very cold on my thigh. Partly awake I felt what I thought to be the cat ... put my hand down and, *mirabili dictu*, found I had hold of a snake. I quickly slung it on the ground and as it was again coming at me jumped out of bed and called Pumpkin. Unfortunately it got away, crawled through the books and on top of the wall. Pumpkin hit it but did not succeed in killing it so it remains an invisible occupant of our domocile.

A few days later Mille, the cook, began shouting one morning that the river was only fifty yards from the house. Father told him to get back to bed but an hour later Pumpkin, who had hitherto placed a sublime faith in Grandfather's 'flood level' calculations when pegging out the house, decided they had best start digging a dam to save the kitchen.

> But before we had even one corner done the water was up to us. We abandoned the kitchen and tried to secure the house but without avail for the water was onto us too soon. We tried to secure the things inside and likewise the rations, but before we

> could do so the water was inside and destroying gunpowder, boxes of clothes and hats . . . While putting other things up higher in the house we could hear the kitchen coming down, so fearing for ourselves in the house we left, the water then being about one foot up on the walls. Taking with us a bit of bread, rifle and cartridges we left the house to its fate. During this time the rain is coming down but not heavily.
>
> In about an hour the water began to recede, to our great delight and was just past the verandah at the break of day. After breakfast we set to work getting what we could from underneath the ruins of the kitchen . . . Many articles completely destroyed . . . all the knives, forks, bucket, chisel and other articles swept down the river. Flood mark up to the door of our room. House undermined and our room partly falling down. Still raining . . .

Father, however, had one glimmering of satisfaction in the incident.

'I must write and tell Father we don't think much of the site he picked,' he told Pumpkin.

The black man pointed reprovingly down the bank to where the brown water was swirling over the tops of the river trees.

'Well, look where you and young Johnnie had the pegs!'

The days that followed were spent ploughing through the bog after stone to repair the damage and rebuild the kitchen, in riding after straying horses and cattle in the driving rain and slosh of one of the heaviest wets on record.

Somehow Bob Button got through from the fields with a bag of gold, a letter from Uncle John and reports of fresh reefs. By this time the level-headed cattle man had been well bitten with the prospecting bug and persuaded Father to spend a day or two fossicking around the quartz outcrops at the foot of Mt Misery. They found nothing but worked up some reason for going together into the gulf, a journey of which my father wrote on his return to Argyle at the end of March.

> We came to the Ord and found it too high to cross without a swim. After an anxious wait of eleven days we succeeded in getting across through the kind assistance of Long Michael who built a boat in which we brought all our goods and chattels across safely. It was pulled across by the black boys, one of whom, Long Michael's boy young Billy, deserves special mention for his unremitting services. R. Button and myself piloted the horses across. Proceeded after a days rest at Lissadell, found the road very boggy and had

some difficulty in finding a crossing over the Dunham. Got to Twenty Mile at dinner time on the fourth day. Received a letter from Father, the police being there with the mail. Stopped, enjoying the hospitality of August Lucanus. Black boy brought word that the S.S. *Otway* was in port so Lucanus, Button and self proceeded in ... mosquitoes very bad ...

Sent telegram by *Otway* to be sent from Cossack, re rents to Alex Forrest ...

Subtle changes had occurred in the town of Wyndham since the rough and tumble months of its beginning. There was still no attempt to remove to the official site and the chances of the early investors ever realising on their 'town blocks' were beginning to look very thin indeed. Near the landing stage a few more permanent buildings had gone up, including a better class hotel owned and run by the Cable family, whose charming daughters, with the three lively Byrne sisters and the wives of a few of the more 'solid' citizens, were causing the young bloods of the district to look to their laurels. Wyndham was now rather more respectably 'gay', with tea parties daintily served, formal little dinners and dances. The naïve delight in 'keeping the champagne flowing' had passed into a more sophisticated phase and the few 'demi-mondaines' who had danced on table tops and generally 'made free' had been frozen either out of countenance or out of town.

Most prominent among the dashing young blades were two Irishmen named Francis Connor and Dennis Doherty who had been attracted from Sydney to the gold rush, had set up a merchant and general agency business in the town and had recently acquired a pastoral lease adjoining Rosewood and Argyle which they had named 'Newry' after their mutual birthplace in Ireland. They were 'charming fellows' of dash and enterprise and their lusty affiliation with the north-west seemed to augur well for its future. To their neat little establishment opposite a row of Chinese shacks in the single street came cattle men and prospectors to do business and discuss the rosy prospects of Kimberley.

Discussion revolved largely around the problem of markets for local cattle, for with the gradual drifting of the alluvial miners from Hall's Creek the immediate prospects were beginning to look grim. Many, like Grandfather, believed that the real wealth of the Kimberley fields had not yet been tapped, but there was no guarantee of this and if that outlet failed—what then? To encourage the West Australian pastoralists a protective duty had been imposed on all livestock imported for slaughter from other States but there was little sense in encouraging a product that could not be got rid of. Even if jetties were built for shipping cattle from Derby or Wyndham, the southern market in a colony of little over 40,000 people could hardly be described as 'unlimited'.

Connor, however, already spoke of shipments of thousands of head of cattle a year from Wyndham alone. To where? Eastern markets probably—Singapore, South Africa, the Philippines, Japan! Doherty, genial and debonair, urged constant pressure for government facilities that must inevitably open the portals to boundless expansion and enterprise. Meanwhile they organised picnics, riding and shooting parties for which the ladies 'prepared delectable al fresco repasts'. The hardier young women, in blouses and long tight-waisted skirts, gem hats with quantities of flapping gossamer veil, buttoned boots and gloves went 'mountaineering' with their gallants to the top of the stony Bastions where they placed little flags to flutter in the breeze, sipped tea, and thrilled to the awe-inspiring expanse of white salt marsh, flat-topped ranges and winding tide-churned gulf.

When Father rode in with Bob Button in February '88 Dennis Doherty, as no doubt others besides, was courting the charming and statuesque Georgina Cable and rumour had it 'they would make it a match'.

Father agreed to carry out some business for Connor and Doherty in Darwin while banking his gold and he embarked on the SS *Active* with Bob Button and Tudor Shadforth, a dashing young stockman from Ord River Station.

Darwin on its cliff top at the jungle's edge was a dazzle of colour under monsoon skies, the stilted latticed houses of a ragtag makeshift age picturesque in their setting of tropical trees, shrubs, creepers towering over the rank wet-weather grass. Poincianas—Flame of the Forest—glowed in spreading scarlet fans, beside hanging molten gold of the *Cassia fistula*, the pink and cream of frangipani—fragrant temple flowers of the East. Chinese lanterns, Mexican rose, *quis qualis*, Bougainvillaea spilt a concealing glow of warm beauty over the dereliction of the shacks. Father was at this time attracted by the quaint exotic flavour and sheer wild fecundity of the untidy Territory port. At the botanical gardens, started in the seventies by scientist Dr Maurice Holtze, he interviewed the curator and staggered back to the ship with armsful of seedlings in jam tins, seeds in paper packets and cuttings carefully wrapped in wet cloth, for if these things would grow in Darwin why not at Argyle? He would plant a garden too, crotons, amaranthus, spreading ferns and glorious trees to rest the eye and shade the hot little mud-brick homestead on Behn River. And vegetables too, 'acclimatised seeds' of melons, cabbages, cauliflowers, maize, tobacco, sugar cane, cotton. Who knew that any one of them might flourish so well as to start a minor industry?

He and his companions talked to officials of Territory markets for their beef, of mining and Chinese labour and blacks and the 'potentialities of the north' and finally hied themselves to an enterprising Chinese photographer who posed them in heroic attitudes with Shadforth holding a shovel as a symbol of 'digging in'.

Doherty met the SS *Active* on their return and hustled them off to a dance at the Byrnes' Three Mile Hotel where they 'made merry into the early hours'. Bluff Tom Kilfoyle had ridden in from Rosewood and surprised the younger fellows with his gallantry especially towards one of the Misses Byrne.

Many years later I knew the two remaining 'Byrne girls', the Misses Maggie and Joe, when they came to visit their late sister's son Jack Kilfoyle on Rosewood. Little elderly ladies, they had still about them much of the Irish sparkle and sprightliness that made these early day parties and dances at their Three Mile Hotel, among the big white gums on the marsh's edge, occasions to remember.

Miss Maggie painted religious statues for a living and could still coax from the old Argyle piano—all the way from Thylungra—some of the ditties woven around the happenings of her youth—words by all and sundry and the tunes her own. I regret now that I did not record as she sang these jaunty Kimberley folk songs that went with her into oblivion.

Father's plants travelled disappointingly. All the cuttings withered before he got home and most of the seedlings likewise curled up and died. Three poincianas survived and were carefully planted out under hessian shades while Pumpkin and the boys pegged, fenced and dug a kitchen garden on the river bank. Pumpkin put in the seeds and watered them in packing cases as he had done many a year on Thylungra, but the garden was doomed that season. Not many weeks after their return, fever, from which they had been fairly free since the previous year, returned to the Behn with renewed violence.

Father, Mille the cook, even Pumpkin and the boys were intermittently struck down, until Father, on one of the rare occasions in his robust life, actually took to his bed and, oblivious of date and day, neglected his journal.

> It is now sixteen days since I have taken up my diary as today is the 29th of May. On the last day dated I had the worst attack of fever ever during my short time in Kimberley, being for days after

> beset with all manner of imaginations and as if labouring under some great, insurmountable difficulty. Johnny arrived with packs from the fields but scarcely knew him for seven days. Since then I have been but slowly recovering . . .

By June he had rallied and was back in the now established routine of mustering, branding and riding into town. Next time he stayed so long that Uncle John, left in charge at Argyle, 'presumed he had lost either his horses or his heart. Probably the latter.'

Whether his suspicions were well founded I cannot say since the intervening three weeks of Father's life are represented by two non-committal dotted lines. But life returned to the Behn with him; since he was accompanied from the gulf by Grandfather, Uncle 'Galway' Jerry, Long Michael and several others, all excited and bursting with news.

Dennis Doherty and Georgina Cable had been married just after the races and the whole of Wyndham turned out to the event. A man named Barnett, much loved on the fields, had been speared by blacks when on the road with the supply waggons and the police were out with a big party while other self-appointed 'special constables' were also riding the countryside to avenge the death of their mate.

Furthermore, on the track to Argyle they had come upon the carcass of the beautiful Thylungra stallion, Count, wantonly speared and meat cut from its rump.

Grandfather and his brothers had arrived in good heart although business was not then so flourishing in Queensland. Droughts and the low price of wool were causing lack of confidence, pastoral affairs were at a standstill and the Queensland Co-operative had not yet paid up. Still there was hope of a better season and better prices next year, while newly discovered artesian water pointed to the possibility of a big basin underlying the Cooper properties. If this proved true they need no longer fear ruin from drought and the company should soon be able to settle its account. Meantime the three brothers had continued to invest in land around the city, for many considered values would rise still higher as a result of the extension of pastoral leases and a wider use of the artesian flow.

Grandfather had now formed a syndicate called The Argyle Downs Gold Mining and Quartz Crushing Company, had purchased in Sydney for the sum of £700 a plant of machinery soon to arrive in Wyndham, and was now to visit the fields again and select a promising claim.

There was news of racing activities and growing families. Stumpy Michael's eldest boy Ambrose and Grandfather's third son, Pat, were both soon to leave college and come to Kimberley. Galway Jerry's eldest, young Patsy, six years old, had the makings of a first-class jockey, which, since he had horses in his blood, his father thought would be a better life than that of a stockman. The women, in their comfortable homes, led the pleasant, easy lives they deserved after their pioneering years, but Grandmother missed her sons sadly and prayed constantly for their safety.

There were merry times at Argyle during the few days all were together:

> July 30: Today worth chronicling since Father, Uncle Jerry, Long Michael and Jim Minogue up all night playing cards and were this morning suffering a recovery, since Bacchus reigned supreme . . .

Stumpy Michael left for Lissadell with Long Michael. Grandfather, Uncle John and Jim Minogue, despite the effects of their 'Bacchanalian frivolities', set off for the fields and Father, rather smugly brisk and clear-headed, started with a mob of cattle to the gulf.

The town was at this time suffering a reaction from over-optimism.

> Wyndham [he writes], does not appear in the most flourishing state from the fact of so much bad money in circulation, and business people very chary having been often bitten in taking cheques of would-be millionaires.
>
> The town has now formed a Cricket Club, at present all the rage, in fact indulged in to excess being played every afternoon until 'majestic Sol' disappears behind the waters of the Indian Ocean.

The town was a buzz of discussion about the murder of the teamster Barnett, the reported killing of a few cattle and horses in east Kimberley and many sheep on the western side. Isadore Emanuel, as chairman of the Kimberley Pastoral Association, had succeeded in bestirring the authorities to reinforce the police in Derby, but, to the indignation of the settlers, some police officers were attributing extensive loss of sheep less to the wholesale depredations of the blacks than to dry seasons and straying due to the size and understaffing of the properties. These 'misleading statements', the settlers declared, were caused by reluctance on the part of the police to patrol dangerous areas, for it was plain to see the blacks were not only trying to burn the settlers out of the country, but were stealing or killing sheep faster than the grower could breed them. Personal deputations to Alexander Forrest resulted in his proposal of an expedition of special constables 'strong enough to resist, subdue and leave a lasting impression on the aborigines . . .'

No sooner was this news released than the steady trickle of criticism against the northern settlers became a flood in the southern press. Letters, some three and four columns in length, told of atrocities and massacres of natives throughout the entire north-west of the State. Replies, some in hot denial and some in forthright defence of the allegations, filled further columns. 'Onlooker', endeavouring to throw the cool water of reason on the fierce dispute, wrote saying unfortunately the Aborigines were doomed in any case. To this the Catholic Bishop Gibney bent the full blast of his Irish eloquence:

> 'The aboriginal races of Australia are doomed to disappear before the advances of the white man.' So say the well-groomed armchair philosophers, talking of a matter with which they have no practical acquaintance. 'Doomed to disappear!' Blessed phrase! Over how many bloody outrages, over what an amount of greed on the part of some, weakness on the part of the Government, and apathy on the part of the public does this convenient euphemism throw a thin but decent disguise. Our blackfellows do, indeed, seem fated to disappear but not because of any inherent inability to adapt themselves to the conditions of civilisation. Nor is it solely, nor chiefly because the easily-acquired vices of the white man prove fatal to them. Their misfortune is that they stand in the way of unchecked spread of flocks and herds. Insatiable earth hunger and monstrous unscrupulousness are main factors in that process of 'removal' of which they are the victims. They disappear rapidly on the outskirts of civilisation because in such a situation the white man is practically beyond the cognisance of the law, shoots straight and shoots often . . .

He was requested, in reply, to go out himself among the Kimberley tribespeople, 'protected by nothing other than the word of God' and see how he fared. The writer may have been unaware that this taunt was directed at the same man who in 1880 had entered the blazing inn at Glenrowan where Ned Kelly and his band had taken their final stand, in order to render the last rites to the dying outlaws. Nor did he hesitate in taking up the challenge, for not long afterwards we find him out in the wilds of Beagle Bay and Cape Leveque, unarmed and surrounded by tribes of Aborigines, selecting the site for a Trappist mission.

Disappointment was expressed throughout the north when, owing to the protests of so many 'uninformed sentimentalists' in safely settled areas, Forrest's motion was thrown out. What, demanded the bush people, was a handful of pioneers, menaced by savage tribes hundreds, perhaps thousands strong, supposed to do? Were they to admit defeat, clear out and give the country back to the Aborigines, or quietly turn the other cheek, confident that 'sweet reason' would at length prevail while their relatives and friends were murdered and their stock destroyed?

Young Jim Durack contributed to the discussion with a string of verses dedicated to his late brother Big Johnnie, 'feloniously slain by the Kimberley blacks'. In no less than 100 rhyming couplets he poured forth his opinion of all outsiders so ignorant as to suggest that the black man might have a point of view.

> The counter-jumper with his well-oiled head
> Who measures ribbons for his daily bread

and 'the civic merchant'

> Passing his days in comfort ease and peace
> Guarded by the metropolitan police

came in for his bitterest scorn.

> You who tread safe the city's beaten tracks,
> May well believe in kindness to the blacks.
> Would you still hold your dusky friend so dear
> If he was dodging round you with a spear?
> Suppose yourself by great and wondrous change
> Camped in the heart of some dark mountain range . . .
> Would not a deadly rage upon you creep
> When tired, distressed and much in need of sleep,
> You dare not close your over-wary eye
> Because you know to do so were to die?
> Young man, before you judge another's case
> In fancy put yourself in that man's place . . .
> How else than cold the lonely stockman's heart
> Who sees his horse lie slain by savage dart?
> Picture the frenzy on the squatter's brain
> When speared bullocks dot the spreading plain,
> Or how the solitary traveller feels
> When round his camp the sneaking nigger steals . . .
> No suppliants they save who would disguise
> Their bloody purpose from their victim's eyes . . .
> Thoughtless he turns towards his waiting hack,

Too late—too late! The spear is in his back . . .
Ah who shall judge the bushman's hasty crime
Justified both by circumstance and clime?
Righteous the hate with which the soul is filled
When man must slaughter or himself be killed . . .

Although his verses would no doubt have lent more weight to the other side of the argument, young Jim's indignation at the city critic was not unjustified for whatever principles men professed while 1,000 miles away, once in Kimberley they all more or less subscribed to the philosophy of 'us or them'. A way of dealing with the situation was extremely hard to impose from the outside and as long as the insiders, black and white, went in fear of their lives there could be little hope of a reasonable relationship.

At least a temporary compromise was reached in a decree that the law, not the individual, must deal with erring blacks. Any white found guilty of murdering an Aboriginal must suffer the supreme penalty in the same way as black murdering white. But the decree was no more than a pious statement of principle. No native brought to justice in Kimberley was acquitted nor was any white found guilty on a charge involving the treatment of an Aboriginal.

To satisfy the outcry of the inhabitants after the death of Barnett and others, sentence of death was passed on several natives sent to Fremantle for trial. These were returned to Hall's Creek so that justice could be carried out on the spot and as many of their countrymen as possible gathered in to witness the execution and take heed therefrom. But after all the moral was lost on the blacks. Some laughed and applauded, believing the hanging to have been staged for their entertainment. Others shrugged in disgust at the white man's perverted sense of humour. One of the condemned men had gripped the rope with his strong teeth and refused to fall, but though some of the assembled diggers cried out that he should be cut down and let go, the law stood firm, until the fellow dropped from exhaustion.

Police were from now on to patrol the outlying areas and 'apprehend' suspected murderers or cattle-spearers. As it would be impossible to hold them otherwise, when being brought in to trial they might be chained, together with native witnesses, but not ill-treated. For cattle-spearing offences sentence of flogging might be passed and the culprit at once turned bush with his sorry tale and bearing the marks of the lash. In this way it was hoped that many might learn from the experience of the few and much trouble and suffering be saved all round.

In this, however, it was soon to be seen that they had miscalculated both the character and calibre of the enemy, for when an Aboriginal has passed through the tests of tribal initiation he is not only a man of proud physical endurance but a man of faith.

30

Nemesis

The years late '88 to '91. Horse thieves on Argyle. The Ruby Queen. Dissatisfaction on the fields. Financial ruin. Mrs Patsy Durack comes to Kimberley. Family life at Argyle and Rosewood. Depression in Queensland. Death of Tudor Shadforth. Ulysses and Boxer. The Buchanans in search of markets. M. P. Durack and T. Kilfoyle droving to the Territory. Conditions at Pine Creek. Aled Meith. Return to Wyndham.

Pumpkin was the mainstay of the station on Behn River. Stockman, horse-tailer, blacksmith, butcher, gardener and general handyman, he gave for love and pride of being a good man, of everything he had.

> Pumpkin up the Creek after some horses got away in hobbles. Back this evening bringing in the Grey Stallion and his mob . . .
>
> Pumpkin down the Ord after cattle and horses ... went in at the junction to try a crossing and got swept down, himself and mare managing to swim across.
>
> Pumpkin repairing yard damaged in a recent fire . . .

This man of the Boontamurra tribe of Cooper's Creek owed no loyalty to the 'myall blackfellows' of the north. They were no countrymen of his, and relentlessly he rode their tracks, reporting where they had chased and sometimes speared cattle and horses.

With all the death bones of the Mirriwun tribespeople pointed at the heart of this stranger who looked like an Aboriginal but thought and acted like a white, Pumpkin did not sicken or fail, but continued to ride the plains and gullies, his eyes on the ground ahead looking out for blacks. One day, riding after cattle with Father, he observed a maze of horse tracks on a patch of red soil.

> Pumpkin, [Father wrote] was convinced from what we saw that the persons in possession were making good their escape and insisted we follow them . . . Being now quite certain of his theory we rode into camp of police sergeant camped nearby in pursuit of

> his regular rounds and together we followed the tracks into a pocket, nicely hidden away as the thieves no doubt had thought. They turned out to be no other than . . . on their way to the fields there to sell our horses at a good price, cross branded. They were hastily putting away the remnants of a meal when we came upon them. A daring project that would no doubt have succeeded but for Pumpkin's sagacity.

The sergeant escorted the downcast little band into Wyndham where the men stood their trial and served a short sentence. Local juries were loath to find white men guilty in those days, since no one knew when he might be up on a similar charge himself or thrown in close association with a man he had helped to convict. Spartan-like, the disgrace lay more in being caught red-handed than in the actual crime, for many who would not have stolen money if their lives depended on it thought of the appropriation of stock as part of the game. This tendency became more marked as time went on and a number of tough Queensland stockmen with no capital began to drift into Kimberley and take up small holdings around the larger estates. One of these horse-thieves in fact later became a small squatter who stocked his run almost entirely from his 'poddy dodging' exploits.

Meanwhile Grandfather had thrown himself wholeheartedly into his mining venture at Ruby Creek. His brothers returned to Queensland, Stumpy Michael with power of attorney in the handling of his affairs, but Grandfather, with headquarters at the fields, remained for over twelve months. He spent much of this time moving to and fro from the gulf, up to Darwin to purchase equipment, and over to see how things were faring at Argyle, his claim meanwhile a hive of activity, with two full-time engineers at work on the ten-head battery, men in the shafts, well sinkers and carriers bringing supplies and equipment from the gulf at £50 a ton. This charge was considered reasonable since at the height of the rush in '86 the price had been £100 a ton. He had twenty-five men, including carriers, on his books over this period, among the 'permanents' his cousin Jerry Brice, son John, Barney Lamond, Jim Dillon, Jim Minogue and Tom Pethic. The last was one of many around at this time who signed their name with a cross and when travelling with a companion who knew no more of letters than himself was one day searching for some pepper among the many tins and bottles in their supply waggon. Unable to read the labels it seemed they would have to break open every tin until they came to the right one, when Pethic suddenly had an inspiration.

'I've 'eard there's a hell uv a lot of "P's" in pepper, mate,' he said, 'and

P's the one letter I know on account of it's being at the start of me own name.'

From this clue the pepper was quickly identified.

This homely old bushman dismissed as hopeless namby-pambies all such as Father and Uncle John who 'read books and wore pyjamas'.

'What did you want 'em learned in a school for?' he asked Grandfather. 'That tripe ain't gonna help 'em round up the poddies.'

Grandfather trained a couple of racehorses for meetings in Wyndham and on the Behn River in July '89, when all the young bloods and many of the Wyndham ladies flocked to Argyle for three glorious days and nights of racing, sports and revelry. To Grandfather, gatherings of this sort were an essential part of life, not a mere sideline as they became for his sons in the worried absorption of their business lives. Up to this time wherever Grandfather went the joy and zest of life followed on his heels. Bush shacks became homely rendezvous and lonely outposts were peopled with lively, laughing, singing, hard-riding folk. If things were going well he found cause to celebrate, if badly, all the more need for 'a bit of shinanakin' to keep up morale. His capacity for enjoyment was as unlimited as his energy.

There were still intermittent bursts of life at the fields, but as the year went on and even Patsy Durack, with his machinery and staff of experienced men, had failed by a long way to cover expenses, the drift towards the Murchison became a steady stream. With the obvious decline in the goldfields the West Australian government, in the grip of depression, began to reconsider its intentions of carrying our further public works in Kimberley. Spirits dropped and the general outlook was bleak. Everyone complained bitterly of the climate, the fever, the lack of government interest and the blacks, the blacks, the blacks.

There was something of desperation in the way Grandfather continued doggedly to pour money into his Ruby Queen show as the wet of '89 closed in. News from Queensland was really disturbing by this time. There was nowhere any confidence in the future of the State and land values had already begun to fall. The Queensland Co-operative, far from being able to pay up, was now in worse financial straits.

When a telegram came from his brother Michael asking him to return at his 'earliest convenience', Grandfather reluctantly paid off his men, stacked his machinery under canvas and hurried to catch the first ship from the gulf. Anyone travelling to Hall's Creek may still see the remains of Patsy Durack's plant—the better part of £5,000 worth of machinery in rust and ruin where he left it that day in December '89

He returned to nemesis. It was difficult to realise at first that everything was gone, a lifetime of assets carefully built to spell security. After his return from Kimberley the year before, Stumpy Michael had speculated further, no doubt recklessly, in land and land shares on behalf of both himself and Grandfather. The land shares were a swindle. Land values dropped to zero and the whole of Queensland, and much of Victoria and New South Wales, were teetering on the edge of financial ruin. The general smash came in '91, but Grandfather and his brothers and many besides were already ruined a year before. The Queensland Co-operative went out of business. Thylungra and Galway Downs passed into the hands of the Union Bank. Clamouring creditors closed in on every side, bailiffs moved in on Grandfather's house at Albion while his brothers, forced to sell their properties at Archerfield and Ipswich, raised a mortgage on their Kimberley interest with which to carry on. Grandfather, having signed Argyle over to his sons, had no asset left on which to raise anything at all. Only the few possessions in Grandmother's name survived the holocaust—a few pieces of furniture and some wedding presents. The rest were spirited away. With a little money of her own, Grandmother took her two girls to Goulburn, hiding from them the starker facts of their father's destitution, and left them in the care of the Mercy nuns with whom she had been at school.

Mary was already seventeen and Birdie fifteen but they were young for their years and had led extremely sheltered lives. Kimberley, their brothers insisted, would be no place for them at that time whereas in Goulburn they would be surrounded by old friends and relatives including their Grandmother Costello. For once old Mrs Costello had had no word of reproach for her son-in-law, for whether the land smash was an act of God or of the devil she regarded it, at all events, as a misfortune beyond the control of man. Her own son John had been hard hit at the same time but he still had certain 'assets'. These were the 3,000-square mile Lake Nash lease where he had a manager in charge, another 2,000 square miles in the centre, and a chunk of country extending for about 300 miles from the McArthur to the Roper River, where he and his family were now established.

'And you all still have your old home at Tea-Tree to come back to if everything else fails,' Mrs Costello told her daughter.

In the midst of the confusion Great-grandmother Bridget took to her bed in Galway Jerry's home near Ipswich and died suddenly, sorrowing for the misfortune of her sons.

Grandfather, unable at first to realise the sudden and complete evaporation of an estate reckoned at its height as nearly three-quarters of a million pounds between himself and his two brothers, rallied at last to write to his sons in Kimberley:

> ... so ye're Mama and me must now come to Kimberley to live at Argyle for ye understand that we have not at present any home of our own. When the markets are opened up and ye are getting a price for yere cattle I hope I can pick up again on the Ruby Queen where I am still satisfied we should strike it rich. Pat is to come with us and ye will be pleased to have his help and the girls are to school in Goulburn and little Jerry will stay at college in Brisbane.
>
> I know ye will be wanting them, especially ye're brother Jerry, who is a smart boy and head of his class to have the advantages of education that ye have already received. But for this I am not now in a position to pay, for all that is left belongs to you according to the agreament made and to which I shall not be holding ye, as regards the payments, since ye must now be keeping the children at school and ye're mama and me and other things of which I must talk to ye. For myself I have only now my old moleskins, riding saddle and pack and what experience I have at your disposal.

Apart from recording the arrival of a letter from Grandfather telling of the decision to come to Argyle, Father makes no mention whatever in his journal of the financial disaster that had befallen the family. The only hint of misfortune is that from this time onwards he frequently refers to 'poor Father' in the way they always referred to 'Poor Mary' Skeahan. For Father the loss of estate seems to have implied a certain loss of status and he found the whole affair too painful ever to be discussed. Although he knew well enough that the long drought, the collapse of false land values and the resulting bank smash was a disaster on a national scale, he was always a little impatient with his father for having been so deeply involved and for having, at what he should have known to be a critical time, left his brother in charge of his affairs. Grandfather had always said himself that Stumpy Michael had little head for business and yet he had given him full power of attorney to buy and sell as he thought fit. Meanwhile precious time and money had been squandered on the Ruby Queen long after most responsible people had given Hall's Creek up as a bad job. Grandfather accepted the scarcely spoken criticism with unexpected humility and with it the fact that neither of his two elder sons would ever afterwards quite trust his judgement.

It was a quaint little procession that moved out of Wyndham and along the winding, rough track through Button's Gap and the Cockatoo Sands. The buggy, driven by Grandfather, with Grandmother at his side, was followed by the horse-drawn station waggon containing a bedstead with elaborate brass knobs, a heavily carved sideboard, the piano, bookcase, iron press, writing desk with a green baize top, three ornamental clocks and a crate of Muscovy ducks.

With a white woman installed at Argyle the black community began to grow. One day, shortly after Grandmother's arrival, Pumpkin turned up with a broad smile and a shy young girl

'My wife,' he said proudly.

Everyone was astonished, for since Pumpkin's original wife, a woman much older than himself, had died on Thylungra he had appeared quite uninterested in romance.

Pumpkin declared that the girl belonged to his 'proper marriage skin' and had come willingly. He had been carrying on negotiations, he said, since he first heard that 'the missus' was coming to live at Argyle and had realised she would need help in the house. The tribal wives whom the younger boys might have claimed were all old women, but he, being an elder, had the right to a young girl of amenable age, and here she was.

'I pick her up over that way,' he said, signing with his chin in the manner of his people, 'in that Ord River valley. What about you find her a good whitefellow name?'

'What would be wrong with Valley at all?' Grandfather suggested. 'Seeing as you found her there.'

Everyone was satisfied, but young Pat who inherited much of his father's simple-hearted exuberance felt there should be a ceremony of some sort to impress the happiness and importance of the occasion. He had them stand before him in their best clothes, dipped their heads in a bucket of water to make a lasting impression and read the marriage ceremony.

From all accounts the marriage was a happy one, though seven years later a man turned up from some far country claiming Valley as his promised bride. He and his supporters came into the camp one day and speared the girl in the leg while another older woman, trying to protect her from further harm, was fatally wounded.

Inevitably Valley's relatives soon drifted into the station and some remained. The boys in the camp on the river were no longer lonely and cut off from their kind and at night from around their fire on the river bank rose the familiar sound of corroboree.

'I never thought,' Grandmother said, 'I could be so happy to hear the noise that used to frighten me when we first came to Cooper's Creek. It's like coming home.'

Grandfather's old cheerful spirit returned as he dug and delved in the garden on the creek and the pumpkins and runner beans flourished under his practised hands. He made pieces of furniture for his wife, rode after cattle and horses and gave a hand wherever required, but he never for a moment accepted his financial disaster as final. He regarded it as no more than one of the misfortunes among the many ups and downs of life. He had been down often enough before, but by hanging on and keeping faith in God and in himself when others were talking ruin, he had always managed to come to the top again. It was important that one had a plan and kept to it steadily. Sooner or later the financial crisis would lift as depressions always did. The market for Kimberley cattle would open up and settlement would follow as it had done elsewhere. So much seemed only common sense. He would then borrow enough from the boys to start again in the deserted shafts and rusting machinery at the Ruby Queen. That there was gold there he had no doubt and he yearned to see the population come flocking back and the mushroom mining towns dotting the deserted land.

'But what if you do not find it?' Grandmother asked.

'I will give it a few months only,' Grandfather assured her, 'and if I get nothing then I will give up, but by that time the boys should be in a position to make a home in Fremantle for ourselves and the girls and it can be a headquarters for them all when they come down. They should be shipping cattle south by that time and I will be able to look after their affairs for them at that end.'

But there were times when he was haunted by the debts he had perforce left unpaid at the time of his downfall—the cheques he had written out before he knew that there was nothing left in the bank to meet them.

'That I who have spared so many from the humiliation of debt should be unable to meet my own is the greatest affliction the Lord could have sent me,' he said.

To which Grandmother replied as always in times of stress and trouble, 'But affliction, you see, my dear, is the love of God. For how can you wear a crown if you have not borne a cross?'

Everything was different for the boys with a woman in the house. Mattresses and clean linen appeared on their bunks in place of the rough greenhides and coarse blankets. Clothes were carefully laundered, meals daintily served. The water bags were never allowed to be drained and left to dry. The hessian safe, made by Grandfather, was kept damp and cool by a steady dripping of water from pieces of hanging saddle cloth. The black women, respectably clothed in loose, ankle-length dresses of turkey twill or calico with coloured borders, moved quietly about the place, working cheerfully under the gentle and expert direction of 'the missus'.

Shortly after Grandmother came to Argyle, Uncle Galway Jerry brought to Rosewood his wife and young family of two boys and two girls. Aunt Fan had with her, as companion and governess to the children, the charming little gentlewoman Miss Cameron, referred to frequently by Father in courtly terms. She appears to have been as often at Argyle with one or another of the children as at Rosewood and was the cause of a great deal of banter among the boys. Father made arch references, no doubt reciprocated, to his brother Pat's 'amorous intentions', though Duncan McCaully, who was 'like a bull in a crockery shop' outside the cattle camp, does not seem to have been considered in the race at the time.

Uncle Stumpy Michael and his tall quiet son Ambrose were to and fro from Lissadell, but Aunt Kate and her younger children, mostly at school, remained in Brisbane. For all his reverses Stumpy Michael was confident that 'when the markets opened up' he would quickly reduce his mortgage and that Lissadell would continue to provide handsomely for his dependants.

A peacefulness, clearly reflected in Father's journals, descended over Argyle.

> The evening is serene and calm [he writes]. Father and Mother sitting together outside on the verandah, their conversation of old associations. The piano emits sweet music from the fairy fingers of Miss Cameron who is here from Rosewood for a few days with little Patsy. Brother John and the youngster in mirthful mood tramping round the bouse without a care.

Not long afterwards Tom Kilfoyle brought his bride, the former Miss Byrne, and her sister Miss Maggie to join the Rosewood establishment and life in Kimberley became more like that of western Queensland. A larger dining table was 'knocked up' and the piano was never left long enough, as in later years, to become a lodging house for cockroaches and bush mice.

The year 1890 was disturbed by news from Queensland relatives of the prolonged and disastrous drought and of the ruin of so many of their old friends. Bullocks were bringing no more than £1 a head and boiling-down works coped with the surplus. The Tullys at Wathagurra had dug in their heels, determined at all costs to stick to their land. Poor Mary Skeahan was living with them while her husband and two younger sons ranged the countryside for work, and the Scanlans hung on to Springvale by the skin of their teeth.

Reports from the Costellos were no more cheerful. After six years' valiant struggle to build up their Territory properties, the family had at last retreated from their home on the Limmen River to their Lake Nash property near

Camooweal. Costello had left his old employee Jack Farrar in charge at the Valley of Springs and hoped they might have suffered only a temporary defeat in that area. Perhaps in time they would find some means of controlling the growing scourge of cattle tick and the increasing depredations of the blacks. They might manage to shoot out the ''gators' in the rivers, discover an antidote for malaria and even overcome the seemingly invincible, teeming, silent army of white ants. Perhaps, too, someone might persuade the government that the only hope of settling the Territory lay in decreasing the land rents rather than in raising them as had recently been done. Then it would only remain to find a market for Territory beef and all would be well.

No doubt the family at Argyle lived better at this time than their Queensland relatives, but money was very short and lack of markets was a haunting fear. The goldfields were almost dead. There was no outlet from either Wyndham or Derby and letters to Darwin enquiring about the beef market in the Territory were unanswered.

News that the State of Western Australia had been granted self-government, that Kimberley had been divided into an eastern and western electorate and that nominations were being sought for local representatives caused no great interest outback. Few bothered to enrol and the two candidates, Alexander Forrest for west and William Baker, a Wyndham storekeeper, for east Kimberley were returned unopposed. The sheep and cattle men were too worried about their immediate future to think in terms of political development. Adversity, however, drew the settlers together as prosperity would never do. Those hard put to find stockmen's wages helped each other at mustering and branding times while the few men who were not fossicking around Hall's Creek or following the golden trail to the Murchison found employment on company properties with capital to tide them over the hard times.

Duncan McCaully, 'The Scrub Bull', took a job on Ord River Station while Bob Button, the manager, who 'had the gold fever bad', went prospecting. Here Duncan struck up a firm friendship with young Tudor Shadforth, the head stockman, who in August, when the two were mustering on Osmond River, was struck down by a spear. McCaully had drawn the weapon from the lifeless body, lifted it on to the saddle in front of him and ridden twenty miles on a dark night into the Ord. The tough old bushman never forgot that Shadforth's last words, when they separated to muster opposite sides of the river, had been 'See you anon', and thirty years later, a dying man, he rode from Ivanhoe so that he might be buried beside his mate.

Police raids and the inevitable unauthorised punitive expeditions followed the murder on Osmond River. The police left terse records for official files and the rest is silence.

From this time on, however, the name of another boy, Ulysses, appears in the Argyle journals. Nothing is recorded of how he got there but Ulysses himself told me, many years later at Ivanhoe, that he and his sister Maggie were the only survivors of a raid on a big encampment of blacks around the Ord River after the spearing of Tudor Shadforth. Without a trace of rancour, in fact with the suggestion of a reminiscent chuckle, the genial old man in his pensioner's camp on the river told how he and his sister had been discovered crouching behind a tree.

'"Better shoot 'em," one of the white men said. "This little boy only gonna grow up to put a spear in some poor whitefulla and this little girl—well she gonna breed more blackfellas." Then big Duncan McCaully come up. "I can do with a boy," he says, and he put me up on his saddle and somebody else take Maggie and by-'n'-by we come into Argyle.'

It was a good day's work on McCaully's part since both Ulysses and his sister grew to become the backbone of station communities at Ivanhoe and Auvergne.

Almost at once Ulysses appears in Father's journals as his almost constant companion.

> The boy [he records] for his tender years undoubtedly bears the fatigue of late travelling well and on no one occasion have I had to upbraid him for lagging behind.

This was really remarkable, for few men could keep their mounts up to the brisk pace that Father got out of his horses. He was undoubtedly a splendid rider and a good judge of horseflesh, but unlike Grandfather, who felt for a mount as part of himself, they were primarily tools to him. Frequently he records with a note of exasperation the sudden collapse of his horse which he attributes to excessive heat or the possibility of its having been exhausted by galloping from blacks.

Young Boxer, generally conceded to be the cleverest of the Argyle boys, was at this time proving the least reliable. Sent after horses he would sometimes disappear for a week at a time, causing both inconvenience and anxiety for his safety, since he belonged to a Queensland tribe.

> Even if he could give a reason for his conduct it would not be so aggravating [Father writes] but he appears to have spent his time doing nothing but idly commune with nature or perhaps catch fish or lizards, though he declines to explain . . .

Father did not then realise that Boxer spent these stolen holidays with the bush blacks, and it later often puzzled him how the Queensland boy was not only so fluent in the various local tongues but so knowledgeable in their ways, projected movements and hideouts.

All over the country young natives like this were being recruited for station work and the old bogy of 'outside criticism' was being raised against the settlers for 'blackbirding aboriginal boys into slavery'. This was always a very touchy point with the station owners, for couched in certain terms their methods of native employment sounded as near to the general conception of slavery as might be. A black received no payment other than the basic necessities of life. His time off was at the convenience of the boss and his station activities. If he 'cleared out' he would be tracked down and brought back, while any other white man employing him without the consent of his original master would be breaking an unwritten law of the country. The station people, however, looked at the matter differently. In a letter of the time my father put the station owner's point of view:

> Let people who know nothing of the blacks and the conditions of the country come and learn for themselves in the hard school of experience. The station blacks are neither chained down nor locked up. They are out on their own every day after cattle and horses and they come back. Why? Because the new arrangement happens to suit them. They like the white man's tucker. They like riding and mustering stock. Hunting is in their blood and this is a more exciting form of hunting than anything they have known before. The black boy feels like a king in the saddle galloping over the plains where his fathers footed it for thousands of years, and what's more he likes his white boss, providing he is a man who knows his own mind, gives an order and sticks to it, even if it doesn't make sense to the blackfellow.
>
> As for being forced to return if he absconds—do we teach a white boy not to play truant from school by letting him turn up uncorrected when he feels so disposed? The station blacks have a great deal of free time and long walkabouts in the bush, but will never be given any sense of responsibility if allowed to come and go at their will. They are told that if they want to go bush without permission they have to stay bush, but they don't want this. In tribal life they are used to having personal decisions made for them by acting in accordance with their ancient laws and are only

> confused if handled in a weak and indecisive manner and constantly given a choice of action.
>
> Our monetary system is as yet a mystery to the blackfellow. Even were there shops where he could spend the money he would not know the value of it, but he values food, clothing, tobacco and such things and is willing to work for them. In so doing he feels a cut above his 'wild-munjong' relatives skulking in the hills. The station people should be subsidised, not criticised for training such boys for useful work.

When news spread over the 'bush telegraph' that young Gordie Buchanan was taking 300 head of Wave Hill bullocks from Sturt Creek into Derby and that 'old Bluey' was to take an experimental thirty head up to Singapore hopes again soared in Kimberley. Connor and Doherty, daily expecting word of a big market in the Far East, made tentative arrangements to act as agents for the primary producers. Buchanan, however, returned a disappointed man. Expenses had panned out at £5 a head. The bullocks brought no more than £8 each and even that 'on sufferance', for a local meat combine had stamped down on any continuance of the trade.

Following this, one or two small experimental shipments were sent from Derby to Fremantle, under primitive conditions, and obtained a fair price but there were heavy losses on the voyage and the demand was limited. Altogether an ironical situation now faced the Kimberley cattle man, for here was the country of their heart's desire—seasons vastly more reliable than those that had defeated or threatened to defeat them in Queensland, rich pastures on which the stock fattened and multiplied to a remarkable degree, and no outlet for their produce.

In desperation old Buchanan and his brothers-in-law Hugh and Wattie Gordon started 1,000 head from Elvire River down the Ninety Mile Beach to the upper Murchison—blazing what is still known as 'Buchanan's Track' from the De Grey River to the Gascoyne where Lennie Darlot of Birringarra purchased their entire mob. This result was encouraging, but the Murchison was a far cry from East Kimberley. Early in '91 Father and Tom Kilfoyle, weary of waiting for replies from Darwin about prospects in the Territory, decided to test for themselves the goldfields market at Pine Creek, about 120 miles south of Darwin, with a small mob of 169 bullocks and 17 horses.

They were to pioneer a new route of about 350 miles, striking out north-east from Argyle, following the Baines River down to the Victoria, making out towards the Katherine and thence due north to the mining town.

Grandfather presented them on departure with a pumpkin from his garden and a sacred relic that he assured Father would keep him safe under all circumstances.

'It is one I have always carried,' he said. 'I give it to you now because you are the pathfinder and I am the old man who stays at home and grows vegetables.'

Any one of Father's many droving trips from this time on is a story in itself but this book would quickly become unwieldy were I to more than briefly summarise the journeys so closely packed with incident.

The two natives, Pumpkin and Sultan, were their only assistants on this trip.

> Pumpkin [Father writes] each morning taking on the bullocks while we follow with the horses. We catch them up, leave him his dinner and go ahead to form a camp while he follows on at his leisure.

None of the party had yet visited McCartney's Auvergne Station on the Baines River and it was little wonder that, misled by numerous very similar 'Razor Back Mountains' and branching creeks, they were three days locating it. Years later, when travelling the rough road to Auvergne by car, Father would speak of his first impressions of this station, then in his control, as 'the weirdest place ever I struck'. Since its formation in '86 it had already acquired a name for tragedy and the wonder is that after the violent death or grave misfortune of at least half a dozen managers they could get anyone to run it at all.

Barney Flinn, the man then in charge, welcomed the drovers to the little shack on the high, wild bank of the Baines and conversation continued normally until he confided in his visitors what Father describes as 'a number of extraordinary hallucinations . . .' Among these was that the station was nightly surrounded by wild blacks and that he was doomed to die by a spear.

> About midnight, when all were asleep, he leaped from his bunk and yelling like a maniac ran into the yard where he discharged the contents of his revolver. A most nerve racking experience.

In fact Flinn left soon afterwards, declaring the blacks would surely 'settle' him at Auvergne. He went buffalo shooting in Arnhem Land where he was promptly despatched by a spear while asleep.

When the droving party arrived at the Victoria River Depot the supply boat was about to leave for Darwin and Bill Hutchins, the storekeeper, was observed hastily stuffing handfuls of cheques from a tea cask into a sugar bag. He remarked to the visitors that he supposed it was time he was paying the Darwin merchants for the supplies sent 'on tick'.

'Have you counted it?' someone asked.

'Can't count,' said Hutchins. 'The blighters'll let me know if it ain't enough and come it's too much they won't be worrying me.'

From this stage Father was suffering from the effects of a severe jar to his right hand.

> April 1. With a strong effort I take hold of my pencil, for the pain of my hand still intense, after eight or nine days, during which time, as Milton says, 'Sleep hath forsook and given me over.'
>
> April 7th . . . Six days have elapsed since last entry and now make an attempt to write with my left hand for the suffering of my right by no means eased . . . Blacks appear on hill close to cattle—seem friendly disposed and Sultan and Pumpkin have conversation with them.
>
> April 8th. Find we are four head cattle short. Pumpkin starts back after them returning without them. Reports that blacks encountered yesterday had chased them over the range . . .
>
> Got spill going down a bank to water stock. Heavy shock for the sore hand . . . Rain came on suddenly at night—no tent rigged, all got drenched.
>
> April 15th. Last night blacks appeared close by on the hill and about daylight made a war-like uproar, one fellow challenging us to mortal combat: 'Come on now, you white b——!' They remained all the morning but kept very quiet after first greeting . . . Travelling on, precipitous hills on either side and somewhat apprehensive of ambush. Reach good open flat at last without further incident.
>
> April 17th. Discovered this evening that I have lost the relic given to me by poor Father on my departure from the station. Whilst myself attaching little credence to its miraculous or safe-guarding qualities and suspecting that it was as likely sold to Father by some rogue masquerading as a man of faith I am reluctant to proceed without it or to tell him on return that I have lost that which he has valued so highly for many years.
>
> April 18th. Resolve to ride back with Pumpkin to yesterday's dinner camp where I had stripped off for a dip, and *mirabili dictu*

Pumpkin discovers it in the crevice of a rock whereon I had left my clothes. The good fellow as delighted at its discovery as myself and Kilfoyle equally pleased on our return.

April 30th. Reached New Delamere Station. Only one man here—W. Wade, but blacks camped around. Black arrived this evening with mail from Springvale. Latest news eagerly absorbed Pt. Darwin paper April 24th, Sydney *Bulletin* April 11th. Much bitterness over issue shearers' strike in which labour appears to have suffered major defeat. Strikers disbanded with fines and imprisonment for rioting and industry may now be permitted to carry on. Wade most interestingly regales us with the history of his ups and downs on this planet. Pumpkin and I bring bullocks in here to drink, but they refuse water, smell of blacks camped about too repugnant for them.

Pumpkin rides back after 'Goaty', our beaviest beast, somewhat lame after coming through gorge.

May 4th. On to Sardine Creek . . . 'Goaty' still very lame, doubt he can go much farther . . .

Passed large lagoon, surrounded by pandanus, crocodiles very numerous.

May 8th. Crossed large creek running into the Katherine . . . At last we have to leave poor Goaty, the pride of the Behn, at the mercy of blacks, disease and alligators. Was half a mind to destroy him but who knows he may recover and come through, and Life is sweet, no doubt to dumb animals as to ourselves.

This concern for 'poor Goaty' is typical of the affection with which drovers often came to regard certain beasts in their mob, though hardly logical in view of the fact that they were being driven to slaughter anyway!

Threading through bog swamps and ant hills over fourteen feet high the drovers noticed symptoms of disease in the mob and before reaching Pine Creek eight had dropped out, dead or dying. Anxious to dispose of the cattle before further losses, Kilfoyle rode in to Fountain Head to negotiate with the local butcher, Bill Lawrie, while the mob followed quietly on. The announcement that he had Kimberley cattle for sale, however, was received without enthusiasm, for beef was no longer at a premium with outside markets closed to the Territory cattle men. Kilfoyle brusquely turned down Lawrie's offer of £5 a head and leaving Father to hold and inoculate the cattle, took the train into Darwin to negotiate for better terms.

Meanwhile Father interviewed a Chinese butcher named Ah Tin, 'who being unusually big for his race, with pointed beard and a good seat in the saddle, might have been Genghis Khan himself in a somewhat unusual setting'. Father had a liking and respect for the Oriental that was unusual in the north at this time and he made no apologies for his enjoyment of the Chinese butcher's company as they rode together inspecting the mines, 'being hospitably entertained with Square Face and Lager' and arriving, in a very roundabout manner, at a tentative agreement for the sale of beef at 4d a pound and the horses at £17 a head.

A complicated vendetta following the theft of a bag of nuggets from one Chin-ah-din was in full swing around Pine Creek, 'the rights and wrongs of which', Father writes, 'are so far as I can make out, beyond human solution, but a source of endless discussion among our oriental friends'.

Father's hand had recovered and he was back in form again, reflecting upon the irony of down and out Australians working for Chinese when

> The Celestials as everyone calls them hereabouts were after all introduced by the South Australian Government to supply that cheap and servile coolie labour necessary to the development of a new colony. Of a local population two-thirds Chinese I see no evidence of any working but for himself and not in such ways likely to develop the country since the gold they find will be taken out, smuggled if possible, and the gardens they have grown will be abandoned to the wilderness when the gardeners have amassed such as will constitute a fortune in the Land of the Dragon. One must mention in all fairness, however, that we owe to the Chinese the rapid completion of the railway from Fountain Head to the port since white labour would have lacked not only in numbers but in hardiness and energy to have achieved a mile of it under Territory conditions.

Of the 10,000 Chinese who came to the Territory, perhaps half returned to their native land. The rest would remain to settle in Darwin, Wyndham, Derby and Broome or to drift about the country as station cooks. Great numbers died by misadventure, many while attempting to make back overland into Queensland to avoid the heavy poll-tax imposed on gold leaving Darwin.

Kilfoyle returned from Darwin where no one had been prepared to make any offer for the cattle at all. They thereupon ran up a bough shed and a butcher's gallows and began slaughtering and salting their beef for distribution by Ah Tin around Brocks Creek and Yam Creek where most of the miners were congregated.

A June entry records the acquisition of a new stockboy in a casual manner typical of the times.

> Black boy called Dick came to our camp this evening bringing with him nice little fellow named 'Aled Meith'. He, Dick, consents to leave boy with me to care for him.

A few weeks later when Long Michael was returning to Wyndham after a short visit to his relatives in the Territory, Father sent the boy around with him to be left in charge of his brother John who was then managing Connor and Doherty's store in Wyndham. By this time the child had become so attached to Father that

> he most reluctantly stopped behind when I left on the train, caught hold of the bars endeavouring to get in after me. M.J.D. led him away weeping—poor little chap, unable to understand that he will see me soon again.

After three months in the butchering business, results seemed to justify Father's returning for another mob while Kilfoyle, now joined by his wife, carried on at Pine Creek. Father and Pumpkin took the train to the port—still referred to as Palmerston

> . . . that same rather unpleasant habitat where every person thinks himself wiser than his brother and bears himself with that same languid and sardonic air. Find myself looking forward to the return to Wyndham which monotonous shambles though it is has the friendly familiarity of one's home town.

31

LIFE AND DEATH IN KIMBERLEY

The years 1891 to 1893. First Durack born in Kimberley. Mrs Patsy Durack visits Goulburn. M. P. Durack and Tom Hayes droving to the Territory. Stock disease. Further droving trips to Territory market. Murder of Sam Croaker at Auvergne. Controversy on the native question—Bishop Gibney versus Chas. Harper. Sergeant Lavery arrests natives on Argyle. Death of Mrs Patsy Durack from fever at Argyle. Rise of Connor and Doherty. M. P. and M. J. Durack drove cattle to Derby. Shipping to Fremantle.

Back at Argyle, where Grandfather and young Pat had been left in charge, news awaited of the birth of a fifth child to Uncle Jerry and Aunt Fan at Rosewood. 'This making no less than eighteen Duracks in the district,' Father writes, but he does not add a local wit's description of contemporary East Kimberley as 'the land of blacks, Sacks and bloody Duracks', the 'Sacks' referred to being another prolific local clan.

A feeling of depression hung over the station, for Grandmother had taken ship around the north coast to visit her daughters in Goulburn. Grandfather thought the girls should return to Kimberley with their mother, for it now seemed that the house in Fremantle might not be possible for another year or two. So far there was barely enough money to carry on at Argyle and except for old Mrs Costello's insistence upon paying for her daughter's trip even that could not have been considered.

'We'll have them both nuns if we leave them in that convent much longer,' Grandfather complained. 'There's Mary nineteen already and whatever chance of meeting an eligible man?'

'I don't think much of her chances of meeting one here,' Father said, for he had already set an almost impossibly high standard of eligibility for his sisters' suitors. 'Besides, what on earth would they do with themselves?'

'What do girls do anywhere?' Grandfather asked. 'Help their mother, make pretty clothes, go riding—'

'In this climate? With skins like theirs?'

Father would not hear of it and already it was he who had the last word on family affairs.

At the beginning of October he was off again into the Territory with a second mob of 118 head. This time his companions, besides Pumpkin, were Tom Hayes and his boy Ned Kelly from Rosewood. This combination seems hardly to have been a successful one, for Father, the 'book-reading' young fellow who would not be told, and Hayes, the seasoned, opinionated overlander, were incompatible travelling companions. Since it had fallen to Father's lot to undertake these rather tedious droving trips he saw no reason why they should not occasionally break a day's travelling record or follow an unconventional procedure. Not so Tom Hayes, for whom there was only one way of handling cattle and that was as they had handled them 'on the overland'. They came one day to a waterhole where Hayes considered the approach unsuitable for stock and insisted on riding downstream to find a better place, leaving Father, fuming with impatience, to hold the thirsty mob. After waiting half an hour Father, with Pumpkin's help, started the cattle in to drink:

> We have no difficulty whatever [he writes] in getting the cattle down where my friend tried to persuade me they could not be got in.

The boy Ned Kelly kept going to sleep on watch and letting the cattle stray and when Hayes took to him with a stockwhip retaliated by attacking his master with a tomahawk:

> Indeed [Father remarks] had I not appeared at that moment to wrench the implement from the boy's hands there may well have been serious consequences. Pumpkin in some disgust of the scene.

Blacks dogged their footsteps from the Territory border, set fire to the grass and disturbed the cattle continuously. Hayes was for firing shots to disperse them, Father for 'making parley, since an understanding must be arrived at if this is to become a regular stock route'. A watering place where a bullock was speared and the mob deliberately stampeded they named 'Humbug Camp' as it is still known today.

Here and there, however, the blacks now appeared anxious to compromise:

> October 25th. Whilst packing up four of our sable brethren come into our camp, one giving his name as 'George', very generously offering me his paramour. I politely decline, and when packed up, finding his companions with spears carried in their toes through

> the grass, I order them away. They follow a short distance but are soon lost to sight . . .

Disease struck the cattle at Delamere and thirty-five animals dropped dead by the wayside before they reached Brock's Creek. 'Alas for this mysterious affliction,' Fathers writes, for red-water fever had not yet been traced to infection from cattle tick that was soon to prove a major challenge to the pioneers.

The year '92 was unsettled for everyone. The Territory market remained limited and the price poor but there was no better alternative and Father, with various companions, including his brother John and cousin Jim Durack, the forthright versifier, made the weary journey five times in twelve months. These three got on very well together, however. They broke their own records on each successive trip and achieved a number of quite unnecessary feats that the overlanding drovers would have refused to attempt on principle. Father and Uncle John recited Homer and Milton to their hearts' content and their cousin reeled off interminable verses of his own.

The blacks seem gradually to have discovered certain advantages to be gained from the droving parties and would close in on the camps as the white men moved out, scavenging for beef bones or plugs of tobacco left as gestures of goodwill.

Towards the end of the year Father and Uncle John arrived at Auvergne to find that Jock McPhee and the Chinese cook had just buried the latest manager, that pioneer drover of the Gulf route to Kimberley, 'Greenhide' Sam Croaker, who had been shot by his half-caste stockman Flanigan. They were probably the first to hear the story, so often told in after years, of a resentment that had smouldered to hate in the oppressive atmosphere of the Territory wet, ending with the shooting of Croaker over a game of cards.

The rest of the story had reached Pine Creek before the droving party. Flanigan had ridden the dead man's horse to Ord River Station and told his story to Jack Kelly, the manager, convinced that he had only to have his case presented by a white man and it would be seen at once that his action was fully justifed.

Kelly humoured him all the way in to Hall's Creek where he delivered him into the hands of the police. When the time came Flanigan had nothing to say in his own defence and six months later was hanged at Fanny Bay jail in Darwin.

At Argyle the old year '92 was ushered out to the tune of 'Auld Lang Syne' lustily rendered by the family and a large police party under Sergeant Lavery, then organising a 'surprise drive' on the persistent cattle-spearers. With the settlers on the one side still demanding 'some effective action' against the depredations of the blacks and the 'outside critics' on the other loudly condemning atrocities, the dispute had continued in the southern press. Bishop Gibney, long since safely returned from establishing a mission at Beagle Bay, his estimate of the native character if anything higher than before, took up the cudgels once more on behalf of the blacks, this time finding an equally eloquent opponent in Charles Harper of De Grey Station outside Port Hedland. The good bishop, in a public meeting at the Town Hall in Perth, made what seems to have been a tactical mistake in declaring that 'for every sheep killed by the blacks and for which they were most cruelly treated, God has punished the settlers by taking away a hundred or more sheep in the drought'. This statement, seized upon, analysed in the light of Biblical interpretation, commonsense logic and the Irish question, became a red herring across the main track of the argument. The bishop refused to retract a word of it and rose to the bait in defending the Nationalist cause in his home land:

> Mr Harper's allusion to the cause of Ireland by way of analogy to the native question is an unfortunate one . . . The few real atrocities committed by the Irish were those of the weak against the strong and founded on centuries of misrule. Many manifestos have been issued by Nationalist leaders against genuine atrocities but I have never seen the squatters of this colony, as a body, or their representatives do anything but take part against the Government to stamp out the wilful and deliberate murders and cruelties against the original owners of the soil by the alleged 'few'.

When this correspondence reached Argyle, Grandfather, somewhat to the embarrassment of his family, waved and quoted it at all comers. A keen admirer of the forthright bishop and a loyal supporter of Parnell and the Nationalist movement, much of his old fire returned as he now denounced the increased powers of the police and the flogging of cattle-spearers. His brother Galway Jerry disagreed with him, insisting that nothing short of flogging was merited by blacks who would cut the tongues and tails from living animals.

'And how are we to teach them that such things are cruel and that the branding, ear-marking and castrating that we do to the living beasts are not?' Grandfather demanded. 'Just read here now what the bishop has to say of it all.'

Galway Jerry glanced cursorily through the letters.

'What! Not the Irish question again!'

'The Irish question!' Grandfather exclaimed indignantly. 'And you but for the Grace of God born to starve in the poor famine-stricken country! Ye are like the rest of them, Jerry, born with a silver spoon in your mouth and little thought in your head for the under-dog.'

'It's precious little silver we can lay our hands on these days,' Jerry laughed, 'and there'd be none at all soon if we left the running of the country to you and the bishop.'

Grandfather had no higher opinion of the police in Kimberley than he had had for the same body in Queensland.

'Ye're all useless anyway without the blacks to help you with the dirty work,' he remarked in reply to the sergeant's complaint that they had found the patrolling of the countryside a thankless task.

The police claimed to have ridden out at great personal risk, followed every black's track and every smoke in sight, only to find the camps deserted, except sometimes for a few old men, women or children. When they brought these in as better than nothing, they were laughed at. If they shot blacks down in the act of 'resisting arrest' they were reprimanded or disbelieved by authorities in the south. At long last, however, the department had increased the Kimberley force, offering as an extra incentive a bonus of so much a day on the road in for every prisoner secured.

Lavery had heard that the blacks, always vigilant in the dry season, relaxed during the wet, confident that the police valued their comfort too highly to venture into the bog and brave the flooded rivers and creeks. Hence his present resolve to make a wet-weather raid with a party of four white men and five black trackers. It is rather surprising that so cumbersome a party succeeded in bagging even the 'five gins, four piccaninnies and two buck niggers' recorded as being brought into Argyle a week later. Father made a cryptic comment on the incident:

> After some debate in which the pater expressed himself with unusual vehemence the police decide to let go the gins and piccaninnies and take in only the two bucks with the purpose of introducing the lash to them.

It was a heavy wet, almost intolerably hot, and the fever was bad. McCaully, Pumpkin, Boxer and other blacks went down with it and became so weak that Grandmother, long since returned from her trip to Goulburn, sent her sons out to shoot duck, hoping to tempt them with the broth. Two of the black women let off by the police came in with children, one suffering from terrible burns, another with bad eyes, to be healed by the white woman's 'magic'. Grandmother was cooking and caring for her patients day and night until she too succumbed to the prevalent fever.

Father's journals tell the familiar story of the malarial victim:

> Mother still suffering fever and very weak.
>
> Mother still poorly but a little better since yesterday.
>
> Mother suffering violent attacks fever and ague today.
>
> Mother feeling well in early part of day but towards evening had to take to her bed again, very weak and suffering much from want of sleep. Administered five drops of laudanum.
>
> Mother slightly better this morning, and has taken her sewing to the verandah.

Somewhat reassured, he went to Rosewood to discuss a boundary muster, stayed the night with his uncle and aunt and was packing to return in the morning when Boxer came riding from Argyle, lagging in his reluctance to be the bearer of such news.

> He evidently did not hurry himself [Father writes on the black-rimmed page of his journal] for he could have been here three hours earlier judging from the time he left . . .

The girl, Valley, sent to her mistress with a cup of tea, had returned to say that she was asleep. That was a good sign, they thought, since she had been resting so poorly, and Grandfather went on quietly with his work in the blacksmith shop. Pumpkin appeared in the doorway with stricken face and shaking from head to foot.

'Boonari,' he said, using the old western Queensland word of endearment and respect, 'Boonari,' and sank sobbing to the ground.

She lay relaxed in the chair, her sewing in her lap, her fingers clasped on the nun's beads that had been her lifeline of spiritual strength.

Family members came from Rosewood and Lissadell.

> Jan. 23/93. James Clarke comes from Lagoon to make a coffin. Brother Pat and self assist. The remains of our poor dear Mother buried at sundown. We place a cross at the head of grave inscribed:
>
> J. M. J.
>
> Pray For Her
>
> Jan. 28. Pat, Pumpkin and Ulysses prepare to go to gulf to inform brother John. Father accompanies Uncle, Aunt and children to Rosewood. Miss Cameron likewise goes . . . What a strange change

> has come over the place! Gone the cheerful look and greeting smile that formerly associated itself with home. Decide to leave at once for Rosewood myself as find it too desolate even for a night.

The brief notes of the journal record the quiet grief and sympathy of the bush people as they gathered at Argyle on Grandfather's return. Old hands from the goldfields, a few former associates from Cooper's Creek, old 'Pepper Tin' Pethic, weeping so uncontrollably that Grandfather must bid him 'pull himself together', the blacks wailing on the river bank. Grandfather had as yet found neither words nor tears in the shock of his grief, doing whatever was suggested like a man in a dream, pulling the broken girths from a rafter in the saddle shed and quietly setting to work on them, weeding his patch of corn. Nat Buchanan and his wife, who had come to Kimberley not long after Grandmother, drove by buggy all the way from Flora Valley. Grandfather took his old friends' hands, thanking them wordlessly, and turned to talking of the horses in Buchanan's plant, of a fine colt one of his brood mares had got from the stallion Sultan that had near been taken by horse-thieves. But his effort at control had been too great and in leading his guests to the verandah he had reeled and fallen in a dead faint. Buchanan and Father lifted him to a bunk where he quickly recovered, made his apologies and went on with talk of everyday affairs.

Mustering continued through the wet, a procedure long since abandoned for sake of both man and beast.

A February 20 entry is evidence of its effect.

> Boy Bob loses his mare shortly after taking bullocks out. I go out after her riding the grey 'School Boy'. Find mare and return for home when my horse gives in and have to leave him and walk back. Return shortly after only to find horse quite dead. Cause attributed to 'dry puffs' brought on by former hard galloping. Rain and terrific heat all throughout day.

The necessity for grasping any possible market seems to have dictated this unseasonable work and in the wet of early '93 the pace was increased by a new turn of events. When Baker, the first member for East Kimberley, died in January a by-election was held in which Francis Connor was returned unopposed. This undoubtedly marked a new era of progress for the district, for Connor and Alex Forrest, member for West Kimberley, together began to organise the cattle trade. They had plenty of incentive, for both had business interests in the Kimberley district and a keen desire to make their fortunes. Before March the firm of Connor and Doherty began to make itself felt in the community. With Connor back and forth from Fremantle and Doherty operating around Wyndham, communications were sent out offering to act as middlemen for the pastoralists. There were now shipping facilities of a sort at Derby and the SS *Colak* had been chartered to bring cattle from there to Fremantle. Father and Long Michael at once closed a deal to deliver a mob of 500 Argyle and Lissadell bullocks to Derby, 750 miles west, by the first week in May.

This party consisted of Long Michael, Father, Pumpkin, Ulysses, Ned Kelly and two Lissadell boys Barney and Billy.

No need to follow in detail the long, slow trip to the west, with the restless night-watching of cattle on wet camps, the fear of stampede, the difficulty of getting stock to drink where they sensed the musky Aboriginal smell, the disappointment of stock losses caused from eating poison bush. Frank Connor met them at Hall's Creek, discussing the familiar Kimberley topics of numbers, dates, prices, weights and condition. Connor would be in Fremantle when the cattle arrived, Doherty down from Wyndham to see them at Derby.

From Hall's Creek the East Kimberley station men were on new ground, but meeting old friends. Willie MacDonald welcomed them to his shack at Fossil Downs and they discussed the problems of the industry. MacDonald said he had been living 'on credit' since he arrived and looked like continuing to do so for another couple of years. A storekeeper in Derby had carried him all that time, but he would not regret it. Every penny would be paid back now the markets were opening up.

At the spot where the prospectors had crossed the Fitzroy on their way to Hall's Creek there was now a Telegraph Station and homestead shanty cum hotel run up by Joe Blythe, who then little knew he had founded the townsite of Fitzroy Crossing. How cheered would have been this hardy battler whom they met on the road with his team to know that the Glenroy run he was soon to take up in 'the underworld' behind the Leopolds would become, through the faith and enterprise of his sons, the centre of the Kimberley air-beef project, with abattoirs from which carcasses would be flown from almost inaccessible back regions to the Wyndham freezing-works.

At Quanbun they met Edwin Rose, a member of another West Kimberley pioneering family, whose 'place showed the result of that industry and perseverance that are the basis and root of prosperity'.

Other encounters of the journey were Will McClarty, who had received members of the Durack-Emanuel expedition towards the end of their journey in 1882, and farther on Solomon Emanuel's son Isadore whom the drovers found at Emanuel's original station some forty-five miles outside Derby. Emanuels were at that time the largest single lessees in the Kimberleys and had extended their holdings to include Gogo, Noonkanbah, Lower Liveringa and Rarriwell. So far, Isadore told Father, they had made nothing whatever out of the country, although they had sunk some £50,000 into it. For all people might talk of encouraging the small men to the district, it seemed clear to him that it was at this stage a big man's country. Already a number of small-holders who had taken up land in West Kimberley had been overwhelmed by the difficulties of holding out against poor markets, depredations by the blacks and stock losses through disease, and had been bought out by men with capital such as Alex Forrest and themselves.

The drovers' arrival at the port coincided with that of the *Rob Roy* from Wyndham bringing Dennis Doherty to see the cattle shipped and Grandfather on his way round to Goulburn, via Fremantle, to escort his daughters to Kimberley as a solace to his lonely heart. Even Father had to admit by this time that to leave them any longer in the Goulburn convent was ridiculous, for Mary was now almost twenty-one and Birdie nineteen. It seemed now, however, that with the southern market opening up, the long talked of 'house in Fremantle', where the girls could make a home for their sorrowing father and a city headquarters for their brothers, might soon become a reality.

Grandfather rode out to the cattle and helped bring in and yard the first eighty head at the port. The *Colak* swayed in and then began the slow clumsy process of drafting the cattle into cages at the head of the race and swinging them into the ship's hold.

> Work continuing all night up to three a.m. and on again after 6 a.m. Process slow enough apart from lack of energy or interest on part of men working on the boat. Away by mid-day.

The *Rob Roy* continued south. Doherty returned to Wyndham in the *Australind*. Long Michael rode back with most of the plant and boys, while Father awaited the return of the *Colak* on which he was to travel south with the remainder of the mob.

He had been looking forward to this first holiday since his arrival in Kimberley seven years before but he had not bargained on the effects of the sudden cold of a southern winter.

Francis Connor was at the ship to meet him and together they supervised the swimming ashore of the cattle from Owen's Anchorage, the poor beasts, after the bumping and rolling of a stormy voyage, now forced shivering down the race and into a cold rough sea. Father, clutching a flapping overcoat, pitied the animals with which he had become familiar in the two months' journey from Argyle to Derby.

> Manner of landing very crude indeed to say the least of it. Cattle pretty knocked about. Ten lost on voyage.

32

PROSPERITY—AT A PRICE

The years 1893 to 1894. M. P. Durack writes impressions of Perth and its people. Discovery of gold at Kalgoorlie and implications for Kimberley market. Arrival of the Misses M. and B. Durack and their father in Fremantle and Wyndham. Survey of Ivanhoe country. Spearing of Constable Collins on Rosewood and criticism in southern press. Optimism in Wyndham. Selection of Ivanhoe lease. Illness and departure for Queensland of Stumpy Michael Durack.

Father, who often enough in his journals had mused on the comparative comforts and advantages of city life and had become restless on receiving news of his college friends forging ahead in their white-collar businesses and professions, was now shocked, not only by the wet and cold but by the ugliness of city life:

> ... the mob of gaping faces threading a most abominable thoroughfare ... buildings of antiquated design with bedaubed sign-boards—ungrammatical at that ... indeed a poor little country town compared to the eastern capitals. Fremantle as the main business centre is brisk enough but Perth, though very prettily situated on the Swan River, is quite dead and alive and gives the impression that there is little real prosperity or progress over here. As far as the beef market is concerned with the population more or less at a standstill there is little here to boost it beyond what it is at present ...

The rather disgruntled tone of his journal may have been due in part to finding himself something of an outsider. The name of Durack cut little ice with the entrenched families of the West to whom his people, if known of at all, were a crowd of Irish blow-ins from 'the Eastern States'. The Irish background that had become so shadowy a thing to himself loomed large for others:

> ... it's being somewhat taken for granted that I entertain certain subscribed views or prejudices on current affairs and notably that of the Irish question.

This nettled Father who had, in fact, given precious little thought to the matter at all but who, since the Irish were undoubtedly a pretty impossible sort of people to deal with, would not have considered the case against Home Rule entirely unjustified. He began to wonder whether his father would get on so well down here after all and whether he might be prevailed upon to express himself generally with a little more 'tact and discretion'. The old man had been so accustomed to ruling the roost in his own little kingdom and to holding forth freely on all occasions and all subjects. Although in many respects fairly tolerant of other men's views, there were certain issues on which he became increasingly dogmatic and would not hesitate in dubbing a man of the opposite opinion 'a rogue, a hypocrite and a mountebank'. Father liked hearing both sides of an argument propounded, not necessarily without fire, but in such a way that all sides parted on a basis of mutual respect and with a sense of having participated in an improving discussion.

Meeting certain west Kimberley pioneers on their home ground, Father could see for himself that there were essential differences between them and those rugged, self-made men who had entered via the Territory. These Westerners, whatever privations they might have suffered or to whatever menial tasks they might descend, had this indestructible background of British gentility and even if defeated could always return to their stronghold in the south where success had little bearing on social acceptability.

He discussed the matter with Dennis Doherty who expressed himself humorously on the stuffiness of Perth society but was little concerned about it. He and his charming wife, herself a West Australian, had a big circle of friends and acquaintances, by no means all of the Irish Catholic community, and it was not long before Father was writing of garden parties, 'cake fairs', musical evenings and concerts with 'items altogether of a classical order and rendered by the most beguiling cherubs', and various other forms of 'fruitful pleasure' that passed the weeks of waiting for the arrival of his father and sisters with whom he was to return north. The lean, rather gawky youth who had arrived in Kimberley seven years before was now a distinguished-looking young man, tall, broad-shouldered, courtly and with neatly clipped beard and moustache. Mrs Doherty, declaring he had the air of a Spanish grandee, had dubbed him 'Miguel' which thereafter stuck to him and helped dispel a little of the general confusion of family names.

But there was a more important reason for Father's change of attitude towards life in Perth, for within a short time of his arrival it became apparent that the tide of history had turned for the Cinderella colony. A man called Paddy Hannan had found a nugget in a desolate little place called Kalgoorlie about 350 miles east of Perth, and as fast as carriages, horses, camels or human legs could travel the goldseekers were flocking to the scene. Soon the news had got abroad and shiploads of prospectors were making for the port of Fremantle.

> Anyone not knowing the circumstances [Father wrote] might well wonder at the sudden change that has come upon the sleepy little city of Perth as though life from some mysterious source had been breathed into it and its inhabitants. Perhaps after all we are to be compensated for our bitter disappointment at Hall's Creek, for gold anywhere in the State will bring population and population will bring markets for Kimberley beef.

Frank Connor and Alex Forrest as Members for the district approached the Premier to close loopholes in the Stock Act of '88 which taxed the entry of all livestock imported for slaughter. The amended Act imposed a duty on all livestock except stud crossing the Kimberley border, thus safeguarding the Kimberley cattle men from a rush of stock out of Queensland and the Territory to swamp their market. It also put an immediate end to overland droving treks from the east by cattle men eager to take up land in Kimberley. 'Hungry' Jimmy Tyson had to disband a big mob already on the way to stock new country around Hall's Creek. It would not, however, stop the steady flow of individualists, tough little men driven out of Queensland by the drought, the flood, the bank smash or the defeated shearers' strike. In fact, as the small men moved out of West Kimberley, others were moving in on the east side to start the brief but stirring era of the 'poddy dodgers' between Wyndham and Hall's Creek.

Grandfather arrived with his girls, in better spirits than he had departed. He dearly loved the excitement of a gold rush and he was delighted as well by these two charming grown-up young daughters who fussed and adored him. Birdie, heartbroken at the death of her mother, deeply attached to the nuns with whom she had spent those four impressionable years and having, unlike her sister, no hankering for bush life, had wanted to enter the noviciate but had been persuaded that her duty at this juncture lay with her family. That Mary should return alone with their father to Kimberley seemed unthinkable, but in a year or two, the Reverend Mother said, when, please God, the family would have a home in the city she could return to the convent if she so desired. Every month, until her death, the good nun would write to her 'dearest child'.

> Pray always and be steadfast, my little one, for well I know that the devil will strew distractions in the way of your true heart's desire. Do not let him blind you to the narrow way of the cross or muffle your ears to His call . . . You are so kind, my child, so gentle and reluctant to offend any living soul, only draw the line always between gentleness and weakness, for the two are allied but may be kept a world apart.

'Why does Reverend Mother write always to you, and send me only her love at the end?' her sister would ask and Birdie, touching her sweetly, would reply:

'Because you are strong, my dear, and I am just a poor little weakling birdie tossed out of its nest.'

That arrival in Wyndham, early in August '93, was a flutter of veils, parasols and petticoats among the bobbing of topees and twirling of moustaches as the fresh-faced young girls were welcomed with moist handshakes and frilly embraces.

'Miguel, you old oyster! Why didn't you warn us you had such pretty sisters? We won't have a young man left in Wyndham once they get to Argyle.'

'Mind you don't step on a crocodile! They often bask on the jetty, you know, but they're tamer than the brutes up the Ord.'

Aunt Mary laughing and excited, Aunt Birdie smiling nervously, half inclined to believe any tale of this stark, torrid land, both mindful of the warnings and tearful prayers of the nuns, of Reverend Mother's parting homily delivered through trembling lips:

'It is God's will, my dears, a great test of your strength and courage. You must make the station a home for them now and look after them. It is so easy for men to fall into careless ways in the outback. You have a great calling, a great responsibility.'

The picnic journey from Wyndham to Argyle was quite an expedition with Uncle Galway Jerry, Aunt Fan and the children from Rosewood, Uncle John down from Argyle, and two young would-be pastoralists, Joe and Jack Hart, who had come north on the same ship. Along the road, droving stud bulls inland from Wyndham, they met a young man who was at last recognised among cries of surprise as brother Pat, taller than Miguel now, and no longer the smooth-faced boy they had last seen in Brisbane three years before.

They camped at the Ord River crossing, bulls and all, while Grandfather and his boys rode looking at country 'well watered and with some excellent pockets of good grass and picturesque beyond description along the range where there are the most entrancing pools of cold water overhung with fern'.

Grandfather named Valentine Creek after the camp horse he was riding and the family determined then and there to take up this chunk of country, embracing ranges, river and lagoons—Ivanhoe, the lovely lonely playground of our youth.

Meanwhile the family camped and gossiped, Aunt Mary happy and excited in the adventure of the new life, Aunt Birdie fussily attaching nets and veils to the children's hats, brushing the flies and ants from their food, loving and mothering and deploring the beasties of the bush. It was Birdie, however, who requested that their picturesque camping site be named Carlton Reach 'after a dear friend in New South Wales'.[1]

Again Argyle was full of movement and life. Hacks must be trained and saddles adapted for the girls and a new homestead pegged out higher on the river bank. This time it was to be of local stone with cement floors, the walls plastered inside, the rafters decently hidden behind tin ceilings. Joe and Jack Hart had agreed to assist with the building between expeditions with Father looking for a suitable station block. Grandfather, older and whiter since his wife's death, found relief in hard work, the company of his children and frequent visits from his brothers, Galway Jerry from Rosewood and Stumpy Michael from Lissadell. No doubt this concern for others helped divert his thoughts, for although the control had slipped from his hands into those of his eldest son he never ceased to plan and advise. His greatest worry at this time was for his brother Stumpy Michael who at forty-five was now a shadow of his old robust frame but who struggled on at Lissadell with his son Ambrose, determined to build this last asset into a going concern for the wife and family he yearned to be with.

Black Pat was also now at Lissadell, having sold his store and taken up a tentative holding some thirty miles from Wyndham where his brother Jim was camped.[2] The Mantinea run, however, was soon abandoned to become part of Ivanhoe.

At the end of August a police patrol including Constables Collins and

[1] Carlton Reach—site of the first Kimberley Agricultural Research Station—established by 'Miguel' Durack's son Kimberley some fifty years later.

[2] Jim Durack went prospecting to the Murchison goldfields is '94 and roved the outback as miner and stockman until his untimely death fom beriberi while droving for Sidney Kidman around Camooweal in 1907.

August Lucanus, who had again joined the force, arrived at Argyle, this time with a new policy. Collins, a big man with a wealth of flowing beard, claimed long experience with blacks in other parts of the State, and entertained the family with stories of his exploits and adventures, his knowledge of native law and psychology. He was a humane man with a real interest in tribal customs, was no adherent of the policy of wholesale slaughter, and had been posted to East Kimberley by reason of a reputation for having some influence with the black people.

'The news of my coming has always been signalled ahead of me,' he said. 'For some reason I am associated with one of their tribal heroes and am known to them all by my beard. It is my talisman, for no black dare harm a hair of it.'

Galway Jerry was sceptical.

'You need more than a talisman with the niggers round these parts,' he said. 'As for this idea of reasoning with them—it's a case of "first catch your bird".'

'The rest of you may carry weapons if you wish,' Collins said. 'For myself—I have no need of them.'

Jerry thought it a 'damn fool idea', but was willing to try anything to prevent the further killing of Rosewood stock.

Young Boxer volunteered to contact the natives, giving false clues as to the whereabouts and intentions of the police. The encampment was located and the raid organised. The fateful dawn came and Collins rode into the midst of the sleeping blacks. Pandemonium followed, the blacks shouting and flourishing their spears as they disappeared into a nearby thicket. Collins rode towards them with hand outstretched. A spear flashed from the scrub and he fell heavily, grasping the long-handled weapon in his side.

His companions hurried to his aid. Spears came from all directions, rifles barked out above the din of rage and terror as the blacks fell dead and dying and the survivors fled in confusion.

'But they didn't harm a hair of my beard,' Collins said when they returned to him.

Galway Jerry galloped to fetch a buggy but when he returned to the scene of the fight the brave man was already dead and his companions digging his grave.

As after the death of Big Johnnie Durack, a chain of fires blazed defiance from range to range. Lucanus marshalled his forces and rode the countryside, and slowly the fires went out.

The incident touched off another spate of correspondence in the southern press and an unsigned article in the Catholic *Record*, in which we surely detect the outraged eloquence of the bishop, denounced 'another blood-stained page' in the State's history:

> The following is the official account, sent by wire, of a most painful incident:
>
> 'From Sub-Inspector Drewry of Derby—On the 18th September 1893, whilst police were endeavouring to arrest some natives for horse and cattle killing, Constable Collins was speared through the body. He died next day and was buried on the spot, on the Behn River, 140 miles from Wyndham. There were other narrow escapes. A borrowed horse was killed. Twenty-three natives were shot before they could be driven off.'
>
> Filling in with the help of experience the meagre details supplied in this cautious message we may take it that the trooper and his companions acted in the usual manner . . . Even if we take it that their tactics were intended merely to awe the natives, what other course could they have than to cause a conflict? . . . Had they any reason to suppose that by laying down their arms they might have saved their lives, even at the expense of their liberty? . . . We doubt whether in the circumstances they saw any alternative than to kill or be killed . . . We know how the unequal struggle fared. There is no glory in an achievement where there is so little risk. The swiftness of his horse and the long range of his rifle make the white man complete master of such a situation . . . In the affair on Behn River, therefore, the troopers had the game in their own hands. And on their own showing, brutally did they use their advantage. It is not credible that the natives obstinately stood their ground and threw futile spears until the whole twenty-three had fallen.
>
> . . . It is perfectly clear that in this case no choice of surrender was given to them. Some were slain fighting and some as they ran and how many of these deliberately followed up and shot down as they made off? This was no 'fight'. It was a massacre. A white man fell too, one who is described as having been a good and useful officer. His death is much regretted, but still more the manner of it, for putting aside the question of colour, is one life to be considered an equivalent for twenty-three—or more?
>
> A pile of dead victims sacrificed to the ruthless Moloch of Australian civilisation, at this moment lies rotting under the

> tropical sun of Kimberley. And surely every gaping wound in their bodies calls incessantly to the Creator for justice. For after all of what crime were these men guilty at the worst? . . . The story of their accusers we have heard but their defence we shall never hear . . .

At Argyle Miss Cameron's fairy fingers accompanied Aunt Mary's singing of Irish melodies while Aunt Birdie unpacked copies of classic art executed at school—'Mariana of the Moated Grange', 'The Courtship', 'The Monarch of the Glen.'

As Mrs Doherty had predicted, the girls at Argyle brought a constant stream of visitors. The young men of the district seldom from this time used the 'back road' to Hall's Creek but took the longer road through Button's Gap and the Cockatoo Sands for the sake of a day or two at Durack's station, while the bridle tracks between Argyle, Rosewood and Lissadell became well worn with the constant coming and going of the girls and their escorts, friends and relatives.

At the end of October, Argyle cattle were mustered to stock country thirty miles from Wyndham that Father had helped select for the brothers Hart.

The general feeling of expansion since the Kalgoorlie gold boom is reflected in a jotting made in Wyndham at this time:

> Sent wire to Lands Department. Mr Hart Senior telegraphs to have £1300 transferred our account for stock delivered Carlton. Send telegram Goldsborough and Mort asking quotation for 500 or 1000 unbranded weaner heifers for ourselves. Doherty has dinner with Harts and self when we break a bottle of Rhine to drink their success . . . Champagne drinking again becoming fashionable. Three bottles broken today in Cable's dining room. The luck of Doherty phenomenal. Nobody able to put him down at dice . . .

Despatches to the Lands Department were for the lease of some 800,000 acres for stud property on the lower Ord, later to be known as Ivanhoe.

One night, camped with Ulysses near the Ord crossing during his inspection of the area, Father had fallen asleep while reading Scott's *Ivanhoe* and left the red and green buggy lamp burning at his head. Towards dawn he was awakened by a hue and cry of natives fleeing in terror and young Ulysses doubled up with laughter under the net beside him.

'Boss,' he said, 'they reckon you got the debbil-debbil eye all right. They properly frightened this time.'

To the end of his days Ulysses would dissolve in mirth at recollection of this incident from which the new station was to derive the name of Ivanhoe.

As Father always read himself to sleep, he believed he owed his life on more than one occasion to having left alight the kerosene lamp. When packing to leave Argyle for the last time, a few weeks before his death, he put it in his bag.

> To me [he noted in his journal] that little lamp not only stood for my safety but was the means of taking me on many a voyage of discovery and adventure. By its light I read all the great masters of literature so that my lonely rides in the bush were peopled with classical heroes and heroines . . . It saved not only my life but my mind.

Christmas at Argyle was this year an occasion of forced merriment, for Grandfather could no longer keep back his tears at thought of other days gladdened by the company of his life's love, or overcome his distress at the 'Rosewood incident' and its condemnatiion in the Catholic press. He was worried too by the ill-health of his brother Stumpy Michael, reduced by fever and with a persistent cough that gave him little rest. The girls insisted their uncle remain at Argyle where they could care for him but the thought of causing trouble distressed him more than his illness. As his coughing fits became increasingly violent he decided that a few weeks in hospital in Fremantle might put him in better shape.

'My poor Kate has had so many shocks of late years,' he said. 'I don't want to go back to her a living skeleton.'

Father set out with him by buggy for the river crossing to Lissadell but all the forces of nature combined to keep the sick man prisoner. Lightning shattered trees across the track, rent the shirt on Father's back when he dismounted to clear the way. The rain pelted in torrents and the river came thundering down. When they bogged back to the station it was clear that Stumpy Michael was a dying man, but when the weather cleared for a time he insisted on starting to Wyndham by the other track. This time both Father and Grandfather accompanied him, catching up on the way with a mob of fat Lissadell bullocks that was to comprise the first shipment of stock from Wyndham to Fremantle. The sick man was cheered at sight of the sleek beasts from the property he had pioneered and borrowing Long Michael's horse rode round them with appraising eye.

'Thank God,' he said, 'that whatever may become of me Kate and the children will be well provided for with Lissadell.'

Grandfather ventured to question him about his mortgages and other entanglements, but he dismissed all anxiety with an optimism that may have been a symptom of his illness.

'With the markets opening up like this, everything will be paid off within a couple of years and we shall all be on clover.'

Wyndham at the beginning of '94 gave every indication that this might be the case, for since Connor and Doherty had succeeded in chartering *Eddystone* for shipment of cattle from the gulf, the long talked of 'facilities' in the form of a new jetty and stockyards had quickly been completed. On his arrival Father was called upon to drive in the last spike of the town cattleyards, and the new era of East Kimberley expansion was ceremoniously ushered in with speeches and toasts. Later the cattle were driven down the race into the ship's hold while Stumpy Michael, waving goodbye from the deck, looked down the gulf and down the years to the day he had landed with his little party on that lonely shore in '82.

33

EXPANDING BOUNDARIES

The years 1894 to 1895. Exploration of country and incidents of the time. Native 'art galleries' on the Keep River. Patsy Durack takes a road contract. Pumpkin and Ulysses at the Ivanhoe 'stud'. Death of Stumpy Michael Durack and his brother's visit to New South Wales and Queensland. Dr Gallagher of 'St Pat's'. Queensland relatives. The case of Mrs M. Durack versus Lumley Hill.

Though money was still fairly short for the pioneers, their prospects were now as bright as the lucky nugget that had trebled the State's population within a few months. The immediate reaction of the men with a good foothold in the country, however, was not to sit back and consider how to double the carrying capacity of the land they already held but to ride forth and double its area. This after all was in the good old tradition of the open range, a policy that the government found hard to improve upon for encouraging the opening up of new and untried country. Conditions were made as attractive as authority considered justified, though naturally the pastoralists, like all other men in this land of free for all, fought an unremitting and fairly fruitful battle for better terms. Whatever the land rentals, they were described as 'crippling'. Talk of resumption within whatever stipulated time was 'this sword of Damocles stultifying to development' and any limitation of acreage was 'a dog-in-the-manger government attitude'. There was something, however, in the pastoralists' contention that their holdings sounded fantastically large mainly by reason of the vast tracts of useless rough range, claypan and cajuput swamp that lay between the good grazing areas, and that any Kimberley block under a million acres was hardly worth considering.

An uninformed reader, casually perusing a pioneering journal of the time, might wonder at the long accounts of seemingly aimless riding around—not mustering, for no stock had penetrated as far as the horsemen probed, not prospecting or searching for lost explorers—just 'looking at country'.

Released from the anxious toil of long droving trips to uncertain markets, the stations running on organised lines, Father with his brother John or a native boy spent much of the winter months of '94 and '95 in this way. The result of their activities was reflected in the gradually expanding boundaries of Argyle and Ivanhoe, which from being two isolated holdings on the east side of the Ord gradually drew together and merged along a vast fertile tract of river frontage.

Although most of the bigger watercourses and ranges had been identified, the more detailed exploration and naming of landmarks fell, as elsewhere, to the first settlers. Aboriginal words they found hard to remember and harder to spell, so simple names like Confusion Swamp, Wild Dog Gully, Skeleton Creek, Dead Horse Crossing, Blackfellow Gorge and Crocodile Hole began to fill blank spaces on the map as they rode around. Father's diary of such expeditions reads like the summary of some Davy Crockett serial in an Australian setting. He and his companions were constantly being surprised, followed, surrounded or attacked by blacks. One morning at Emu crossing he and Ulysses awoke to discover that a shower of spears had penetrated their tent while they slept. Another time, startled by a warning shout from Boxer while riding through a gorge, Father glanced up to find a group of warriors with spears poised about ten feet above his head. Boxer shouted a remark at which they hurriedly lowered their weapons and disappeared, but the boy would give no satisfactory explanation of what he had said.

Natural wonders and phenomena, dear to all bushmen's hearts, were the subject of endless anecdotes that delighted our childhood. I have little doubt that in some stories, such as that of the fabulous serpent whose tail disappeared on one side of Cockatoo Lagoon as its head rose on the other, he drew the long bow. For others, however, like that of the daddy of all man-eating crocodiles in the Baines and the snake that left a track twelve inches wide through the grass, he would call witnesses. From the blacks he collected strange tales that challenged investigation—a white man living among the tribespeople of the Leopold Ranges, 'a canary coloured goddess' roaming with the Arnhem Land blacks.

Then too there are terrible incidents, as when the tracker, sent to spy on a native encampment, was caught and hacked to pieces by his infuriated countrymen. Nipper, a boy who often accompanied Father at this time, one night rolled into the fire so that his shirt caught alight and burned the skin almost entirely from his chest and back. Father tells the story of the boy's incredible endurance, as tied to his horse and sometimes fainting in agony he rode forty miles back to Argyle. For a while his life hung in the balance, but he recovered with the care of my aunts, and was soon on the track again, terribly scarred but otherwise none the worse. The Territory boy Aled Meid whom Father brought from Pine Creek was less fortunate. He became paralysed after a fall from a horse, was brought to Wyndham for medical care, but died soon afterwards.

Also running through the journals of these years is a record of Father's varied enthusiasms and often rather ludicrous experiments. He was from this time on a keen but inexpert photographer, taking hundreds of shots of local scenery or groups of people balanced at precarious angles, all developed and printed with a maximum of assistance and mess. One of these, long since faded almost to extinction, recalls a typical experiment of the nineties when he reared a clutch of emus for the purpose of training them to draw a buggy. A similar attempt with kangaroos likewise failed, but Father never lost his boyish enthusiasm for utilising the natural fauna. His most successful inspiration was having a suite of furniture upholstered from crocodile hides, not exactly comfortable, but certainly unique.

Sometimes major incidents are recorded with tantalising brevity while at others the writer expands to long descriptive passages like those written when exploring the Keep River in the winter of '94:

> . . . The stream now bearing to the north. Mark a boab, MPD, 21/8/94 at point of a small volcanic hill. Country too low for cattle, but picturesque and plenty of fresh water. Many crocodiles observed, especially at junction of salt and fresh streams. Turned south 22 miles. Natives saluted us with warlike words. We anticipated an attack when they faced us, stamping to the time of their martial song sounding like the words 'Yap Yah! Yap Yah!' ejaculated with great force. Proceeded until interrupted by a precipitous gorge on the one side and a large expanse of glistening water on the other, and behold here are the natives again on our trail. They quickly receded however, into concealment. Cautiously we tried the passage on the left-hand bank and 5 p.m. found us on 'the salvation side of the gorge' as brother John remarked. We camp and have no sooner breakfasted than the smoke of a native fire springs up close by. We saddle up and proceed towards it but find only fresh footprints. About seven or eight miles on we have to pass through another gorge more formidable than the last the distance through being much greater and the cliffs towering above our heads for hundreds of feet. On passing through we found many native art galleries but in so outlandish and inaccessible a place that few are likely to witness these depictions of animal life—the formidable alligator, venomous reptile, sleepy turtle, majestic kangaroo and

> feathered emu, all portrayed with that instinct born of intimate relationship. On getting through we breathed a sigh of relief seeing so many fresh footprints all through the passage and knowing how easily a man might be intercepted in such a place . . .

Between journeys such as this and his station work Father moved briskly between Argyle and Wyndham, just as Grandfather in his prime had ridden between Thylungra and Charleville. Grandfather was proud of his sons and pleased to see young Michael's personality developing on lines rather different from his own, but he did not always agree with the views and outlook of this younger generation. Since Grandmother's death he had felt increasingly depressed at Argyle and at night would often slip away from the music and banter of the young people to stand by his wife's grave or call upon Pumpkin in his camp and talk of other days. He hardly liked to admit how lost he felt when Pumpkin, with Ulysses as his offsider, was put in charge of the new stud holding at Ivanhoe, but after this little differences between himself and his sons became more frequent. There were times when he could no longer contain his impatience, and his Irish temper, long held in check, would flare unexpectedly as over the issue of the road between Wyndham and Ivanhoe. Up to this time travellers on the route had either to cut a new track or follow the waggon ruts of the teamsters and hope for the best. The pass through Button's Gap near Ivanhoe had not yet been cut and buggies were sometimes hours negotiating a matter of half a mile. The local Road Board had answered the complaints of the settlers with talk of money and labour shortage.

'But surely the government can do something for us?' the settlers grumbled. 'And what about all these useless, big nigger prisoners? Why can't the police bring them out and put them to some useful work?'

It was pointed out that whereas it was easy enough to control a chain gang working about the town with a lock-up to return them to at night, it would take a complete force to hold them, chains or no chains, out in the bush. The dispute had continued for over a year when Grandfather lost patience with them all.

'Great heavens!' he exclaimed. 'I don't know what's come over the young fellows these times. Out in western Queensland if we wanted a road we went out and made it ourselves—never mind waiting for money from the government or black labour.'

Father had retorted indignantly:

'Do you think we've nothing better to do than make roads?'

'There's a lot of things ye do that are waste of time in my opinion,'

Grandfather said, 'but making a road is time well spent by any man. Ye could take it on a roster week and week about.'

Finding his suggestion put to scorn, Grandfather left off working on the new house at Argyle, rode into Wyndham and submitted a contract to complete the road. His tender was so modest that a flabbergasted secretary accepted it without further question.

For the next four or five months, with the help of a white man named Littleton and a native boy, he cut down trees, removed stakes and stones, graded precipitous creek and river crossings and made a cutting through the more rugged stages of Button's Gap. If he had any headquarters during this time it was at the little camp on the Ivanhoe billabong where, in the rugged grandeur of the Kimberley landscape, he pined with a son of the Boontamurra for the unbroken horizons and shallow river channels of Cooper's Creek.

Often during this time Father mentions spending an evening at 'the Stud'.

> Pater [he writes] passing some time in reminiscence of Thylungra days, calling upon Pumpkin to refresh his memory of various incidents. Pumpkin's memory is, I must say, excellent, but I do not know that so much looking back is in a measure good for either, since they appear often much moved to sadness by even the happier recollections.

One detects a hint of impatience that Grandfather, once a man of considerable wealth and influence, should not only content himself with a labourer's task but should turn for companionship to one who, for all his sterling qualities, was after all but a simple Aboriginal.

It is a sad reflection on the irony of life that since his wife's death it seemed to Grandfather that only Pumpkin still really believed in him. To the rest, he felt, it was as though in having lost his money the great efforts of his life had after all been wasted, that he had become a forlorn and tragic figure of failure. In letters to his youngest son Jerry—the little 'Sunny' who had so gladdened his life at Thylungra in what he now referred to as 'the happy days'—he fumbled for words in which to express the rift of values widening between himself and his elder sons:

> Yere brothers, Michael and Johnnie are getting on their feet at last and should do well. They have certain of their own views and opinions which are not my own but are not wanting my advise, so that I keep it to myself. Pat is more to my way of thinking but

he is young yet and not so much of a man of the world and does not care much for books. Now ye have all had a good education and have learned a grate deal and may think yere father but an ignorant old fool but in experience I have learned a few things that could be of use to ye all and I would want ye all to make good and do well in life but to remember that everything is not in the making of a fortune or in the losing of it . . . A man may still have led a profitable life and have little proof of it in his pocket . . .

After another of his visits to Ivanhoe, Father wrote:

Pater now informs me that Pumpkin is undoubtedly homesick and should be sent on a visit to his countrymen. It may be some measure of poor Father's own homesickness and loneliness that he sees reflected in his old associate, since Pumpkin has at no time mentioned to me his desire for a holiday and he must know full well that no request he might make of any reasonable nature would be refused.

A brief note some months later, however, remarks the return of Pumpkin 'much refreshed after a visit to his countrymen'.

In all justice to Father it must be said that he probably never refused a request made him by an Aboriginal. The station blacks might have persuaded him to indulge even fantastic whims had they but realised his eager responsiveness to any evidence of ambition or initiative. For the most part their requests were simple and few, though on the rare occasions when a native employee expressed a wish to see the big city, Father, to our intense delight, would bring him south to our home in Perth and show him the sights.

Boxer was probably the only one of the old station boys who ever exploited Father's sincere wish to compensate the blacks for the service of their youth, but even his requests were modest enough—a plant of horses to go prospecting and his tucker bags filled whenever he returned to Argyle. Somehow Boxer was to work out a track of his own between the white world and the black, never belonging to either and answerable to himself alone. The blacks, even his boyhood companion Ulysses, distrusted him and many whites said he was a rogue but Father regarded him, apart from Pumpkin, as the most remarkable native he had ever known, and when the old Queenslander died in 1908, it was Boxer on whom was bestowed the title of 'King of Argyle'. This was a purely white man investiture, consisting of a brass plaque on a chain to be worn around the neck. Boxer received the honour with gracious thanks and handed it back.

'You keep it for me, Umpy. More better I travel light.'

(Father, from his initials 'M. P.' was usually 'old Umpy' to the blacks.)

If a station boy wished to visit a relative in another part of the country he would be issued wth a 'passport', requesting stations *en route* to supply the bearer with rations on account and arrange his return transport when required. One of these remarkable documents dated 1905 was years later returned to Father with a note from the manager of Sturt Creek:

> Found the enclosed when turning out the old store. Hardly evidence of the indifference of station owners to their aboriginal employees!

When the news came through in August '94 that his brother Stumpy Michael had died at his house near Brisbane, leaving his affairs in a bad way, Grandfather laid down his pick and shovel and said he must go home at once. When in Kimberley 'home' to Grandfather seems to have been anywhere between Goulburn, Brisbane and Cooper's Creek, but when on that side of the continent 'home' was the station on the Behn.

He left with Uncle John by the first south-bound ship from Wyndham, carrying with him a small box for burial in the Goulburn cemetery, for he had felt that Grandmother would never rest peacefully until brought to lie in hallowed soil beside her little ones. Tbe task of disinterment had fallen to Father, who wrote sadly:

> It is of importance to Pater that this be done, but alas how little remains of what was so dear, everything having mouldered away in so short a time to but a few poor bones.

Uncle John took up his erratic diary to record their trip, the reunion in Sydney with his youngest brother Jerry and Grandmother Costello from her home then at Blackney Creek near Yass. In Goulburn they went at once to visit Dr Gallagher of St Pat's, who had continued an animated and regular correspondence with his ex-pupils throughout the years. Removed for a while from headmastership of the college to a parish post he had been quickly brought back to his old job when, with the financial ruin of so many established families and competition from new secondary schools in other colonies, the college faced disaster. The priestly scholar had girded his loins, his tongue never more eloquent, his pen never busier than in presenting the cause of the institution whose reputation he had done so much to build.

A bundle of letters, cherished for fifty years, tell of the steady return of the college to solvency and the rebuilding of the bursary schemes that had lapsed in the depression. Uncle John's request for a suitable motto for their venture in Kimberley Dr Gallagher had taken most earnestly, writing no less than three times as further inspirations came to him.

> My idea is that it shall suggest some historical association or classical memory, or thought taken at least in part from the Inspired Vol. or some elevating sentiment consecrated by ancient use while fitting in also with the present surroundings of time and place.
>
> Now all my acquaintance with the classics does not bring to me a single sentiment which would be entirely apposite. Nearly all classical allusions (Greek and Latin) suggest the pastoral life as connected with quietude and repose—the shepherds pipe and seed and song. In a word it is idyllic, while our current of thought connects it more with progress and the development of a country's resources. Those, on the other hand, which I have culled here from the Old Testament seem much more appropriate and one or two are wonderfully suggestive . . . I cannot say that any satisfy me, but you might take the Bible upon your journeys, and as I have marked chapter and verse, read the context. Then you might by a little change, or by blending the most appropriate parts of two or three of them together, work out one to fit in with the vignette.
>
> To these I would add one of my own viz the Latin Equivalent of Tennyson's line in the 'Passing of Arthur':
>
> 'The old order changeth, yielding place to new.'
> Vetera cedunt novis.
>
> which is true, as the old race is yielding to the progress of civilisation and to the white man . . .

In Brisbane they were met by a flock of relatives, Tullys, Scanlans, Skeahans and Moores with their tales of bare subsistence through droughts and floods and the big bank smash of '91.

'You would hardly know Thylungra,' Sarah Tully told them, 'the fences and yards falling into ruin and no life about the homestead any more. Oh Patsy, what came over the Cooper when you all went away?'

Grandfather comforted her with soothing words.

'You did right to stay. We would all have done better to remain and battle through together.'

'But they tell us it's splendid country over there and that you're doing well now with the great gold strikes.'

Grandfather agreed.

'Yes, it's good country enough, and thank God the boys are getting on at last and our debts near paid, but for myself it was too late to put down new roots. For my liking there is too much of the rough mountain scenery. I miss the big level plains and the skyline nice and clear upon all sides.'

For his sister Poor Mary Skeahan he had news of her two boys Jack and young Jerry who had joined the family recently in Kimberley. Jack had proved a good, resourceful stockman and did not apparently regret having stowed away on the *Rajputana* in '86 and young Jerry was putting up a good, straight line of fencing on Argyle. Later he hoped that the two boys would get a block of land of their own and that perhaps their mother and father and the two elder boys would join them. Poor Mary, however, seems long since to have lost hope of anything turning out trumps for the Skeahans and could only nod through her tears.

In 1905 after the terrible news that her son Jerry had been clubbed to death by blacks with the rest of the passengers on a lugger making for Darwin from Bradshaw's run, she gave voice to the grief and frustration of her life in one memorable remark:

'Only one prayer the good Lord saw fit to grant me—that he gave me no daughter to face the sort of life that I have lived.'

In the sorrowing house of his sister-in-law Kate, Grandfather heard the tragic story of his brother's end—how he had stayed in hospital in Fremantle until the doctor wrote saying he must be persuaded to return while there was still time. There had been a few weeks only together after all the years of waiting and they had made the most of the precious hours. Michael had said she must not be worried when she heard of his debts, for Lissadell was a wonderful property and with the new markets his mortgage would soon be paid. Father Dunham had come from Roma to be with his old friend at the last and to preside at his funeral and had paid a beautiful tribute to his great goodness and character, and John Costello had had his son Michael write a long *In Memoriam* poem which had been printed and sent to friends and family:

> I think I hear your hopeful voice
> As in 'the early sixties' when
> We dared the desert's toil, and then
> Faced the bush hardships as our choice.
>
> Your courage and your kindness rare
> Would that I had the words to praise.
> Oh pioneer who raised the herds
> And trod the unfrequented ways . . .

Grandfather undertook to go into the widow's financial position and although prepared to find the estate in poor shape he was shocked and shaken to discover the full extent of his brother's indebtedness. The land smash had left Michael in a hopeless position with assets whose value on the market was far below the amount of his mortgages and time had done nothing to solve his problems. Not only was he deeply in debt to the banks to the tune of nearly £34,000 but he had mortgaged his interest in Lissadell to his friend and partner Lumley Hill, who, finding himself in the invidious position of being a co-executor of the will as well as a creditor of the heavily encumbered estate, quickly resigned his office in favour of a Trustee Company. The 'equity of redemption' in Stumpy Michael's mortgaged property was now up for public auction from which the widow hoped, rather unrealistically, to derive at least a modest income after the debt was cleared.

In Sydney Grandfather and his son stayed at Kimberley House, a hotel in York Street that had recently been taken over by his Uncle Darby's widow and her unmarried daughters. This establishment was quite a step up from the country hotel at Molong and the family was now in comfortable circumstances with the two youngest boys training for professions—Lawrence for dentistry and Will for medicine. From here Grandfather wrote his family at Argyle:

Kimberley House.
Jan. 21st '95.

> ... A few lines to let you know Johnny, Sonnie and myself are all quite well thank God and hope the arrival of this will find you Michael, Pat and Mary and Birdie all enjoying the same blessing.
>
> Dear Michael I received a long letter from you the day I sent the wire from Goulburn after the interment of your dear mother's remains ...
>
> Tell Birdie on today I bought her a watch. It was thirty guineas but as I was buying two I got a shade nocked off. It is a real beauty. The other was for Sunnie, a gold one also, and I think my poor boy is deserving of it as you know I have promised it to him four years ago if he passed his Junior before his cousin Ambrose, and he has done better even than we had hoped with all these honours and distinctions ...
>
> Mr Dunn, the finder of The Wealth of Nations is here and we have had a long chat last night and he would make people mad concerning the reefs at Coolgardie. He tells us about 200 miles from Coolgardie there is splendid saltbush country, well grassed

> and mulga country on a lake called Lake Carey. Another Lake he told us of is 90 miles long but brackish though his camels would drink it and while there they got fat.
>
> Dear Michael, if you were here with Johnnie that country would be worth going to see. If it is as good as he tells us there is a fortune in it on account of it being so near the Murchison and Coolgardie goldfields. You could send your bullocks overland to there and we have been told they are now making a stock route on up to the Kimberleys. Dunn is going back again and tells us he is going to explore up north from the Wealth of Nations in our direction . . . Only for this infernal pain I have in my hip I would never go back to the Kimberleys until I would see it as them that goes there first they have the pick of the country besides a chance of dropping on to some golden country or reefs as you would be in the middle of the golden country as well as the cattle country. Dunn tells us there is fresh water creeks running into this big lake. It is very level country he tells us. When you get this letter we will be in Perth and if you suggest anything you could send a wire care of Connor.
>
> Sunnie is going back to Brisbane on tomorrow when ye're Uncle Michael's part of Lissadell is to be put up for sale. Cousin M. J. D. (Long Michael) is in Brisbane and we will wait here until he comes after the auction. I cannot say when we will leave with the cattle as we have not as yet heard whether Connor has arranged with the Melbourne people for the boat. They are to let us know.
>
> My darling children I am your ever loving father
>
> P.D.

The boys, however, were too much occupied in other directions to pay any attention to these suggestions, and felt that Grandfather should now be encouraged to continue work on the new house at Argyle that still stood as he left it when he took his job on the road.

> House still in abeyance [Father remarks during this time], matters of more vital moment requiring our full attention but all here agree it will be more fitting that the pater should proceed with this than take on work with the Road Board which we cannot but feel to be unnecessary and somewhat humiliating to the rest of us.

Grandfather, although willing enough to go on with the house on his return, did not refrain from mentioning how, in the days of his great energy, he had taken building in the stride of his many activities.

He now hung doors, fixed windows with real panes of glass, plastered, painted and paved, but as the work neared completion depression closed in on him again.

Poor Aunt Kate wrote desperately of an intrigue to rob herself and her children of their heritage, telling how before the sale of her husband's share of Lissadell it was being whispered around that the property was practically worthless and that it would be twenty years at least before it would be clear of encumbrances. Only one man had bid at the auction, acquiring the sole right to Lissadell, except for such stock as was owned by Long Michael, for £1 over the mortgage. The bidder was Lumley Hill. Aunt Kate had put her case in the hands of a solicitor named Charles Lilley, who felt so keenly for the widow that he had agreed, despite her penniless state, to institute proceedings requesting that the sale be set aside on the ground of 'breach of trust' on the part of Mr Hill.

After a long hearing the Judge had declared that if Kate Durack had a case at all it should be based on fraud rather than breach of trust, whereupon Lilley marshalled fresh evidence for a new hearing, alleging that Lumley Hill had fraudulently deprived the estate of a valuable asset.

In an effort to compromise, the widow was offered a yearly allowance of £200 from the proceeds of the estate, but John Walsh, one of her husband's executors, then refused to sign the transfer of country. Exasperated, Lumley Hill declared that the allowance would be forfeited unless all claim to Lissadell was waived in a signed acknowledgement that the payment was a voluntary and charitable concession on the part of the present partners in the property—Long Michael and himself.

Grandfather was deeply distressed over this affair and felt the helplessness of his position keenly, particularly when letters from Charles Lilley made known that the widow and her family were existing at that time only by the patience and charity of the tradespeople. He blamed himself bitterly for not having enquired more deeply into his brother's affairs before his death and we read in Father's diaries how he tracked back and forth between Argle and Lissadell 'in an effort to thrash this painful matter out with Long Michael'. I can find no evidence, however, that Grandfather blamed his cousin for his part in the affair. The two had always held each other in high regard and one gathers that although Long Michael's role throughout is somewhat vague, he must have put his case quite clearly to Grandfather. Certainly his evidence at the hearing did not assist the widow's cause. Testimony of the potential value of Lissadell might well have done so, but Long Michael spoke only of the many disabilities and uncertainties facing the Kimberley pioneer. He may well have spoken from conviction for it would have been difficult to testify with any accuracy to the potential value of the property at that time. It would, moreover, have been hardly human to boost its possibilities when he stood to lose by doing so. It may have been taken as a matter of luck that the output of the station over the following years was some four times his reckoning, for who was to have known that Kalgoorlie gold was no flash in the pan, that Western Australia was now the golden colony of the continent, its population to rise from some 50,000 at the time of the first strikes to over 184,000 within six years? It would seem that all attempts at compromise were at Long Michael's instigation and after his marriage in 1905 he offered to adopt one of Stumpy Michael's daughters. Kate Durack, however, declined the offer and would hear nothing in his defence.

Tall and straight by nature, the very idea of accepting charity never allowed her to unbend her back again. She hung, beside the photo of her beloved husband, the gilt-framed family tree of the McInnes-McLeods, showing their descent from many royal lines, took in boarders and continued valiantly to fight her already defeated cause.

As for Lissadell—Long Michael was to become sole owner after the death of his partner and in 1927, with no family of his own to carry on, was to sell out to William Naughton for the sum of £72,000.

34

GLIMPSES OF 'THE NAUGHTY NINETIES'

The years 1895 to 1896. Social life in east Kimberley. The Pierce family. Police and settlers. Native prisoners. Women in the cattle camps. The half-caste question. Killing for the blacks. Patsy Durack interviews black miscreants. Perth, Melbourne, Sydney and Brisbane in '95. The tick question arises.

From the beginning of '94 there had been a definite feeling that Wyndham was to become a port of substance, but the idea of moving to the official site seems never again to have been mooted. The town was nobody's special pride and responsibility. To the station people it was no more than a business depot and its residents were for the most part government officials serving three-year terms of which they made the best or the worst according to temperament. Many of the younger people assuredly made the best of it and social life in east Kimberley was never as lively and convivial as at this time.

When Magistrate Frederick Pierce, his lovely wife and daughters took over the residency on the slope of Mt Albany the young men of the district began finding more frequent and pressing business in town. A racing association organised several meetings a year, while picnic parties were extended to camping expeditions, when the young people, heavily chaperoned, rigged mosquito nets on the banks of lily lagoons and sang plantation songs around blazing camp fires. Apprehension of dawn attacks from natives added zest to the adventure and even Miss Norma Pierce's experience of discovering a snake in the voluminous sleeve of her nightgown did nothing to dampen their enthusiasm for the great outdoors.

The station men vied with each other in escorting the pretty Misses Pierce, mounted on their race-horses, for long rides across the white salt marsh. The sisters, two at a time, were as often at Argyle as my aunts, Mary and Birdie, were in Wyndham, the arrivals causing a stir of excitement either at the station or the town. Aunt Mary often pointed out to us a little thicket by a spring, a few miles outside Wyndham, where after the long hot buggy rides from inland they had bathed and changed for their triumphant entries. In these days of carefree sun dresses and shorts, the elaborate outfits they wore seem incredible, photographs of picnics and tennis parties at Wyndham and Argyle in temperatures soaring over one hundred degrees showing the men complete with coats and ties and the girls in veiled gem hats, leg o' mutton sleeves, heavily tucked and embroidered blouses, pinched waists, long, substantial skirts and buttoned boots.

Father, making sly digs in his journals at the 'amorous delights' of his brothers and cousins, himself became deeply absorbed in the project of establishing a racing stables at Connor and Doherty's Ascot depot a few miles outside Wyndham. Romantic musings on 'the captivating brunette' whom it is his 'happy lot' to escort on riding and duck-shooting expeditions run through his diaries for quite three years, with delicate references to 'stolen tresses' and letters 'written in a clearly defined, beautiful hand which would at once betray a mind capable of no intrigue and a spirit filled wth the loftiest human feelings of her divine sex'.

It is surprising, however, that none of the family married any of the Wyndham belles of that time and that Father did not meet his fate until another 'captivating brunette' crossed his path some fifteen years later.

At Argyle the two spare rooms and wide verandahs were often taxed to capacity with visitors and the Chinese cook constantly threatened to go on strike. Amusing young men rode to and fro. Will Mansbridge, youthful magistrate for Hall's Creek, played merry pranks; Frederick Booty, an Oxford graduate and nephew of Osmond, owner of Ord River Station, enchanted the company with long recitals from Milton and Wordsworth; and the handsome young baronet Sir Alexander Cockburn Campbell, travelling the country in some official capacity, lent an aristocratic flavour to the gathering. Mr and Mrs Nat Buchanan called when travelling to town, as did Mr Stretch, brother of the Bishop of Newcastle, and his cultured wife from Denison Downs. The 'fairy fingered Miss Cameron', having surprised the community by becoming Mrs Duncan McCaully a year before, also visited frequently with her baby daughter.

On July 22, 1895, Father records at Argyle:

> Receiving congratulations this morning from sister Birdie and Miss Pierce I remember that this is my 30th birthday. My reflections upon the occasion are intermixed with grief and joy. A wide and seemingly unbounded prospect yet lies before me but clouds as ever shadow the horizon ... I am much exercised in my mind with our problem regarding the blacks and resolve upon this day to make every effort

> at reaching an understanding. It must be admitted that one is far from edified by the sight of so many of these unfortunates bound in chains. In fact some of our fair companions, in the gentleness of their hearts, have taken us to task for it.

Father's troubled state of mind is hardly surprising in view of the fact that his father's predictions on the native question were working out so much nearer the truth than those of the opposite faction. The flogging of the blacks had done nothing to subdue their spirit; rather it had incited them to more daring acts of bravado, and although sometimes roused to indignation by allegations that he considered ill-informed or 'grossly overstated', Father was extremely sensitive to the ill-opinion of a growing faction in the south. Generally respectful of authority he had, moreover, lately been at variance with the police over a matter touching on his integrity.

Early in April he had recorded:

> . . . a heated discussion with Inspector Orme, who openly asserted that the squatters are afraid to venture far enough afield to properly round up their cattle. I defiantly threw back the taunt.

The mutual taunt of cowardice had started in west Kimberley some years before, police accusing the station people of letting their cattle stray so far afield that they were frightened to venture after them, settlers blaming the police for the inadequacy of their patrol and their failure to arrest the real culprits. However, where not long before the police had been laughed at for their failure to make sufficient arrests, they were now denounced for making too many. With an increased number of reliable black trackers, and a fairly elaborate system of espionage, their tactics had increased in subtlety so that they were able to round up big encampments in well planned dawn raids. Moreover, a daily living allowance of 2s 5d 'per knob' for all natives arrested as suspects and witnesses made it profitable to bring in as many as they could manage. Chained together neck to neck, wrist to wrist, the long lines of prisoners, men, women and children, wound their miserable way over the bush tracks to receive sentence in Wyndham, Derby or Hall's Creek. Their crimes were murder, sheep or cattle spearing or breaking insulators to make spear heads, and acquittals were nil.

Brief, scattered entries reveal Father's growing sense of discomfiture at the situation:

> Am disgusted at the spectacle of a party of niggers on the road with police, the chains in many instances much too short from neck to neck, chafing and pulling as they move along and all

> appearing half starved. Constables —— and —— making no secret of sending the women bush to catch lizards and snakes so that they may pocket the greater part of the food allowance.
>
> Just witnessed the separation of a black youngster, about four years old, from its mother, being taken off to Darwin as a 'witness' to some crime or another. The wailing of this poor little devil was pitiful, refusing every attempt at solace from other members of his tribe, pelting them with stones, throwing himself on the ground and rolling in desperation, casting imploring glances after his retreating mother with loud cries of 'Walya ca! Walya ca!' until his voice grew husky and faded into the bay of a dingo.

As time went on there was less talk of the inferiority of the Kimberley natives to those of Queensland and New South Wales. The anonymous 'buck niggers' and 'gins' were becoming entities with human attributes and likeable ways and steadily more indispensable as the big gold strikes in the south lured away white labour from Kimberley. At Auvergne about this time Father records a discussion with the manager, T. K. White, 'on a somewhat different level to that usually adopted in this country'.

> ... pleasantly discoursing upon the maladministration of the Territory, the works of Rabelais, Racine, Moliere, Rousseau, Talleyrand and the merits of Boswell's *Life of Johnson*. Thence to philosophy, the littleness of the part we play in this vast universe and the future that may lie ahead for some of the aboriginal people of this community. Mr White points out to me three young children here of most pleasant and intelligent features upon whom he had experimented with surprising results in the teaching of the alphabet and minor arithmetical problems. He declares us mistaken in considering their intelligence of the lower orders of man ... Altogether I find White a man of most interesting and humane outlook.

In more isolated areas the power of the soft-eyed native women was already apparent. Some of the bigger resident landholders had their wives and families to dispel the loneliness of the bush but many a small battler or solitary manager for some absentee owner was glad enough of the dusky companions whose only terms were the right to live and to serve. The following entry, made when visiting Wave Hill Station around this time, is significant of a changing order:

> Sunday on one of the most isolated stations in Australia. The musterers, Sam Kelly, Horace Bennison, three blk. boys, five gins. What a transformation! The many-coloured dresses of the women have now given place to shirts, moleskin pants and stockwhips slung across their shoulders. They are not now easily to be distinguished from the sterner sex but for their fuller posterial curves. Took a camera shot of men, women and piccaninnies all jumbled together. Living conditions very crude indeed and am moved to remark that the owners of such properties would do well to give some thought to those who work for them on such outlandish places, separated as they are from all social comforts and associations and surrounded by half savages . . .

From this time, until a Native Administration Act put a stop to the employment of women in the cattle camps, was probably the heyday of the black women who never before or since enjoyed such status and sense of importance. Small-boned and timid-seeming, they soon proved themselves to have more endurance and intelligence than their men in the cattle game. They loved the life of the stock camps, the thrill of riding the plains where they had dug for yams and scratched for lizards and if they served other ends than mustering and holding cattle little evil was prevented by confining them to the boredom of the homestead wurlies on the creek banks.

Other aspects of this increasing compatibility began to reveal themselves from this time onwards. Father records having noticed a black stockwoman riding into Wyndham with cattle, a half-caste baby in a coolamon strapped to her back. It would seem to have been the first half-caste child he had seen at Kimberley and he reacted forthrightly:

> It is greatly to be hoped [he wrote] that such is not to become a commonplace in our community for the strain resulting will assuredly be no asset its being common knowledge that the half-breed inherits the worst characteristics of both races, nor would I feel disposed ever to trust or to employ one of the kind. The problem will therefore inevitably arise as to what can be done with such unfortunate unemployables who through no fault of their own are brought into the world in evidence of the unlicensed and irresponsible conduct of the poorer products of both black and white societies.

In this Father was voicing opinions to which all 'right thinking' people of the day subscribed, but I never heard him deny the reliability or efficiency of his various half-caste workers of after years. In fact the Kimberley 'yella-fellas' were to prove genetically remarkably good specimens, better adapted to the environment than the white man and better to the new way of life and philosophy than their full black brothers. The men who fathered them were after all mostly hardy individualists with guts and staying power and their mothers selected from the more attractive and healthy specimens of black womanhood.

It is clear that from now on Father began acting on lines previously dismissed as 'impractical'. His journals show that he lost no opportunity of investigating native tracks or camp fires and of trying, with the help of an interpreter, to come to some understanding. On Inspector Orme's next visit to Argyle he records a further

> . . . heated interview on what measures he intends taking in regard to the recent mischief and I especially request that he takes no prisoners into town—that after he arrests the malefactors he sends me word when it is my intention to take a bullock and shoot it for them.

Meanwhile Grandfather, having finished the Argyle house and joined Pumpkin and Ulysses at the Ivanhoe stud, was dealing with the situation along lines of his own. Here, where the stock consisted at this time of valuable imported strains, every beast speared represented a serious loss, and Pumpkin, who felt his responsibility keenly, was at his wits' end when Grandfather arrived. Together they had followed tracks, watched and waited at strategic places and one morning surprised a party of about six men in the act of pushing a raft piled with fresh beef from the river bank.

> Pater informs me that the blacks made a great noise and show of weapons [Father writes], but appeared nonetheless somewhat abashed to have been caught red-handed. He ordered them to take some of the steak from the raft while Ulysses got a fire going. They thereupon cooked and distributed it around, eating some themselves and communicating, as far as possible, that a beast would be killed at the station on request if they left the cattle alone on the run. Pater and Pumpkin thereupon entertain their company with stories of the different hunting methods employed in western Queensland to those used in Kimberley. It is to be seen in how far this parley will prove successful.

This little incident is a good example of Grandfather's extraordinary tact and insight in the handling of the Aborigines, and it is the only instance in any of these early journals of an attempt to establish a basis of common human understanding. It may have had much to do with the fact that there were fewer instances of cattle-spearing at Ivanhoe than elsewhere after this time and that there was never any difficulty in recruiting abundant native labour for this station.

Towards the end of the year Father persuaded his younger sister Birdie to accompany him on a holiday. She went without much enthusiasm, being at that time 'deep in the throes of romance' with a charming and personable young warden for the Hall's Creek goldfields. Perth they found lively and much grown up in two years, 'with the subject of Coolgardie still foremost upon all lips', though compared to Melbourne still a mere country town.

> How strange [Father writes] to get into the bustle and *throng* of crowded humanity again and although Melbourne is said still to be very dull since the depression it seems much alive to us after the back blocks of Kimberley, and the shops beautifully decorated and lit. How many years will it yet be before our now prosperous Perth approaches anything within reasonable comparison? As I sit here on my hotel bed my thoughts are carried back to dear old Kimberley, to poor old Pater, his sadness forgotten, I trust in healthful sleep, sister Mary dreaming of happy times to come and brother Patriens, perhaps somewhere out on the run doing a nocturnal watch around the cattle . . .

While in Melbourne Father ran into an old school friend who, now much a man of the world, determined to introduce the innocent from outback to a taste of real life.

> The scenes tonight [we read] superceded anything it has yet been my lot to witness. Firstly, the Dynamite works where wheels are seen going with 1500 revolutions to the minute apparently to the eye quite motionless where this *electricity* is generated and sparks flying without any heat whatever. Such works are so great that they make a man feel of little individual moment in this world.
>
> The other sight takes us to the deplorable state of society and never did I conceive that such a miserable and piteous sight was to be presented. Here, lying on a wooden bed, her head resting on pillows was a beautiful young girl in the bloom of life, dressed to taste, bodice of delicate white folded material, red and white crepe skirt, surrounded with clouds of opium smoke between two hideous old Chinese and in a dreamy kind of lethargic state with

> her eyes languidly shutting and opening regardless of anyone about her. Her head was decked with a kind of crown which she repeatedly kept pressing down with her hand. On another chair sat a depraved looking girl with heavy eyes imploring alms for to procure opium, while soon there came in a youth about 17 or 18, smart looking and well dressed—another victim, I suppose to that terrible drug and begging our acceptance of a smoke 'to soothe our nerves'. Truly we are blind to the conditions of this life and in leaving necessary contribution of 1/- did we not do wrong as lending sanction to the further continuance of this vice?

Christmas in Goulburn was a time for visiting friends and relatives and catching up with the years between. Aunt Birdie attended midnight Mass in the Mercy Convent chapel and confided to her best-loved nuns the shy secret of her romance. The nuns, disappointed no doubt that their beloved 'little one' had been after all diverted from 'the narrow way' of religious life, were concerned to hear that the young man in question was not of her faith.

'But his attitude to religion is most serious and respectful,' Birdie assured them, 'and he hints that he will no doubt become converted in time.'

At the Goulburn Cathedral Father listened to a Christmas sermon preached by his old teacher Dr Gallagher, soon to be elected Coadjutor Bishop of the diocese.

> I am delighted to find [Father writes] that his eloquence was no illusion of inexperienced youth and that he still has the same power to stir our vacillating hearts to fresh resolve, sentiments that might on other lips appear but commonplace transmuted by some individual magic to utterances of new and vital appeal. Yet, when asked what he has told us I can only say it is the time honoured exhortation to attend our spiritual duties, throw old feuds aside and greet our fellow men with cordial wishes and open hearts . . .

In Sydney, at Kimberley House, the family headquarters in York Street, there had been a joyous meeting with the youngest brother, Jerry, who having won a mathematical scholarship was then attending the Sydney Unversity.

> Together we embark on a round of visitations, races and theatres with such programmes as 'The Pirates of Penzance', 'The Magistrate', carried out, but 'Robinson Crusoe' and 'Pat or the Bells of Rathbeal' the latter providing many a good, solid laugh.

> At Her Majesty's Theatre witnessed an Australian play 'To the West', a very good and true representation of life in a mining camp. The sensational acting of Dampier was indeed exceptional but his playing of the man dying of thirst was, I consider, rather overdrawn. The explosion in the mine was a scene very well the representation of the Fremantle Gaol incorrect, its being built of brick and the original in stone . . .
>
> The city of Sydney this month indicates a tone of prosperity the regime of Free Trade auguring for many a new era of startling possibilities while others assert it to be a fallacious policy . . . For myself I regard a policy of partial protection infinitely more desirable . . .

Further somewhat quaint comments on contemporary Sydney life may have historical interest:

> I notice here a strong propensity for music . . . with numerous itinerant musicians parading throughout the night and day and superior bands drawing big assemblies. Many, I must say however, are subsidised less for the tunefulness of their performances than for the obvious misfortune of their circumstances . . . Nor can I here refrain from remarking upon those ladies who are 'bound apprentice to the wanton trade'. In none of the colonies have I found them so persistent for man's welfare, greeting him with winning smiles in streets and restaurants, commiserating with the inconvenience of his late hours should they encounter him after ten or eleven at night. I am told that homeliness and familiarity is a virtue that they carry to excess. One is reminded of the letters of Goldsmith and his story of the Chinese merchant writing so eloquently to his friend the ambassador in China of the generosity of the English woman for whom he prepared verses of the most eulogistic quality only to find himself most woefully deceived . . .
>
> Jerry and myself have pleasant walks through the city and discuss ardently the physique and manners of the Sydney people who on the whole strike one as rather small and thin in stature, contrary to the general conception of Australian manhood. There seems less of the larrikin element in the main streets of the town however and certainly less of that vile whistling than one finds in some of the rural towns. I cannot speak for the lower suburbs.
>
> The love of rapid aerial motion appears to have taken strong possession of the city and the spirit of cycling has captured the

populace, even the ladies. There is visible in the main street a girl who rides a bicycle advertising Don Marino cigars and it is still a matter of dispute whether the divided skirts or the bloomers are the proper dress for the symmetrical female form indulging in this mode of travel. Some say the fad will pass but it is my opinion that the bicycle has come to stay and has in many instances superceded the use of the horse which I suppose will suffer further unemployment on the introduction of the now spoken of motor-cycle which has been tried in America with some success . . .

A Sunday stroll on the domain to hear the stump orators expatiating on Temperance, Religion, Socialism. The trait of sincerity would appear wanting in many of them.

Attended a cricket match the enthusiasm showing that this game is regarded as the great national sport in N.S.W. as football in Victoria. A great number of ladies present not so much from admiration or understanding of the game as of putting in evidence their new Sunday frocks and hats . . .

Father records at some length his righteous anger when a young Sydney solicitor brashly deprecated the morals of the bush.

The most convincing practical argument would be to have felled him on the spot but I had to bring the philosophy of my silent hours in the bush to bear and so averted the enactment of a scene.

I emphasised that what he said might in some measure be true of the weak minded led by the dictates of others into giving way to their animal propensities in places yet lacking the elevating influence of women or of entertainment of any sort.

I remark that we assuredly lack such edifying influences as high kicking ballet girls and daily scenes of debauchery and lawlessness. The appearance at this stage of a depraved and drunken woman added some weight to my remarks on this boasted city morality. Should therefore, any casual reader peruse these lines, let him not hold up for my admiration the high standards of the city as against those of the bush nor yet accuse us of callous indifference to fellow beings who deal to the best of our ability and conscience and within the limits of our present circumstances with the daily exigencies of our isolated lives . . .

In Brisbane the inevitable family contacts included Aunt Kate, still in the throes of legal battle, Aunt Sarah and Uncle Pat Tully with stories

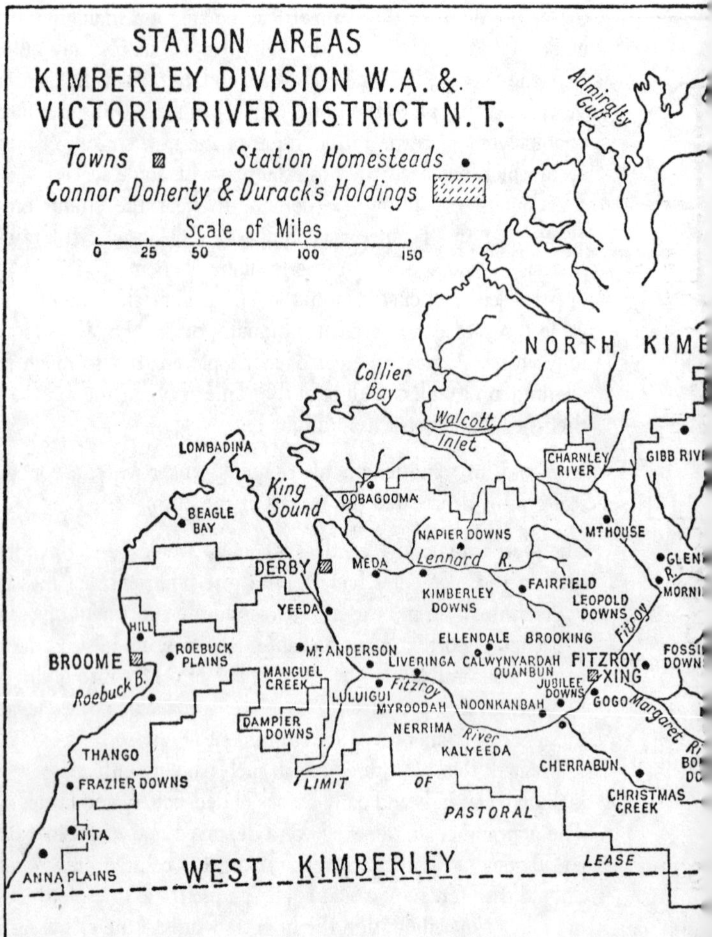
STATION AREAS
KIMBERLEY DIVISION W.A. &
VICTORIA RIVER DISTRICT N.T.
Towns
Station Homesteads
Connor Doherty & Durack's Holdings
Scale of Miles
0 25 50 100 150
Admiralty Gulf
NORTH KIMB
Collier Bay
Walcott Inlet
LOMBADINA
King Sound
CHARNLEY RIVER
GIBB RIV
OOBAGOOMA
BEAGLE BAY
NAPIER DOWNS
MT HOUSE
DERBY
MEDA
Lennard R.
FAIRFIELD
KIMBERLEY DOWNS
LEOPOLD DOWNS
YEEDA
HILL
ROEBUCK PLAINS
MT ANDERSON
ELLENDALE
BROOKING
BROOME
LIVERINGA
CALWYNYARDAH
QUANBUN
FITZROY XING
Roebuck B.
MANGUEL CREEK
LULUIGUI
Fitzroy
MYROODAH
NOONKANBAH
JUBILEE DOWNS
GOGO
Margaret
DAMPIER DOWNS
NERRIMA
River
KALYEEDA
THANGO
CHERRABUN
FRAZIER DOWNS
LIMIT OF PASTORAL LEASE
CHRISTMAS CREEK
NITA
ANNA PLAINS
WEST KIMBERLEY

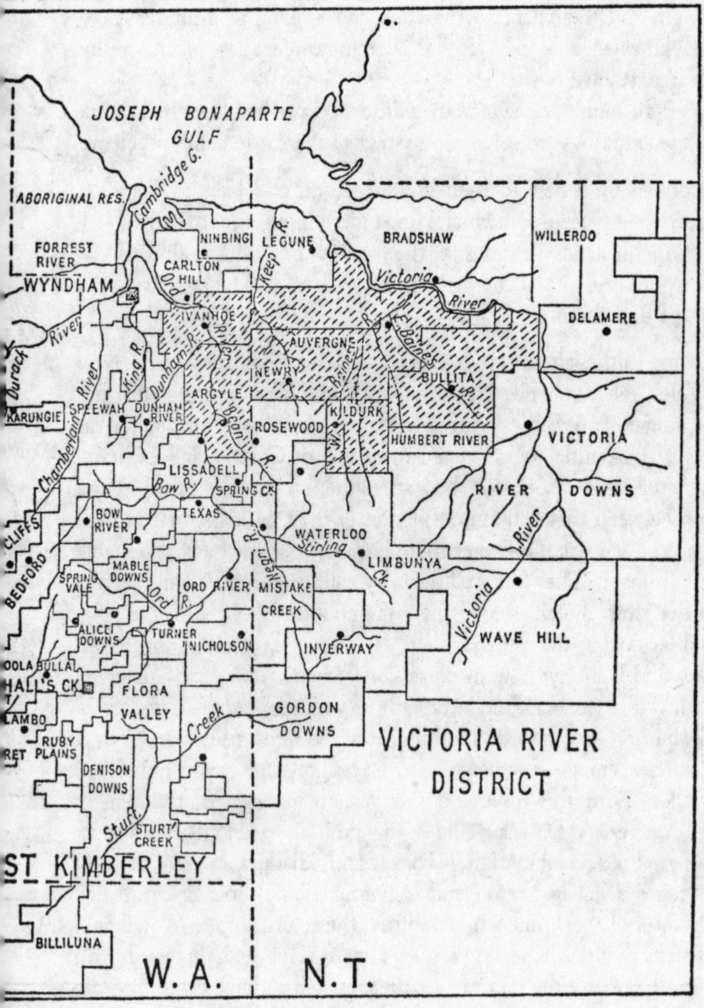

JOSEPH BONAPARTE
GULF
Cambridge G.
ABORIGINAL RES.
FORREST
RIVER
WYNDHAM
NINBING
LEGUNE
BRADSHAW
WILLEROO
CARLTON
HILL
Keep R.
Victoria
River
Ord
IVANHOE
DELAMERE
AUVERGNE
NEWRY
BULLITA
ARGYLE
KILDURK
Durack
Chamberlain River
King R.
Dunham R.
KARUNGIE
SPEEWAH
DUNHAM
RIVER
ROSEWOOD
HUMBERT RIVER
VICTORIA
RIVER
DOWNS
LISSADELL
Bow R.
SPRING CK.
TEXAS
CLIFFS
BOW
RIVER
WATERLOO
Stirling
Ck.
LIMBUNYA
BEDFORD
MABLE
DOWNS
SPRING
VALE
ORD RIVER
MISTAKE
CREEK
Victoria
River
ALICE
DOWNS
TURNER
NICHOLSON
WAVE HILL
INVERWAY
HALL'S CK.
FLORA
VALLEY
GORDON
DOWNS
Creek
RUBY
PLAINS
DENISON
DOWNS
VICTORIA RIVER
DISTRICT
Sturt
STURT
CREEK
ST KIMBERLEY
BILLILUNA
W.A.
N.T.

of the recent inroads of rabbits to match the growing worry of tick infestation in the north. But things were improving in western Queensland. The Tullys with 22,000 sheep, 3,000 cattle and 400 horses were rapidly wiping off their debt to the bank and looking to a future where increasing knowledge of the artesian system would allay much of the constant anxiety of drought.

Father's old Kimberley acquaintance Ernest Baynes had branched out in an experiment that was to solve yet another of the cattle man's problems.

> Am driven by Ernest to their chilling rooms and later to their meatworks at Queensport which I find indeed inspiring and thought provoking in its implications for the future of our industry. In this process not one iota of the beast goes to waste . . . The process of *tinning* I find amazing . . .

By this time, although drawn by associations to Queensland and New South Wales, the Kimberley branch of the family definitely regarded the West as home, and Father voices sentiments of warm satisfaction at returning to Fremantle to the hearty welcome of Connor and Doherty. Every year of their association had strengthened the ties of trust and friendship between them and an affiliation of their business interests had already been discussed. To Father there had never seemed any reasonable argument against it. They followed the same calling, knew the same people, went to the same church, shared the same politics, belonged to the same clubs and laughed at the same jokes.

Connor and Doherty, now in possession of both Newry and Auvergne stations, had a large area of country with its western border—unfenced of course—abutting on Argyle so that altogether the properties would form a sizeable pastoral empire of some six to seven million acres or roughly 10,000 square miles. With this asset and the Wyndham business, the firm of Connor, Doherty and Durack would be in a position to hold its own against even so powerful a combination as Forrest and Emanuel.

The proposed amalgamation and the troublesome topic of cattle tick occupied most of their time while awaiting the return ship to Wyndham.

In January Long Michael's partner Lumley Hill had discussed with Connor and Doherty the danger of tick, supposed to have come into the north from Batavia in the seventies, being allowed to penetrate freely into Kimberley from heavily infested areas in Queensland and the Territory. The idea was rapidly gaining ground that the parasite *Ixodes bovis* was directly responsible for red-water fever that had decimated many good herds over the past ten or twelve years. So far Kimberley had been relatively free of the pest, but if unchecked it would no doubt soon become a major challenge to the industry.

Connor, Lumley Hill and other east Kimberley pastoralists had thereupon waited on the Commissioner for Crown Lands asking for an implementation of the Stock Diseases Act to prevent the import of cattle from the Territory—except from border properties owned by Kimberley interests such as Wave Hill, Newry and Auvergne. It no doubt seemed a shrewd move at the time to have protected the east Kimberley market at the same time as preventing the further introduction of tick, but no sooner was the regulation agreed upon than some busybody stock inspector reported cases of tick and resultant red-water fever as far west as Hall's Creek!

East Kimberley pastoralists at once began clouding the issue by referring to the difficulty of distinguishing true cattle tick from other harmless varieties and of how many infested areas had never known a case of red-water fever, whereas red-water fever had occurred where no one had yet seen a tick. An entomologist named Helms had now been sent up to make a thorough investigation of all stations and it was hoped by his associates in Fremantle that Father would be able to bring to his notice 'the many anomalies that appeared so far to have escaped the notice of the inspectors'.

And so began the battle of *Ixodes bovis* that was to rage between east and west Kimberley pastoralists for many years to come, uncovering the worst aspects of self interest on either side—a story actually more interesting to the psychologist than to the entomologist who was in little doubt from the beginning as to the true nature and implications of the pest. The fight was to drag on long after the limit I have set for this chronicle of the pioneering days, until the issue was resolved in the gradual immunity built up by the cattle against infection, when the regulations, quarantine lines and dipping troughs would fall, one by one, into disuse, almost without the participants in the long struggle realising that it was drawing to an end. By this time, however, little semblance of friendship would remain between Connor, Doherty and Durack in the east and their old associates Forrest and Emanuel in the west. Nor did it help to dispel the undercurrent of class consciousness that existed between the 'old families' of the State and the 'Irish element' from 'the other side'.

In the first round the Duracks came out rather well, being put on record by the government entomologist Richard Helms as the only settlers in the district from whom he received any co-operation. This may not have been unrelated to the fact that Father and the scientist enjoyed each other's company, finding much in common in their literary tastes. Together they rode around collecting specimens in tin match boxes and discussing the 'anomalies of the tick question' with the anomalies of various philosophers far into the night.

> Apropos of the many abortive arguments upon which we mortals embark, [Father writes] I quote from the *Rubaiyat* of Omar Khayyam:
>
> Myself when young did eagerly frequent
> Doctor and saint and heard great argument
> About it and about: but evermore
> Came out by the same door wherein I went.
>
> Helms shares my admiration of the philosophy expressed, poor Father, on the other hand, somewhat contemptuous of 'the heathen nincompoop!'

Grandfather had no patience with the pastoralists in deliberately keeping the tick question 'anomalous' and he had frankly laid before the inspector a number of aspects that did not favour the immediate policy of the east Kimberley cattle men. He had expressed himself on this subject forthrightly from the outset:

'Why don't ye get down to tin-tacks about this tick business?'

'What do you mean—tin-tacks?' his sons countered. 'What would you do about it, anyway?'

'I'd find out whether the tick really was the cause of this red-water and set to work to get rid of it even if ye sell no cattle for a couple of years.'

'But we're sure it's not the cause,' the boys insisted. 'It's a big scare put up by the west Kimberley people to collar the market.'

Grandfather however had an inconvenient memory in some respects:

'Ye were willing to blame the little creature when it suited yere own ends to keep the Territory cattle out. I tell ye ye'll not solve yere problems by playing politics.'

'But we've to sell our stock haven't we? It's a matter of business.'

'It's bad business,' the old man told them. 'There's a cattle disease in this country and ye should be fighting it together, both sides of the fence, instead of trying to hoodwink the government for the sake of a temporary gain.'

But his protests carried little weight with his sons, or for that matter with any other Kimberley residents. An attitude had taken hold of the country that he could neither define nor understand. He could only shake his head in a bewildered way, wondering where the dream had failed, why this rich and beautiful land seemed loved by neither God nor man. The towns and the homes had not come as he had hoped. The only made road within hundreds of miles was one he had hacked out with his own hands. The boys showed no signs of marrying and it was clear that Argyle would be a home only as long as the girls remained. When they went away it would become a desolate shell of a place, full of dust and cobwebs and white ants like the womanless shack over the river at Lissadell. Was the lack of progress in the land a matter of the climate, the fever, the isolation, and the cattle tick or was there something lacking towards it in the hearts of the pioneers?

35

Return to Ireland

The years 1896 to 1897. Patsy Durack sails for Ireland, visits his birthplace in County Clare and Mr Healy in Kilkenny and returns to Australia. A broken romance.

Grandfather was depressed, restless and 'inclined to be cantankerous'. He complained that nobody now confided in him or took his advice. His suggestion for linking up the Kimberley properties with land in the goldfields district had been turned down, his recommendation that the boys purchase a piece of land known as Mt Eliza, overlooking the Swan River and city of Perth, then going for a song, swept aside as 'another airy speculation'. His son now appeared more inclined to rely upon the business advice of Connor and Doherty and talked of an amalgamation that he regarded as the utmost folly. Let them remain friends and business associates, but partners, never! His brother Galway Jerry's recent move in selling his Rosewood interest for an inferior lump of country on the Dunham River—for which he should have his head read, Grandfather declared—was nonetheless an example of the troubles that could arise in such partnerships.

In the middle of '96 the old man was persuaded to act on his long-professed wish to visit the land of his birth and to see Mr Healy who, supposedly a dying man when he left Brisbane ten years before, was now well over eighty. A business angle was given the trip by commissioning Grandfather to purchase a couple of much-coveted stud bulls from a dealer in Penzance.

And so, after forty-four crowded years, Grandfather returned to Ireland and the scenes of his boyhood and to his few remaining relatives and friends. In most respects he returned to disillusionment, for although in the intervening years he had sent regular remittances to relieve the poverty of his people and had brought out and settled in Australia as many as possible, his welcome seemed less genuine than he had expected. He felt that after all his name had been associated mainly with a source of revenue, and that when he was found to be no more than an ageing and rather impecunious colonial there was little interest in his homecoming. Few cared to know what his life had been, to hear of his beloved wife or of his family, and even in the matter of politics he felt somehow let down. The high ideals he had upheld in the face of so much argument seemed, with many he met, to have dissolved in pettiness and the totally 'unreasonable' attitude of which so many complained. Even his hero Parnell had brought dishonour on the Nationalist cause through being cited as co-respondent in a divorce suit. Moreover, although well aware of historical causes he was grieved by so much evidence of apathy and neglect. Surely a stable door could be fixed 'in two shakes of a cow's tail' without the purchase of a single pennyworth of new materials. All his life he had been fighting circumstances, contriving, improvising, calling upon St Patrick and all the saints for miracles and achieving them with his own bare hands. And now, out of the turmoil of busy years and forward striving he was back in the slow-moving changeless land of procrastination where, because there seemed so little future, people found solace and inspiration only in the past.

> There is much idle talk [he wrote to his family from Scariff] of again shifting a boundary between the Counties Galway and Clare but nothing practical of removing the mess from the laneways and clearing of the ditches. This change will be putting the birthplace of yere Grandfather onto the Clare side and for that it is written he was a Galwayman on his tombstone and proud of it I would not have it changed.
>
> I have seen the old home and the barn where I received what little schooling was then possible for the poor Irish. Of the Hedge schools, as we were after calling them, I have spoken to ye, for that they were sometimes indade held among the hedges for the fear of detection, but this before my time a little.
>
> Of the sorrows of Ireland I have not spoke much for ye will not understand it, dear children, as here they will not understand that a property in Australia may be the size of all Ireland and a single paddock the size and more of Galway or Clare, so that I hold my tongue unless they be taking me for the millionaire I am not.
>
> But some day ye must be seeing it that ye will know of the green that burns on the eye for that it is so bright and of the colour of heath that I am sending ye but will soon be dry. The snow on the mountains of New South Wales is not as here where it is in a white winter lying everywhere and very quiet in the frost.
>
> The tinkers are here still with all their lies and nonsense for the tune of a coin and I believing them and all as a boy. From here I go to Kilkenny for to visit ye're old tutor Mr Healy who is near blind I hear, but well enough by the grace of God, and all

the years since ye're dear Mama and me have sent him home to die after his terrible experience, all the skin burnt clean from his body by the sun and him shouting out and delirious. My dear boys, John and Pat there is no doubt ye're Guardian Angels were minding ye on that day and do not be forgetting in ye're prayers for to thank them.

I am in touch with the dealer in Penzanse from whom I shall purchase the bulls and will be bringing them with me on the ship and hope ye shall be to Sydney to meet me. I have a present for each of ye and from Father Feeney who got it from France some of the Water of Leward for to cure the sick.

I am not sure yet the ship only that it will be a finer one than brought me the same way in '53 when we were glad of the passage alone without the luxury for those were hard times as ye would not understand or be needing now to know . . .

How should they understand since he himself had all but forgotten until he stood again on the mountain he had climbed as a boy and played upon his flute the songs of the bards?

Gold, silver and jewels were only
As dust in his hand,
But his sword, like a lightning flash blasted
The foes of the land . . .

For all he had worked hard, there had been time then to dream of heroes such as the valiant Boru and the noble Mahon but men did not dream of the past in the new land where life was a pressing forward and a riding on, to the next horizon and the next.

How should they understand that here a hundred years ago was as yesterday and that the Irish born, like a child of Israel, carries within him the past of his race? He felt now that he had spoken perhaps too little of the old land and of his own youth, telling few but the happy things—of trout fishing in the Shannon, of market days in Gort, of wielding the cudgels and 'hurling' and dancing 'The Walls of Limerick' as they used in the village of Scariff on the quiet Loch where he was born. He had spoken more of the splendour of the Galway Blazers than of himself as the struggling farmer's son—watching and dreaming.

He had said little of the blight of '45, the curse that fell in the autumn and the next again, the foliage black overnight and the stems brittle to the touch and the potatoes but the size of pigeon's eggs. And of how the memory was there then of all the famines of the past from the *bliadhain an air*, the year of the slaughter and other years when even the skies seemed hung with the dark draperies of death.

'And what can the Irish be wanting now?'

'They're starving and dying, Your Majesty, some in barns and some upon the frozen highways, living and dead huddled beneath a covering of bags, and babies new-born with never a garment to wrap them.'

'You cannot live in Ireland. To get up you must first get out.'

He had hardly spoken of the struggle it was to save from the sale of stock as various branches of the family went on their way to the colonies, of waiting for letters and hoping, with the winter coming on, for good news and a 'little something' in the envelope. He had told his children a simple tale of a shining sovereign tossed by an English nobleman whose carriage he had lifted from the bog—a magic coin that multiplied to a whole heap of money that brought them all to the land of opportunity. Why explain that 'the fortune' they paid as assisted immigrants was but £8 in all? It had been wealth to them then, when they had gathered, family on family, waiting in the cold with the dogged patience of the poor for a turn of the wind to send the sailing packet on its way.

He had given his family release from hunger and cold in a warm land where the poorest hardly knew the meaning of poverty as the Irish had known it. He had given them the benefits of education for which generations of Irish had yearned and risked their very lives—and yet he had failed them. By his foolishness he had deprived them of what he had reared them to expect of life, but to what after all did it amount? Money to squander on enjoyment, a fine home in the city, a life of ease? Was it not perhaps, as his wife had said, the goodness of Providence that had divested him of his fortune while there was still time to save their souls?

A yokel seeing him as he wandered on Slieve Aughty Mountain, picking little sprigs of heather and bog cotton, might well have wondered at this strange old man who spoke and dressed like a foreigner but who, with his flowing white beard and silver hair, was like enough to the picture of St Patrick in the village church.

Mr Healy had welcomed him to the ruined portals of his ancestral seat in Kilkenny. The old man had forgotten being informed by letter of Grandmother's death and peered about expecting that she had playfully hidden herself behind her husband.

'Come my dear, you do not need to hide from me, for I am blind enough as it is.'

Grandfather took the old tutor's hands.

'She is gone now three years back. Michael wrote you of it but you could not have realised. I am hardly yet able to realise it myself.'

Weeping, the old man led his visitor into the house.

'So she was never to see the land of her forefathers, but her heart was here. She was a true daughter of Ireland—a saintly woman, a woman of prayer . . . And you, my dear old friend, I knew you would come. You were always a man of your word—a great one for getting about the country—a thousand miles—two thousand miles—nothing at all! But they laugh at me here you know. They are a people of most terrible ignorance. Australia, I tell them—God's chosen country, the loveliest country in the whole world, I have relations there, I tell them, wonderful people rich and with a grand mansion, carriages, horses, servants—and they laugh at me . . .'

'And well they might,' Grandfather smiled, but it was clear that the old man's mind was fixed on the past. Why distress him with the story of his ruin? There had been no need to break the news to him at the time for on his departure from Brisbane Grandfather had paid a sum of money into his bank account from which he continued to derive a small income.

'Ah, the rascals they were, attending to nothing but to watch for the shadow at the door and forever interrupting my prayers. And how is that poor fellow now, that idiot Lutheran who came for to convert the blacks?'

The increasing tempo of business in Kimberley had prevented any of the boys, except young Jerry, from meeting their father on his return to Sydney. The two spent a few days together in close companionship before Grandfather left for Fremantle from where, soon after his arrival, he wrote back to his youngest son.

Fremantle.
April '97.

My dear son,

I am to leave here for home in two days with the bulls which are doing well.

When I got your telegram I was pleased to hear that ye got on so well with your exams. Let me know how long from now until ye expect your B.A. degree . . .

Now concerning this malgimation I cannot say anything but from what they tell me it is all trumps according to their view and opinion of the affair. I have explained to Johnnie who is with me here everything I know which would be likely to crop up hereafter. I wired up to Michael, Pat and Johnnie that I would not give

Argyle for all the places Connor and Doherty has got and every wire I sent them and since Johnnie came down I had no reply to. Since Johnnie came down it has taken them all their time arranging about the Wyndham Store buildings. I am of the same opinion as you that by working on along steady as they are would be the better way of it and then they would always be their own masters, but their opinion of the affair is not mine.

I have made on request to Johnnie today to have an agreament for Mary and Birdie for 500 head of cattle each or the money if they would prefer it. It is not much to ask as they would brand that many from Argyle in three months and it would add years to my life to see yere dear sisters comfortable as well as yeselves.

Another thing I want to say is that the property of Durack Bros. in east Kimberley is equal between the four of ye and make no change concerning your interest in the same. Surely to God what is made yearly by the sale of bullocks should be more than what is paid for yere schooling. I had to pay for them and I never kept any a/c against them. Please God I shall go to Goulburn in August next and shall see ye then and yere Grandmother Costello. I should go now but that I want to see them all at home first and it is cool weather in Kimberley now and gets warm in October.

Concerning Birdie's marriage, by what Johnnie tells me it is broken off on account of some scandal rumour they heard concerning the man and if the rumour was true I hope in God they have done it all for her welfare . . .

I am sending to ye by Steve Brogan a prayerbook and some of the Water of Leward I have brought with me for ye all. Of the handkerchiefs I am sending ye one of them is worth over five pounds.[1]

Tell Scanlan he should not join the police I would have none of them. Let me know how is yere cousin Will Durack doing with his medical studies so I can let his brothers know at Lissadell . . .

This letter indicates that Grandfather was not returning to Kimberley much less 'cantankerous' than he had gone away, and the resolution of his sons,

[1] Uncle Dermot who sent me this letter among others from Ireland explained that there were five sovereigns in the border of one handkerchief—a thought that meant a good deal to him in his student days.

at this stage of their careers, to put even family affairs on a purely business basis obviously irritated him. When told that they could not yet afford to be as generous with all and sundry as he urged, Grandfather would remind them of the battling days in western Queensland when they had never failed to proffer a helping hand to friend, relative or wayfarer.

'If ye must wait till the time is convenient then ye shall find yereselves waiting at the gates of paradise.'

Grandfather's reference to Aunt Birdie's broken engagement uncovers a story seldom mentioned in the family. Everything had been ready for the wedding at Argyle and Father Kelly present to officiate when the scandal that had caused the bridegroom to seek refuge in the colonies somehow caught up with him in Kimberley. What exactly the scandal was we can only surmise from the fact that the young man had been an associate of Oscar Wilde, then still languishing in Reading gaol, and of the young Lord Alfred Douglas who had also left England to seek adventure around the Kalgoorlie goldfields. Ambrose Durack galloped all night to get the bad news through from Wyndham in time to stop the ceremony and Father Kelly was left the unenviable task of endeavouring to explain 'the unspeakable' to the heart-broken and bewildered girl. Aunt Birdie, quite at a loss to understand, turned from one to another to be met on all sides by an implacable blank wall.

'But I promised. I said that whatever I might come to hear of him, provided he was not married, would make no difference. The past is over and done with and I love him.'

'My dear girl,' Father said, 'it is quite impossible. I have sent him away and you must never mention his name again.'

It was Mrs Doherty who made the practical suggestion that the frustrated girl should accompany herself and her family on a trip to Ireland. For Aunt Birdie, the most tender-hearted and generous of women, this was only the beginning of a series of unfortunate romances. She was never to marry and never to set foot in Kimberley again after her departure, of which Father writes at the end of May:

> The SS *Albany* leaves this morning and poor little Bird takes passage on it for Fremantle thence with Mrs Doherty to Newry in Ireland. The dear girl kept up her spirits very well knowing that her tour is to extend over twelve months. Father Kelly also a passenger . . .

The Hall's Creek police files record the end of the story for the unhappy young warden who, evidently realising the impossibility of making a fresh start in even so remote a wilderness, shortly afterwards put an end to his own life, and Aunt Birdie, an old woman weary of living, reading again the cherished letters from her beloved nuns, bemourned 'the narrow way' she had forsaken in the frustrated innocence of her youth.

36
End of an Era

The years 1897 to 1898. Amalgamation of Durack Bros. with Connor and Doherty. Problems—Aborigines and cattle tick. M. P. Durack overlands store cattle to Camooweal. Reunion with John Costello at Lake Nash. Death of Patsy Durack in Fremantle.

After his father's departure Uncle John remained in Fremantle to finalise the new company, of which he wrote his brother Jerry early in May:

> ... Well, we put in our property Argyle and the Stud and my one third interest in the Wyndham business against C. and D.'s third in same and their Newry and Auvergne stations, Wyndham paddocks and Fremantle business ...
>
> We form on these properties a limited liability company of £80,000 capital ...
>
> We four brothers mutually agree to give Mary and Bird £1500 cash each as soon as we can ... You must confirm this assent and power of attorney to us until you are 21 years of age.
>
> This is the night previous to the General Election. Doherty is putting up for East Fremantle and I think he must get in. Connor is member for our district E. Kimberley. He was unopposed.
>
> Sir John Forrest Premier goes home to join in Jubilee festivities.
>
> Connor and I were invited to the opening of Harbour Work—a great day. I have enjoyed myself well and regret my short stay. All business so far adjusted satisfactorily.
>
> Bird's marriage is broken off and she goes to England with Mrs Doherty and children. There is a great scare on about *ticks* in cattle but it is all bosh we think.
>
> Your fond frere,
> J.W.D.

From this time on Father and his brothers John and Pat entered upon a new phase. Under the terms of their partnership all business in Kimberley was to be under their direct control. Father was to be general manager of the four stations and all business involving the purchase, sale and movements of cattle. Pat, with his headquarters at Argyle, was to manage station stock-work and John the Wyndham merchant business. Connor and Doherty were to direct affairs from Fremantle, to arrange stock contracts, control shipments and deliveries of cattle, attend their political careers and generally seek to secure the best end of the stick for East Kimberley pastoralists. And so the players, for better or worse, in seeking to strengthen their positions were now bound in complicated association as precarious as any situation they sought to avoid.

The tick question loomed large in the first years of the new company and prospects that had seemed so rosy at the outset took on something of the depressed hue of earlier years. Despite a deal of lobbying and many deputations on the part of Connor and Doherty, the entry of all livestock from Queensland and the Northern Territory was prohibited until these areas were declared 'clean'. Protests against this limitation of the Wyndham export market were in vain and Connor, Doherty and Durack were fined for ignoring the regulation and shipping to Fremantle a mob which, although tick free, had originated in the Territory. Connor threatened a motion of non-confidence in the government if the regulations were not removed and openly accused 'certain parties' of deliberately urging the restrictions in their own interests. A deal of malicious cross-correspondence enlivened the daily papers for some time to follow. Father wrote of

> ... southern pastoralists, unscrupulous of the truth, and studying only their own personal aggrandisement at a loss to the country and starvation to the miner.

A mob of Wave Hill bullocks was held on the border until the Premier, Sir John Forrest, threatened with the removal of east Kimberley support, sanctioned their entry on condition of a certificate of cleanliness. Father rode round the cattle with the stock inspector, pointing out the splendid condition and health of the mob:

> ... and whilst not asking Mr Alston to depart from his duty I do ask him to facilitate entry of this mob in the name of justice and common sense.

The inspector complied and that mob went through, but general restrictions were maintained. Later in the year Connor and Doherty wrote from Fremantle of good prospects for the lifting of the Territory barrier that they had earlier sought to impose. Now, with the possibility of a South African market opening up, they were anxious, as stock agents, to encourage a steady supply of cattle to Wyndham from all directions. Father, therefore, accompanied by Pumpkin and another boy, set out for the Territory to enquire into the possibilities of buying cattle if the market was confirmed.

There is a persistent strain of sadness through his record of this journey:

> Riding today with a certain heaviness of spirit and sinking of heart transferred by the master pen of Byron through medium of his Prisoner of Chillon. My thoughts keep turning back to the days I first travelled this track with Tom Kilfoyle. Our situation has certainly improved financially, despite our present problems, but many associates have in so short a time gone to their bourne beyond, and of those the majority in a somewhat violent or untimely manner. Good old Pumpkin however, appears to have aged little and carries on his duties with the same quietness and efficiency as ever . . .
>
> What a wearisome track where few are encountered but our sable brethren with their unpredictable habits and where lonely graves by the way tell of murder by the blacks, suicide under the influence of drink or the delirium of fever . . .

What a picture is contained in these brief jottings of this land of lost men and buried hopes, crude, rich and violent beyond the capacity of the toughest men to tame. On his weary 800-mile trek via Daly Waters to the border town of Camooweal he speaks of lonely stations and a variety of managers, the garrulous and entertaining, the 'carping pessimists', generous and hospitable or mean and misanthropic, venting their ill-humour on fellow beings and dumb animals. Quaint encounters on the track in a land of apt nicknames were the fiery old teamster known as 'Roaring Anger', a downright itinerant carpenter called 'Hammer and Gad' and a querulous old gasbag well-named 'The Squeaking Gimlet'. The diarist speaks of wild buffalo herds, of 'festal boards prepared by ebony hands', of camps so infested with tick that the flanks of his horses were heavily studded with the parasites as they moved along. The blacks no longer hindered drovers as in earlier years, in fact on one stage Father remarked upon a party of 'myall nigger footmen' assisting in bringing along the tail-end of a mob they encountered on their way. But oddly incongruous with so crude a country practically every wayfarer had books in his swag—many no doubt 'borrowed' from the Carnegie bequest of classical literature some philanthropist had seen fit to bestow on the dead-end Territory town of Borroloola. Father was much touched by one traveller who could not read himself carrying a volume of Shakespeare always in hope of meeting someone who would read to him. His own current reading included Cardinal Newman,

Mark Twain and Olive Schreiner's *Story of an African Farm*, reflections upon all of which mingle with observations on the habits of tick, the state of local cattle and the distance covered each day.

At a lonely station on the Limmen River 'where everything betokened ruin and want of care' he met an old Queensland friend, Jack Farrar, whom John Costello had left in charge of what remained of his vast Gulf properties—Lake Ellen, Wickham Park, Wangalara, Valley of Springs. Farrar told the story of their fruitless struggle against all the forces imaginable with which nature could frustrate the pioneer. Not only black marauders but crocodiles that abounded in the gulf streams took a daily toll of horses and cattle, dingo packs destroyed the new-born calves and cattle tick became thicker every year. Add to this the virulence of fever and beriberi that accounted for any graves on the river bank not attributable to native spears and you had the reason why Costello from his headquarters at Lake Nash, some seventy miles south of Camooweal, had at last decided to remove what stock remained on his Territory properties and thereafter abandon them to the wilds.

> The only cheering thing about the place [Father remarks in conclusion] are the two bright, healthy little Farrar boys, Johnny and Billy, who for all the bitter story of fruitless struggle inform me they want to be stockmen when they grow up—and own a station in the Territory! So much for the unfailing optimism of youth, while others I have met prophesy that in a few years the Territory will be more or less abandoned to the blacks and the white ants, as has indeed already happened in the case of many properties.

Hoping daily for news of the lifting of the border restrictions, Father made contracts for the purchase of cattle from Creswell and Brunette Downs, and left Pumpkin to hold the mob at Anthony's Lagoon and rode on to interview the stock inspector at Camooweal.

Somewhere on the track he had picked up a native stockman who accompanied him with his packs into the dusty, sweltering little town:

> . . . surely unique in its appearance of utter desolation, and yet boasting about seventy women and prolific at that, with twins a common occurrence I am told, as indeed I can well believe from the appearance of the vast majority—a character study in themselves, bantering as freely with the men about their 'delicate condition' as though among themselves!

The stock inspector raised his spirits by propounding the theory of tick immunity based on the fact that of 9,000 head travelling through from the heavily infested Gulf country in the past year none had died. In these times everyone talked tick and carried 'specimens' of different varieties in their pockets and every bushman had learned to recognise *Ixodes*, the true villain of the piece, by his little straight white legs.

Since no further word had come through from his partners, Father rode south from Camooweal to visit John Costello and family at Lake Nash. His uncle, whom he had not seen for twenty years, met him as a stranger on the verandah of his quaint two-storey homestead.

'Good-day sir! Where do you hail from?'

'Kimberley.'

'I've got relatives over that way.'

'That's funny, I've got relatives over here!'

And so the game went on as each member of the family appeared, and lastly Father's cousin and schoolmate, Michael Costello, who in turn he failed to recognise 'having pictured him still as in college days'.

> How eagerly we enter into conversation, recalling old times and exchanging news of various friends and family members. Uncle John telling me of the failure or success of his many ventures. He declares himself finished forever with the Territory wherein he placed such high hopes some years back. He is however optimistic of Queensland and declares times to be improving.
>
> My cousin Michael later lets me into his confidence, permitting me to peruse his sacred epistles leading from diffidence to confidence and so to the grand climax and ordering of the ring . . .
>
> My Aunt discoursing with lively interest the political issues of the day. Her memory is indeed wonderfully retentive and she vividly recalls many incidents of our childhood I had almost forgotten.

Already this last stronghold of Costello's pastoral empire, as vast at one stage as the map of Ireland, was threatened with calamity. Having survived the long drought and the flood that followed, he was to embark on a big programme of experimental water boring and although successful at last in striking the subartesian flow he went broke in the process. The banks closed down on his overdraft and he was left with nothing but the modest 1,000 acres that comprised the first Costello property near Grabben Gullen—Teatree Station, now badly run down through years of mismanagement. To this the brave-hearted old optimist returned with his family, built the place up again, sold it for a good price and purchased a fine property on the Lachlan River near Hillston—Tocabil—the home of his ripe old age.

When Father parted with his Costello relatives, however, they little realised that their days at Lake Nash were numbered, and John Costello spoke of ways and means by which Grandfather might catch the ship from Darwin to Burketown and from there travel down to visit them.

'He so often talks of you all,' Father told him, 'and a little jaunt over to see you might be just what he needs. He gets so low-spirited at times that we hardly know what to do with him.'

'And would I not be the same,' Costello said, 'but for the companionship of my own dear wife?'

January closed in with no more than an isolated storm and the mob at Anthony's Lagoon was in poor shape. Day after day, Father and his two black helpers, still awaiting the expected permission to proceed west, anxiously scanning the skies for rain, hauled perishing beasts from the mud of the lagoon, burned carcasses, and watched the miserable survivors supporting themselves against the trunks of meagre trees.

Every few days Father rode to the nearest telegraph station but the answer was always the same—'No mail, no messages.'

Down south the battle of the border raged on, Connor, Doherty and their supporters still contending that the connection between red-water fever and cattle tick had not been satisfactorily established and that in any case it was too late to make discriminatory regulations as with the constant intermingling of herds in this fenceless land, there were probably as many tick in the west Kimberley as in the east. The suggestion that tick investigations be extended to the western side was, however, defeated by the Forrests, and in the middle of January a bill was passed declaring east Kimberley an infected area and thus prohibited from exporting livestock to any other part of the State.

Father received this news with a letter from his sister Mary written from Wyndham early in December to say that she was leaving for Fremantle with Grandfather. Many years afterwards, when together at Argyle, my aunt would tell me of Grandfather's increasing melancholy, of how he would go back and back over the past, analysing his every action to discover why God had forsaken him in his old age.

'He has stripped me of everything, Mary, my money, my position, my beloved wife, my good health, even my self respect, for the people who took my advice and failed with myself and for the debts I can never pay.'

'But Father, you've still got your children and your home.'

'My boys lost faith in me. They don't listen to me any more—and this house, since your mother was never here, is no home to me.'

At night, when missing from his bed, his daughter would find him wandering around the first mud-brick place, that now did service as a store, or kneeling on the spot where his wife had been buried.

'But she is not here, Mary. She has nothing to say to me.'

His brother Galway Jerry came from the Dunham, trying to rally him with the cheerful nonsense that had never before failed to bring a smile to Grandfather's lips.

'Take him away, Mary,' her Uncle Jerry suggested. 'He always got bored when he was in one place for more than a month. He needs shaking out of himself.'

'But he's sick,' the girl protested. 'I'm afraid he's going to die.'

'Nonsense! He's not an old man yet and there's nothing really the matter with him. Get him out of this God-forsaken place and he'll be all right.'

But in Fremantle Grandfather took to his bed in the home that had been thrown open to them by kindly friends. The doctor was unable to diagnose his complaint and he could only say that he was apparently near the end.

He was conscious to the last but would sink into fitful dozes and on waking murmur on of his distressful dreams.

'All the little kings in their grass castles, Mary, and the wind and the water sweeping them away. The gullies are creeping up about the house, my dear. Tell the boys . . .'

'What shall I tell them, father?'

'Tell them . . . How should I know, a poor ignorant old man. They would not listen to me. Tell them . . .'

But on the last morning of his life he woke from sleep seeming peaceful and content:

'She came,' he said simply, 'and explained it all to me. I go out of the world as I came into it, with nothing but my immortal soul, apart from the watch she gave me on our wedding day, with her picture and one of St Patrick at the back. You must give it to poor Pumpkin for his faith in it was as great as my own and he was the best friend I ever had.'

Long Michael, returning from a business trip to Brisbane, hurried to the bedside of his dying cousin. Grandfather roused himself from the gathering shades:

'Who is it?'

'It is Long Michael, Father, just back from Queensland.'

'How are they all at home? Did you fix it up with poor Kate?'

'She would not see me, Patsy.'

'I am sorry. The family has always been ... except for this—nothing could ever break the family.'

And last of all, with a faint echo of his old spirit at the outset of a journey:

'Tell Pumpkin to fetch up the horses, Mary. I am ready now.'

A rider brought two telegrams to Father at Anthony's Lagoon—one from his partners about the ban on east Kimberley stock, the continued ban on Territory cattle entering W.A. and the failure of negotiations to ship cattle to South Africa. This meant the closing of all immediate markets except Queensland, which State was already entering upon the biggest drought in history. The second message was from Aunt Mary, telling of Grandfather's death.

> Remarkable [Father wrote] that it should be the anniversary of poor Mother's also, four years ago. I had anticipated the worst from an earlier telegram, but had hoped that his old strength might stand at least until I could have reached him. It seems that only Mary and Long Michael were with him at the end, John in Wyndham, Pat at Argyle, Jerry in Sydney and Birdie in Ireland ... Had dreamed last night that I saw him at Argyle, stirring before any of us as he always did, and actively engaged, finding happiness and consolation in the work at his hand.
>
> Would I could now consult him, as so often in the past. Where do we go from here? Fortunately we have had several storms and the season appears to have broken at last, so that we can at least proceed to Camooweal with the remains of this poor mob. I have asked Pumpkin whether he wishes from there to visit his countrymen at Cooper's Creek, but he tells me he has not the heart to return to the scene of happier days, and sits now, poor, faithful fellow, hunched in his grief.
>
> At present we would seem to have come to an 'impasse', but I know that somehow we will battle through as we have always done and in one of my bleakest hours I have hit upon a motto that I often sought in brighter circumstances: '*Travel hopefully*'.

Index